AMERICAN

TRAVEL SMART

Monument Valley, Utah

© Dainel B. Gibson

AMERICAN SOUTHWEST
TRAVEL ✦ SMART®

Daniel Gibson

John Muir Publications
Santa Fe, New Mexico

Dedication
This book is dedicated to my mother, Virginia Whipple, who first opened my eyes to the beauty of our world, and to my children, Travis and Isabel Gibson, who will hopefully one day inherit it.

John Muir Publications, P.O. Box 613, Santa Fe, New Mexico 87504

Printed in the United States of America.
First edition. First printing April 1998.

ISSN 1097-6108
ISBN 1-56261-406-1

Editors: Sarah Baldwin, Heidi Utz
Graphics Editor: Tom Gaukel
Production: Janine Lehmann
Design: Janine Lehmann, Linda Braun
Cover Design: Janine Lehmann
Typesetting: Fabian West
Map Style Development: American Custom Maps, Albuquerque, NM USA
Map Illustration: Kathleen Sparkes, White Hart Designs, Albuquerque, NM USA
Printer: Publishers Press
Front Cover Photos: *large:* Leo de Wys Inc./Siegfried Tauquer
　　　　　　　　　　small: © Chris Corrie
Back Cover Photo: © Janine Lehmann

Distributed to the book trade by
Publishers Group West
Berkeley, California

HOW TO USE THIS BOOK

The *American Southwest Travel•Smart* is organized in 22 destination chapters, each covering the best sights and activities, restaurants, and lodging available in that specific destination. Thanks to thorough research and experience, the author is able to bring you only the best options, saving you time and money in your travels. The chapters are presented in a logical sequence so you can follow an easy route from one place to the next. If you were to visit each destination in chapter order, you'd enjoy a complete tour of the best of the American Southwest.

Each chapter contains:

• User-friendly maps of the area, showing all recommended sights, restaurants, and accommodations.
• "A Perfect Day" description—how the author would spend his time if he had just one day in that destination.
• Sightseeing highlights, each rated by degree of importance: ★★★ Don't miss; ★★ Try hard to see; ★ See if you have time; and No stars—Worth knowing about.
• Selected restaurant, lodging, and camping recommendations to suit a variety of budgets.
• Helpful hints, fitness and recreation ideas, insights, and random tidbits of information to enhance your trip.

The Importance of Planning. Developing an itinerary is the best way to get the most satisfaction from your travels, and this guidebook makes it easy. First, read through the book and choose the places you'd most like to visit. Then study the color map on the inside cover flap and the mileage chart (page 12) to determine which you can realistically see in the time you have available and at the travel pace you prefer. Using the Planning Map (pages 10–11), map out your route. Finally, use the lodging recommendations to determine your accommodations.

Some Suggested Itineraries. To get you started, six itineraries of varying lengths and based on specific interests follow. Mix and match according to your interests and time constraints, or follow a given itinerary from start to finish. The possibilities are endless. *Happy travels!*

SUGGESTED ITINERARIES

With the *American Southwest Travel•Smart*, you can plan a trip of any length—a one-day excursion, a getaway weekend, or a three-week vacation—around any special interest. To get you started, the following pages contain six suggested itineraries geared toward a variety of interests. For more information, refer to the chapters listed—chapter names are bolded and chapter numbers appear inside black bullets. You can follow a suggested itinerary in its entirety, or shorten, lengthen, or combine parts of each, depending on your starting and ending points.

Discuss alternative routes and schedules with your travel companions—it's a great way to have fun, even before you leave home. And remember: don't hesitate to change your itinerary once you're on the road. Careful study and planning ahead will help you make informed decisions as you go, but spontaneity is the extra ingredient that will make your trip memorable.

© Andre Jenny/Unicorn Stock Photos

Albuquerque, New Mexico

Best of the American Southwest Tour

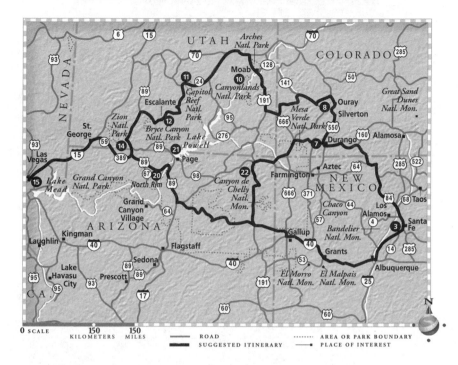

❸ **Santa Fe** (Palace of the Governors, Museum of Fine Arts, Georgia O'Keeffe Museum, Canyon Road, Pecos National Monument)

❼ **Southwest Colorado** (Mesa Verde, Durango & Silverton Narrow Gauge Railroad)

❽ **San Juan Mountains** (San Juan Skyway, Silverton, Ouray, Telluride)

❿ **Moab Area** (The Needles District, Islands in the Sky District, Arches National Park)

⓫ **Capitol Reef National Park** (Park Scenic Drive, Fruita, Aquarius Plateau)

⓬ **Grand Staircase** (UT 12 Drive, Escalante Petrified Forest State Park, Kodachrome Basin State Park)

⓮ **Zion National Park** (East Entrance and Zion Canyon Scenic Drives)

⓯ **Las Vegas** (Downtown, The Strip)

⓴ **Grand Canyon: North Rim** (Cape Royal Drive)

㉒ **Indian Country** (Monument Valley, Hopi Mesas, Canyon de Chelly National Monument, Petrified Forest National Park)

Time needed: 2 to 3 weeks

Nature Lover's Tour

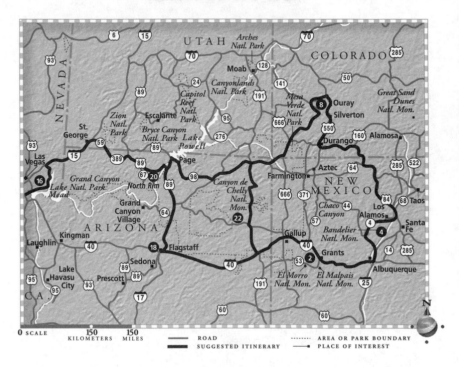

To see the tremendous diversity of landforms, natural wonders, ecosystems, plants, and animals in the Southwest, you'd need many weeks. But here's one itinerary that offers a good look at what's out there.

❷ **Gallup and Grants Area** (El Malpais National Monument, Mt. Taylor drive)

❹ **Jemez Area** (Bandelier National Monument, Valle Grande)

❽ **San Juan Mountains** (San Juan Skyway, hikes)

㉒ **Indian Country** (Petrified Forest National Park, Canyon de Chelly)

⓲ **Flagstaff Area** (San Francisco Peaks, Sunset Crater/Wupatki National Monuments, Walnut Canyon National Monument)

⓴ **Grand Canyon: North Rim** (Toroweap Overlook, Cape Royal drive)

⓰ **Outside Las Vegas** (Mt. Charleston, Lake Mead Scenic Drive, Valley of Fires State Park)

Time needed: 2 weeks

Art Lover's Tour

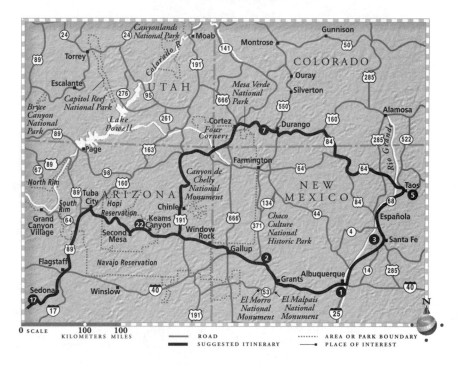

The Southwest is a flourishing arts center, with work ranging from traditional Indian and Hispanic arts to a wide range of contemporary art that goes well beyond cowboys and howling coyotes.

❶ **Albuquerque** (museums and galleries)

❸ **Santa Fe** (museums and galleries, Santa Fe Opera, chamber music, Indian Market, Spanish Market)

❺ **Taos** (Millicent Rogers Museum, Harwood Foundation, D.H. Lawrence Ranch, Blumenschein Home, downtown galleries, Taos Pueblo studios)

❼ **Southwestern Colorado** (Mesa Verde National Park museum, Durango galleries, Indian Village on Southern Ute reservation)

㉒ **Indian Country** (roadside vendors, trading posts, Navajo Museum, artist studios, Hopi Cultural Center)

⓱ **Sedona Area**

❷ **Gallup and Grants Area** (Gallup hock shops, Red Rocks State Park museum, Zuni Indian Reservation shops and studios, Acoma Pueblo)

Time needed: 2 weeks

Family Fun Tour

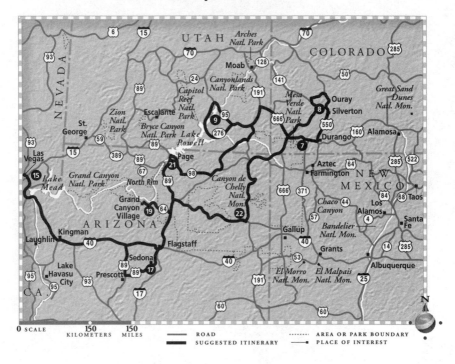

Here's an itinerary to keep the kids wide-eyed and on their toes.

- ㉑ **Lake Powell Area** (Glen Canyon Dam tour, boat excursions on Lake Powell, lake swimming and fishing, Lee's Ferry launch site)
- ⑨ **Southeastern Utah** (Bridges National Monument, San Juan River raft trip, Valley of the Gods car tour, Muley Overlook)
- ⑧ **San Juan Mountains** (skiing at Telluride, jeep tours, Ouray hot springs, summer hiking, Silverton's National Historic District walk)
- ⑦ **Southwestern Colorado** (Durango & Silverton Narrow Gauge Railroad, Mesa Verde National Park)
- ㉒ **Indian Country** (parks, horse tours, Hopi Indian dances)
- ⑲ **South Rim of the Grand Canyon** (scenic drives, Tusayan Museum, Hopi House, burro rides, hikes)
- ⑰ **Sedona Area** (Verde Canyon Railroad, jeep rides, horseback rides, Tuzigoot National Monument, Jerome State Park, swimming)
- ⑮ **Las Vegas** (casino amusement arcades and parks, Wet 'n' Wild waterpark, Liberace Museum, Ripley's Believe It or Not! Museum)

Time needed: 2 weeks

Indian, Hispanic, and Mormon History and Culture Tour

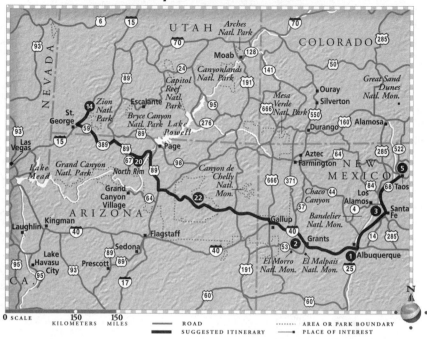

The Southwest has the oldest human history of any region in the nation, with an unbroken interplay of different cultures. This tour captures the history of three of the region's most distinct cultural groups.

❺ **Taos** (Millicent Rogers Museum, Taos Pueblo)

❸ **Santa Fe Area** (Pecos National Historic Park, Wheelwright Museum, Palace of the Governors portal, Bandelier National Monument)

❶ **Albuquerque** (Albuquerque Museum of Art, History, and Science; Petroglyph National Monument; Indian Pueblo Cultural Center; Coronado Monument drive)

❷ **Gallup and Grants Area** (Chaco Canyon National Historic Park, Zuni Indian Reservation, Acoma Pueblo, Laguna Pueblo)

㉒ **Indian Country** (Navajo National Monument, Hopi Mesas, Canyon de Chelly, Window Rock, Hubbell and other local trading posts)

⑳ **Grand Canyon: North Rim** (Pipe Springs National Monument)

⑭ **Zion National Park Area** (St. George, Hurricane, Zion National Park)

Time needed: 2 weeks

Outdoor Recreation Tour

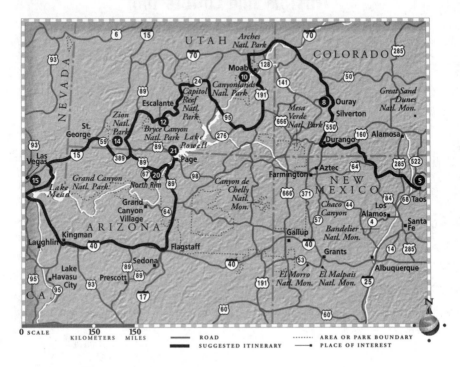

| 0 SCALE | 150 KILOMETERS | 150 MILES | ━━━ ROAD | ········ AREA OR PARK BOUNDARY |
| | | | ▬▬▬ SUGGESTED ITINERARY | ━━• PLACE OF INTEREST |

Outdoor rec enthusiasts can set down in almost every locale in this book and find a world of recreational possibilities. Here are some highlights.

⑤ Taos (skiing, Rio Grande white-water outings, hiking, fishing, hunting, mountain biking)

⑧ San Juan Mountains (skiing, hiking, jeep drives, fishing, hunting)

⑩ Moab Area (river trips on the Green or Colorado, four-wheel driving, hiking, mountain biking)

⑫ Grand Staircase (hiking in the Escalante Canyons, horseback riding in Kodachrome Basin, mountain biking, hunting, fishing)

⑭ Zion National Park Area (hiking, dune riding at Snow Canyon)

⑮ Outside Las Vegas (water sports on Lake Mead, hiking and skiing at Mt. Charleston and at Red Rocks and Valley of Fires State Parks)

⑳ Grand Canyon: North Rim (hiking into the canyon and on rim trails, hunting, burro rides, cross-country skiing)

㉑ Lake Powell Area (sailing, Jet Skiing, motorboating, waterskiing, lake and river fishing, four-wheel driving, hiking slot canyons)

Time needed: 2 weeks

USING THE PLANNING MAP

A major aspect of itinerary planning is determining your mode of transportation and the route you will follow as you travel from destination to destination. The Planning Map on the following pages will allow you to do just that.

First, read through the destination chapters carefully and note the sights that intrigue you. Then photocopy the Planning Map so you can try out several different routes that will take you to these destinations. (The mileage chart that follows will help you to calculate your travel distances.) Decide where you will be starting your tour of the region. Will you fly into Albuquerque, Flagstaff, or Las Vegas, or will you start from somewhere in between? Will you be driving from place to place or flying into major transportation hubs and renting a car for day trips? The answers to these questions will form the basis for your travel route design.

Once you have a firm idea of where your travels will take you, copy your route onto the additional Planning Map in the Appendix. You won't have to worry about where your map is, and the information you need on each destination will always be close at hand.

Zion National Park

Planning Map: American Southwest

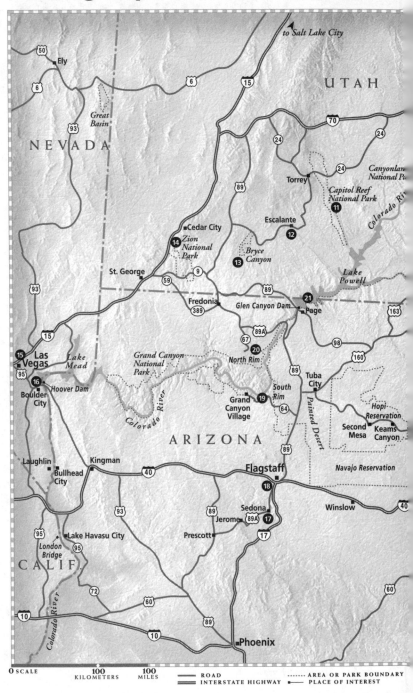

to Salt Lake City

UTAH

Ely

Great Basin

NEVADA

Canyonlan National P.

Torrey

Capitol Reef National Park

Colorado Ri

Cedar City

Escalante

Zion National Park

Bryce Canyon

St. George

Lake Powell

Fredonia

Glen Canyon Dam

Page

Las Vegas

Lake Mead

Grand Canyon National Park

North Rim

Tuba City

Boulder City

Hoover Dam

South Rim

Hopi Reservation

Grand Canyon Village

Colorado River

Second Mesa

Keams Canyon

ARIZONA

Painted Desert

Laughlin

Kingman

Flagstaff

Navajo Reservation

Bullhead City

Sedona

Winslow

Jerome

Prescott

Lake Havasu City

London Bridge

CALIF.

Colorado River

Phoenix

SCALE

100 KILOMETERS

100 MILES

ROAD

INTERSTATE HIGHWAY

AREA OR PARK BOUNDARY

PLACE OF INTEREST

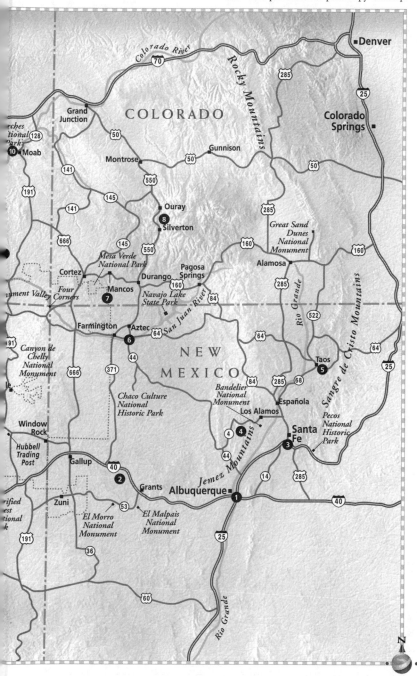

AMERICAN SOUTHWEST MILEAGE CHART

	Albuquerque, NM	Aztec, NM	Bryce Canyon	Chinle, AZ	Durango, CO	Flagstaff, AZ	Gallup, NM	GC Village, AZ	Kingman, AZ	Las Vegas, NV	Los Alamos, NM	Moab, UT	No. Rim, GC, AZ	Page, AZ	Prescott, AZ	Santa Fe, NM	St. George, UT	Taos, NM
Aztec, NM	196																	
Bryce Canyon, UT	557	395																
Chinle, AZ	227	163	366															
Durango, CO	273	39	417	184														
Flagstaff, AZ	324	320	286	203	356													
Gallup, NM	138	134	466	89	170	186												
GC Village, AZ	396	282	290	236	318	84	267											
Kingman, AZ	468	461	352	347	500	144	330	174										
Las Vegas, NV	580	601	234	471	564	248	437	176	101									
Los Alamos, NM	93	181	542	317	208	417	228	489	559	670								
Moab, UT	385	168	270	195	159	322	247	326	466	440	376							
No. Rim, GC, AZ	497	364	164	337	419	211	359	215	268	268	518	394						
Page, AZ	371	238	157	174	306	136	233	140	314	275	392	268	122					
Prescott, AZ	410	406	385	286	442	86	285	129	141	276	503	408	297	222				
Santa Fe, NM	60	222	617	286	214	384	197	455	527	640	45	444	556	430	469			
St. George, UT	578	536	126	418	500	292	440	296	226	119	669	341	168	156	378	368		
Taos, NM	133	197	583	365	206		276	534	606	710	73	365	637	517	548		657	
Torrey, UT	549	371	120	321	286	422	290	352	336	512	199	253	261	385	246	79	557	649

WHY VISIT THE AMERICAN SOUTHWEST?

W hat is it about the American Southwest that casts such a spell over residents and visitors alike? Certain images come to mind: a hand gently smoothing the wall of a clay pot; a bright red chile *ristra* hanging from a tin roof; a cold, clear stream falling over a shelf of yellow limestone; a mariachi band tuning guitars; a kayaker bounding down a roaring river. Beams of sunlight piercing immense clouds while rain falls like a veil over a distant mesa. The smell of piñon smoke on a snowy afternoon. The cry of a Hopi singer leading the dance in the dusty pueblo. Bobcats, black bears, eagles, and rattlesnakes; dark canyons, blazing deserts, ice-locked summits, and vast empty spaces. All of these things evoke the spirit that draws so many people to the American Southwest.

Beyond the seductive iconography, however, is a complex region full of contrasts. Here ancient worlds exist side by side with jetports, nuclear scientists, and powerful hydro turbines spinning away in the bowels of Hoover Dam. Here you can live in homes that have been occupied for almost a millennium or in high-rise hotels on Las Vegas' Strip. The people of the Southwest range from the descendants of the hard-edged Mormons, who carved out a miniature empire in the rocks of Utah, and the Hispanic farmers of New Mexico, cut off from the rest of the world for more than 200 years, to Albuquerque's blue-collar construction workers, throwing up frame homes as fast as their nail guns will shoot, and the wealthy newcomers building adobe mansions in the hills of Santa Fe and Sedona.

One nearly universal quality of these people is a willingness to live and let live in the midst of a vast and awesomely beautiful land. I look forward to sharing some of its secrets with you.

HISTORY AND CULTURES

W hile much of North America was under the glaciers of the last ice age some 11,000 years ago, Paleolithic hunter-gatherer societies occupied the Southwest, where the perpetual snows were limited to the high mountains. Over time, these people, called Paleo-Indians, acquired the secrets of agriculture from Mexican Indian cultures, allowing them to settle into semipermanent villages beginning around

500 B.C. Known as the Basketmakers, they lived in pit houses—
subterranean pockets carved into the earth and covered with logs
and dirt—concentrated in the San Juan River drainage of the Four
Corners area.

Around A.D. 500–700 this culture began to make substantial
advances, moving into above-ground living quarters, expanding trade
networks, and refining their arts and religious rituals. Archeologists
label these people the Pueblo I culture, but they are also known as the
Anasazi, a Navajo word for "Ancient Enemies." (The term *Anasazi*
is falling out of favor but is used here because of its still-common
usage.) Meanwhile, elsewhere in the Southwest, parallel cultures were
emerging: the Hohokam in southern Arizona, the Mogollon in southern New Mexico, and, somewhat later, the Fremont people in central
Utah.

The period of A.D. 900–1170 saw the Anasazi culture peak and
then vanish at New Mexico's Chaco Canyon. Similarly, the Hohokam
and the Mogollon cultures disappeared. Activity shifted to the Sinagua
culture of north-central Arizona and to the cliff dwellings of Mesa
Verde, Keet Seel, and other late Anasazi sites to the west and north of
Chaco. But except for a few Sinagua sites, these settlements were also
abandoned by the beginning of the fourteenth century. Why?

The answer remains a haunting mystery, though an extended
drought, resource consumption, and the arrival of warring nomads
probably played a role. Modern New Mexican Pueblo Indians and the
Hopi of Arizona have long claimed to descend from the Anasazi,
whom they prefer to simply call "ancestors." Archeologists now support this theory.

About the same time these new Indian cultures arrived on the
scene, the first Europeans showed up. In 1540 Francisco Coronado led
the first major expedition into what is now the United States. He
marched from Mexico's Sea of Cortez across eastern Arizona and into
the Rio Grande Valley of New Mexico, where he spent a winter holed
up in Kuaua Pueblo (near present-day Bernalillo). He came seeking
gold and other riches, like those found in Mexico by earlier conquistadors, but instead found a farming culture with a highly evolved cultural
and religious life. Disappointed, Spain and Mexico temporarily abandoned the region.

But in 1598, Don Juan de Oñate, a band of Mexican settlers, and
Franciscan friars returned to the Rio Grande Valley, lured by its potential for agriculture and for converts to the One Religion. Near present-

day Española, they established the second European colony in what is now the United States: San Gabriel (see Scenic Route, page 85). The Spanish Crown's recognition of the Pueblo people as people, and as potential converts to Catholicism, was a double-edged sword. While European colonists elsewhere labeled Indians heathens unworthy of conversion and slaughtered them, here the Indians were allowed to retain their ancestral homes and livelihoods while priests tried to convert them.

By the mid- to late 1600s, Hispanic settlements dotted the Rio Grande Valley, and the Pueblo people were reeling under the combined oppression of secular and religious authorities. In 1680 the Pueblo people rose in one of only two successful Native revolts ever undertaken in North America, and the Hispanics were forced out of New Mexico. However, in 1692 Don Diego de Vargas led them back—this time for good. The two cultures settled into a relationship that varied—depending on the individuals, the political climate, and other circumstances—from extremely close to wary, with a great deal of cross-cultural exchange of everything from food to language and genes.

When Mexico broke free of Spain in 1821, New Mexico fell under Mexican authority. This allowed entrepreneurs in Missouri—the closest U.S. lands—to launch wagon trade over the famed Santa Fe Trail. In 1846, at the outbreak of the Mexican-American War, U.S. troops under General Kearny occupied New Mexico, leading it and Arizona to become U.S. territories two years later. Up until this period, non-Indian occupation of the rest of the Southwest, other than a few missions in southern Arizona, was quite limited because of the fierce resistance by the Comanche, Ute, Paiute, Apache, and Navajo peoples. The U.S. cavalry, however, finally broke them, and the next wave of change swept the region.

Around the same time, the first Mormon emigrants from the Midwest arrived in central Utah seeking a place to practice their religion without persecution. After establishing themselves in the Salt Lake City area, colonists were sent southward to occupy portions of northern Arizona, southeastern Nevada, northwestern New Mexico, and southeastern Utah.

Toward the end of the nineteenth century, ranching, industrial-scale mining, railroads, massive timber harvesting, and the founding of many towns added chapters to the region's already complex history. The twentieth century has provided still more. Much of the Southwest rested in easy slumber up to World War II, enlivened by the arrival of artists and early tourists in the 1920s and 1930s. However, the 1940s saw the creation of immense U.S. military bases throughout the region. These provided an economic spark that is still smoldering. Small towns like Albuquerque and Phoenix have blown up into cities, with growth in the 1980s and 1990s spurred by increased tourism, telecommuters, retirees looking for a home in the sun, and high-tech corporations seeking a better quality of life. Even with all this growth, Indian and Hispanic cultures remain strong, subtly informing and transforming the new arrivals—the ancient continues to affect the modern.

Note: Throughout this book I make many references to "prehistoric" sites and cultures. This rather Eurocentric description simply refers to any time prior to contact between Indians and Europeans.

THE ARTS

More than 1,000 years before Georgia O'Keeffe came to the area, the ancestors of New Mexico's Pueblo Indians and the Hopi of Arizona were creating masterful artwork. The earliest surviving works consist of petroglyphs (pecked into rock) and pictographs (painted on rock) found across the Southwest, some dating back to A.D. 800. Modern Pueblo artisans are noted for their abilities in ceramics and jewelry, and, to lesser degrees, in weaving, drum making, and carving, as well as in most of the contemporary arts. The Navajos became some of the world's finest weavers and silversmiths in the eighteenth century and continue to produce beautiful silver jewelry, rugs, and tapestries today, with the addition of micaceous pottery and folk art.

New Mexico's Hispanic settlers, cut off from their Mexican roots, had to create almost everything they needed from scratch; they continue to be skilled wood carvers, tin workers, weavers, furniture makers, and creators of varied religious art.

Early in the twentieth century, pockets of the Southwest, particularly Santa Fe and Taos, were "discovered" by East Coast artists fascinated and inspired by the still-flourishing artistic and cultural traditions of the Indian and Hispanic peoples as well as the area's stark beauty. They settled in and spread the word to their friends. In subsequent decades, the making and selling of art has become a mainstay in the Southwest's economic and social fabric. Santa Fe, Sedona, Taos, and even Albuquerque, Flagstaff, Gallup, Durango, and Telluride have become nationally renowned art centers, and others—like Las Vegas—are rushing to catch up.

Southwestern arts today reflect the great diversity of the area's inhabitants. In tiny Jerome, Arizona, someone is working on a potter's wheel. Near Mexican Hat, Utah, a Navajo woman is preparing her loom. In Trampas, New Mexico, a *santero* sharpens his whittling knife. In the orchestra pit at the Santa Fe Opera, a violinist tunes her instrument. In Sedona, a photographer finishes shooting a roll of film as the sun sets over the red rock hills. At Zuni, a silversmith carefully pours liquid silver into his jewelry mold. And at Telluride, a Joffrey Ballet dancer stretches in preparation for a performance.

CUISINE

L ike the arts of the region, the cuisine is diverse, echoing the cultural variety. Basic ranch food, heavy on the beef and potatoes, and fiery New Mexican fare spiced with green and red chile are two of the most common types. But the area also has Pueblo Indian food, which mixes such modern American fare as hamburgers and bologna sandwiches with traditional Pueblo and Hispanic elements. Navajo favorites include mutton dishes. And in Santa Fe, Sedona, Telluride, and Las Vegas, you'll find high-end restaurants specializing in the artful blending of traditional regional foods with unexpected ingredients and international culinary styles.

In other words, the Southwest has more than one regional cuisine. That said, the food that originated in New Mexico with the melding of Pueblo Indian and Hispanic colonial cuisine is undoubtedly the most famous. Long called "Mexican food" by outsiders, it is really *New Mexican*, as anyone who has eaten in both places knows. Though Mexican and New Mexican food share certain basic ingredients—such as beans and tortillas—and certain dishes—such as enchiladas, *posole*, and *carne adovada*—there the similarities end. Mexican food uses many ingredients not found in traditional New Mexican food, and New Mexican cuisine has more Native American influences; for example, sopaipillas—the puffy fried dough best smothered with honey and eaten warm for dessert—are unique to the area.

But the key to New Mexican cuisine, and the thing that makes it distinctive, is chile, which is used more extensively and imaginatively here than anywhere else in the world. The state has festivals and even a magazine (*Chile Pepper*, based in Albuquerque) devoted to subject. When you eat out, don't be surprised if your waiter asks, "Red or green?" The question refers to the two types of chile widely available in the region. They are different in taste, look, and tongue-burning quotient, but no hard rules apply to the latter. Take a shot and discover for yourself. By the way, milk is a good antidote for "flame face."

FLORA AND FAUNA

The American Southwest sits in the crossroads of North America. Within its vast expanse merge the Great Plains of the Midwest, the Rocky Mountains and Basin and Range provinces to the north, the Great Basin Desert to the west, and the Sonoran desert to the south. Combine that enormity with terrain that runs from sea level to more than 14,000 feet high and you have the makings of the greatest variety of animals and plants in North America: from cactus to tundra flowers, rattlesnakes to black bear.

Southwestern geography tends to isolate species from each other, with plants and animals marooned on mountain chains separated by desert and canyon lowlands. Temperatures can and do vary tremendously only miles apart. Thus, one can encounter a wide range of plants and animals that have adapted to these specific local conditions.

And while the Southwest has been pounded by grazing, hunting, logging, mining, and other extractive industries for centuries, it is still often wild, allowing plant and animal kingdoms to flourish. In fact, except for the extirpation of the grizzly bear and the Mexican wolf, all of its original major mammals are still here, and the lobo is scheduled for reintroduction in 1998. However, many plant and animal species are endangered—from the rare Apache trout to the willow flycatcher. A growing appreciation for the region's rich plant and animal heritage may come just in time to stave off its loss.

THE LAY OF THE LAND

The American Southwest has a widely varying geography, its convoluted face crinkled by massive fault lines, upthrust ranges, dropped basins, volcanic intrusions, and carved canyons, mesas, buttes, spires, stone arches, and bridges. It is rarely level. Along its southern edge lie the Chihuahua and Sonoran Deserts. Adjoining its western fringe are the Mojave and Great Basin Deserts, while its interior encompasses other, sometimes large patches of high desert terrain; thus the common impression that this area is strictly desert. Indeed, it can be very dry, and its few major rivers—the Rio Grande, the Green, and even the Colorado—are not very voluminous. They are, though, precious and welcome in the arid environment—linear green oases penned in by rock and bare dirt.

Much of the ground covered in this book is part of the Colorado Plateau, which sits over the Four Corners area and extends westward to the edge of Nevada, south through north-central Arizona to the deserts, and southeastward into northwestern New Mexico. This immense plateau contains rock that is more than 500 million years old, some of the oldest on Earth. Most of the massive sheets of exposed rock were deposited on sea floors when much of the region lay at sea level near the equator, or were wind-driven dunes when it was part of huge deserts.

Widespread erosion of these sediments began about 10 million years ago, when the Colorado Plateau was uplifted by continental drift forces. The higher mountain ranges, created by volcanic eruptions and fault thrusting, receive much more moisture than the low-lying terrain. As the moisture flows off the summits and across the plateau heading toward the distant Pacific and Atlantic Oceans, it has slowly but inexorably cut and carved the Grand Canyon and thousands of other land features seen today in this fantastic rock realm. And the process continues.

The Southwest's northern realm is split by finger ranges of the Rocky Mountains, including the Sangre de Cristos of New Mexico and the San Juans of southwestern Colorado, which tower above 13,000 and 14,000 feet elevations. Other ranges poke up in majestic isolation, including the Abajos, La Sals, and Henry Mountains of Utah; the San Francisco Peaks of Arizona; and the Spring Mountains of Nevada. They provide the region with totally different sub-climates and geography from the surrounding lowlands and give life to its streams, creeks, springs, and rivers.

OUTDOOR ACTIVITIES

The geographical, topographical, and climatic variations of the Southwest lend themselves to diverse outdoor activities. Save ocean sports, it's hard to think of any form of outdoor recreation that's not enjoyed here.

What are the best activities? That would depend on whom you ask. A downhill skier might talk of the feathery powder and plunging ridge lines of Telluride or Taos Ski Valley. A hiker might rhapsodize about a descent of Utah's Paria Canyon. A climber might recall summiting Granite Mountain near Prescott. Visions of the wave that flipped a rafter in the Grand Canyon's Lava Falls might haunt a boater. You can find lands set aside for Off-Road Vehicles (ORVs) and four-wheeling; tiny trout streams you have to wade through, hunched under the bower of branches; land calling out for a fast gallop on a horse; and immense lakes on which you can run a motorboat for hours without turning the wheel. Further details on these and many other activities are in the Fitness and Recreation sections of each destination chapter in this book.

PRACTICAL TIPS

HOW MUCH WILL IT COST?

Many different trips at many different costs are possible in the vast five-state area included in this book. You can rack up substantial bills by staying at posh resorts or drop a small fortune in Vegas in a single night. On the other hand, you can camp your way through the region and spend little more than gasoline and grocery money. In between these two extremes are many moderate options. I'd suggest you sample some of all the possibilities. You can't have a total Southwest experience without getting into the land, picking up some dust, and maybe washing it off in a river or lake. But a steady diet of this kind of living will give you fresh appreciation for a hot shower, a prepared meal, and a warm bed.

Since many of the region's prime sightseeing highlights are found inside national parks and monuments, purchase of the Golden Eagle Pass is a smart idea. The pass costs $50 and provides free admission to all national parks and monuments for a year. United States residents over 62 can purchase a $10 Golden Age Passport that also provides free park and monument access. Either can be obtained at most park and monument visitor centers or admission booths. Gasoline will be a major expense if you cover all the ground in this book—the entire loop, including side drives, encompasses about 3,000 miles.

WHEN TO GO

Prime time for this portion of the Southwest is early May through late October. However, because the region has a wide variety of climates, when you decide to go depends in part on where you want to spend most of your time. For instance, the lowest area of the region, around Las Vegas, can be brutally hot from May through September. I suggest visiting there earlier or later in the year. Also, some of the warmer national parks, including Zion, the South Rim of the Grand Canyon, and Sedona might be best seen in winter to avoid crowds.

On the other hand, to many people's surprise, winters can be quite rough and lengthy in many parts of the region. Santa Fe, at 7,000 feet, and even Flagstaff, at 6,000 feet, can have prolonged and snowy winters—good for skiing but not for winter-weary travelers looking for a desert retreat. The San Juans of southern Colorado are slammed by winter, and even the windswept mesas and canyons of southern Utah are no picnic then. In New Mexico, I love the days of autumn most, when the sun still shines warmly, the sky assumes a deep turquoise glow, and the world seems to hold its breath, awaiting the first gentle snows of winter.

TRANSPORTATION

The best way to get around the Southwest is by car, preferably a four-wheel-drive vehicle so you can cut through a winter storm or negotiate dirt roads without getting stranded. Rentals are widely available, particularly in large urban centers. Rental RVs are also seen more and more in the Southwest. Available in major cities, including Albuquerque, Las Vegas, and Phoenix, they rent for anywhere from $380 to $1,100 a week.

AMERICAN SOUTHWEST CLIMATE

Average daily high and low temperatures in degrees Fahrenheit, plus monthly precipitation in inches.

	Santa Fe	Grand Canyon	Moab	Durango
Jan.	40/19	42/21	41/17	41/10
	.7	1.2	.7	18
Mar.	51/28	59/31	62/32	51/21
	.7	1.3	.8	10.9
May	68/43	69/37	81/47	69/36
	1.4	.5	.6	1.4
July	81/56	94/65	98/63	85/49
	1.4	1.4	.5	1.8
Sept.	74/49	85/57	87/51	78/40
	1.4	1.0	.8	1.7
Nov.	50/28	53/26	57/27	53/23
	.6	.8	.6	5.2

Local and regional bus lines do crisscross the region, but many of the most celebrated and interesting sights lie away from towns, so bus travel isn't very practical. Nor is train travel: the region is served by the historic Southwest Chief line (run today by Amtrak), which travels between Chicago and Los Angeles and passes near Santa Fe at the Lamy stop, on through Albuquerque, and westward to Flagstaff and Kingman, Arizona. While this scenic rail line provides a great way to arrive, it leaves you without local mobility.

Air travel in this region is increasing constantly. Major jetports are located in Albuquerque and Las Vegas, but regular jet service is now available in Durango and Telluride/Montrose, Colorado; St. George, Utah; and Farmington, New Mexico. Smaller commercial airports also exist in Flagstaff and Page, Arizona. You can even fly onto the South Rim of the Grand Canyon on regularly scheduled flights from Las Vegas.

Emergency Road Conditions

To check on road conditions during summer or winter storms, contact the authorities at the following numbers: Arizona, (520) 573-7623; Colorado, (303) 639-1111/1234; New Mexico, (800) 432-4269; southern Nevada, (702) 486-3116; Utah, (800) 492-2400.

CAMPING, LODGING, AND DINING

You can find deluxe lodgings in Las Vegas, Santa Fe, and Telluride, or almost as much in Sedona, Taos, and Albuquerque. But you can also find a charming bed-and-breakfast you'll always remember for as little as $60. And if the weather's right, a night under the stars is the best bargain around. These options are detailed within this book. During summer, I'd suggest reserving campgrounds ahead whenever possible (see the Camping sections in the destination chapters), since many campgrounds fill up nightly and, in some cases, alternatives may be far away.

You'll find an abundance of dining options in Santa Fe, Las Vegas, and Albuquerque, and to a lesser degree in Sedona, Taos, Durango, and Flagstaff. Santa Fe in particular is a dining mecca, with several nationally known restaurants specializing in the latest "Nouvelle Southwestern" cuisine. The larger urban centers offer a variety of ethnic choices, including Asian, East Indian, and Italian, in addition to the expected Southwestern fare. Throughout the area you can find good steaks and other meats, befitting the Southwest's ranching and livestock heritage. Be sure to have some green chile when you're in New Mexico. And, of course, you'll never have to travel too far to find a fast-food joint if you need a quick fix.

RECOMMENDED READING

A great deal of wonderful literature, both expository and fictional, has been written in and about the American Southwest. The sheer volume and variety is daunting, but here's a list to get you started. In addition, you might want to bring a good pair of binoculars and a bird identification book on your journey, as well as guidebooks for cacti and wildflowers.

Paul Horgan's *Great River*, which won him the Pulitzer Prize in 1955, will undoubtedly stand as the primary historical reference for the Spanish Southwest for many years to come. But smaller treasures also exist, such as J. Frank Dobie's *Coronado's Children*, and Louisa Weatherill's *Traders to the Navajo*, portraying her family's life among the Navajo in the nineteenth century. David Grant Noble's *Ancient Ruins of the Southwest* provides the best overview of the region's prehistoric Indian ruins.

Exploration of the Colorado River of the West and its Tributaries is the amazing but true story of the first expedition to run the Colorado through the Grand Canyon, led by its author, the one-armed John Wesley Powell. The book was reissued by Penguin in 1989. *In the House of Stone and Light: A Human History of the Grand Canyon*, by J. Donald Hughes, is a very interesting and authoritative book on its subject. If you want to learn more about Colorado's origins, pick up *A Colorado History*, edited by Carl Ubbelohde, Maxine Benson, and Duane Smith.

For an inside look at the Taos society of artists in the 1920s and '30s, see Mabel Dodge Lujan's *Movers and Shakers*. The great Fray Angelico Chavez's *My Penitente Land* is a sensitive and evocative look at the lives and customs of the little-known *Penitente* sect of Roman Catholics in New Mexico's small Hispanic communities. Read it along with Sabine Ulabari's *My Grandmother Smoked Cigars* and the still-resonant *Mayordomo*, by Stanley Crawford, about lives along a small irrigation ditch in north-central New Mexico.

On the top of the fiction list are Rudolfo Anaya's *Bless Me, Ultima*, a magical look at the Indio-Hispanic soul of New Mexico; Willa

Cather's beautiful and rich portrait of Archbishop Lamy of Santa Fe, during the transition from Mexican to U.S. rule in the mid-1800s, in *Death Comes to the Archbishop*; and Frank Waters' *People of the Valley*, about San Luis Valley villagers, and *The Man Who Killed the Deer*, set in Taos Pueblo. For a hilarious, dead-ringer glimpse into New Mexico of the 1960s and early '70s, see John Nichols' *The Milagro Beanfield War*.

Tony Hillerman, of course, has become a one-man publishing dynasty with his series of contemporary thrillers set on the Navajo reservation. His nonfiction talents are less known, but you can check them out by reading his *New Mexico, Rio Grande and Other Essays*.

One-time baseball player and dentist Zane Grey visited the Arizona Strip country (see North Rim chapter) and shortly thereafter penned his first great book, *Riders of the Purple Sage*, a classic western novel. Edward Abbey gave the world a vision of the beauty he found as a ranger at Arches National Monument in his nonfiction book *Desert Solitaire*, then conceived a biting fictional satire on the Southwest's exploitation, *The Monkey Wrench Gang*. For a slightly twisted look at Las Vegas, see Hunter S. Thompson's *Fear and Loathing in Las Vegas* or Tom Wolfe's *The Kandy-Kolored Tangerine-Flake Streamline Baby*.

RESOURCES

In addition to the following resources, many other addresses and phone numbers accompany specific listings in the destination chapters. The map titled "Indian Country," distributed throughout the region by the Southwest Parks and Monuments Association, (602) 622-1999, is a great resource.

Regional

American Park Network: www.AmericanParkNetwork.com
National Forest Service: Camping reservations, (800) 280-CAMP
National Forest Service: Intermountain Region (CO, NV, UT) general information: 324 25th St., Ogden, UT 84401; (801) 625-5306
National Forest Service: Southwestern Region (AZ, NM) general information: 517 Gold SW, Albuquerque, NM 87102; (505) 842-3292
National Park Service: Intermountain Region, 12795 W. Alameda Parkway, Lakewood, CO 80225; (303) 969-2000
National Park Service: Southwestern Region, 1100 Old Santa Fe Trail, Box 728, Santa Fe, NM 87504-0728; (505) 988-6940

Arizona

Arizona Office of Tourism: 2702 N. 3rd St., Suite 4015, Phoenix, AZ 85004; (602) 230-7733 or (800) 842-8257; www.arizonaguide.com

Arizona State Parks Department: 1300 W. Washington St., Suite 415, Phoenix, AZ 85007; (602) 542-4174

Canyon de Chelly National Monument: P.O. Box 588, Chinle, AZ 86503; (520) 674-5436

Flagstaff: Convention and Visitors Bureau, 211 W. Aspen Ave., Flagstaff, AZ 86001; (520) 779-7611

Glen Canyon National Recreation Area: P.O. Box 1507, Page, AZ 86040; (520) 645-2471

Grand Canyon National Park: P.O. Box 129, Grand Canyon, AZ 86023; (520) 638-7888; for camping reservations, (800) 365-2267

Hopi: Office of Public Relations, P.O. Box 123, Kykotsmovi, AZ 86039; (520) 734-2441/6648

Jerome: Chamber of Commerce, P.O. Drawer K, Jerome, AZ 96331, (520) 634-2900

Navajo Nation: Navajo Tourism Office, P.O. Box 663, Window Rock, AZ 85615; (520) 871-6436/6659

Page/Lake Powell: Chamber of Commerce, 106 S. Lake Powell Blvd., P.O. Box 727, Page, AZ 86040; (520) 645-2741

Petrified Forest National Park: P.O. Box 2217, Petrified Forest, AZ 86028; (520) 387-6849

Prescott: Chamber of Commerce, 117 W. Goodwin, P.O. Box 1147, Prescott, AZ 86302; (520) 445-2000 or (800) 266-7534

Sedona: Oak Creek Chamber of Commerce, P.O. Box 478, Sedona, AZ 86336; (520) 282-7722 or (800) 288-7336

Williams: Williams/U.S. Forest Service Visitor Center, 200 W. Railroad Ave., Williams, AZ 86046-2556; (520) 635-4061

Colorado

Colorado Division of Parks and Outdoor Recreation: 1313 Sherman St., Suite 618, Denver, CO 80203; (303) 866-3437

Colorado Division of Wildlife: 6060 Broadway, Denver, CO 80216; general information, (303) 297-1192; fishing, (303) 291-7533

Colorado Travel and Tourism Authority: 1625 Broadway, Suite 1700, Denver, CO 80202; (800) 433-2656; www.colorado.com

Durango: Durango Area Chamber Resort Association, Box 2587, Durango, CO 81302; (800) 463-8726

Mesa Verde Country: Visitor Information Bureau, P.O. Box HH, Cortez, CO 81321-0990; (800) 253-1616; reservations, (800) 449-2288
Mesa Verde National Park: MVNP, CO 81330; (303) 529-4465
Southwest Colorado Travel Region: 295-A Girard, Durango, CO 81301; (970) 385-7884, (800) 933-4340; www.swcolotravel.org
Telluride: Chamber Resort Association Visitors Center, 666 W. Colorado Ave., P.O. Box 653, Telluride, CO 81435; (970) 728-6265 or (800) 525-9717; central reservations, (800) 525-3455; www.telluridemm.com

Nevada
Nevada Commission on Tourism: Capitol Complex, Carson City, NV 89710; (702) 687-6779 or (800) NEVADA-8; www.travelnevada.com
Nevada Division of State Parks: Capitol Complex, Carson City, NV 89710; (800) 237 0774
Boulder City: 100 Nevada Hwy., Boulder City, NV 89005; (702) 294-1220
Lake Mead National Recreation Area: LMNRA, 601 Nevada Hwy., Boulder City, NV 89005-2426; (702) 293-8990
Las Vegas: Vegas Visitors Information Center, 3150 Paradise Blvd., Las Vegas, NV 89109-9096; (702) 892-7575 or (800) 332-5333
Laughlin: Visitors Bureau, 1555 S. Casino Dr., Laughlin, NV 89029; (720) 298-3022 or (800) 367-5284

New Mexico
New Mexico Department of Tourism: 491 Old Santa Fe Trail, Santa Fe, NM 87501-2753; (505) 827-7400 or (800) 733-6396; www.newmexico.org
New Mexico Department of Game and Fish: Villagra Building, 408 Galisteo, Box 25112, Santa Fe, NM 87503; (505) 827-7911
New Mexico Public Lands Information Center: 1474 Rodeo Rd., Santa Fe, NM 87505; (505) 438-7542. Provides details on the region's national forests, national parks, state parks, and Bureau of Land Management holdings
Albuquerque: Convention and Visitor's Bureau, 401 2nd St. NW, P.O. Box 25100, Albuquerque, NM 87125; (505) 842-9918 or (800) 284-2282
Bandelier National Monument: HCR 1, Box 1, Suite 15, Los Alamos, NM 87544; (505) 682-3861
Gallup: Convention and Visitors Bureau, P.O. Box 600, Gallup, NM 87305; (800) 242-4282

Pecos National Monument: P.O. Box 418, Pecos, NM 87552; (505) 757-6414

Petroglyph National Monument: P.O. Box 1293, Albuquerque, NM 87103; (505) 839-4429

Santa Fe Convention and Visitors Bureau: P.O. Box 909, Santa Fe, NM 87504-0909; (505) 984-6760 or (800) 777-2489

Taos: Chamber of Commerce, P.O. Drawer I, Taos, NM 87571; (505) 758-3873 or (800) 732-8267

Zuni Pueblo: Pueblo of Zuni, P.O. Box 339, Zuni, NM 87327; (505) 782-4481

Utah

Utah Division of State Parks and Recreation: 1594 W. North Temple, Suite 116, Box 146001, Salt Lake City, UT 84114-6001; (801) 538-7220; for park camping reservations, (800) 322-3770

Utah Travel Council: Council Hall/Capitol Hill, Salt Lake City, UT 84114; (801) 538-1030 or (800) 200-1160; www.utah.com

Arches National Park: Box 907, Moab, UT 84532; (435) 259-8161

Bryce Canyon National Park: BCNP, Bryce Canyon, UT 84717; (435) 834-5322; www.brycecanyon.com

Canyonlands National Park: CNP, Moab, UT 84532; (435) 259-7164

Capitol Reef/Wayne County: Travel Council, P.O. Box 7, Teasdale, UT 84773, (800) 858-7951; or CRNP, Superintendent, Torrey, UT 84775

Kane County: Travel Council, P.O. Box 728, Kanab, UT 84741; (435) 644-5033

Moab: Visitor Multi-Agency Information Center, Moab, UT 84532; (435) 259-8825 or (800) 635-6622

Monticello: Visitor Multi-Agency Information Center, 117 S. Main, P.O. Box 490, Monticello, UT 84535; (435) 587-3235 or (800) 574-4FUN

St. George: Visitor Multi-Agency Information Center, 345 E. Riverside Dr., St. George, UT 84770; (435) 673-4654; or Travel and Convention Bureau, 425 South East 700 East, St. George, UT 84770; (435) 634-5747 or (800) 869-6635

Zion National Park: P.O. Box 1099, Springdale, UT 84767; (435) 772-3256

1
ALBUQUERQUE

The center of commerce, education, industry, medicine, and population in New Mexico, Albuquerque is the perfect gateway to the American Southwest. Its international airport and two intersecting interstate highways provide easy access to the region. It is also my hometown and a natural spot to begin our American Southwest tour.

Like many Rocky Mountain and western cities, Albuquerque is booming—fueled in part by the computer giant Intel's production plants. The city has a vibrant economy, a youthful population, and a Phoenix-like sprawl beginning to occur at its edges. Thus, it feels like a new city, but it's actually one of the nation's oldest, founded in the Old Town district in 1706. Like much of New Mexico, the city has a multicultural flavor, with its old Spanish/Hispanic core, the Anglo elements developed largely since World War II, and the subtle influences of the area's original Indian cultures.

For a modern metropolis, Albuquerque is refreshingly close to nature. From almost anywhere in the city you can see the looming face of the Sandia Mountains, its colors constantly shifting with the changing light throughout the day. A string of dormant volcanic cones dots Albuquerque's western skyline, and the city is bisected by the green swath of the fabled Rio Grande. By far and away the city's most popular event is the annual Kodak Albuquerque International Balloon Fiesta, held for ten days in early October. The mass ascension of more than 850 balloons is an unforgettable sight. ∎

ALBUQUERQUE

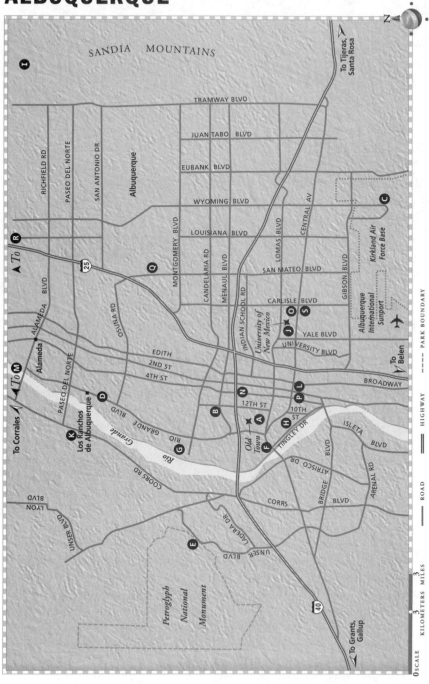

SANDIA MOUNTAINS

To Tijeras,
Santa Rosa

TRAMWAY BLVD

JUAN TABO BLVD

EUBANK BLVD

WYOMING BLVD

RICHFIELD RD

PASEO DEL NORTE

SAN ANTONIO DR

Albuquerque

LOUISIANA BLVD

MONTGOMERY BLVD

CANDELARIA RD

MENAUL BLVD

SAN LOMAS BLVD

CENTRAL AV

Kirkland Air
Force Base

OSUNA RD

CARLISLE BLVD

SAN MATEO BLVD

GIBSON BLVD

Albuquerque
International
Sunport

To
Belen

INDIAN SCHOOL RD

University of
New Mexico

YALE BLVD

UNIVERSITY BLVD

BROADWAY

EDITH
2ND ST
4TH ST

12TH ST

10TH
ST

ISLETA

TINGLEY DR

ATRISCO DR

BRIDGE BLVD

ARENAL RD

CORRS

BLVD

Old
Town

PASEO DEL NORTE

GRANDE BLVD

RIO GRANDE BLVD

Rio Grande

COORS RD

Los Ranchos
de Albuquerque

To Corrales

Alameda

ALAMEDA BLVD

ALAMEDA

To

To

LYON BLVD

UNSER BLVD

LADERA DR

UNSER BLVD

Petroglyph
National
Monument

To Grants,
Gallup

SCALE 0   3   3
       KILOMETERS MILES

PARK BOUNDARY
HIGHWAY
ROAD

Sights

Ⓐ Albuquerque Museum of Arts, History and Science

Ⓑ Indian Pueblo Cultural Center

Ⓒ National Atomic Museum

Ⓐ New Mexico Museum of Natural History

Ⓓ North Valley/Corrales/ Coronado State Monument

Ⓐ Old Town Plaza

Ⓔ Petroglyph National Monument

Ⓐ Rattlesnake Museum

Ⓕ Rio Grande Botanic Garden and Albuquerque Aquarium

Ⓖ Rio Grande Nature Center

Ⓗ Rio Grande Zoo

Ⓘ Sandia Mountains

Ⓐ San Felipe de Neri Church

Ⓐ Turquoise Museum

Ⓙ UNM Art Museum

Food

Ⓚ André's

Ⓛ Artichoke Café

Ⓜ Casa Vieja

Ⓝ Garcia's Kitchen

Ⓘ High Finance Restaurant and Tavern

Ⓞ Il Vicino

Ⓐ La Crepe Michele

Ⓐ La Placita

Ⓐ Maria Teresa's

Ⓟ M&J Sanitary Tortilla Factory

Ⓠ Oasis

Ⓡ Range Café

Ⓢ Scalo Northern Italian Grill

Note: Items with the same letter are located in the same area.

A PERFECT DAY IN ALBUQUERQUE

After an early breakfast at Garcia's Kitchen, visit Petroglyph National Monument on the West Mesa to get an overview of the city and some grounding in its prehistoric past. Then visit Old Town to soak up its Hispanic flavor, shop, visit museums, and have lunch at La Crepe Michele or La Placita. A short drive takes you to the Indian Pueblo Cultural Center for an introduction to the art, culture, and history of the state's 19 Pueblo tribes. End the day with a ride on the tramway to Sandia Crest for a spectacular sunset. Then take a drive through the North Valley to Corrales for dinner at Casa Vieja.

SIGHTSEEING HIGHLIGHTS

★★★ **Indian Pueblo Cultural Center**—This is a great place to introduce yourself to New Mexico's Pueblo Indians, arguably the most culturally intact of all the nation's Indian people. The center is owned and run by the Pueblo people themselves, which alone makes it unique. Here you can tour permanent exhibits on the arts and history of each of the 19 different pueblos, see changing contemporary art shows, watch live dances and arts-and-crafts demonstrations on weekends, and even take in a meal—all in the Indian way. The center also houses a children's museum, excellent gift shop, and bookstore.

Details: *2401 12th St. NW (a few blocks north of I-40 [exit 157B] at the corner of 12th St. and Indian School Rd.); (505) 843-7270 or (800) 766-4405. Open daily 9–5:30. Admission is $3 for adults, $1.50 for students, free to children under 6. (2 hours)*

★★★ **Old Town Plaza**—Here is where Albuquerque got its start, as a small village founded by Hispanic farmers in 1706. Around the charming, shady plaza—much calmer and prettier than the highly touted central plazas of Santa Fe and Taos—and down side streets perfect for strolling are hundreds of one-of-a-kind retail stores, art galleries, craft shops, tacky-but-fun souvenir dives, and a handful of restaurants. Bargain directly with the Indian arts-and-crafts vendors who display their excellent goods on blankets under the portal on the east side of the Plaza.

On Sundays, **Wild West Shootouts** are held on Romero Street, and on special occasions, mariachi and other music is played on the central bandstand. **Christmas Eve** is particularly memorable here, as tens of thousands of *luminarias* (votive candles placed in small brown paper sacks with sand in the bottom) are set along walks and walls.

The **Old Town Visitors Center** offers tips on the area's attractions and distributes a free walking-tour guide. Complimentary guided walking tours are also conducted by the Albuquerque Museum (see below), from April through October at 11 a.m. daily (except Monday). Tours last about an hour.

Details: *The visitor center is located at 305 Romero St. NW; (505) 243-3215. Open Monday through Saturday 9–5, Sunday 10–5. (30 minutes to 2 hours)*

★★★ **Rio Grande Nature Center**—This 270-acre preserve is set amidst the largest river cottonwood forest in the world, stretching along the Rio Grande from Cochiti Pueblo in the north to Socorro in the south. Here, city thoughts quickly disappear. A wonderful nature center is sunk into ground of the *bosque* (Spanish for woodland), providing an underwater glimpse into a wetland pond where migratory ducks bob for food and turtles dive. A foot trail winds through the forest and along the great irrigation channel locals call the Clear Ditch. It's great birding ground, with excellent year-round viewing of Canada geese and mallard ducks. In the winter months you can see wood and ring-necked ducks, gadwall, and American wigeon; in the spring look for blue grosbeaks, cinnamon teal, red-winged blackbirds, and roadrunners.

Details: *2901 Candelaria Rd. NW (off Rio Grande Blvd. NW); (505) 344-7240. Open daily 9–5. Admission is $4.25 for adults, $2.25 for kids under 16. (1 to 2 hours)*

✰✰✰ **Sandia Mountains**—The Sandias are Albuquerque's ever-changing artistic canvas, rearing up in the east like a wave whose colors and form constantly shift with the changing light. Their name is Spanish for "watermelon"—a color they often assume at dusk. They offer both a visual orientation for the city and a nearby getaway for walks, hiking, picnicking, skiing, bird watching, and other outdoor activities.

The **Sandia Peak Aerial Tramway** rises some 3,000 feet up the fractured western face of the Sandias in a ride that thrills both kids and adults. One of North America's longest cable tramways, it requires at least 90 minutes for a round trip, more if you plan to walk one of the rim trails. You can also drive to the **Sandia Crest** via NM 536, a national scenic byway, which cuts off of NM 14 (the Turquoise Trail). From the summit, at an elevation of 10,678 feet, you seem to see half of New Mexico: 125-mile views in all directions are often possible. The rim is frequently 30 to 40 degrees cooler than town, a welcome break in summer or a teeth-chattering encounter in winter, so dress appropriately.

There are two nice foot trails at the Crest: one dips into deep conifer forest, the other runs along the face just under the rim. In the early morning and late afternoon, you'll see a lot of wildlife, including Abert and red squirrel, chipmunks, mule deer, and many bird species, including eagles and other raptors. The **Sandia Crest House**, (505) 243-0605, carries snacks, sandwiches, and small gifts. The Crest also hosts the Steel Forest, one of the world's greatest concentrations of radio and television antennas in the world—not the place to be in a summer lightning storm! A number of cars have also had their car alarms go wacky here, in some cases shutting down their ignition systems. Know how to override your car's security system.

Details: For driving directions, see the Turquoise Trail Scenic Drive section. To get to the tram's base station, take I-25 north to Tramway Blvd., head east to Tramway Loop, and turn left; (505) 856-7325. Hours of operation shift seasonally; call first. A round-trip ticket costs $13.50 for adults, $11.50 for kids. Additional information is available from the Cibola National Forest at (505) 842-3292, or the Sandia Ranger Station, located in Tijeras village on NM 337, at (505) 281-3304. (1½ to 3 hours)

★★ **Albuquerque Museum of Arts, History and Science**—This museum houses the nation's largest collection of Spanish Colonial artifacts, including a pair of life-size conquistadors in original chain mail and armor. Interesting photos and artifacts from the city's past accompany excellent historical and contemporary exhibits drawn from the city's vibrant art community. Outside, visit the museum's terrific sculpture garden.

Details: 2000 Mountain Rd. NW (on the eastern edge of Old Town); (505) 243-7255. Open Tuesday through Sunday 9–5. Free. (2 hours)

★★ **New Mexico Museum of Natural History**—This outstanding museum has fascinating and fun displays on the region's prehistoric critters and landforms, from life-size dinos (including a model of one of the largest specimens ever found) to "erupting" volcanoes. Several beautiful dioramas include one depicting New Mexico in the last ice age, with a real woolly mammoth skeleton beside it. Kids love the Evolator, a shaking, baking box that simulates a descent into the Earth and back in time. The museum also has a decent lunch room, a Dynamax Theater, and a great educational gift shop.

Details: 1801 Mountain Rd. NW (on the eastern edge of Old Town, just a few minutes walk from the Plaza); (505) 841-2800. Open daily 9–5. Admission is $4 adults, $3 seniors, $1 children 3–11. (2 hours)

★★ **North Valley/Corrales/Coronado State Monument**—This linear drive parallels the lovely Rio Grande Valley. Head north on Rio Grande Boulevard from its intersection with Central Avenue, which gets prettier and prettier as you head into what was a major farming area 25 years ago. At the T intersection with Alameda, turn left and cross the Rio Grande. At the first stoplight west of the river, turn right onto Corrales Road (NM 448) and continue north to the village of **Corrales**, dotted with art galleries, small restaurants, bed-and-breakfasts, and roadside produce stands.

Eventually you'll climb out of the valley floor and onto the mesa. At the intersection with NM 528, turn right and proceed 5 miles or so north to NM 44, and turn right. In a few hundred yards you'll see the entrance to Coronado State Monument on your left. The monument preserves prehistoric Kuaua Pueblo, from which you'll see beautiful views of the Rio Grande and the Sandias. You can enter a restored, roofed kiva bedecked with rare wall paintings. A nice visitor center displays materials recovered from the now-disintegrating pueblo. There is talk of shutting down this monument because of nearby development pressure, so call first.

Details: The monument is on the west bank of the Rio Grande, just off NM 44, west of Bernalillo; (505) 867-5351. Open daily 9–6 from mid-May through mid-September, and 10–6 the rest of the year. Admission is $2; under 17 free. (2 to 3 hours)

★★ **Petroglyph National Monument**—Long before there was an Albuquerque, Indian people recorded their habitation and travel on the dark basalt rock cliffs and boulders of the West Mesa in one of the world's greatest assembly of petroglyphs. Among the 15,000 or so drawings pecked into the dark surface of boulders and cliff overhangs are a tropical parrot, reflective of prehistoric trade with Mexico; spirals believed to represent the cosmos or eternity; and the hunchbacked flute-player Kokopelli, a god of fertility and frivolity. The images span more than 3,000 years, including some rare Spanish and territorial period works

Details: 4735 Unser Boulevard NW; (505) 839-4429. Take I-40 West over the Rio Grande to NM 448, then a left off Coors onto Unser Blvd. Open daily 8–5. Admission is $1 per car weekdays, $2 weekends. (2 hours)

★★ **Rio Grande Botanic Garden and Albuquerque Aquarium**—Opened to great and deserved fanfare in December 1996, the $33-million facility includes 450,000 gallons of exhibition aquariums and 10 acres of landscaped gardens. Both the gardens and the aquariums focus on life forms of the Rio Grande and trace its long journey from the Colorado mountains to the Gulf of Mexico.

Details: 2601 Central Ave. at New York Ave. NW; (505) 764-6200. Open daily 9–5. Admission is $6 adults, $4 children. (2 to 3 hours)

★★ **Rio Grande Zoo**—A few minutes' drive from the botanic gardens is one of the nation's better midsized zoos. Set on 60 acres under ancient, arching river cottonwoods are spacious, naturalistic settings for some 1,300 different species of mammals, reptiles, and birds, including rare lobos (Mexican wolves), California condors (the world's largest bird), orangutans, and buffalo. There's also a rainforest and a wonderful seal tank with underwater viewing ports. The museum has a decent cafeteria, a snack counter, and a gift shop.
Details: 903 10th St. NW; (505) 764-6200. Open daily 9–5. Admission is $4.25 adults, $2.25 seniors and children. (2 hours)

★★ **San Felipe de Neri Church**—On the north side of Old Town Plaza is this attractive, historic 1706 church. The sparse interior has a quiet elegance, with a spiral staircase winding up to a small balcony and an altar with hand-carved *retablos* (carved and painted panels). The church also maintains an attached museum and gift shop.
Details: 2005 N. Plaza, (505) 243-4628. The church is open daily 7–6, with Sunday mass at 8:30 a.m.; the museum is open Monday through Friday 1–4, Saturday noon to 3. Free. (30 minutes)

★ **National Atomic Museum**—This unique tribute to technology will either thrill or appall you, depending on your view of nuclear energy and weaponry. It includes replicas of Fat Man and Little Boy, the bombs dropped on Hiroshima and Nagasaki. *Ten Seconds That Shook the World*, about the making of the atomic bomb, screens four times daily.
Details: Kirtland Air Force base, through the Wyoming gate; (505) 284-3243. Open daily 9–5. Free. (1 hour)

★ **Rattlesnake Museum**—Housing the world's largest collection of live rattling snakes from around the Southwest and the world, this private museum in Old Town is popular with kids. The owner stresses the ecological importance of rattlesnakes.
Details: 202 San Felipe St. NW, (505) 242-6569. Open daily 10–9 in summer, 10–6 otherwise. Admission is $2 for adults, $1 for kids under 17. (30 minutes)

★ **Turquoise Museum**—This eye-popping small museum displays an amazing array of the state's official gemstone: the sky-matching turquoise. There are immense nuggets, examples of fake turquoise, and samples from different mines worldwide.

Details: 2107 Central Ave. NW; (505) 247-8650 or (800) 821-7443. Open Monday through Saturday 9–5. Admission is $3. (1 hour)

✦ **University of New Mexico Art Museum**—Believe it or not, this relatively small institution houses one of the nation's better photo collections, including both American and world masters, in many photographic and print media. It also hangs ambitious, often-excellent, changing fine art exhibitions, as well as faculty and student shows. It's an important adjunct to the university's thriving arts program.

Details: Fine Arts Building next to Popejoy Hall, just off Central at Cornell St.; (505) 277-4001. Open Tuesday through Friday 9–4, Sunday 1–4; closed Saturday. Admission is by donation. (1 hour)

KIDS' STUFF

Kids particularly like the already-noted Museum of Natural History, Rattlesnake Museum, Rio Grande Zoo, Rio Grande Botanic Garden and Albuquerque Aquarium, and the dances at the Indian Pueblo Cultural Center. Also popular are Petroglyph National Monument, the Sandias, and Rio Grande Nature Center. The **Albuquerque Children's Museum**, 800 Rio Grande Blvd. NW, (505) 842-5525, within a shopping arcade attached to the Old Town Sheraton, is also outstanding. In the summer heat there's **The Beach**, 3 Desert Surf Circle at Montaño and I-25, (505) 345-6066. Outside of town, on the Turquoise Trail, is the Tinkertown Museum (see Scenic Route, below).

FITNESS AND RECREATION

Albuquerque has a host of outdoor recreation possibilities, as well as many public and commercial fitness centers. Walking, biking, and jogging trails can be found along the forested Rio Grande valley floor and in the foothills of the Sandias. A 5-mile public asphalt trail in the Valley, **Paseo del Bosque**, is a great place to stretch the legs or ride a bike. Bike rentals and guided tours can be secured at **Old Town Bicycles**, 2209-B Central Ave. NW, (505) 247-4926. Another biking resource is the **Albuquerque Wheelmen** group, (505) 291-9835.

On the city's eastern edge is **Elena Gallegos-Simms Park**, (505)

291-6224, a 640-acre preserve of lovely grasslands overlooking the city, set beneath the towering Sandias, with hiking, biking, and picnic areas. The **Domingo Baca Trail** leads to an area frequented by mule deer. Its water tank with a blind is a good place to view bird life. The park entrance is on the east side of Tramway Boulevard, about ⅛-mile north of Montgomery Boulevard. It's open 7 a.m. to 9 p.m. in summer, 7 to 7 otherwise. Admission is $1 per car on weekdays, $2 on weekends.

The **Sandias** offer wonderful short to multi-day hikes, both along the high rim (good in summer) and at lower elevations close to the city (good in winter). A terrific 7-mile hike can be had on **La Luz Trail**, which switchbacks up from high desert terrain in the foothills to subalpine forests at the summit, opening up views of the Rio Grande Valley below. Ideally, you'd have a car waiting for you at the crest. Be sure to bring along your own water, and be extremely alert for ice on the trail, even in spring. To get to the trailhead, take I-25 north to the Tramway exit and head east; at the first left turn, proceed on Forest Service Road 444 which runs to the trail parking lot. For additional trail information, contact the Sandia Ranger Station, (505) 281-3304.

In winter, the wedge-shaped range also provides for cross-country and downhill skiing on its eastern slope at **Sandia Peak Ski Area**, (505) 242-9133, a small but surprisingly good area that receives more than 100 inches of snow a year. I stepped into cable bindings here in 1961, and the mountain has introduced thousands to the sport before and since. Most runs are relatively short, geared for beginners and intermediates. Weekends can be quite crowded in nice weather. The Sandia Tram (see Sightseeing Highlights) provides quick and easy access to its summit, or you can drive around to its base via the Turquoise Trail (see the Scenic Route, below). In summer, you can rent mountain bikes or hike here, taking advantage of the chairlift for the uphill climb. The chairlift operates from 10 a.m. to 4 p.m. on weekends.

If you like horseback riding, check out **Sandia Trails** in the Valley, 10601 N. 4th St. NW, (505) 281-1772, or **Turkey Track Stables**, 1306 US 66 East, Tijeras, (505) 281-1772, in the Manzano Mountain foothills. The city also maintains four public golf courses, numerous indoor and outdoor pools, and tennis courts. For details on city walking and biking trails or these other activities, call the Albuquerque Cultural and Recreation Services Department, (505) 768-3550. Albuquerque is also famous for its hot-air balloons, and a handful of companies (see the Yellow Pages) can take you up for a bird's-eye view of the city.

SPECTATOR SPORTS

Albuquerque *loooves* its sports. Especially popular are the **University of New Mexico Lobos**, (505) 277-2116 or (800) 905-3315, in particular their basketball games in the infamous 18,000-seat Pit at the corner of University Boulevard and Avenida César Chavez. It's also hard to beat a summer night at the **Albuquerque Dukes'** baseball stadium, 1601 Avenida César Chavez, (505) 243-1791, with a soft breeze accompanying the crack of bat on ball. This is the Dodgers' Triple-A farm team—Orel Hershiser is an alumnus.

The city is also home to the world's largest hot-air balloon gathering—the **Albuquerque Kodak International Balloon Fiesta**. Held annually from the first through the second weekends in October, it draws more than 850 balloonists from across the globe. Highlights are the weekend morning mass ascensions and the Special Shapes events, when balloons of almost every imaginable form—hot dogs, wine bottles, rolled-up newspapers, castles, pigs, and spaceships—take to the air. The $4 admission allows you to wander among the launching balloons. With more than 1.5 million spectators, finding a room or dining reservation in the city on short notice is almost impossible. The launch site is located in 77-acre Balloon Fiesta Park, on the northwestern edge of the city between Paseo del Norte and Alameda Boulevard. Shuttle buses run between major hotels and the site. For general information, call (505) 821-1000; for recorded events, call (505) 243-3696.

FOOD

Albuquerque may not be a dining mecca, but its sheer size and growing sophistication provide it with an ample selection of restaurants. Right on the Plaza is **La Placita**, 206 San Felipe St. NW, (505) 247-2204, serving traditional New Mexican dishes, plus a wide selection of American dishes, including fine steaks, with a full bar. The wonderful building dates to 1706. Also exuding historic flavor is **Maria Teresa's**, 618 Rio Grande Blvd. NW (next to the Old Town Sheraton), (505) 242-3900. This national landmark property serves pricey but delicious Continental specialties as well as New Mexican fare and includes a pleasant courtyard. **La Crepe Michele**, 400 C-2 San Felipe St. NW (tucked into the intimate Patio del Norte), (505) 242-1251, is an excellent French bistro offering something different for those burned out on chile. Its proximity to San Felipe de Neri church precludes liquor.

For some excellent New Mexican food outside the plaza area, check out the **M&J Sanitary Tortilla Factory**, 403 2nd St. SW, (505) 242-4890, which supplies Air Force One with takeout. They have incendiary salsa and the best sopaipillas in the state. Another locally beloved spot is **Garcia's Kitchen**, 1113 N. 4th St. NW, (505) 247-9149. You won't believe the oddball collectible decor. A seat at the counter provides quick service, or dive into a booth and dig into a bowl of steamy *carne adovada* (pork marinated in red chile) with a fried egg for breakfast—it's guaranteed to clear the cobwebs!

In Nob Hill, a popular shopping and nightlife district, many a revealing comment has been dropped around the animated tables of **Scalo Northern Italian Grill**, 3500 Central Ave. NE, (505) 255-8781. Meals range from salmon salads to veal scaloppine with toasted almonds and cranberries. **Il Vicino**, 3403 Central Ave. NE, (505) 266-7855, serves wood-fired-oven pizza, as well as salads, pasta, and several microbrews.

Elsewhere in the city, locals head to the **Artichoke Café**, 424 Central Ave. SE, (505) 243-0200, for some of the city's best French, new American, and Italian fare, such as grilled duck or pumpkin ravioli with fresh spinach. **Oasis**, 5400 San Mateo, (505) 884-2324, presents modestly priced fine Greek and Mediterranean food, including dolmas, *spanikopita*, Greek salads, moussaka, and skewered lamb. On the West Mesa, to the west of the Rio Grande, is **André's**, 9401 Coors Blvd. NW, (505) 890-2725. Food here is both imaginative and well-priced, including the tasty daily specials. They offer an extensive wine list and unusual beers.

Outside Albuquerque, my favorite local restaurant is in the charming village of Corrales—**Casa Vieja**, 4541 Corrales Rd., (505) 898-7489. Housed in a building almost three centuries old, its small dining rooms, several with fireplaces, envelop one in the relaxing atmosphere of old New Mexico. The French and northern Italian food is outstanding, as is the service. A jacket and tie are required. Not open for lunch. In nearby Bernalillo is the less expensive and equally good **Range Café**, 264 Camino del Pueblo (the main drag), (505) 867-1700, with meatloaf like Mom used to cook, all fresh ingredients, and excellent breads, pastry, breakfasts, and desserts.

The **High Finance Restaurant and Tavern**, (505) 243-9742, is at the summit of the Sandia Peak Tramway. Although it's a bit pricey, the tab for standard steaks, seafood, pasta, and New Mexican fare includes tremendous views of sunsets and the city lights. If you have a reservation, the tram ride is reduced by two dollars.

LODGING

The city and surrounding area have a diverse selection of accommodations, ranging from all the major brand-name hotels and motels to many one-of-a-kind bed-and-breakfasts.

The nicest of the corporate hotels is the **Hyatt Regency**, 330 Tijeras Ave. NW, (505) 842-1234. Located downtown, it's popular with business travelers and has a slick art deco interior and restful ambiance. Within it is a good restaurant, McGraths's, an outdoor pool, health club, and shopping arcade. Rates are $135–$175. While not as fancy as the Regency, the **Old Town Sheraton**, 800 Rio Grande Blvd. NW, (505) 842-9863, is a nice place offering accommodations close to Old Town, museums, the North Valley, and downtown. Amenities include two on-site restaurants, an outdoor pool with a hot tub, and the attached Albuquerque Children's Museum. Rates are $100–$120.

Also downtown is the charming **La Posada de Albuquerque**, 125 2nd St. NW, (505) 242-9090 or (800) 777-5732. Opened in 1939 by New Mexico native Conrad Hilton as his first endeavor outside of Texas, it is now an independent property undergoing a $4.5-million expansion to add a six-floor, 90-room tower. The hotel's older section boasts many attractive features, from murals to architectural elements, reflecting the early decades of Southwestern tourism. The on-premises Conrad's restaurant features good food from the Mexican Yucatan region. Rates are $69–$115.

At the airport is **Best Western Wyndham Albuquerque Hotel**, 2910 Yale Blvd. SE, (505) 843-7000 or (800) 227-1117, which completed an $8-million renovation in 1997; rooms are $89. Also in the airport area are the **Radisson Inn**, 1901 University Blvd. SE, (505) 247-0512 or (800) 333-3333, which has standard rooms but a year-round pool, a bar, and a decent restaurant, Diamond Back's Café. Rates are $79–$95. The **Comfort Inn**, 2300 Yale Blvd. SE, (505) 243-2244 or (800) 221-2222, has rooms for less than $65 a night. Another mid-priced option is the **Best Western Rio Grande Inn**, 1015 Rio Grande Blvd. NW, (505) 843-9500 or (800) 959-4726, offering easy access to the Old Town area, rooms with handmade furniture and local art, a laundry facility, and dining at the Albuquerque Grill. Rates are $88.

Among the cheapest accommodations is the **Route 66 Hostel**, 1012 Central Ave. SW, (505) 247-1813, with dormitory bunk beds at $12 for members, $14 for nonmembers. Central Avenue has a slew of cheap motels, including the **Gas Light**, 601 Central Ave. NE, (505)

ALBUQUERQUE

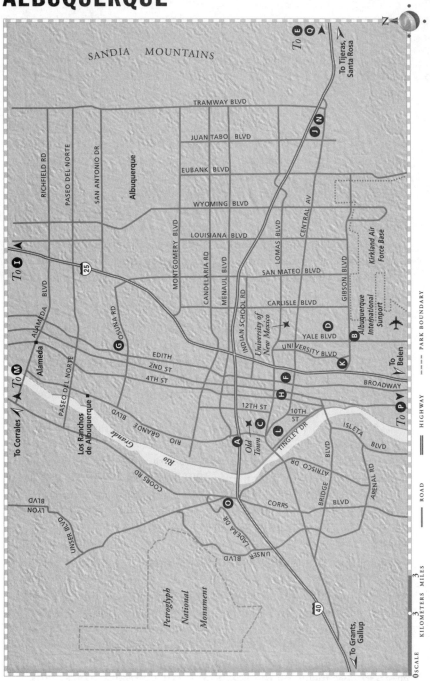

SANDIA MOUNTAINS

TRAMWAY BLVD

JUAN TABO BLVD

EUBANK BLVD

WYOMING BLVD

LOUISIANA BLVD

Albuquerque

RICHFIELD RD

PASEO DEL NORTE

SAN ANTONIO DR

MONTGOMERY BLVD

CANDELARIA RD

MENAUL BLVD

LOMAS BLVD

CENTRAL AV

SAN MATEO BLVD

CARLISLE BLVD

GIBSON BLVD

Kirkland Air
Force Base

Albuquerque
International
Sunport

INDIAN SCHOOL RD

University of
New Mexico

YALE BLVD

UNIVERSITY BLVD

To
Belen

To Tijeras,
Santa Rosa

To Tijeras

25

GOSUNA RD

ALAMEDA BLVD

Alameda

PASEO DEL NORTE

To Corrales

Los Ranchos
de Albuquerque

RIO GRANDE BLVD

Rio Grande

COORS RD

LYON BLVD

UNSER BLVD

Petroglyph
National
Monument

EDITH

2ND ST

4TH ST

12TH ST

10TH ST

Old Town

TINGLEY DR

ISLETA BLVD

ATRISCO DR

BRIDGE BLVD

ARENAL RD

CORRS BLVD

LADERA DR

UNSER BLVD

BROADWAY

To Grants,
Gallup

40

N

To E
To Q

To I

To M

To P

Lodging

Ⓐ Best Western Rio Grande Inn

Ⓑ Best Western Wyndham
   Albuquerque Hotel

Ⓒ Bottger Mansion

Ⓒ Casas de Sueños

Ⓓ Comfort Inn

Ⓔ Elaine's

Ⓕ Gas Light

Ⓖ Hacienda Antigua

Ⓗ Hyatt Regency

Ⓘ La Hacienda Grande

Ⓗ La Posada de Albuquerque

Ⓙ Motel 6

Ⓒ Old Town B&B

Lodging *(continued)*

Ⓒ Old Town Sheraton

Ⓚ Radisson Inn

Ⓛ Route 66 Hostel

Ⓜ Sandhill Crane

Ⓕ Travel Inn

Camping

Ⓝ Albuquerque Central KOA

Ⓘ Albuquerque North KOA

Ⓞ Albuquerque West KOA

Ⓟ Isleta Lakes

Ⓠ Sandia Mountains

Ⓠ Turquoise Trail Campground

Note: Items with the same letter are located in the same area.

242-6020; and the **Travel Inn**, 615 Central Ave. NE, (505) 247-8897—both with doubles for around $30. On the far eastern edge of town is one of several **Motel 6**s, 13141 Central Ave. NW, (505) 294-4600, with rooms for $36.

If you dare to leave the beaten path, you'll find many excellent and unusual bed-and-breakfasts in and around Albuquerque. Within Old Town is the **Bottger Mansion**, 110 San Felipe St. NW, (505) 243-3639, a historic and handsome American foursquare home built in 1912. Victorian-era rooms have original pressed-tin ceilings and roomy brass beds. Try the breakfast burritos smothered in green chile. Rates are $79–$139.

Adjacent to Old Town in the Country Club district, **Casas de Sueños**, 310 Rio Grande Blvd. SW, (505) 247-4560 or (800) 242-8987, has 17 comfortable casitas that ramble over 2 acres dotted with gardens, patios, and fountains. Some feature fireplaces, kitchens, and private hot tubs. Rates are $90–$250. The **Old Town Bed-and-Breakfast**, 707 17th St. NW, (505) 764-9144, is on the edge of Old Town in a quiet residential neighborhood. Built by adobe residential design pioneer Leon Watson, this comfortable residence has one outstanding new suite with a kiva fireplace, and an inexpensive, small but pleasant second-floor room with good views. Rates are $65–$80.

Out in the pastoral, cottonwood-shaded North Valley, you'll find the 200-year-old **Hacienda Antigua**, 6708 Tierra Dr., (505) 345-5399 or (800) 201-2987. This historic adobe stayed in the same family for 150 years and served as a stop for travelers on the Camino Real and later for stagecoach travelers. The hacienda has been beautifully renovated in the Spanish Colonial style by the current innkeepers. The building features a lovely courtyard with gardens and a pool. A hearty Southwestern breakfast is served. Rates are $105–$160.

Further north, in the village of Corrales, is the **Sandhill Crane**, 389 Camino Hermosa, (505) 898-2445 or (800) 375-2445, a rambling hacienda with pretty gardens, pleasant rooms, and great views of the Sandias. Rates are $75–$150. In Bernalillo, the 250-plus-year-old **La Hacienda Grande**, 21 Baros Lane, (505) 876-1887, offers a cozy sitting room with fireplace, a brick-floored dining room, and charming bedrooms. Rates are $89–$119.

To the east of the city, on the "backside" of the Sandias and along the Turquoise Trail (see Scenic Route, below), is **Elaine's**, 72 Snowline Rd., Cedar Crest, (505) 281-2467 or (800) 821-3092, a three-story log structure with massive stone fireplaces that perfectly suits its mountain setting. Rates are $80–$90.

CAMPING

Several commercial campgrounds in and near town include the **Albuquerque KOA Central**, 12400 Skyline Rd. (exit 166 off I-40 on the city's eastern edge), (505) 296-2729, with 169 RV sites, 30 tent sites, and 16 cabins. Amenities are hot showers, LP gas, a grocery and pool, and miniature golf; however, you'll find little shade in summer. **Albuquerque North KOA**, 555 Hill Rd., 12 miles north of the city in Bernalillo, (505) 867-5227 or (800) 624-9767, has 57 RV sites and 36 tent sites, an outdoor café, horseshoes, and a heated pool. **Albuquerque West KOA**, 5739 Ouray Rd. NW (a half-mile north of the I-40 Coors Rd. exit, 505-831-1991) is another in-town option.

Out of town, **Isleta Lakes**, 15 miles south of Albuquerque on the

Isleta Pueblo Reservation (take I-25 exit 215 south onto NM 47), (505) 877-0370, has 40 RV sites and 100 tent sites next to fishing and boating lakes, along with hot showers, and grocery and laundry facilities. **Turquoise Trail Campground**, 22 Calvary Rd., in the Sandias at Cedar Crest (head east on I-40 15 miles to exit 175, then follow NM 14 north for 5 miles), (505) 281-2005, has 57 RV sites and two tent sites. The closest U.S. Forest grounds are in the **Sandias**, almost an hour from central Albuquerque. For details, call the Sandia Ranger Station, (505) 281-3304.

NIGHTLIFE

Albuquerque hosts many "high culture" events. To find out more about these events, call the **New Mexico Symphony Orchestra**, (505) 881-9595; **Albuquerque Civic Light Opera**, (505) 345-6577; **Albuquerque Little Theater**, (505) 242-4750; or the bilingual drama troupe **La Compania de Teatro de Albuquerque**, (505) 242-7929. For events in the University of New Mexico's fine **Popejoy Hall**, call (505) 851-5050 or (800) 905-3315.

The city has two main entertainment areas: downtown along Central Avenue and the Nob Hill district. In the dowtown area is the **KiMo Theater**, 423 Central Ave. NW, (505) 848-1370, a former movie palace of fantastic Pueblo Deco design that now hosts live music, dance, performance, and other cultural events. It's usually open for free tours during the day. **La Posada de Albuquerque**, 125 2nd St. NW, (505) 242-9090, a historic hotel (see Lodging, above), has a lobby bar that features jazz and blues on weekend nights and piano on weekdays.

Also downtown, **The Zone** and **Z-Pub** share a space in the former and grand Sunshine Theater, 120 Central Ave. NE, (505) 343-7933, and present live shows occasionally. Nearby is the **Dingo Bar**, 313 Gold Ave. SW, (505) 243-0663, a music hole that's hosted some surprisingly major acts of all stripes over the years, as well as a regular lineup of up-and-comers. **Brewster's**, 312 Central Ave. SW, (505) 247-2533, is a college hangout, with 24 beers on tap and nonstop barbecue for lunch and dinner, live entertainment Wednesday through Saturday, and big-screen TV. At the **Launchpad**, 618 Central Ave. SW, (505) 764-8887, you can hear local alternative bands in a space-age environment. The venerable **El Rey** and **Golden West Saloon**, both on 7th and Central, (505) 764-2624, offer live music and atmosphere.

In Nob Hill, **The Pulse**, 4100 Central Ave. SE, (505) 255-3334, caters to the gay and gay-friendly crowd with occasional touring shows and the city's cutting-edge DJs. This is also ka-boy country; don't miss one of the West's longest-running pointy-toed shuffle spots, with more than 30 years of service, at the **Caravan East**, 7605 Central Ave. NE, (505) 265-7877—two live bands a night and a free buffet and half-price drinks during the 4:30 to 7 p.m. happy hour. The state's best comedy club, **Laff's**, 3100 Juan Tabo NE, (505) 296-5653, is also a full-service restaurant and bar.

There are also a number of Indian casinos just outside Albuquerque, all offering poker, blackjack, craps, roulette, slots, and bingo. To the south at 11000 Broadway SE (take I-40 south to exit 215) is the **Isleta Gaming Palace**, (505) 869-2614 or (800) 460-5686; to the northwest of Bernalillo on NM 44 is the **Santa Ana Star**, (505) 867-0000.

Scenic Route: The Turquoise Trail

If you choose to follow the full loop presented in this book, you'll go to Grants before you head to Santa Fe, but you'll still want to go to Santa Fe via Albuquerque. You can zip up the interstate between Albuquerque and Santa Fe in less than an hour. It's actually a beautiful drive; I've done it countless times, and it still holds my attention. But if you're looking to get off the beaten track and see a slice of life in rural New Mexico, check out the Turquoise Trail. It's dotted with ghost towns that are springing back to life, old mines, and landscapes that vary from bone-dry flats to piñon-juniper hill country.

From the "Big I" in Albuquerque (where I-40 and I-25 intersect), head east 15 miles on I-40 to the village of Tijeras and take exit 175. Turn north (left) onto NM 14. Six miles up the road in **Sandia Park**—past the small rural communities of **San Antonio**, **Cedar Crest**, and **Cañoncito**—you'll pass the turnoff to NM 536, a National Scenic Byway that winds through lovely forests to **Sandia Crest**. You may want to make a quick detour here to visit the charming **Tinkertown Museum**, featuring an immense, animated Western town and circus carved entirely out of wood. Tinkertown is open April through October daily from 9 a.m. to 6 p.m. Admission is $2.50 for

THE TURQUOISE TRAIL

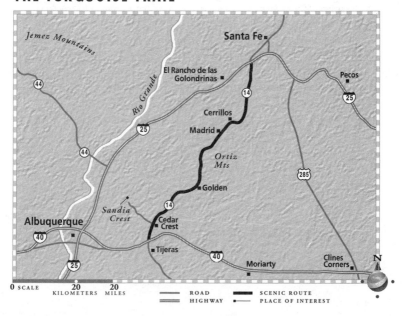

adults and $1 for children. Turn left at the Triangle Grocery Store, head up the road leading to Sandia Peak, and follow the signs.

Back on NM 14 North, just a shout down the road is **Pete's Mexican Restaurant** (a favorite with the locals). Next you'll roll on into tiny **Golden.** It sits in the foothills of the nearby **San Pedro Mountains**, site of the first gold strike (1825) west of the Mississippi. There's a rock shop, mercantile store, and pretty adobe church built in the 1830s to honor St. Francis of Assisi. **La Casita**, the shop at the north side of town, serves as the unofficial information center.

Outside of Golden, you'll ascend a narrow pass through the mountains and then descend into a valley with breathtaking views toward Santa Fe. At the bottom of the valley lies the small, funky village of **Madrid**, a thriving coal-mining company town in the 1800s, with 2,500 residents. By the early 1960s it was almost totally abandoned, but by the end of the decade, it was reoccupied by hippies and today is home to many artists and craftspeople. On its main street you'll find the venerable **Mine Shaft Tavern**, which fronts the **Old Coal Mine Museum**, both (505) 473-0743, where you can tour an underground mine. Also adjoining is the **Engine House Theater**, (505) 438-3780, which presents summer melodramas. If you have time, explore Madrid's many shops; but if you have only a few minutes, make sure you stop at **Primitiva**, specializing in Mexican furniture and crafts, located on the town's main street.

Last stop is **Cerrillos**, an 1880s boom town of silver, gold, and turquoise mines. Several film projects have been shot here (*Young Guns* and *Lonesome Dove* among them), and it harbors a few interesting shops, including **Casa Grande**, (505) 438-3008, which contains mining exhibits, a gift shop, and a petting zoo. Between Cerrillos and Santa Fe on NM 14 is an area called **Garden of the Gods**, where beautiful sandstones have been stood on end by New Mexico's various uplifts. At the turnout you can pull off the road to marvel at these incredible rocks. NM 14 hits I-25 on Santa Fe's southern edge. The entire drive, without stops, takes about 90 minutes. ◼

2

GALLUP AND GRANTS AREA

While Mesa Verde may be more spectacular, the ruins of Keet Seel more beautiful, and the cliff dwellings of Canyon de Chelly more sublime, for me no Anasazi site in the Southwest matches the grandeur and mystifying draw of Chaco Canyon. And while it is the leading attraction in the greater Gallup and Grants area, it is certainly not the only destination worth visiting in the lands flanking I-40 west of Albuquerque.

Though not nearly as popular as the Rio Grande Valley or northern New Mexico, there is much to see and do in this west-central patch of the state. With its mix of Navajo, Zuni, Acoma, and Laguna Indians, Anglo and Hispanic ranchers, miners, small retail businesspeople, artists, and the occasional tourist, it is a down-to-earth slice of the state that represents a slower-paced and unpretentious lifestyle that is disappearing in the West. It's both Main Street USA and foreign nations within a nation.

Here is a land of great beauty, with starkly contrasting microclimates and landforms: high, snowcapped peaks; sun-blasted deserts; mesas and plateaus; small streams; lava fields; and verdant valleys. ◼

GALLUP AND GRANTS AREA

N

To Cuba
197

9

Whitehorse

San Mateo
Mt. Taylor

To Albuquerque
40

G

A
Acoma

38   43

H   547
Grants
M

Acoma Indian Reservation

509

605

C
57

9

Crownpoint

40

Cibola National Forest

D

117

53

El Malpais National Monument

A To B
371

Thoreau
612

Zuni Mountains

El Morro National Monument

Ramah Navajo Indian Reservation

36

36

J

Ramah
L

E

F I
Gallup

602

36

Zuni
K

Zuni Indian Reservation

53

NEW MEXICO
ARIZONA

666

Window Rock

40

61

191

191

St. Johns

264

Navajo Indian Reservation

Ganado

191

Petrified Forest National Park

180

Navajo Indian Reservation

264

Holbrook
40

0 SCALE

25
KILOMETERS   MILES   25

ROAD
INTERSTATE

PARK BOUNDARY
RESERVATION BOUNDARY

STATE BOUNDARY

Sights

Ⓐ Acoma Pueblo

Ⓑ Bisti Badlands Wilderness Area

Ⓒ Chaco Culture National Historic Park

Ⓓ El Malpais National Monument and Conservation Area

Ⓔ El Morro National Monument

Ⓕ Gallup

Ⓖ Laguna Pueblo

Ⓗ Mount Taylor Drive

Ⓘ Red Rocks State Park

Ⓙ Route 66

Ⓚ Zuni Pueblo

Food

Ⓛ Blue Corn Restaurant

Ⓔ Eagle Café

Ⓔ Earl's

Ⓕ El Rancho

Ⓜ Grants Station

Ⓜ La Ventana

Ⓔ Panz Alegra

Ⓔ Shush Yaz Trading Post

Ⓔ Vergie's

Note: Items with the same letter are located in the same town or area.

A PERFECT DAY IN THE GALLUP AND GRANTS AREA

Begin the day with an early arrival at Chaco Canyon, or, better yet, camp there the night before. Visit the canyon's main sites on the valley floor, and have a picnic lunch under the cottonwoods along the Chaco River. Then head into Gallup for an afternoon of shopping and exploring the town's history. Or visit El Malpais National Monument, El Morro National Monument, or Acoma Pueblo. If you end up in Gallup for the night, have a drink at El Rancho and dinner at Earl's or Vergie's.

SIGHTSEEING HIGHLIGHTS

★★★ **Acoma Pueblo**—Most of the 19 New Mexico pueblos still in existence feature wonderful settings—but none can beat this one. Set atop a 376-foot-high sandstone butte, it is aptly called Sky City.

Accessible only via a rough foot trail until this century, Acoma fiercely resisted acculturation, aided by the impregnability of its mesa. In a three-day battle in January 1599, however, Spanish troops succeeded in mounting the mesa and burned the pueblo. Afterward, a handful of males over 25 years old had a foot chopped off, while younger males and females were sent to Mexico as slaves. Still, the Acomans clung to their independence and old ways, and even now, Sky City does not have running water or electricity.

Today open warfare is behind them, and the Acoma welcome visitors to Sky City, as many tribal members earn their living from the sale of their outstanding pottery and, to a lesser degree, jewelry. Tourists must begin at the visitor center, where you purchase a ticket for the van ride up to the mesatop. Before setting off, browse through the gift shop or an interesting display on pueblo history that emphasizes its pottery traditions.

At Sky City, Acoma guides will lead you on an hourlong tour. Highlights include **San Esteban del Rey Church**, one of the most remarkable buildings in the state. Winding through the village's narrow lanes, you can purchase pottery directly from the artisans, or perhaps grab a loaf of their wonderful bread baked in the beehive-shaped, wood-fired *hornos*. End your tour by walking back down the foot trail.

© Daniel B. Gibson

Acoma Pueblo

Details: Acoma Pueblo is between Grants and Albuquerque. Take I-40 exit 102 and head south 12 miles on Tribal Road 38. Park at the visitor center, (505) 470-4966 or (800) 747-0181, open April through October 8–7 daily, with the final tour leaving at 6 p.m. November through March, hours are 8–4:30. Due to tribal ceremonies, tours are not held on June 24, June 29, July 10–13, July 25, and the first or second weekend of October. Tours cost $7 for adults, $6 for seniors, $5 for children. A camera permit is $10. (2 to 3 hours)

★★★ **Chaco Culture National Historic Park**—As all roads once led to Rome, in the Southwest they led to Chaco. For several centuries Chaco was the heart of the Anasazi world, which stretched from Nevada across north-central Arizona and southern Utah into southwestern Colorado and northwestern New Mexico. But where Rome tied its empire together through conquest and brute force, the Anasazi realm was woven together by delicate threads of trade, spiritual association, and cultural community.

Chaco began to flower around A.D. 900. Trade goods from the Pacific coast, tropical Mexico, and the Great Plains flowed into its canyon center. Messengers sped outward on a prehistoric road network, while artists and craftspeople created beautiful pottery, turquoise jewelry, and weavings. Farmers built intricate irrigation systems, and villages of finely shaped stone with astronomical observatories and sunken ceremonial chambers emerged out of the wilderness. Complex social, political, religious, and administrative systems were devised to hold it all together. Then, almost overnight, around A.D. 1200, the center collapsed and its people dispersed, leaving behind intriguing, palpable, and haunting echoes of their once grand culture.

It remains off the main tourist track, despite its accessibility once you're there. Visitors can drive up to half of its 13 primary ruins, or step out on short trails that wind through the multistoried pueblos and earthbound kivas. Or you can enjoy solitude, unexcavated ruins, and the sound of low wind, which seems almost ever-present here, on isolated backcountry trails (see Fitness and Recreation section).

A one-way gravel loop road drive on the valley floor should begin with a stop at the visitor center, where models, artifacts, a video, photos, maps, and other informative materials lay the groundwork for your understanding of the Anasazi and the specifics of Chaco. Here you can arrange tours guided by rangers (May through September) or pick up self-guiding brochures.

The first major site along the loop road is **Chetro Ketl**, one of the valley's "great houses," with more than 500 rooms, 16 kivas, and an enclosed plaza. Just past it is the largest ruin in Chaco, **Pueblo Bonito**, which was occupied from A.D. 900 to almost 1200. It once had more than 600 rooms and 40 kivas, and rose at least four stories. It has been called "America's first condominium complex."

On the south side of the canyon is **Casa Riconada**, which harbors Chaco's largest kiva. One can imagine what it must have felt like when it was roofed and one had to crawl through its entrance tunnel and emerge through a hole in its floor during a ceremony. Flickering firelight would have illuminated people singing and drumming, the air scented with incense. At sunset, as the canyon walls turn a golden red, mule deer wander down from the higher slopes, and coyotes announce their presence with eerie calls. Perhaps the people will return tonight.

Details: From the south on I-40, exit at Thoreau (29 miles west of Grants and 33 miles east of Gallup) onto NM 371. About 5 miles north of Crownpoint, turn east (right) onto Navajo Road 9 and proceed 13.5 miles to Seven Lakes. Turn north (left) onto NM 57, a dirt road, which runs 20 miles directly into Chaco. From the north, approach on NM 44. Just west of mile marker 112, exit onto the new entrance road, CR 1700. The old road from Nageezi is now closed, despite what your map may indicate. The road heads southwest. Its first portion is paved, but the last 16 miles are washboard dirt roads that are occasionally graded. They have no steep sections and are passable for RVs and ordinary cars in good weather.

Chaco is open year-round, but the best time to visit is fall. There is a campground but no food or lodging. The visitor center, (505) 786-7014, is open 8–6 in summer; 8–5 otherwise. Admission is $4 per vehicle. (3 hours minimum on-site)

☆☆ **El Malpais National Monument and Conservation Area**—A little over 1,000 years ago, rivers of molten rock coursed across this landscape in what must have been a fantastic display of volcanic fury. Here and there the seas of stone failed to bury a patch of land, and today they stand as green islands—called *kupukas*, Hawaiian for islands —amidst bays of blackened rock. One *kupuka* is more than 6,000 acres, and another shelters the world's oldest-known Douglas fir, which wriggled out of the soil near the year 1062! In some places the lava ran downhill in streams, and its surface hardened. The interior flow eventually was cut off and poured from the shell, leaving behind formations known as lava tubes. One series of tubes—the nation's longest—spans 17 miles.

Scorched by summer heat, the blackened rock shelters other secrets. The lava, permeated by tiny air bubbles, is actually a great natural insulator, and water sinking into it from light winter snows and heavier summer rains has collected in lava tubes and other hollows, forming permanent caches of ice.

Altogether within the monument's 377,000 acres—a mixture of wilderness conservation and national parklands set aside for protection in 1987—are the remnants of 30 volcanoes, 80 vents, sinkholes, lava trenches, older lava flows, and numerous smaller spatter cones. Around the edges of the lava flows, which the Spanish explorers labeled *malpais*, or "badlands," are sandstone ridges and cliffs, including New Mexico's most accessible natural arch, petroglyphs, ruins, and cabins of later-day homesteaders.

On the east side of the monument, NM 117 passes **Sandstone Bluffs Overlook** about 11 miles south of I-40, where a picnic area offers outstanding views of the lava field. A few miles south on NM 117 is the trailhead for the **Zuni–Acoma Trail**, which runs 7.5 miles (one way) across four major lava flows to another paved road, NM 53, on the west side of the monument. Some 17 miles south of I-40 off NM 117 is **La Ventana Arch**, reached via a short hike from the road. From the top of **The Narrows** sandstone rim, enjoy great views of the recent McCarty's lava flow.

Details: Access from either NM 117 or NM 53 south of Grants. Grants' visitor information center, 620 E. Santa Fe Ave., (505) 285-4641, is open daily in summer 8–5 and the rest of the year 8–4:30. A ranger information center is about 10 miles south of I-40 on NM 117, and is open daily 8:30–5. Backcountry camping is allowed with a free permit. The monument is open year-round,. Admission is free. (2 to 4 hours)

✪✪ **El Morro National Monument**—Call it America's first scratch pad or the original graffiti corner. For centuries this prominent landmark with a permanent water source along a natural travel corridor has served as a type of rock blackboard for people passing by. Some 700 years ago, Indians recorded their journeys and occupation on the mesatop above. The oldest non-Indian marks were left by Don Juan de Oñate, who wrote *paso por aqui*—"passed by here"—in 1605. In 1857 a U.S. Army contingent using camels as pack animals tromped through, leaving some beautiful carved inscriptions. Such work led to the bluff's name, "Inscription Rock."

Don't, however, try to add *your* name to the rock. In 1906 it fell under the protection of the federal government as the nation's first national monument, and defacing it is a crime.

A visitor center provides information on the monument and other associated points of interest. Just outside the door a half-mile asphalt loop trail leads to the inscriptions. If you have an extra hour or two, continue on this trail another 1.5 miles (round trip), as it turns to dirt and climbs to the top of the 200-foot-high mesa, where you'll find a beautiful landscape of yellow sandstone dotted with junipers, ponderosa pine, and the thirteenth-century ruin of **Atsinna**, once an outlying village of Zuni Pueblo.

Details: El Morro is located along NM 53, 43 miles southwest of Grants; (505) 783-4226. Open in summer 8–8, the rest of the year 8–5. Admission is $3 per vehicle. (1 to 3 hours)

★★ **Gallup**—The area's commercial center, this town of 22,000 is an interesting place to poke around. It is the focus of the area's vast Indian arts and crafts industry, with an estimated 45,000 people employed at least part time in some facet of this trade. Its pawnshops are renowned for hiding terrific, often old and valuable, jewelry and other goods. (They are carefully regulated, by the way, by federal and state laws.) **Richardsons Trading Co.**, 222 W. Rt. 66, is a notable establishment, with its hardwood floors and pressed-tin ceilings. It's been wheeling and dealing since 1938 and has more than 1,100 saddles in pawn. While not a pawnshop, **City Electric Shoe Shop**, 3rd and Coal, makes for a great visit: it has almost anything in leather (except halter tops—visit New York City for those) you can think of.

Launched as a railroad boomtown in 1881, and later a prime stop on fabled Route 66, which runs through its heart, Gallup has many fine old brick and stone buildings that echo its role as a travel corridor. Visit the 1922 Mission Pueblo Revival–style **Santa Fe Railroad Depot**, 201 E. Rt. 66, (800) 242-4282, today the city's visitor center, where free nightly Indian dances are held in summer.

Gallup also served as home base to many major Hollywood films, dating back to *The Great Divide* (1915), *Red Skin* (with Richard Dix, 1928), *Pursued* (with Robert Mitchum, 1946), *The Bad Man* (with Ronald Reagan), *Sea of Grass* (with Hepburn and Tracy), *Streets of Loredo* (with William Holden), *Rocky Mountain* (with Errol Flynn and Slim Pickens) and *Natural Born Killers* (directed by Oliver Stone, 1993). A great deal of the area's film history can be seen today in the many photos found in the **El Rancho Hotel**, 1000 E. Rt 66. It was opened in 1937 by the brother of legendary director D.W. Griffith, and served as the center of film life in Gallup.

One of the oldest, biggest, and friendliest Indian cultural festivals in the nation, the Intertribal Indian Ceremonial, is held annually during the second week of August in and around Gallup.

Details: 138 miles west of Albuquerque on I-40; (800) 242-4282. (1 to 4 hours)

★★ **Zuni Pueblo**—As one of the state's oldest pueblos, Zuni has played a central role in New Mexico's long history. Its current primary village may be only 300 years old, but outlying ruins such as **Hawikuh** and **Taaiyalone** attest to much earlier occupation. In fact, the latter site has pit houses dating to A.D. 700. Zuni was the first population center encountered in 1540 on the first Spanish exploration of New Mexico by Francisco Coronado. Expecting to find the "Seven Cities of Gold," he discovered instead a basically poor adobe village whose mud walls often glowed a golden hue in the colorful sunsets.

Today Zuni has the largest population and land base of New Mexico's 19 pueblos. While its residents share many cultural and religious traits with other Pueblo people, it has a completely unique language and also resembles the Hopi of Arizona, who are geographically closer than many of the Rio Grande pueblos.

Zunis are master jewelers, working with tiny inlaid stones in a style known as needlepoint and petit point. They are also the only New Mexico pueblo group to produce significant numbers of kachina figures (carved wooden deities), weavings, and tiny carved animal figures called fetishes. These arts can be purchased from many authentic shops on the reservation, the Zuni Craftsmen Cooperative on NM 53, or the artists themselves.

Also of note at Zuni is its Spanish mission church, **Our Lady of Guadalupe**, (505) 782-4477. On its inner walls are a series of beautiful, large murals originally painted between 1175 and 1780. They depict views of the nearby mesas; the four seasons; and figures of mudheads, Rain Dancers, Father of the Kivas, and the fantastic giant birdlike figure of Shalako, as well as Catholic saints—as remarkable a melding of faiths as you'll find anywhere in the world. The church is open erratically on weekdays, and for Sunday Mass at 10 a.m.

Details: Zuni village is 34 miles south of Gallup on NM 53, just west of its intersection with NM 602. It is open year-round, but its central plaza may be closed during occasional ceremonies. For additional information, contact Pueblo of Zuni, P.O. Box 339, Zuni, NM 87327; (505) 782-4481. (1 to 3 hours)

☆ **Bisti Badlands Wilderness Area**—If you like weird, even unearthly, desert landscapes, you'll love this place. While at first glance it seems desolate, if you get out and walk among its wind- and water-carved earthen formations—small mesas, buttes, hoodoos, mushrooms, spires, and caps—you may find it fascinating... or still simply desolate!

Details: 64 miles north of I-40 off NM 371, north of Crownpoint and south of Farmington. It is administered by the Bureau of Land Management in Farmington, (505) 599-8900. Open daily year-round. Admission is free. (2 to 4 hours on site)

☆ **Laguna Pueblo**—This large reservation along I-40 between Grants and Albuquerque has at least six different villages, but visitors are generally most interested in Old Laguna, which sits just off the interstate. Most noticeable is the graceful, whitewashed **San Jose de Laguna Mission Church**, built in 1705 atop a small hill, with an altar and decorations made by Laguna artisans.

Details: Old Laguna is 34 miles east of Grants and 46 miles west of Albuquerque. Take I-40 exit 108; (505) 552-6654 or (505) 243-7616. (1 hour)

☆ **Mount Taylor Drive**—Towering over this swath of west-central New Mexico is 11,301-foot Mount Taylor, the Navajos' sacred mountain of the south. A volcanic eruption remnant now weathered into a graceful profile, until June its brilliant white snowcapped top shines in the sun like a beacon for more than 100 miles in all directions. Round trip from Grants to La Mosca Saddle is 46 miles.

Details: Take NM 547 (Lobo Canyon Road) out of Grants. The pavement ends at milepost 13, and gravel Forest Road 239 begins. Continue 3 miles and turn right onto Forest Road 453 to the La Mosca fire tower lookout. The road gets very rough at this point, but continues another 2 miles to La Mosca Saddle. For details, call the Forest Service, (505) 287-8833. It is open June through October and is passable for normal vehicles in good weather. (3 hours)

☆ **Red Rocks State Park**—This park 6 miles east of Gallup is the home of the annual August Intertribal Indian Ceremonial. It also has a museum of local Indian arts and crafts, and prehistoric Indian artifacts, plus a gift shop and trading post. Located at the foot of a red-rock mesa carved into wonderful spires and domes, it offers short trails that wind back into these formations.

Details: Head east out of Gallup on I-40 or Route 66, then north on NM 566; (505) 722-3829. The museum is open weekdays 8:30–4:40, with extended summer hours. (1 hour)

✿ **Route 66**—Several long sections of the original Route 66, the fabled road of Western adventure and escape, parallel I-40 in western New Mexico. Crumbling souvenir shops, gas stations, motels, and towns that modern life blew by lie along its sides, paint peeling, plaster cracking, signs fading. If you like this sort of thing, you'll be in nostalgia nirvana (see also Scenic Route, page 234).

Details: The old roadway begins in the west, just over the Arizona line, and loops back and forth under I-40, occasionally ending and then resuming before finally heading past Laguna Pueblo and on to Los Lunas. You can cruise it all, or short sections, hopping on and off I-40. (3 hours to a full day)

FITNESS AND RECREATION

West-central New Mexico is a land of great physical contrasts, with opportunities for many diverse outdoor activities.

While most visitors to **Chaco Canyon** stay close to their cars and the major ruins on the main valley floor, backcountry trails allow you to experience Chaco as it used to be: deathly quiet, with a supreme sense of antiquity and isolation.

Three of these trails climb out of the canyon, providing awesome views of the imposing canyon ramparts on all sides as well as expansive views of the surrounding San Juan Basin and region. From on high, the vast distances that meet the eye and the forbidding character of the larger landscape make the Chaco phenomenon all the more impressive.

Pueblo Alto Trail is the most popular backcountry trail, and for good reason. Situated on the north mesa of the canyon, it provides wonderful views directly down on Chaco's largest ruin, Pueblo Bonito, as well as of Chetro Ketl. If you hike just to the Pueblo Bonito overlook, the round-trip distance is 1.6 miles. A round trip to Pueblo Alto is 3.2 miles. If you continue on past Pueblo Alto and take the loop trail back to the starting point, the distance is 5.4 miles.

Wijiji Trail is the park's only backcountry trail open to mountain biking as well as to hiking. The ride is rather tame by mountan-biking standards, with a round-trip distance of 3 miles.

South Mesa Trail is perhaps the most visually captivating of the park's backcountry trails. It climbs 450 vertical feet out of the main canyon, giving you a bird's-eye view of the imposing rock walls of side canyons and of the entire region. Hike to the isolated ruins of **Tsin Kletsin** and back on the same trail (3 miles), or continue on the loop trail into South Gap, for a total distance of 4.1 miles.

Peñasco Blanco Trail has several intriguing aspects, including fascinating petroglyphs, a walk under cottonwood trees along the Chaco River, and the mesa-top ruins of **Pueblo Peñasco Blanco**. Round-trip, this trail covers 6.4 miles.

Because of the archeological ruins, backcountry camping is not allowed at Chaco, and a backcountry permit (obtain at visitor center) is required even for day hikes.

Mountain biking is OK at **El Malpais Monument**, on the rough roads in the **Cerritos de Jaspe** area, reached via a primitive road off NM 53. Biking is also allowed on primitive roads in the **Chain of Craters** wilderness study area and in **Brazos Canyon**. The monument also has both short and long hiking trails (see Sightseeing Highlights). At the **Bisti Wilderness Area**, hiking is obviously *the* thing to do.

The **Zuni Mountains**, south of I-40 between Gallup and Grants, offer stream and lake fishing, as well as waterskiing at **Blue Lake**. The latter, at I-40 exit 63, then 6 miles south on NM 412, (505) 876-2391, has a 2,350-acre lake, marina, boat rentals, grocery store, and campground; day use is $3. Trout-fish on the Zuni Reservation at **Nutria Lakes**. Call Zuni Fish and Wildlife, (505) 782-5851, for details.

Just north of Grants, **Mt. Taylor** offers cool forests for hiking and hunting, and winter cross-country skiing. It is also the site of the annual Mt. Taylor Quadrathon, held the second week of February, which combines cycling, running, Nordic skiing, and snowshoeing.

FOOD

Don't look for fine dining, but decent, modestly priced options abound.

In Gallup, one of the fancier places is the dining room of **El Rancho**, 1000 E. Rt. 66, (505) 863-9311. **Panz Alegra**, 1201 E. Rt. 66, (505) 722-7229, has somewhat pricey New Mexico food and some American standards, but it's a popular place, even crowded on weekends. **Earl's**, 1400 E. Rt. 66, (505) 863-4201, serves some tasty dishes, such as the green chile enchiladas. The **Eagle Café**, 200 W. Rt. 66, (505) 722-3220, has been serving travelers since 1917, with almost the exact same interior, owners, and simple but good food. For something different, try the mutton stew, fry bread, and other Indian food at **Shush Yaz Trading Post**, 214 W. Aztec; closed Sunday. **Vergie's**, 2720 W. Rt. 66, (505) 863-5152, offers fine Mexican food, as well as steaks, a full bar, and some classic neon outside.

In Grants, I like the atmosphere and food at **La Ventana**, 110½ Geis, (505) 287-9393, with worthy New Mexican fare, as well as prime rib, steak, a fish dish, and salads. It's closed Sunday. A major meal runs about $15. Cheaper is the locally popular **Grants Station**, 200 W. Santa Fe. Ave., (505) 287-2334, serving American and New Mexican food.

At Acoma Pueblo you can eat in the Sky City Visitor Center restaurant, which has a few Indian-style meals, burgers, and other simple fare. Zuni has a few cafés right on NM 53 in the village center. In Ramah is the **Blue Corn Restaurant**, NM 53, with excellent New Mexican food and daily specials. It's open Wednesday through Sunday 11–9.

LODGING

The most colorful lodging in Gallup by far is **El Rancho**, 1000 E. Rt. 66, (505) 863-9311 or (800) 543-6351, built in 1937 by the brother of film director D.W. Griffith. It served as the base of operations for many movies shot nearby and hosted guests like Humphrey Bogart, Carole Lombard, Clark Gable, Gene Kelly, William Holden, Joan Crawford, Kirk Douglas, and Jean Harlow. Though it fell on hard times, it is now on the rebound. Rates of $32–$39 include a summer pool, gift shop, restaurant, and the 49er Lounge, which hosts live music on weekends.

Gallup has motel rows on both the east and west entrances to town, where one can find accommodations ranging from upscale chains properties ($75 and up), such as the **Holiday Inn**, 2915 W. Rt. 66, (505) 722-2201 or (800) 432-2211; to modest ($40)—**Motel 6**, 3306 W. Rt. 66, (505) 863-4492; and cheap ($25–$35)—**Hopi Motel**, 2305 W. Rt. 66, (505) 863-4172.

Grants has more than a dozen motels, encompassing **Econo Lodge**, 1509 E. Santa Fe Ave., (505) 287-4426 or (800) 424-4777 ($50 rates include a pool); and one of the cheapest joints in the region (under $20), the **Wayside**, 903 E. Santa Fe Ave., (505) 287-4268. Perhaps the nicest is the **Best Western Grants Inn**, 1501 E. Santa Fe

GALLUP AND GRANTS AREA

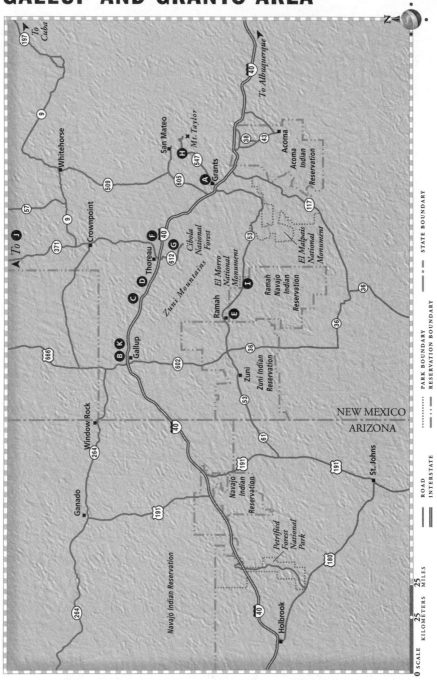

Lodging

A Best Western Grants Inn

A Econo Lodge

B El Rancho

B Holiday Inn

B Hopi Motel

B Motel 6

C Navajo Lodge

D Stauder's Navajo Lodge

E Voight Ranch

A Wayside

F Zuni Mt. Lodge

Camping

G Blue Water Lake State Park

H Cibola National Forest

A Cibola Sands RV Park

H Coal Mine Campground

I El Morro National Monument

I El Morro RV Park

J Gallo Campground

B Gallup KOA

H Lobo Canyon Campground

K Red Rock State Park

Note: Items with the same letter are located in the same town or area.

Ave., (505) 287-7901, with indoor pool, hot tub, sauna, game room, room service, and coin and valet laundry, for $70–$85.

The few B&B choices in the area include **Stauder's Navajo Lodge,** (505) 862-7553, outside of town, and **Navajo Lodge,** 20 miles from Gallup in Coolidge, (505) 862-7553, providing two cottages with kitchens, living rooms, and bathrooms for $78. The **Voight Ranch,** 1 mile south of Ramah, (505) 783-4362, was built in 1915 from Anasazi ruin rocks. It offers two rooms with private baths, for $75 from mid-March through December. Another option is the **Zuni Mt. Lodge** in Thoreau, (505) 862-7769.

CAMPING

At Chaco Canyon is the **Gallo Campground,** (505) 786-7014, with 68 sites, restrooms, and drinking water (no showers) for $8. Tucked up against the walls of a sandstone cove, this pretty spot is the only camping for more than 60 miles; it's usually full in summer by early afternoon. It operates on a first-come, first-served basis year-round. **El Morro National Monument** has a nine-site campground that also operates on a first-come, first-served basis. One mile west on NM 53 is **El Morro RV Park**, charging $15 for full hookups, $8 without.

Gallup has several commercial options, including the **KOA**, 2925 W. Rt. 66, (505) 863-5021, with $22 RV sites with hookups, laundry, swimming pool, playground, and grocery store; it's open April to mid-October. **Red Rock State Park**, (505) 722-3839, 6 miles from town, is open year-round, with 100 sites, showers, laundry, grocery store, and horse rentals; $12 for hookups, $8 for tents. Grants' **Cibola Sands RV Park**, on NM 53 a half-mile south of I-40 off exit 81, has store, showers, laundry, and 54 sites at $10 for tents and $14 for RV hookups.

Free dispersed camping and developed campgrounds exist on Mt. Taylor and in the Zuni Mountains, in the **Cibola National Forest**, (505) 287-8833. Outside of Grants is the **Lobo Canyon Campground**, 8 miles northeast on Lobo Canyon Rd., then 1.5 miles east on unpaved Forest Road 193, with pit toilets. Two miles further up Lobo Canyon is the shady **Coal Mine Campground**, providing drinking water and restrooms. Both facilities are free and open mid-May to late October. **Blue Water Lake State Park** has a campground with laundry and showers; tent sites are $8 and RV hookups, $12.

NIGHTLIFE

A few bars in Gallup have live music, particularly on weekends: the **Holiday Inn**, **El Rancho**, and **Vergie's**. Acoma Pueblo also operates the **Sky City Casino**, exit 102 on I-40 east of Grants, (505) 552-6017 or (888) SKY-CITY, with card games, slots, roulette, craps, and bingo.

3
SANTA FE

The City Different is definitely that—almost everything about Santa Fe is unlike anything else in the country. It has been described as America's most foreign capital, and with good reason. Founded circa 1608, Santa Fe was the political capital of what was once the northernmost province of New Spain, with territory encompassing almost all of what is now called the American Southwest. The city has a rich history resulting from the complex interplay of Indians, the Hispanic descendants of the Spanish and Mexican colonialists, and the "Anglo" or "gringo" influx that began in the mid-1800s. This tri-cultural mix has created a vibrant city with a distinctive architecture and a flourishing arts scene, ranging from opera to ethnic arts, literature to painting and photography.

Above all, Santa Fe is beautiful: sitting at an elevation of 7,000 feet, with mountains at its back climbing to almost 13,000 feet, the city has an invigorating climate with four distinct seasons (including surprisingly cold, snowy winters). The high, generally dry climate gives the air a clarity and sparkle that is, well, enchanting. To the west and south, plateaus descend in steps to great dry basins, their distant edges 100 miles away punctuated by sawtooth mountain ridges. Visitors should make a point to get out of town and see some of the lovely countryside, pocketed with Indian ruins, pretty valleys with cool rivers running through them, Hispanic villages, and other hidden treasures. ◼

SANTA FE

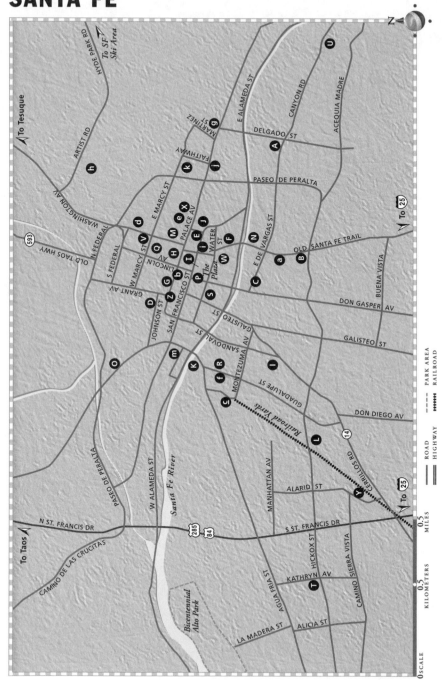

Sights

- Ⓐ Canyon Road
- Ⓑ Capitol Building
- Ⓒ De Vargas Street
- Ⓓ Georgia O'Keeffe Museum
- Ⓔ Institute of American Indian Arts Museum
- Ⓕ Loretto Chapel
- Ⓖ Museum of Fine Arts
- Ⓗ Palace of the Governors
- Ⓘ The Plaza
- Ⓙ St. Francis Cathedral
- Ⓚ Santuario de Guadalupe
- Ⓛ SITE Santa Fe

Food

- Ⓜ Anasazi Restaurant
- Ⓝ Bistro 315
- Ⓞ Burt's Burger Bowl
- Ⓟ Café Pasqual's
- Ⓠ Carlos' Gospel Café
- Ⓡ Cowgirl Hall of Fame
- Ⓢ Coyote Café
- Ⓣ Dave's Not Here

Food (continued)

- Ⓤ Geronimo
- Ⓥ Il Piatto
- Ⓦ India Palace
- Ⓧ La Casa Sena
- Ⓨ La Choza
- Ⓩ The Palace
- ⓐ Pink Adobe
- ⓑ Plaza Restaurant
- ⓒ Pranzo
- ⓓ Santacafé
- ⓔ The Shed
- ⓕ Zia Diner

Lodging

- ⓖ Alexander's Inn
- ⓗ Fort Marcy Compound
- ⓜ Inn of the Anasazi
- ⓘ La Fonda
- ⓙ La Posada
- ⓚ Preston House
- ⓛ Santa Fe Motel
- ⓜ Water Street Inn

Note: Items with the same letter are located in the same place.

A PERFECT DAY IN SANTA FE

Begin on the Plaza with a stop at the Palace of the Governors. Shop on its portal for Indian arts and crafts, walk next door to the Museum of Fine Arts, then to the Georgia O'Keeffe Museum several blocks away. Drop into La Fonda hotel for a glimpse of its storied lobby, then saunter over to St. Francis Cathedral and its fascinating older *capilla* (chapel) located inside in the back left corner. After lunch at The Shed, head up Canyon Road for a walk. In the late afternoon take a drive up to the ski basin for a shot of the outdoors and, if you're lucky, a dramatic sunset. Have a drink at the Dragon Room of the Pink Adobe before eating at one of Santa Fe's many fine restaurants. On summer nights, the Santa Fe Opera beckons.

SIGHTSEEING HIGHLIGHTS

★★★ **Canyon Road**—Nicknamed the "Art and Soul of Santa Fe," this narrow street running up the Santa Fe River canyon away from the Plaza was first an Indian trail, then a route for Hispanic woodcutters and berry-pickers traveling out of the Sangre de Cristo Mountains rising to the east. In the 1920s a handful of painters (including Fremont Ellis and other members of the Cinco Pintores), writers (including Mary Austin), and craftspeople settled on and around the street, sparking the creation of the Santa Fe arts colony, which continues unabated today. The street houses many of Santa Fe's 200-plus art galleries, as well as unique shops and restaurants. It's a great street to walk, especially with parking hard to find.

Be sure to check out the Bandelier Gardens at **El Zaquan**, 545 Canyon Rd., one of the oldest residences in town and now home to the Santa Fe Historical Society. At the corner of Upper Canyon and Alameda, you'll find **Cristo Rey Church**, 1120 Canyon Rd., said to be the largest adobe structure in the nation, with an impressive Mexican-made stone altar.

Details: The bottom of Canyon Road begins on Paseo de Peralta just south of Alameda. (1 to 4 hours)

★★★ **Georgia O'Keeffe Museum**—In July 1997 the world's first museum dedicated to a twentieth-century woman artist opened in Santa Fe. Georgia O'Keeffe was one of the many eastern-seaboard artists who emigrated to New Mexico from the 1920s through the

1940s. She proved to be the best of them all, and her legacy has created a one-gal mini-industry in north-central New Mexico. She lived an hour north, in Abiquiu (see Scenic Route, below).

The museum manages at least 80 of O'Keeffe's pieces, making it the largest repository of her creations. Shows are supplemented by work lent from other collections. Many of her large signature oil paintings are here, but you'll also find some rarely seen sculpture, delightful watercolor sketches, and striking charcoal studies. The museum maintains a gift shop (no T-shirts!) on the premises.

Details: *217 Johnson St.; (505) 995-0785. Open Tuesday through Sunday 10–5, Friday to 8 p.m. Admission is $5, free for ages 16 and under; $1 for New Mexico residents on Sunday (bring a driver's license); free for New Mexico seniors on Wednesday; free to all Friday 5–8. Four-day pass good here. (1 hour)*

✯✯✯ **Museum of Fine Arts**—Arguably the Southwest's best museum, this graceful Isaac Rapp–designed adobe facing the northwest corner of the Plaza defined the Santa Fe form of Pueblo Revival architecture. Be sure to see selections from its second-floor permanent collection for a fine overview of the amazing array of artists who have worked in New Mexico. Downstairs are changing exhibitions, usually of high quality and interest. A very pretty patio contains precious murals by Will Shuster and fountains by Jesus Morales. If you have a chance to attend a performance of any kind at its **St. Francis Auditorium**, go— it's a beautiful building of classic Spanish Mission form and decor with fine acoustics.

Details: *107 W. Palace Ave. (kitty-corner to the Plaza); (505) 827-4455. Open Tuesday through Sunday 10–5, Friday to 8. Admission is $5, free for ages 16 and under; $1 for New Mexico residents on Sunday (bring a driver's license); free for New Mexico seniors on Wednesday; free to all Friday 5–8. Four-day pass good here. (1 to 2 hours)*

✯✯✯ **Palace of the Governors**—This humble-looking one-story building on the north side of the Plaza has seen an incredible number of bizarre and important events unfold within its thick adobe walls. The oldest government building in the United States (circa 1607), it has flown the flags of the Spanish empire, the Republic of Mexico, the Confederacy (for a few weeks), and the U.S. Territory that preceded its statehood in 1912. It was also ruled from 1680 to 1692 by an uneasy alliance of Pueblo people, who carried off one of the two successful

Indian revolts in all the Americas. Many men and women died within its walls, and plots were hatched for *coups d'etat*. Zebulon Pike, the first U.S. explorer to enter New Mexico, was imprisoned here briefly, and the first U.S. Territorial Governor, Lew Wallace, author of *Ben Hur*, complained about the dirt settling out of its adobe ceilings as he tried to write.

Now the state's history museum, it provides a great introduction to the region's past. Kids love the stage wagons in the interior patio. There's a working hand-press shop that produces beautiful books, a great gift shop, and a bookstore of local relevance. On the building's portal facing the Plaza, Pueblo artisans gather daily to display and sell their handmade jewelry, pottery, and other goods. Strict oversight by a panel ensures authenticity, so it's a reliable place to shop, and the money goes directly to the artists and craftspeople.

Details: *Palace Avenue between Washington and Lincoln Streets; (505) 827-6483. Open Tuesday through Sunday 10–5, Friday to 8. Admission is $5, free for ages 16 and under; $1 for New Mexico residents on Sunday (bring a driver's license); free for New Mexico seniors on Wednesday; free to all Friday 5–8. Four-day pass good here. (1 to 2 hours)*

★★★ **The Plaza**—This was once the locus of the vast but poor province of New Mexico, the center of its politics, power, and pride, its commerce, culture, and social life. Indians were first attracted to the then-more-bountiful Santa Fe River, and they settled along it in small villages some 700 years ago. They had abandoned the area before the Spanish arrived to build their capital around 1607, when the Crown decreed that an open square would front its government seat. English was not spoken here until the 1820s, when the air cracked with the snap of bullwhips as wagon drovers rolled in at the terminus of the arduous Santa Fe Trail, which ran eastward to the American frontier in Missouri.

Today the roughest thing you're likely to encounter on the Plaza is an errant Hacky Sack. It's a nice place to sit on a bench under the shade of a tree and contemplate Santa Fe's past. Check out the interesting historical statues. While most of the Plaza's local stores have morphed into brand-name boutiques, it's still the focus of city celebrations of all kinds, including **Spanish Market** and **Indian Market** in summer, **Fiesta** in early fall, and Christmas lights and *farolitos* in winter. Even today, the Plaza is the heart of Santa Fe.

Details: *The Plaza is within the square formed by San Francisco*

Street, Old Santa Fe Trail, Palace Avenue, and Lincoln Street. The Santa Fe Visitor Center, 201 W. Marcy St. (between Lincoln and Grant Streets), (505) 984-6760, is one block away, in the Sweeney Convention Center, with public restrooms. (30 minutes)

★★ **El Rancho de las Golondrinas**—Once upon a time, the Ranch of the Swallows was the final *paraje* (overnight stop) on the longest and oldest road in North America—El Camino Real, which wound tortuously north from Mexico City through Chihuahua and into New Mexico. Soldiers, priests, traders, stock drivers, and other Royal Road travelers would spend their final night at this spring-fed oasis before pushing on to Santa Fe. Today the *paraje* is a living museum, the Williamsburg of the Southwest, with operating water mills, fields, and homes, livestock, even a *Penitente morada* (the church of New Mexico's anachronistic order of Catholic penitents). During fall and spring festivals, anvils ring out, loom shuttles fly, aromas waft out of open *posole* kettles, and fiddles hum. Guided tours and living-history weekends are also available.

Details: About 11 miles south of Santa Fe off I-25. At the La Cienega exit, head west on the two-lane road into a verdant valley and follow the signs; (505) 471-2261. Spring festival held the first weekend in April, summer festival the first weekend in June, and harvest festival the first weekend in October. Open June through September Wednesday through Sunday 10–4 for self-guided tours; guided tours available April through October. Admission to the museum is $4, $3 for seniors and teens, $1.50 children; festivals $6 adults, $4 seniors and teens, $2.50 children; under age 5 free. (3 hours to full day)

★★ **Institute of American Indian Arts Museum**—This museum showcases work from the nation's premier Indian arts educational facility of the same name. It houses a superb collection of more than 8,000 contemporary Indian art works created by the likes of Allan Houser, T.C. Cannon, Charles Loloma, Doug Hyde, Fritz Scholder, Earl Biss, Linda Lomahaftewa, Denise Wallace, and other alumni and faculty members. Don't overlook the sculpture garden. The museum also has traveling and revolving exhibitions, as well as a great fine arts and jewelry gift shop.

Details: 108 Cathedral Place (across from St. Francis Cathedral); (505) 988-6211. Open Monday through Saturday 10–5, Sunday noon to 5. Admission is $4 adults, $2 students and seniors, free to those under 16. (1 to 2 hours)

★★ **Museum of Indian Arts and Culture**—This is an attractive, modern institution dedicated to the region's oldest arts—beautiful pottery vessels, stunning silver and turquoise jewelry, fine textiles, and other works created by the state's Pueblo, Apache, and Navajo artists, both historical and living. Its galleries display excellent short-term shows on contemporary Indian arts.

Details: 708 Camino Lejo (off Old Santa Fe Trail); (505) 827-6344. Open Tuesday through Sunday 10–5. Admission is $5, free for ages 16 and under; $1 for New Mexico residents on Sunday (bring a driver's license); free for New Mexico seniors on Wednesday. Four-day pass good here. (1 to 2 hours)

★★ **Museum of International Folk Art**—This gem of a museum shelters one of the world's largest collections of folk art and folk toys—everything from Mexican masks and *milagros* to Zairian hand drums and East Indian dolls. Its Hispanic Heritage wing contains an excellent collection of traditional Hispanic arts of New Mexico, including *retablos* (carved wood panels), *bultos* (carved and painted sculptures), tin, and *colcha* embroidery. In the summer of 1998, it will open a new wing for the Neutrogena Collection, a world-class textile assemblage. The museum has a great gift shop.

Details: 706 Camino Lejo (off Old Santa Fe Trail); (505) 827-6350. Open Tuesday through Sunday 10–5. Admission is $5, free for ages 16 and under; $1 for New Mexico residents on Sunday (bring a driver's license); free for New Mexico seniors on Wednesday. Four-day pass good here. (2 hours)

★★ **Pecos National Historic Park**—This park preserves the remains of Pecos Pueblo, once a major New Mexican pueblo. Located at the mouth of Glorieta Pass, the gateway between the Great Plains and the Rio Grande Valley, it was a huge trading center centuries prior to Spanish arrival. Decimated by introduced diseases, occasional battles with the Spanish, and attacks by Apache, Comanche, and other nomadic tribes, it was finally abandoned in 1838. A self-guided walking tour includes a rare opportunity to enter a functional kiva (the sunken ceremonial chambers of the Pueblo culture), and the ruins of a huge mission church built by the Franciscans—with Indian labor.

An outlying unit, at Pigeon Ranch in Glorieta Canyon, encompasses a decisive Civil War battleground and faint remnants of the historic Santa Fe Trail.

Details: 25 miles southeast of Santa Fe via I-25. From Santa Fe, get off at exit 307 and head east into the village of Pecos, then south 2 miles on

NM 63 to the short entrance road. There is a visitor's center with videos, books, and a ranger on duty to answer questions; (505) 757-6032. Open Memorial Day through Labor Day 8–6, and rest of the year 8–5. Admission is $2 per person or $4 per vehicle. (2 hours)

✯✯ **St. Francis Cathedral**—This solid, handsome Romanesque building designed by the famous Archbishop Lamy and built by imported Italian stonemasons is a downtown landmark and testament to old Santa Fe's Catholic soul. Lamy is buried here in a crypt. But perhaps most appealing is the tiny *capilla* that the larger church was built around, located back in the left-hand corner of the interior. Its colorfully painted wooden altar and other details reflect its humble past and the style still found throughout the northern Hispanic villages. Here the famous *La Conquistadora (Nuestra Señora de la Paz)* is kept in a *nicho*. The oldest Madonna statue in the United States, she accompanied Don Diego de Vargas in his 1692 reconquest of Santa Fe, a victory his followers attributed to the *Señora's* divine intervention. The quiet park outside is cool even on a hot summer afternoon and is great for picnics.

Details: 231 Cathedral Pl.; (505) 982-5619. Open daily, with weekday masses at 7 and 8:15 a.m., 5:15 p.m., and Sunday at 6, 8, and 10 a.m., noon, and 7 p.m. Donations are suggested. (1 hour)

✯✯ **Wheelwright Museum of the American Indian**—Mary Cabot Wheelwright, the Eastern-raised contemporary of Taos' more famous Mabel Dodge Lujan, opened this wonderful, relatively small museum in 1937 to house the work of her friend Hastiin Klah, a Navajo medicine man, weaver, and sandpainter. Its collections have continued to expand, and today it mounts impressive shows of contemporary and historical art by Native Americans. Its Case Trading Post is a great source for excellent Indian arts and crafts, books, and music.

Details: 704 Camino Lejo (off Old Santa Fe Trail); (505) 982-4636. Open daily 10–5, Sunday 1–5. Free. (1 hour)

✯ **Capitol Building**—The only round capitol in the nation, this unique seat of the state legislature and governor's office was designed after the Zia Pueblo's motif of the Circle of Life, which also adorns the state's flag. You can watch the political wrangling from the peanut gallery January through March, or roam the halls' collection of fine art gathered from across the state.

Details: Corner of Old Santa Fe Trail at Paseo de Peralta; (505) 986-4589. Open September through May weekdays 8–5; June through August Monday through Saturday 8–5. Free tours at 10 a.m. and 2 p.m. (1 hour)

✷ **De Vargas Street**—Some of the town's oldest houses are located along a few blocks of this narrow, charming street running along the south bank of the Santa Fe River between Old Santa Fe Trail and Galisteo. At the corner of Old Santa Fe Trail and De Vargas is the **San Miguel Mission**, said to be the oldest church in continual use in the nation; its foundations date to 1625 or so. Its bell is believed to have been cast in Spain in 1356. Inside are priceless statues and paintings.
   Details: The church is at 401 Old Santa Fe Trail; (505) 983-3974. Open daily May through September 9–4:30; October through April 10–4. Admission is by donation. (1 hour)

✷ **Loretto Chapel**—This delicate, pretty Gothic-style church is renowned for its "Miraculous Staircase," which corkscrews up gracefully without a single nail or central support post. The story goes that the Sisters of Loretto prayed for a carpenter, and a nameless man showed up, built the staircase without the use of nails or obvious support systems, and left without pay. Was he St. Joseph? Visit and decide for yourself. The church is owned by the Inn at Loretto and is no longer used for services.
   Details: 211 Old Santa Fe Trail. Open daily 9–5 (on Sunday after services at 10:30). Admission is $1. (30 minutes)

✷ **Santuario de Guadalupe**—Recently renovated, this modest adobe church is reputed to be the oldest existing shrine to Our Lady of Guadalupe in the nation. Its large oil painting by José de Alzibar (1783) was brought up from Mexico on the Camino Real. The canvas work was unscathed by a fire that severely damaged the rest of the church. Though the church is currently used primarily as a space for art shows, recitals, and other cultural events, the parish is fighting to bring back regular services.
   Details: 100 S. Guadalupe (at the corner of Agua Fria Road); (505) 988-2027. Open Monday through Saturday 9–4, Sunday noon–4. Admission is by donation. (30 minutes)

✷ **SITE Santa Fe**—Launched in 1995, this institution has raised the profile of contemporary art in Santa Fe. It hosts a year-round schedule

of regional, national, and international visual art exhibits, as well as frequent literary and musical events and lectures on the arts.
Details: 1606 Paseo de Peralta (near the Railyards); (505) 989-1199. Open Wednesday through Sunday 10–5. Admission is $2.50 adults, $1 students and seniors, free to all on Sunday (1 hour)

✪ **Trader Jack's Flea Market**—For many years Trader Jack's has been a Santa Fe institution. From early spring to late fall, "the Flea" boasts hundreds of booths offering everything from African beads, local crafts, and vintage clothing to used paperbacks and old tools. It's become a little less homespun over the years, with more wholesalers and fewer individuals clearing out their garages, but you can still find great bargains. The gorgeous setting and the colorful scene alone are worth the trip. A snack bar is at the entrance.
Details: About 7 miles north of town on NM 285, turn left just past the Santa Fe Opera. Open late February through November Saturday and Sunday 8–5; also open on Friday during summer. Free. (1 to 3 hours)

KIDS' STUFF

Kids, and many an adult, enjoy the scenic train ride in the restored passenger cars and cabooses of the **Santa Fe Southern Railway**, (505) 989-8600. Trains run Tuesday, Thursday, and Sunday between Santa Fe and Lamy for $21 to $30. Kids also love the **Santa Fe Children's Museum**, 1050 Old Pecos Trail, (505) 989-8359. Admission is $2.50. Also, check out the **International Museum of Folk Art** and **Las Golondrinas** (see Sightseeing Highlights, above); horseback riding and river rafting (see Fitness and Recreation); and the **Southwest Children's Theater**, 142 E. De Vargas, (505) 984-3055.

FITNESS AND RECREATION

Name almost any outdoor recreation, save ocean activities, and you can probably find it near Santa Fe. Take skiing. You have many choices for cross-country outings in the **Sangre de Cristos**, which rise to more than 12,600 feet just above town, or in the gentler **Jemez Mountains**, an hour away. Or you can be on your alpine skis or a snowboard in half an hour at the **Santa Fe Ski Area**, (505) 982-4429 or (800) 776-7669; snowline (505) 983-9155. This relatively compact area skis big, with something for everyone, on top of 250 inches of often light powder.

GREATER SANTA FE

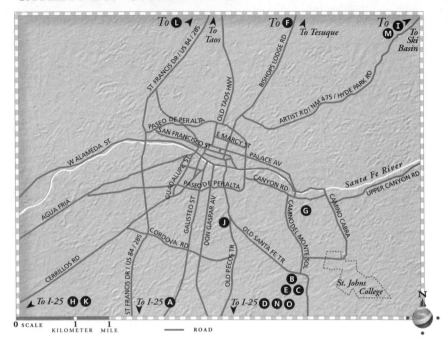

Sights

A El Rancho de las Golondrinas

B International Museum of Folk Art

C Museum of Indian Arts and Culture

D Pecos National Historic Park

E Wheelwright Museum of the American Indian

Lodging

F Bishop's Lodge

G Dunshee's

H El Rey Inn

Lodging (continued)

I Houses of the Moon

J Inn of the Turquoise Bear

Camping

K Babbitt's Los Campos RV Resort

L Camel Rock RV Campground

M Hyde Memorial State Park

N Rancheros de Santa Fe Campground

O Santa Fe KOA

There are buffed ballroom slopes for beginner and intermediate skiers, short chutes, trees, and mogul runs, as well as supreme powder skiing on Big Tesuque Peak. The area has rentals and an instructional program, a children's center, cafeteria, restaurant, bar, and apparel shop. Reach it by heading east on Artist Road from Bishop Lodge Road, which turns into NM 475—also known as Hyde Park Road (road can be tricky in bad weather).

The ski-area road also leads to access to the cool high country in summer, where you can hunt for wildflowers and mushrooms, go birding, or simply lie down in a grassy meadow and watch the thunderheads glide by. The ski-area parking lot and the **Winsor Trail** are jumping-off points for day and multi-day hikes into the 224,000-acre **Pecos Wilderness**, with its superb trout fishing on more than 15 lakes and numerous small rivers and creeks, hunting, horsepack opportunities, and mountain climbing. With elevations reaching 13,103 feet in the Truchas Peaks, one shouldn't just traipse off unprepared here. People can freeze to death in winter or get struck by summer lightning. About 20 minutes up the ski-basin road from town, at a wide pullout, is **Aspen Vista Trail**, an easygoing old Forest Service road now closed to vehicles that is popular with hikers and cross-country skiers. In town, you can stroll or hike the pretty grounds of the **Randall Davey Audubon Center**, Upper Canyon Road, (505) 983-4609, open daily 9 a.m. to 5 p.m. Free guided birding walks are conducted on summer weekend mornings. For further information on outdoor recreation, contact the Santa Fe National Forest, 1220 St. Francis, Box 1689, Santa Fe, NM 87501; (505) 438-7840.

Late spring and early summer are peak seasons for river-running. Many professional tour companies lead guided raft trips down the furious **Rio Grande Box** near Taos, through the more sedate **White Rock Canyon**, and along the tranquil and beautiful **Rio Chama**. There are many local river-running companies (see the phone book for listings). Horse lovers will enjoy rides at **Rancho Encantado**, (505) 982-3537, in the Sangre foothills; the **Broken Saddle**, (505) 470-0074, in the grasslands of Cerrillos half an hour south of town; or **Galarosa Stable**, (505) 983-6565 or (800) 338-6877, in the see-forever Galisteo Basin. The City Parks and Recreation Division, (505) 473-7236, maintains one outdoor and several indoor pools, as well as a few golf courses and tennis courts. Private racquet clubs, golf courses, and fitness centers also exist (see phone book).

FOOD

Santa Fe has the broadest and best dining possibilities in the entire Southwest. However, most of the better restaurants are in the mid-high to high price range. If you're used to New York or San Francisco prices, you won't be shocked, but folks from, say, Truth or Consequences, New Mexico, may be stunned at what a decent meal costs here. Expect tabs of $25 to $45 or more per person (with drinks) at the best spots. But Santa Fe also has a number of more moderately priced, good restaurants, along with the ubiquitous fast-food franchises along Cerrillos Road, so even those on a budget won't starve.

A handful of places vie for the coveted "best" (and most expensive) designation. I love the fireplaces, thick adobe walls, portal dining, and intimate bar of **Geronimo**, 724 Canyon Rd., (505) 982-1500, which serves exquisite, pricey food matched by careful service. The appetizers, such as a crispy red corn *chile relleno* stuffed with roasted duck and black-bean mole and jalapeño-peach salsa, are meals in themselves. Geronimo serves wonderful Sunday brunches as well.

Another popular high-end spot is the **Coyote Café**, 132 Water St., (505) 983-1615, which was the first of chef/owner Mark Miller's impressive establishments. A fixed-price dinner ($39.50) includes appetizer or salad, entree, and dessert. The word here is "inventive." In warm weather, the less-expensive rooftop Coyote Cantina serves equally exotic fare, such as sea bass tacos. The critically acclaimed **Santacafé**, 231 Washington Ave., (505) 984-1788, serves fine food inspired by an eclectic array of local and international styles. The courtyard is a lovely spot for summer dining.

Yet another of the dining elite is the **Anasazi Restaurant**, 113 Washington Ave., (505) 988-3236, with its fanciful blends of local and novel dishes, such as a cinnamon-chile tenderloin of beef, served on a fixed-price dinner basis. Located in the Inn of the Anasazi, this multiple award-winner is one of the world's better hotel restaurants.

For a quiet dinner in a lovely adobe with one of the city's best classic New Mexico art collections, check out **La Casa Sena**, 125 E. Palace Ave. (in Sena Plaza), (505) 982-1500, with its mix of fine local dishes and Continental fare. In summer, dining on the outdoor patio is delightful. There is something faintly decadent, in a pleasurable way, about **The Palace**, 142 W. Palace Ave., (505) 982-9891. Its Continental Italian food is superb, and the service is impeccable, but the crushed red-velvet walls and the lingering air of the 1800s gambling hall and bordello suggest its former indolence. The painting of the Indian girl in the lounge says it all.

Underneath this stratospheric dining level are a host of less expensive but still excellent restaurants. A classic Santa Fe establishment that was *the* place to dine here for many, many years is the **Pink Adobe**, 406 Old Santa Fe Trail, (505) 983-7712. Its animated atmosphere and tasty New Mexican and Continental fare keep 'em coming back. Across the street, **Bistro 315**, 315 Old Santa Fe Trail, (505) 986-9190, is a classic, romantic French bistro that focuses on fresh organic vegetables, meats, and seafood. The well-prepared, diverse, and modestly priced Italian food of **Pranzo**, 540 Montezuma St., (505) 984-2545, has been a hit since the day it opened. Another excellent midrange Italian choice is **Il Piatto**, 95 W. Marcy St., (505) 984-1091, boasting terrific staff and food.

India Palace, 227 Don Gaspar (at the back of the El Centro shopping compound through the Water Street parking lot), (505) 986-5859, serves wonderful East Indian meals in a serene setting, with some of Santa Fe's best waiters. Its lunch buffet is a real bargain, and dining on its covered patio in summer is a treat. Just down the street is **Café Pasqual's**, 121 Don Gaspar, (505) 983-9340, which is particularly popular at breakfast, and for good reason. Homemade pancakes with fresh fruit, log-size burritos, and succulent corned-beef hash are just a few of the dishes that attract throngs of people to this downtown spot every weekend. Get there early or be prepared to wait.

Santa Fe also has a handful of decent restaurants with entrees for less than $10. The **Plaza Restaurant**, 54 Lincoln Ave. (right on the Plaza), (505) 982-1664, is one of the best. It's been a fixture since 1918, and it still boasts red leather booths, black Formica tables, and a 1940s dining counter complete with soda fountain. The menu offers tuna sandwiches, burgers, New Mexico plates, and Greek dishes. Beer and wine are available. Another downtown spot, **Carlos' Gospel Café**, 125 Lincoln Ave. (inside the First Interstate Plaza), (505) 983-1841, is still just open for lunch, despite its cadre of diehard local regulars. Fat sandwiches (half-orders available), fresh salads, the best corn chowder you'll ever find, and the always-beaming Carlos himself shine here. Closed Sunday.

For classic New Mexican food and superior deserts, head to **The Shed**, 113½ E. Palace Ave., (505) 982-9030, which has been around since 1962. It's always full at lunch, and relatively recently it began to serve dinner on a limited basis. Its sister restaurant, **La Choza**, 905

Alarid St. (near the intersection of St. Francis and Cerrillos), (505) 982-0909, has the same menu in a less crowded part of town. West of St. Francis, **Dave's Not Here**, 1115 Hickox St., (505) 983-7060, is a real neighborhood joint with two community tables and several private ones. Hearty burgers, perhaps the best *chile rellenos* in town, yummy tacos, and scrumptious chocolate pie are a few top choices.

In the Guadalupe area, the **Zia Diner**, 326 S. Guadalupe St., (505) 988-7008, was a classic the day it opened, serving hearty home-style food with a flair—meatloaf with piñon nuts, open-faced turkey sandwiches with mashed potatoes, and daily specials. Great pie! Across the street, the **Cowgirl Hall of Fame**, 319 Guadalupe St., (505) 982-2565, serves good grub amid lots of local color. Besides Southwestern standards, specials include wild-game dishes such as buffalo burgers and wild-boar burritos. During warmer months the large, pleasant patio is very popular; at night, live music often fills a hopping bar.

For a burger above, try **Burt's Burger Bowl**, 235 N. Guadalupe St., (505) 982-0215. The green chile cheeseburger is regularly voted the town's best, and you can't go wrong with the excellent posole, pressure-cooked chicken, and old-fashioned shakes.

LODGING

As with its dining, Santa Fe has lots of accommodations choices, but the best don't come cheaply. Expect to pay more than $150 a night for a double at the high end. Summer is peak season, as are winter holidays, and you'll pay more at these times. At the top of the luxury list is the **Inn of the Anasazi**, 113 Washington Ave., (505) 988-3030 or (800) 688-8100, just a half-block off the Plaza. Attention was lavished on every detail of this relatively small hotel, and each one-of-a-kind room has handmade furniture, a kiva-style fireplace, hand-woven blankets, and a beamed ceiling. The hotel also houses one of Santa Fe's best restaurants (see Food section, above).

Outside of town are two fine resorts. The **Bishop's Lodge**, on Bishop's Lodge Road, (505) 983-6377, is only five minutes from the Plaza, but it sits in a stream-fed valley and town seems far removed. First opened in 1918, it has lovely dining rooms, a grand bar, a large outdoor pool, and beautifully landscaped grounds. On the property is a tiny and exquisite chapel—once the private retreat of Archbishop Lamy. Daylong activity programs for kids allow parents to explore their own interests. Horseback riding and skeet shooting are also available. On the road to the ski basin, 4 miles from the Plaza, is the Japanese-style **Houses of the Moon,** (505) 989-5077, on the grounds of the Ten Thousand Waves spa. Six small houses each have brick floors, marble fireplaces, and futon beds. Guests receive discounts on spa services, which include community and private outdoor hot tubs, massages, facials, and herbal wraps.

Dropping down a notch in price, with doubles averaging $100–$150 a night, is a raft of choice spots. Perhaps *the* classic hotel of the Southwest is **La Fonda,** 100 E. San Francisco St., (505) 982-5511 or (800) 523-5002. The only hotel facing the Plaza, it is believed to occupy a spot where a *fonda,* or inn, has stood since 1610. Both Kit Carson and John F. Kennedy stayed here. Each room is unique, there's a lively bar downstairs, and its lobby has seen many historic events and people pass by. Though only a few blocks from the Plaza, **La Posada,** 330 Palace Ave., (505) 986-0000, has a country feeling, with its rambling casitas and gardens spread over 6 acres. An outdoor pool; cozy, historic bar; romantic patio; good restaurant; and even a ghost add to its appeal. Rates range from $89 (single) to $400 (deluxe suite).

One of the finest motels you'll encounter is the **El Rey Inn.** Founded in 1936, its whitewashed buildings with tile trim are flanked by large trees, lawns, and flower gardens. Some rooms have kitchenettes and fireplaces. Rooms can run from less than $65–$150. About the least expensive decent accommodations in the downtown core is the **Santa Fe Motel,** 510 Cerrillos Rd., (505) 982-1039. Expect rates of $65–$100.

Bed-and-breakfasts are a great way to go in Santa Fe, with many eclectic, attractive, and comfortable choices. One of the best, and most expensive ($125–$195), is the **Water Street Inn,** 427 W. Water St., (505) 984-1193. It has imaginative, fun decor; fireplaces; private baths; cable TV in all rooms; and in-room breakfasts. The **Inn of the Turquoise Bear,** 342 E. Buena Vista, (505) 983-0798 or (800) 396-4104, markets itself toward the gay populace. Here previous owner Witter Byner hosted the likes of D.H. Lawrence, Willa Cather, Ansel Adams, Igor Stravinsky, Robert Frost, W.H. Auden, Rita Hayworth, and Errol Flynn. Rooms are $90–$175, and the suite is $250.

You can also find many more moderate bed-and-breakfast options. A top choice is **Alexander's Inn,** 529 Palace Ave., (505) 986-1431. This 1903 two-story Craftsman-style house has a country-cottage ambiance, with fresh flowers everywhere, a veranda shaded by apricot trees and wisteria, and wholesome, all-natural breakfasts. In the heart of the quiet Eastside area, a mile from the Plaza, **Dunshee's**, 986 Acequia Madre, (505) 982-0988, is the pretty home of artist Susan Dunshee, including a suite in the main house and an adobe casita with two bedrooms perfect for a small family. Rates are $120–$130. **Preston House**, 106 Faithway St., (505) 982-3465, is Santa Fe's only Queen Anne–style home. The main house has charming rooms, but for more privacy stay in a casita out back. Rates are $80–$150.

A good choice for families is **Fort Marcy Compound**, 320 Artist Rd., (505) 982-6636. It has 100 one- to three-bedroom suites with full kitchens, fireplaces, and VCRs. Other amenities include laundry facility, hot tub, and great hillside sunsets on a 10-acre site within walking distance of the Plaza. Rates range from $100–$230.

CAMPGROUNDS

Several options exist nearby for public camping, along with a handful of RV and commercial sites. The closest public land camping is at **Hyde Memorial State Park**, (505) 983-7175, about 8 miles up the ski-basin road (NM 475). There's a small fee. Free camping is available in nearby **Santa Fe National Forest**, (505) 438-7840. Other options include **Camel Rock RV Campground**, 10 miles north of Santa Fe on US 84/285, (505) 455-2661. Owned by Tesuque Pueblo, it has 68 full hookups, 26 tent sites, a laundry, showers, and a gift shop. In town is **Babbitt's Los Campos RV Resort**, 3574 Cerrillos Rd., (505) 473-1949, with a swimming pool, showers, LP gas, and picnic tables. Ten miles east of town is **Rancheros de Santa Fe Campground**, 736 Old Las Vegas Highway (NM 3), (505) 466-3482. Set among piñon trees, it offers 95 RV sites, 37 tent sites, a few cabins, hot showers, LP gas, a grocery, laundry, and pool. Also in the area is the **Santa Fe KOA**, 11 miles east of town at I-25 exit 290, (505) 466-1419.

NIGHTLIFE

For a small city, Santa Fe has a lively nightlife, particularly in the summer, when there are more possibilities for fun than any one person can take in. For a current listing of what's happening, check out Friday's "Pasatiempo," the weekly arts and entertainment supplement of the *Santa Fe New Mexican*.

Probably the grandest event of all, drawing people from around the world, is the **Santa Fe Opera**, (505) 986-5900. Located just north of town, the striking opera house has open sides that allow fresh night air to enter and the sounds of thunder to roll in, adding to the pageant on stage. In addition to several classic operas, the Santa Fe Opera performs a world premiere every summer. The building is undergoing remodeling, scheduled to be completed in May 1998. If you find the ticket prices daunting, standing-room tickets can be purchased for $8 on Friday and Saturday, $6 on weekdays, at 10 a.m. or an hour and a half before the performance. People often leave at intermissions, allowing you to grab a cheap seat for the second act.

Another summer event that has been drawing patrons from across the nation since 1973 is the **Santa Fe Chamber Music Festival**, (505) 983-2075, which holds exquisite performances in the lovely St. Francis Auditorium at the Museum of Fine Arts. Launched in 1983, the **Santa Fe Symphony and Chorus**, (505) 983-1414, presents nine or so performances a year, including a free holiday concert in early December.

Contemporary music can be heard at a number of venues. **Corazon de Santa Fe** is a series of free concerts, ranging from R&B to salsa and bluegrass, on Tuesday and Thursday evenings throughout the summer on the Plaza. Also during summer, outstanding shows are held at the wonderful **Paolo Soleri Amphitheater**, 1501 Cerrillos Rd. (on the grounds of the Santa Fe Indian School), which has fantastic sightlines and acoustics. See the local newspapers for details.

A number of nightclubs and bars offer live music. **El Farol**, 808 Canyon Rd., (505) 983-9912, is a popular (and historic) hangout, where the likes of U2's Bono and Joan Baez have stepped out of the crowd and up to the mike. The music ranges from flamenco to blues. El Farol is also a Spanish restaurant with a good selection of tapas and tasty *paella*; for a table, arrive early. The **Dragon Room** of the Pink Adobe, 406 Old Santa Fe Trail, (505) 983-7712, is a long-standing place to see and be seen in Santa Fe. In winter, a fireplace creates a romantic mood, enhanced by flamenco guitar and other live music. Another romantic nightspot is the **Staab House Bar** at La Posada, 330 Palace Ave., (505) 982-6950. If Chris Calloway, Cab's daughter, is singing, go! On the rougher side, **Evangelo's**, downtown at 200 W. San Francisco St., (505) 982-9014, has 200 varieties of imported beer, pool tables in its smoky basement, and live music upstairs on weekends.

Santa Fe isn't known for its dance clubs. However, there are a few that seem to be holding their own. The town's gay population gravitates to the **Drama Club**, 125 N. Guadalupe St., (505) 988-4374, and the excellent sound system and lively DJs encourage a mixed crowd that likes to dance, especially on Wednesday ("Trash Disco" night). Salsa fans should visit **Club Alegria**, Agua Fria two blocks east of Siler Rd., (505) 471-2324, on Friday nights to hear a live salsa band led by a Catholic priest (Father Pretto). For great, danceable Latin jazz, check out Yoboso, who play every Monday and Tuesday at **La Fonda**, 100 E. San Francisco St., (505) 982-5511. If you're in the mood for two-stepping, head for **Rodeo Nites**, 2911 Cerrillos Rd., (505) 473-4138.

Santa Fe has a budding theater scene. **Santa Fe Stages**, (505) 982-6683, produces excellent contemporary and classic shows and dance performances. Throughout July and August on Friday through Sunday nights, the Bard comes alive at the **Shakespeare in Santa Fe** series, (505) 982-2910, presented free at St. John's College, 1160 Camino Cruz Blanca. The surprisingly good **Santa Fe Community Theater**, 142 E. De Vargas, (505) 988-4262, has been offering a variety of works, including the annual Fiesta Melodrama, since 1922.

Both Indian gaming facilities near Santa Fe on US 84/285 offer card games, roulette, craps, slots, and Bingo, along with restaurants and gift shops: **Camel Rock Casino**, (505) 984-8414 or (800) GO-CAMEL; and **Cities of Gold** (505) 455-3313 or (800) 444-3313.

Scenic Route: O'Keeffe Country

Mounds of deep purple and rust-colored dirt. Pale yellow cliffs, banded above by pink and tan sandstone. A flat-topped peak, bones and crosses floating in the turquoise sky. Such are the images left to us by the late great American painter Georgia O'Keeffe, who settled in the once-remote village of Abiquiu in 1949 to pursue her art. Today the area is attracting movie stars building permaculture gardens, but a visit out this way is still well worth the time.

If you are coming from Santa Fe, stop at one of the oldest European colonies in the United States, **San Gabriel**, founded in 1598 by Don Juan de Oñate, just outside present-day Española. To get there, take US 85/284 24 miles northwest from Santa Fe to Española. Staying on the east side of the Rio Grande, head north on NM 68 to the edge of town and turn west (left) onto NM 74—the access road to **San Juan Pueblo**. Wind through the pueblo, past the **Oke Owenge** arts-and-crafts shop, a pretty Gothic-style stone church, and the pueblo plaza. Bear left just past the **Eight Northern Indian Pueblos Center** and cross to the west bank of the Rio Grande. San Gabriel was founded here. Although almost nothing remains, I think

O'KEEFFE COUNTRY

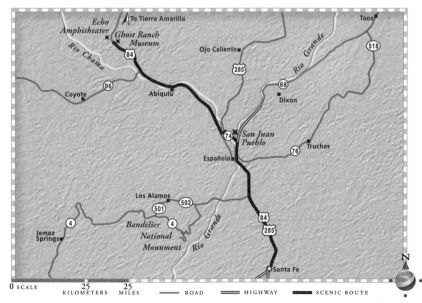

it's an interesting stop, certainly of immense historical significance.

Continue on NM 74 until you hit US 285 coming down from Ojo Caliente. Turn south (left), cross the Rio Chama, and at the intersection with US 84, turn west (right). This road zips up the **Chama Valley** past beautiful bottom land of alfalfa, orchards, and cottonwood trees sheltering ancient adobe homes flanked by the earthen hills and cliffs often painted by O'Keeffe. In about 16 miles you roll into **Abiquiu**. Take a few minutes to visit **Bode's**, a still-functional general mercantile. Then turn off US 84 to Abiquiu's plaza. **Georgia O'Keeffe's house**, (505) 685-4539, is right across the street from Bode's. You can walk around the plaza, but there's not much to see, and some locals will greet you with less than open arms. O'Keeffe's home, however, can be visited on guided tours by advance reservation on Tuesday, Thursday, and Friday.

Another few miles west along US 84 toward Chama is the **Ghost Ranch Living Museum**, (505) 685-4312, with outstanding exhibits of native Southwestern animals and plant life. A few more miles up the road, on the left, tucked under the area's striking yellow, cream, tan, and even light purple cliffs, is **Echo Amphitheater**— a huge natural alcove that bounces your voice around with remarkable clarity. Kids love it.

The round-trip can take as little as four hours or as much as a full day, depending on how much you want to linger. On the way back, dine or recline at the **Abiquiu Inn** and its Abiquiu Café (Middle Eastern and Mediterranean dishes), on US 84 just east of Abiquiu, (505) 685-4378. Twenty minutes away is perhaps the nicest bed-and-breakfast in the entire region, **Rancho de San Juan**, on US 285 a few miles north of the Chama River, (505) 753-6818. It has a gourmet restaurant, beautiful public spaces, and lovely, one-of-a-kind rooms, sporting great views of the countryside O'Keeffe immortalized. ◨

4
JEMEZ AREA

If the Sangre de Cristo Mountains of north-central New Mexico are young, bold, and dramatic, the Jemez Mountains are aged, friendly, and inviting. It's natural, then, that their gently meandering summits and valleys, plentiful water, and lush forests should have harbored the seeds of the Pueblo Indian culture, as seen in the tens of thousands of archeological sites found throughout the range.

The immense Valle Grande once blew its top with a force that scattered debris clear into Kansas. Today mesas drop off unexpectedly in rugged pitches, and geothermal hot waters still bubble to its surface here and there, attesting to the smoldering fires within. Ironically, its eastern-facing Pajarito Plateau is also the site of one of the world's most advanced technological centers, Los Alamos National Laboratory, birthplace and ongoing nursery of the atomic bomb, and the single greatest concentration per capita of super computers and Ph.D.s.

The adjoining town of Los Alamos is the commercial center of the area, with a number of shops, restaurants, and lodging options, as well as several interesting museums that document the lab's role in the development of the atomic bomb. The town's preoccupation with the atomic age is evidenced by the call letters of a popular oldies station—KBOM. All in all, it's an unlikely place—a slice of high-tech suburban America plunked down in the middle of ancient mountains and the Indian and Hispanic communities that have inhabited the area for centuries ◼

A PERFECT DAY IN THE JEMEZ AREA

Pack a picnic and start your day at San Ildefonso Pueblo. Cross the Rio Grande and wind over the mesas to Bandelier National Monument. After touring the ruins and eating your lunch, take a drive along high and cool NM 4, at least as far as the stunning Valle Grande, then return to Los Alamos and visit the technically oriented Bradbury Science Museum, or the Fuller Lodge History Museum for more of a social version of local history. If you're staying in the area, try dinner at Katherine's, in White Rock.

SIGHTSEEING HIGHLIGHTS

★★★ **Bandelier National Monument**—This U.S. Park Service site protects the cultural remnants of the Anasazi, ancestors of today's Pueblo Indians. Protected from the fiercest elements, narrow **Frijoles Canyon** has south-facing cliffs perfect for absorbing warm winter sunlight. Its perennial stream and abundant game once enabled its residents to build elaborate cliff dwellings, canyon-floor residences, ceremonial kivas, and other stone structures along more than a mile of the canyon. An asphalt trail winds through the fourteenth-century ruins, making this an accessible—and, in summer, almost oppressively popular—place.

However, 23,000 backcountry wilderness acres lie outside of this main valley, with some 75 miles of hiking and backpacking trails leading to more isolated ruins and wonderful views. One of the most frequented trails is **Falls Trail**, which leads to a lovely waterfall 1.5 miles from the trailhead. The visitor center contains some beautiful murals, good interpretive displays, and a gift shop.

Details: 40 miles west of Santa Fe. Take US 84/285 north to Pojoaque, then exit onto NM 502 and proceed past San Ildefonso Pueblo. Four miles west of the Rio Grande, exit onto NM 4, and then watch for the entrance sign on your left. Prior to reaching the main monument, you'll pass an outlier, Tsankawi, which offers a beautiful half-hour hike to some unexcavated ruins; (505) 672-3861. Bandelier is open daily Memorial Day to Labor Day 8–6, rest of the year 8–5. Admission is $10 per vehicle. (2 hours to a full day)

★★★ **Bradbury Science Museum**—Los Alamos National Laboratory and the town of Los Alamos are the offspring of America's drive to

Bandelier National Monument

JEMEZ AREA

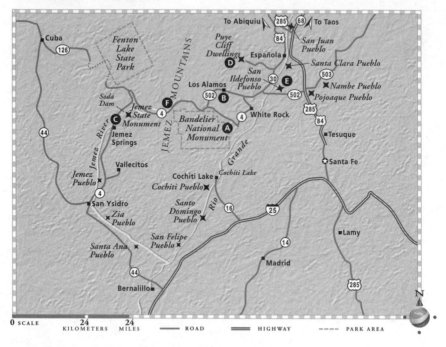

Sights

Ⓐ Bandelier National Monument

Ⓑ Bradbury Science Museum, Los Alamos

Ⓑ Fuller Lodge/Los Alamos County Historical Museum

Ⓒ Jemez Springs

Ⓓ Puye Cliff Dwellings

Ⓔ San Ildefonso Pueblo

Ⓕ Valle Grande

Note: Items with the same letter are located in the same town or area.

build the world's first nuclear bomb. This World War II effort ultimately did end the war when the United States bombed Hiroshima and Nagasaki in 1945. Whether you are a hawk or a dove, this fascinating museum reveals something of the effort that went into the project—even though it tends to glorify the incredible technology and downplay the moral questions surrounding the development and use of weapons of mass destruction. Other displays show Los Alamos' involvement in other sciences, from building space probes to energy research, though weaponeering remains its tour de force today.

Details: 15th St. and Central Ave.; (505) 667-4444. Open Tuesday through Friday 9–5, Saturday through Monday 1–5. Admission is free. (1 hour)

★★★ **San Ildefonso Pueblo**—Scientists like Robert Oppenheimer, director of the atomic bomb project, occasionally used to come down off "The Hill" (as Los Alamos National Laboratory was euphemistically called as late as the 1970s) to watch the age-old ceremonial dances at San Ildefonso Pueblo. What an odd juxtaposition. Around 1919 San Ildefonso potter Maria Martinez helped spark the revival of traditional Pueblo arts when she perfected the process of creating the beautiful black-on-black polished pottery now seen throughout the region and in the impoverished tribal museum. At a handful of pottery studios/galleries you can purchase work from the pueblo's many active ceramic artists. The pueblo also has a fishing pond. The dawn **Winter Hunting Dance** (January 22) is truly memorable. Deer dancers slowly filter down out of the surrounding hills and through the village streets to gather on the main plaza.

Details: Off NM 502 just east of the Rio Grande (see directions to Bandelier, above); (505) 455-3549. Open daily except occasional ceremonial days and major holidays. Admission is $3 per vehicle. A still camera permit costs $5; a video camera permit, $15. (1 hour)

★★ **Fuller Lodge/Los Alamos County Historical Museum**—Fuller Lodge was once the main facility of a boys' school attended by Robert Oppenheimer, a fact that circuitously led to his selection of Los Alamos as the perfect "hideaway" for the atomic bomb project. Today the massive chinked log structure houses an arts center; in an adjoining building is the Los Alamos County Historical Museum. For people interested in this chapter of U.S. history, it's a fascinating stop.

Details: 2132 Central Ave.; (505) 662-9331. Open Monday through Saturday 10–4, Sunday 1–4. Free. (1 to 3 hours)

★★ **Valle Grande**—This is one of the world's largest volcanic calderas—the collapsed rim of an ancient volcano that blew its top a million years ago in an immense cataclysm. You cannot fathom its size until you realize that the specks you see off in the distance are actually elk. For now, you can't enter the privately owned caldera's lush meadows or fish its meandering streams, but pullouts along the road make for grand viewing. The drive to Valle Grande from Bandelier or Los Alamos is lovely, winding through dense stands of quaking aspen, ponderosa pine, Douglas fir, and blue spruce. The aspen make for a great fall-color outing. As this book goes to press, the National Forest and Park Services plan to acquire this area and open it to the public.

    Details: Head west along NM 4 from Bandelier National Monument; from Los Alamos, take Trinity Drive to Diamond Drive, turn south (left) and then west (right) onto West Jemez Drive (NM 501). The roads are open year-round, though winter storms can be treacherous. For further information on the surrounding national forests, contact the Los Alamos Ranger Station,(505) 667-5120. (2 to 3 hours)

★ **Jemez Springs**—This small, rural town is 73 miles southwest of Santa Fe on the southwestern edge of the Jemez; it's equally accessible from Albuquerque via NM 44 and NM 4. Nearby are excellent ruins, along with hiking, fishing, cross-country skiing, and mountain biking opportunities. En route on NM 4 from Valle Grande, just before Jemez Spring and alongside the Jemez River, you'll pass the travertine deposit known as the **Soda Dam**, popular with swimmers. Don't try the cliff jumping—several people have died here. One mile further you'll pass **Jemez State Monument**, (505) 829-3530, which contains impressive Indian and Spanish ruins. In town is the **Jemez Springs Bath House**, (505) 829-3303, which has indoor and outdoor mineral pools. Indoor pools cost $8 an hour, a private tub $30 an hour. Massages, herbal wraps, facials, and other services are also available.

    Details: Continue west and south on NM 4 past Valle Grande. (2 to 3 hours)

★ **Puye Cliff Dwellings**—This rare historical site is run by Indians, in this case **Santa Clara Pueblo**, whose ancestors once lived in the stone and cave structures lining a south-facing canyon wall. A trail takes visitors from the canyon floor up ladders to the mesatop. You can also visit the pueblo itself, which includes a historic Catholic church and several shops selling Santa Clara's acclaimed pottery.

Details: 11 miles off NM 30 (the road that runs between Española and the Los Alamos bridge on the west bank of the Rio Grande) on a gravel Forest Service road; (505) 753-7326. Hours vary. Admission is $5 adults, $4 children and seniors. (2 hours)

FITNESS AND RECREATION

Jemez has a myriad of recreation possibilities. As already noted, within **Bandelier National Monument** are more than 60 miles of backcountry trails that access remote sections of the park. Several of these trails descend and ascend major canyons, which can be extremely hot in midsummer or buried under snow and ice in winter. Prime time for the monument's backcountry is in the late spring or fall. Permits available through the visitor center (see Sightseeing Highlights) are required for backcountry outings.

Just outside of Los Alamos is the **Pajarito Ski Area**, (505) 662-5725. For decades the private ski stash of physicists and other Hilltoppers, the area is now open to the general public on weekends, Wednesdays, and federal holidays throughout the season. It has a 1,400-foot vertical drop, and is noted for its monstrous moguls and occasional major snow dumps of 4 feet or more. Call ahead for conditions and driving directions.

These mountains have a relatively gentle profile, making them ideal for cross-country skiing. A network of Forest Service roads, closed to winter traffic, provide excellent routes. One leads to the **San Antonio Hot Springs**, others into Bandelier. For details, contact the Santa Fe National Forest, Los Alamos, (505) 667-5120, or Jemez Springs Ranger Office, (505) 829-3535, which can also provide information on local summer hiking trails, mountain biking, trout fishing, waterfalls, and the **Jemez National Recreation Area**.

Los Alamos also boasts of one of the state's few outdoor ice-skating rinks, at 4475 West Rd., (505) 662-4500, complete with rentals and snack bar. The nation's highest-altitude indoor Olympic-size pool is at the **Larry Walkup Aquatic Center**, (505) 662-8170.

A few Santa Fe–based rafting companies lead daylong float trips through **White Rock Canyon** of the Rio Grande. This little-visited but significant canyon at the foot of the Jemez has petroglyphs, ruins, and some exciting but relatively tame white water.

JEMEZ AREA

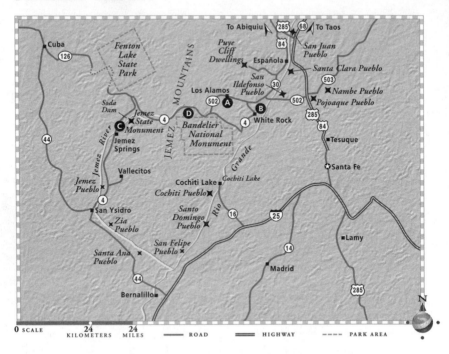

Food

- **A** Blue Window
- **A** Central Avenue Grill
- **A** De Colores
- **A** Hill Diner
- **B** Katherine's
- **C** Los Ojos

Lodging

- **A** Adobe Pines
- **A** Back Porch
- **B** Bandelier Inn
- **A** Hilltop House
- **C** Jemez River
- **A** Los Alamos Inn
- **A** North Road Inn

Camping

- **D** Juniper Campground

Note: Items with the same letter are located in the same town or area.

FOOD

Bandelier National Monument has a snack bar, but for a sit-down meal, stop in White Rock or Los Alamos. A real surprise is **Katherine's,** 121 Longview Dr., White Rock, (505) 672-9661, which offers such fine meals as filet mignon with béarnaise sauce and fresh seafood, table-made Caesar salads, and excellent desserts, including a mouth-watering lemon mousse.

Los Alamos has several decent possibilities, besides a slew of fast-food joints. The **Blue Window**, 800 Trinity Dr., (505) 662-6305, serves soups, crêpes, and New Mexico plates at lunch, and homemade pasta and fresh fish at night. The **Central Avenue Grill**, 1789 Central Ave., (505) 662-2005, dishes up gourmet pizza, salads, and vegetarian lasagna, as well as microbrews. **De Colores**, 820 Trinity Dr., (505) 662-6285, specializes in New Mexico fare but also cooks chicken and steak. It's closed on Sunday. The **Hill Diner**, 1315 Trinity Dr., (505) 662-9745, serves classic diner dishes in a cozy mountain cabin setting. Banana cream pies like you remember!

In Jemez Springs, don't miss **Los Ojos**, downtown, (505) 829-3547, the bar/restaurant nerve center of this community, with pool tables, a huge stone fireplace topped by an elk rack, a jukebox, and wonderful log bar stools that call out for a lazy afternoon sipping brews. Tasty burgers!

LODGING

The lodging closest to Bandelier National Monument is found in White Rock, at the **Bandelier Inn**, 132 NM 4, (505) 672-3838 or (800) 321-3923. It offers reasonably priced rooms, and suites with kitchenettes, cable TV, a hot tub, free breakfasts, and a coin-op laundry for $61 a night.

In Los Alamos, you have the **Hilltop House**, 400 Trinity Dr., (505) 662-2442 or (800) 462-0936, which provides rooms, suites, and kitchenettes, as well as a 24-hour food mart and gas service, outdoor pool, hot tub, and sauna, for $78 a night. Also on the premises is the Trinity Sights Restaurant and Lounge. Another option is the **Los Alamos Inn**, 2201 Trinity Dr., (505) 662-7211 or (800) 279-9279, with an outdoor pool, hot tub, and room service for $79. The inn has two restaurants—Ashley's, with seafood and steaks, and Ashley's Pub.

Los Alamos hosts a handful of bed and breakfasts, all with double rooms in the $50–$75 range. Options include the **Adobe Pines**, 2101 Loma Linda Dr., (505) 662-6761, a modern, elegant adobe with an indoor pool overlooking the Los Alamos Golf Course; the **North Road Inn**, 2127 North Rd., (505) 662-3678 or (800) 279-2898, which features seven suites with private bath, phone, and cable TV; and the **Back Porch**, 13 Karen Circle, (505) 672-9816, where the rooms, which overlook lush gardens and a forested arroyo, have private baths.

In Jemez Springs, a lovely bed-and-breakfast, **Jemez River**, 16445 NM 4, (505) 829-3262 or (800) 809-3262, is a certified hummingbird sanctuary set on 5 riverfront acres. The rooms feature coved ceilings and tile floors opening onto a patio. Rates are $80–$110.

CAMPING

Juniper Campground, (505) 672-3861, at Bandelier National Monument, is a pretty spot on the rim of Frijoles Canyon, with 100 sites (no RV hookups) available on a first-come, first-served basis. The grounds have running water, and rangers lead nightly campfire talks in summer. There are also a few developed campgrounds and dispersed campsites in the surrounding **Santa Fe National Forest**, Los Alamos, (505) 667-5120, or Jemez Springs, (505) 829-3535.

Scenic Route: The High Road to Taos

Most folks heading north from Santa Fe or the Jemez area take the "river route" along the Rio Grande through Española, the Velarde Valley, and the lower Taos canyon. While this is a beautiful drive, there's an even prettier route known as the "High Road." The High Road weaves in and out of the high alpine valleys of the Sangre de Cristos and many small Hispanic villages, as well past the most isolated of the pueblos, Picuris. In fall the aspens and scrub oak create vast swaths of color; in winter soft snow blankets the adobe walls and orchard trees; in spring wildflowers erupt; and in summer green alfalfa and high grass fields shimmer.

The route is best begun in Pojoaque north of Santa Fe, where NM 503 intersects US 84/285. Turn east (right) onto NM 503 and amble up the **Nambe River Valley** and across some eroded "bad-lands." Make a 90-degree turn off NM 503 onto NM 520, which takes you over a rise and into the next valley and the town of **Chimayó**. Just after entering the valley, keep your eyes peeled to your right and you'll see a little plaza and a sign announcing the **Santuario de Chimayó**. This is one of America's most famous and

THE HIGH ROAD TO TAOS

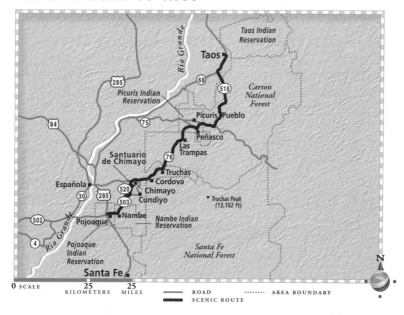

popular places of pilgrimage. Every Easter tens of thousands of faithful walk, crawl, and crank wheelchairs to it—many from as far away as Albuquerque! The tiny, humble chapel with its brightly painted wooden altar is representative of the rural chapels found throughout the region. However, most come to dip their hands in the tiny *pozito*, or well, found in a side room, whose dirt is supposed to hold miraculous powers. A small gift shop sells intriguing religious articles. Continuing north, stop at the neighboring **Rancho de Chimayó**, on the main road, (505) 351-0444, for some good New Mexican food served up in a charming old farmhouse.

A few miles farther along the main road, you might also wish to stop at **Ortega's Weaving Shop**, (505) 351-4215, for a look at the work of this renowned, centuries-old Hispanic weaving center. At the intersection of NM 76, turn east (right). You might want to drop off this road in about 4 miles into the village of **Cordova**, which is famed for its *santeros* who carve and paint incredible folk images of Catholic saints. Next stop is the village of **Truchas**, which has several more art galleries and weaving studios. Seven miles past Truchas is **Las Trampas**, home to the striking adobe church of San Tomas, which dates to 1751.

At the T-intersection with NM 75, turn west (left) if you wish to detour into **Picuris Pueblo**, perhaps the state's most isolated pueblo and the only one found in a mountain setting. The pueblo has a small museum and visitor center with a restaurant featuring Native foods, (505) 587-2957. Its big to-do is the **San Lorenzo Feast Day** on August 10, which includes dances, foot races, pole climbing, and a procession. Return to NM 75 and continue east through the villages of Peñasco, Vadito, and Placitas. Turn north (left) onto NM 518, which joins NM 68 just south of Taos at Ranchos de Taos. The drive, without stops, takes about two hours. ◼

5

TAOS

Taos is the younger sibling of Santa Fe. Like Santa Fe, it has a strong Hispanic and Indian feel, along with frontier and hippie-holdout elements, but without the rarefied atmosphere—and some would say pretension—of Santa Fe. Also like Santa Fe, it is set in an area of tremendous scenic beauty. On one side of the city rises the often snow-capped and mystical Taos Mountain, said to be a power point of the planet. On the other side slices the impressive Taos Gorge, carved by the Rio Grande. To the west great vistas open.

For centuries Taos has been a trading and visiting center. Tribes of the Great Plains, when they weren't at war with the Pueblo Indians, came into Taos to barter with both the Indians of Taos Pueblo and the Spanish, who founded the town of Taos in the early 1600s. In 1898 two American artists, Bert Phillips and Ernest Blumenschein, were on their way to Mexico for a painting trip, when their vehicle broke down outside of Taos. They ended up falling in love with the area and became the nucleus of an art colony that grew to include matron Mabel Dodge Lujan, photographers such as Ansel Adams, painters such as Nicolai Fechin and Georgia O'Keeffe, author D. H. Lawrence, and a slew of lesser-known but highly talented artists in the 1920s through the 1940s. Art remains a major force in the town today.

In the late 1960s the area became a haven for the "back to the country" movement, and world-class skiing was born at nearby Taos Ski Valley. Today elements of all these cultures coexist in the somewhat funky but charming community of greater Taos. ∎

TAOS

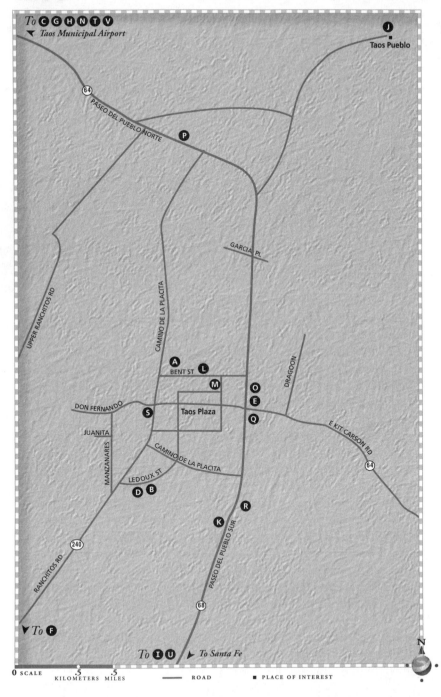

To C G H N T V
Taos Municipal Airport

J
Taos Pueblo

64

PASEO DEL PUEBLO NORTE

P

GARCIA PL

CAMINO DE LA PLACITA

UPPER RANCHITOS RD

DRAGOON

A
BENT ST   L

M

O

E

DON FERNANDO

S   Taos Plaza   Q

E KIT CARSON RD

JUANITA

64

MANZANARES

CAMINO DE LA PLACITA

LEDOUX ST

D B

R

K

PASEO DEL PUEBLO SUR

RANCHITOS RD

240

68

To F

To I U   To Santa Fe

N

0 SCALE   .5   .5
KILOMETERS   MILES   ROAD   ■ PLACE OF INTEREST

Sights

Ⓐ Bent Street

Ⓑ Blumenschein Home

Ⓒ D. H. Lawrence Ranch

Ⓓ Harwood Foundation

Ⓔ Kit Carson Home

Ⓕ Martinez Hacienda

Ⓖ Millicent Rogers Museum

Ⓗ Rio Grande Gorge Bridge

Ⓘ San Francisco de Asis Church

Ⓙ Taos Pueblo

Food

Ⓚ Amigos Natural Grocery & Deli

Ⓛ Apple Tree

Ⓜ Bent Street Deli

Ⓝ Casa Cordova

Ⓞ Doc Martin's

Ⓟ El Pueblo Café

Ⓠ Eske's

Ⓡ Lambert's

Ⓢ Main St. Bakery

Ⓣ Tim's Chile Connection

Ⓤ Trading Post Café

Ⓥ Villa Fontana

A PERFECT DAY IN TAOS

In summer, visit Taos Pueblo early or late in the day to avoid crowds and heat. In town, check out museums, galleries, shops, and historic sites, with lunch at the Main Street Bakery or Bent Street Deli. If you're into outdoor recreation, mix a half-day in town with a half-day of skiing, white-water rafting, hiking, or mountain biking. Finish the day with a drive to the Gorge Bridge and the D. H. Lawrence Ranch, and have dinner at one of the town's many fine restaurants.

SIGHTSEEING HIGHLIGHTS

★★★ **Bent Street**—Just off the town's main plaza, Bent Street has become a center for small galleries, unique retail shops, and restaurants. It also shelters a small but interesting museum. The **Governor Bent Museum** preserves the home of the state's first territorial governor appointed by U.S. authorities, Charles Bent, whose family played a critical role in the success of the Santa Fe Trail. He had his head cut off by a mob in this house during the failed Taos Revolt of 1847, while his wife and children escaped by digging a hole through an adobe wall into an adjoining home.

Details: *117A Bent St.; (505) 758-2376. Open daily 10–5. Admission is $2. For further general information on Taos, contact the Taos Visitors Center on the corner of Paseo del Pueblo Sur and Paseo del Canon, (505) 758-3873 or (800) 732-8267. (1 hour)*

★★★ **Martinez Hacienda**—Within the massive, straw-flecked adobe walls of this compound, a prominent Taos family rose and fell from fortune. The property provides a rare look into the sparse, often harsh, yet fulfilling life on the Spanish frontier, with period rooms re-creating life in the early 1800s. Parts of the home date to the seventeenth century, when it was used as a neighborhood shelter during Comanche raids. During the last weekend in September it hosts the annual Old Taos Trade Fair, when its looms, blacksmith shop, kitchens, and other facilities really come to life.

Details: *Head away from the Plaza on Ranchitos Road (NM 240) and follow a small creek a few miles through the picturesque countryside; (505) 758-1000. Open daily 9–5. Admission is $4. (1 hour)*

★★★ **Taos Pueblo**—The five-story Taos Pueblo is an icon of New Mexico's Pueblo Indian culture. A national historic landmark and UNESCO World Heritage Site, the Pueblo is perhaps the best-preserved of its peers in New Mexico. Originally built circa A.D. 1000–1400, it still lacks electricity or plumbing. Only a handful of families live here year-round today, but many families maintain homes within its condo-like structure for use during their many religious and secular ceremonies.

A dozen or so artists' galleries and shops are scattered about the pueblo. Do not enter any structure unless it is clearly marked as a public facility. Also of note is San Geronimo Church. Built in 1850, it's a lovely example of Spanish Colonial Mission–style architecture. Photography inside is forbidden.

Prime days for visiting include the Fiesta de San Antonio on June 13, the Taos Pueblo Powwow on July 25–26, the Fiesta de San Geronimo on the evening of September 29 and daylong on September 30, Christmas Eve, Christmas Day, and January 1.

Details: *Head north on through Taos on Paseo del Pueblo (NM 68). Just past the Kachina Lodge and post office, take the marked fork to the right and continue a few miles into the pueblo parking lot; (505) 758-9593. It's open April through November daily 8–5:30; December through March 8:30–4:30; and closed one month in late winter. Admission is $5 per vehicle, $5 for a camera permit, and $10 for a video permit. (2 hours)*

★★ **Blumenschein Home**—This funky old adobe, built around 1797, was the home and studio of one of the pioneers of the Taos art colony, Ernest Blumenschein. His terrific work, contents of the house (including an interesting kitchen), and changing displays provide insight into the early days of Taos' still-thriving arts community.

Details: 222 Ledoux Street; (505) 758-0505. Open daily 9–5. Admission is $4 for adults, $2 for children ages 6–15. (1 hour)

★★ **Kit Carson Home**—As interesting and contrary a figure to be found anywhere in the annals of the West was trailblazer, mountain man, family man, trader, trapper, and U.S. Cavalry officer Kit Carson. This low-slung, 12-room adobe preserves the home in which he resided from 1843 to 1868. For history buffs, it's a fascinating stop. Personal and family effects are displayed along with a gun collection and mountain-man artifacts. There's a small gift shop as well.

Details: Kit Carson Road, just off Paseo del Pueblo (the town's main road) near the Plaza; (505) 758-4741. Open November through March daily 9–5; April through September 8–6. Admission is $4 for adults, $2 for children ages 6 –15. (1 hour)

★★ **Millicent Rogers Museum**—An excellent, smallish museum with strong holdings of Pueblo pottery (including those of famed San Ildefonso potter Maria Martinez), Indian silver jewelry and weavings, as well as Hispanic religious and secular arts and crafts, it contains more than 5,000 objects from the personal collection of deceased Standard Oil heiress Millicent Rogers, another of Taos' colorful historical characters. There's also a good gift shop and bookstore.

Details: Take US 64 north. At the stoplight north of town turn west (left) toward Tres Piedras, then left again at the immediate stoplight onto Blue Berry Hill Road, and continue several miles south; (505) 758-2462. It's open year-round daily 9–5. Admission is $4. (1 hour)

★★ **Rio Grande Gorge Bridge**—Once the highest bridge on the U.S. highway system, this structure spanning the Rio Grande's Taos Gorge will put your heart in your mouth if heights scare you. The thin line of the river flowing beneath your feet is some 650 feet down. Park at either side and walk on the sidewalks to reach observation points.

Details: Drive north out of town on US 64, turn left at the stoplight, and continue on US 64 toward Tres Piedras. You can't miss it. It's free and always open. (30 minutes)

✸✸ **San Francisco de Asis Church**—Better known as the Ranchos de Taos Church, after the humble farming community just south of Taos, this eighteenth-century Spanish Colonial church is one of the most-photographed and -painted religious structures in the world. Almost every major artist who has ever lived in or passed through New Mexico has tried to capture its oddly appealing, earthy, abstract form. Mass is still presented here regularly, so don't barge in.

Details: U.S. 64 East, Ranchos de Taos (south of Taos). Its buttressed west wall (best seen in late afternoon) is visible from the highway; (505) 758-2754. Open Monday through Saturday 9–4. Donation requested. (30 minutes)

✸ **D. H. Lawrence Ranch**—A must-see for the literary pilgrim, this 160-acre property was the famed English author's home for some 22 months between 1922 and 1925. The buildings are not open to the public, but one can visit the small shrine where his ashes are buried, and the nearby grave of his wife, Frieda Lawrence. He wrote of this place, "I think New Mexico was the greatest experience from the outside world that I have ever had."

Details: Take US 64 and NM 522 north of Taos about 10 miles. Just before the village of Cristobal, look for a sign on the right, and continue along this gravel road for 4.5 miles. The shrine is about 100 yards uphill from the parking area; (505) 776-2245. Open daily. Admission is free. (1 hour)

✸ **Harwood Foundation**—In almost any other region this would be a top attraction, but in northern New Mexico it is just one of a plethora of good art museums. The Harwood houses a large collection of early Taos artists, as well as work by their contemporary peers.

Details: 238 Ledoux St., Taos; (505) 758-9826. Open weekdays 10–5, Saturday 10–4. Admission is $2. (1 hour)

FITNESS AND RECREATION

Taos is a terrific locale for outdoor recreation. Sitting on a plateau flanked by mountains topping 13,000 feet and one of America's deepest canyons, the Rio Grande Gorge, its microclimates and geography make a wide range of activities possible. In fact, because of the vast differences in altitude, you can both ski and run white water on the same day.

Alpine skiers from around the world head to **Taos Ski Valley**, (505) 776-2291, about 45 minutes from Taos Plaza. This area pioneered the concept of extreme in-bounds skiing off the hike-to ridge of

Highline and West Basin, and it's renowned for its phenomenally light powder (312 inches a year, average!). But it is a large area with lots of terrain for all ability levels. In summer, its chairlift provides hikers and sightseers with a ride into the Sangre de Cristo's highest peaks. To get there, take US 64 to the light at the edge of town, then turn east (right) onto NM 150 through Arroyo Seco. Many options exist for cross-country skiing, too. Contact the Carson National Forest, (505) 758-6200, in Taos, for details; or check out **Enchanted Forest Cross Country Ski Area**, (505) 754-2374, located near Red River.

The other major recreational draw is hour-long, half-day, and full-day white-water outings on the Rio Grande. Various sections run from mild to white-knuckle. For options and information on guided services, or permits to run it yourself (not recommended for amateurs), contact the Taos Visitor Center (see Bent Street, above) or the Bureau of Land Management area office, (505) 758-8851.

Superb options for backpacking and hiking also exist. Some 30 minutes from town is the edge of the 20,000-acre **Wheeler Peak Wilderness Area**. The **Williams Lake Trail**, popular on weekends, climbs 4 miles from the Taos Ski Valley parking lot to a beautiful lake fronting the state's highest summit, 13,160-foot **Wheeler Peak**. Mountain biking is also becoming a major draw, with several trails recently opened, including a track along the Taos Gorge rim (9½ miles one way, with its northern terminus at the Rio Grande Gorge Bridge). For details, including routes and rentals, contact **Gearing Up**, (505) 751-0365, or **Hot Tracks**, (505) 751-0949.

Fishing on local lakes, the Rio Grande, and small streams is also quite good—if you know where and when to try. Get information from several guide services in Taos, or from the Carson National Forest office, (505) 758-6200. Horseback riding is also popular. Particularly notable are rides on Taos Pueblo lands offered by **Taos Indian Horse Ranch**, (505) 758-3212 or (800) 659-3210. If you're a golfer, try the **Taos Country Club**, (505) 758-7300, or the resort town of **Angel Fire**, (505) 377-3055, about an hour from Taos.

FOOD

For a small community, Taos has amazingly diverse and high-quality dining options. At the high end ($20–$30 per person) is my favorite, **Casa Cordova**, just off NM 150 (the Ski Valley road) in Arroyo Seco, (505) 776-2500. Set in an old adobe with fireplaces and an outdoor portal for summer dining, it oozes charm and elegance. Begin with a drink in the sedate bar. The pork loin with jalapeño sauce beckons! Open for dinner only; closed Sunday.

Also topping the price range but well worth a visit, is **Doc Martin's**, in the Taos Inn, 125 Paseo del Pueblo Norte, (505) 758-1977. Nightly specials vie with staples including roasted pheasant or penne pasta with mushrooms, bell pepper, and eggplant. Its wine list is quite impressive. **Lambert's**, 309 Paseo del Pueblo Sur, (505) 758-1009, is known for its contemporary American dishes prepared with fresh ingredients; while **Villa Fontana**, on NM 522 5 miles north of the plaza, (505) 758-5800, serves some terrific classic northern Italian fare in a country-inn setting. A relatively new, highly regarded entry is the **Trading Post Café**, 4179 NM 68 near its intersection with NM 518, in Rancho de Taos, (505) 758-5089.

In the moderate range is the **Bent Street Deli**, 120 Bent Street, (505) 758-5787, which prepares great soups, salads, and sandwiches for lunch; dinners feature pasta or fish. Also in this neighborhood is the **Apple Tree**, 123 Bent Street, (505) 758-1900, which serves daily specials and an international menu including grilled lamb. **Tim's Chile Connection**, just past the turnoff to the Ski Valley road (NM 150), (505) 776-8787, is a sure bet for tasty New Mexican fare, home-brewed beer, and infamous margaritas.

In the inexpensive category, some of the best handcrafted beer found anywhere is tippled into mugs at **Eske's**, 106 DesGeorges Lane (one block southeast of Kit Carson and Paseo del Pueblo), (505) 758-1517. Six to eight brews are on tap at any moment, hauled out of the basement where 22 or so are nursed to life by brewmeister Steve Eskeback and his wife, Wanda. Sandwiches, soups, and other fine pub fare is served, with fresh sushi on Tuesday. Live music often plays at night in this nonsmoking establishment.

The aroma of fresh-baked breads and pastries wafts over you as you arrive for breakfast or lunch at **Main St. Bakery**, just west of the Plaza off Camino de la Placita, (505) 758-9610. Specialties include homemade granola, date-nut/orange French toast, and *huevos rancheros*. For some inexpensive New Mexican food as well as chicken, hamburgers, and such, check out **El Pueblo Café**, 625 Paseo del Pueblo Norte, (505) 758-2053. **Amigos Natural Grocery & Deli**, 326 Paseo del Pueblo Sur, (505) 758-8493, is a great place to stock up on food treats for your condo or sit at the counter for a great sandwich at lunch. Open daily.

LODGING

The **Taos Inn**, 125 Paseo del Pueblo Norte, (505) 758-2233 or (800) 826-7466, has a lot going for it. It's set in the heart of town within walking distance of most of Taos' interesting sites. A historic property composed of centuries-old homes now linked together, it was completely renovated in 1981–82. All rooms have fireplaces, phones, and private baths; $75–$225. The inn has a great restaurant, Doc Martin's (see Food, above), and a fun bar, often with live music.

The **Sagebrush Inn**, 1508 Paseo del Pueblo Sur, (505) 758-2254 or (800) 428-3626, has been Taos' other classic dig since its opening in 1929. Famed painter Georgia O'Keeffe lived for extended periods in one room here, and its lobby—with comfortable leather chairs, Hispanic and Pueblo art and artifacts, a large stone fireplace, and exposed vigas—epitomizes the Taos ambiance. Prices start at $85. The Sagebrush has a rustic bar (often sporting country-western bands at night) and a decent restaurant.

The newest addition to the town's leading hotels is the **Fechin Inn**, 227 Paseo del Pueblo Norte, (505) 751-1000 or (800) 811-2939. Named after renowned artist Nicolai Fechin, its 85 rooms and suites incorporate the artist's original home and reflects his eclectic style and tastes. Amenities include a fitness center, bar, and free Continental breakfast. Pets are allowed. Rates range from $109–$179.

Popular with skiers and families is **Quail Ridge Inn**, just outside of town off the Ski Valley road, (505) 776-2211 or (800) 624-4448. This 110-unit Pueblo-style complex has a 20-meter heated pool, indoor tennis courts, saunas, hot tubs, a coin-op laundry, fireplaces, phones, and maid service. A basic double is $89; condos are $120. A restaurant and bar are also on the premises.

The **Kachina Lodge**, 413 Paseo del Pueblo Norte, (505) 758-2275 or (800) 522-4462, is another unique property—an upscale motel opened in 1961 with a kind of Pueblo Deco decor. Though its bedrooms are nothing special, its lobby, cool Kiva Coffee Shop, and other public spaces feature a superb collection of Indian arts and crafts. Rates are $100–$130. On the north edge of town, it provides quick access to the Ski Valley road.

For those on a budget, check out the **Sun God Lodge**, 919 Paseo del Pueblo Sur, (505) 758-3162 or (800) 821-2437. Its motel rooms are smallish, but Mexican furniture, sculpted walls dividing the bedrooms and bathrooms, and other thoughtful touches makes this a pleasant

TAOS

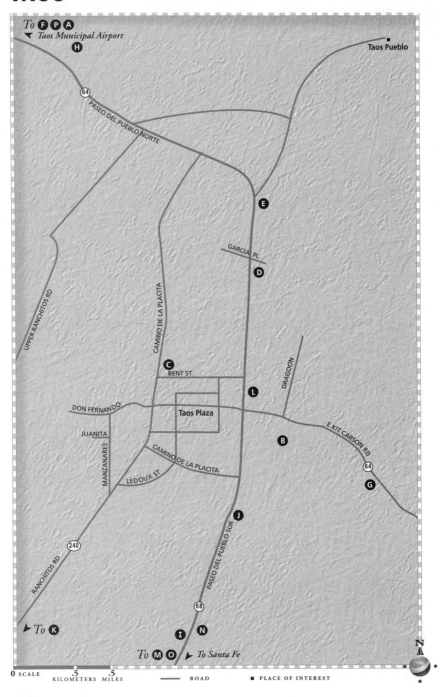

To **F** **P** **A**
▼ *Taos Municipal Airport*
H

Taos Pueblo ■

64

PASEO DEL PUEBLO NORTE

E

GARCIA PL

D

UPPER RANCHITOS RD

CAMINO DE LA PLACITA

DRAGOON

C
BENT ST

L

DON FERNANDO

Taos Plaza

E KIT CARSON RD

JUANITA

MANZANARES

CAMINO DE LA PLACITA

B

64

LEDOUX ST

G

240

PASEO DEL PUEBLO SUR

J

RANCHITOS RD

68

▶ To **K**

I **N**

To **M** **O** ▶ *To Santa Fe*

N

0 SCALE   .5   .5
KILOMETERS MILES   ——— ROAD   ■ PLACE OF INTEREST

Lodging

Ⓐ Abominable Snowmansion

Ⓑ Casa de las Chimeneas

Ⓒ Casa Feliz

Ⓓ Fechin Inn

Ⓔ Kachina Lodge

Ⓕ Mountain Light

Ⓖ Old Taos Guesthouse

Ⓗ Quail Ridge Inn

Ⓘ Sagebrush Inn

Ⓙ Sun God Lodge

Lodging *(continued)*

Ⓚ Taos Country Inn

Ⓛ Taos Inn

Camping

Ⓜ Orilla Verde National Recreation Area

Ⓝ Taos Valley RV Park and Campground

Ⓞ Taos RV Park

Ⓟ Wild and Scenic Rivers National Recreation Area

place to stay. Rates are $59–$82. Taos' least expensive lodging is the **Abominable Snowmansion**, on the Ski Valley road in Arroyo Seco, (505) 776-8298. It's a no-frills but pleasant hostel with private rooms and dormitory rates: $16–$22.

Taos has a great collection of bed and breakfasts, each with its own distinct character. The **Taos Country Inn**, off Ranchitos Road set in fields a few miles west of downtown, (505) 758-4900, has stunning views of sacred Taos Mountain. Saltillo tile floors, local wooden furniture and art, Southwestern textiles, and the adobe structure provide a perfect New Mexico experience. Try the Deveaux Room, with windows on three sides and a fireplace. Rates are $100–$140.

Casa de las Chimeneas, 405 Cordoba Road, (505) 758-4777, is one of Taos' luxury B&Bs. Inside its 7-foot-thick adobe walls are outstanding regional art, tiled hearths, French doors, and lovely furniture. All rooms have private entrances, fireplaces, telephones, mini-refrigerators, and cable TV. In spring, a beautiful garden comes alive. Rates are $130–$160.

Downtown, on historic Bent Street, is **Casa Feliz**, (505) 758-9790. The former home of artist Becky James (who was once married to famed photographer Paul Strand), it radiates charm and tranquillity. Each room has its own bathroom and New Mexico handcrafted furniture. Rates are $85–$110.

Overlooking town on its southeast edge is the **Old Taos Guesthouse**, off Kit Carson Road, (505) 758-5448. Each of the eight rooms has a private entrance and private bath. The friendly owners also cook up a great breakfast. Rates are $70–$110. A simple, inexpensive B&B with see-forever views is **Mountain Light**, out of town in Arroyo Hondo, (505) 776-8474. Rates are $52–$62.

CAMPING

Nine campgrounds sit within 20 miles of Taos in the **Carson National Forest** (505) 758-6200. Developed sites also exist in the **Orilla Verde National Recreation Area,** along the Rio Grande near Pilar (30 minutes south of town off NM 68), administered by the BLM, (505) 758-8851. About 45 minutes north of town is the spectacular **Wild and Scenic Rivers National Recreation Area**, (505) 758-8851; you can camp above the confluence of the Rio Grande and Red River. In Ranchos de Taos, the **Taos RV Park** (505) 758-1667 or (800) 323-6009, offers 29 sites with full hookups. In Taos, try the **Taos Valley RV Park and Campground**, (505) 758-4469, with 92 sites. It's closed November through February.

NIGHTLIFE

In winter, several bars in Taos Ski Valley can be a lot of fun; particularly, **The Bistro** in the venerable Hotel St. Bernard; the **Martini Tree**; and **The Thunderbird**. In town, you can usually do the country shuffle out at the **Sagebrush Inn**. **Eske's** downtown often has live music, too. **Taos Mountain Casino**, on the reservation, (505) 758-4460 or (888)-WIN-TAOS, has smoke-free card games, slots, and roulette, as well as a nice deli restaurant.

6
NORTHWESTERN NEW MEXICO

Northwestern New Mexico is a fascinating intersection of geography and people. It's the transition zone from the Rio Grande Valley/Southern Rocky Mountains and the great Colorado Plateau that dominates southwestern Colorado, northern Arizona, and southern Utah. The region is also the eastern edge of the immense Navajo Reservation and the homeland of the Jicarilla Apache. Most tourists range up and down the Rio Grande Valley from Albuquerque to Taos, leaving the state's northwest corner still a frontier of sorts. Though it lacks luxury tourist amenities, the northwest more than compensates with stunning vistas, outstanding outdoor recreation opportunities, and interesting cultural and historical sites.

Train buffs enjoy the steam-powered Cumbres & Toltec Railroad and wandering around the historic railroad district in Chama. If you like Victorian-era architecture, you'll find the downtown core of Aztec entrancing; if Indian Ruins are your thing, you'll be delighted by the majestic Aztec Ruins National Monument.

With high mountains and the immense Navajo Lake, the area also offers ample opportunities for cross-country skiing, hiking, hunting, fishing, and other outdoor sports; the area is home to the state's largest concentration of snowmobiles. And when the late afternoon sun lights up the soaring walls of Shiprock and casts a great shadow across the dry San Juan Basin, one can envision the jagged rock taking flight once again, true to its Navajo name, *Tse Bi Dahi*, or Rock with Wings. ◪

NORTHWESTERN NEW MEXICO

To Pagosa Springs

Antonito
285
17
D
Toltec Scenic Railway
Rio Brazos
Chama
Cumbres & Toltec
C
I
64 84
K
512
Brazos
Tierra
Amarilla
84
To Taos
Tres Piedras
64
To Taos
285
68
Española
Coyote
96
Rio Grande
Tesuque
To Santa Fe

Heron Lake State Park
N
L
Rio Chama

COLORADO

Dulce
J
Jicarilla
537
E
Apache
Stone Lake
95
44
Cuba

Indian   Reservation

Navajo Lake
Navajo Lake State Park
F
M
527
172
Ignacio
511
539
NEW MEXICO
197
Nageezi
44
197

To Durango
550
B
Aztec Ruins National Monument
A
544
G
Bloomfield
Angel Peak
Chaco Culture National Historic Park

574
Aztec
140
170
Farmington
64
Bisti Badlands
Lake Valley
371

Shiprock
Indian   Reservation
Navajo
Indian   Reservation

Ute Mountain   Reservation

San Juan River
64
H
Shiprock Pinnacle
666
Sheep Springs

UTAH   ARIZONA

0 SCALE
27 KILOMETERS
27 MILES

—— ROAD
═══ HIGHWAY
═ ═ STATE BOUNDARY
- - - - RESERVATION BOUNDARY
++++++ RAILROAD

Sights

Ⓐ Aztec

Ⓑ Aztec Ruins National
Monument

Ⓒ Chama

Ⓓ Cumbres & Toltec Railroad

Ⓔ Jicarilla Apache Reservation

Ⓕ Navajo Lake

Ⓖ Salmon Ruins

Ⓗ Shiprock

Ⓘ Humphries State Wildlife Area

Food

Ⓐ Aztec Restaurant

Ⓒ Elkhorn Café

Ⓐ Frank's

Ⓙ Jicarilla Inn

Ⓒ Viva Vera's Mexican Kitchen

Lodging

Ⓙ Best Western Jicarilla Inn

Ⓚ Corkin's Lodge

Ⓒ Elkhorn Lodge

Ⓐ Enchantment Lodge

Ⓒ Foster Hotel

Ⓒ Gandy Dancer B&B

Ⓒ Jones House

Ⓒ Lodge at Chama

Ⓐ Miss Gail's Inn

Ⓐ Step Back Inn

Camping

Ⓐ Aztec Ruins Road RV Park

Ⓛ Heron Lake State Park

Ⓜ Navajo State Park

Ⓒ Rio Chama RV Campground

Ⓝ Stone Lake

Note: Items with the same letter are located in the same town or area.

A PERFECT DAY IN NORTHWESTERN NEW MEXICO

In this sprawling area, there is no way to take in all the sights in one day. In the Chama region, spend an entire day on the steam-fired railroad, or split the time between visits to town and to Dulce, the capital of the Jicarilla tribe. Go west to enjoy a day at Navajo Lake, or spend the day at Aztec Ruins National Monument and the town of Aztec.

SIGHTSEEING HIGHLIGHTS

★★★ **Aztec Ruins National Monument**—This national park unit provides a rare chance to enter an authentic great kiva, the round, sunken ceremonial chamber of the Anasazi and Pueblo peoples. Almost all Anasazi kiva roofs have long since collapsed, turning them into windswept dirt holes. But in this reconstructed kiva, massive roof beams protect the interior from the elements, providing an inkling of the true kiva experience.

A 400-yard-long trail winds through the surface ruins, which take their name from the early mistaken belief that the site was associated with the great Mexican Indian culture. The pueblo reached its zenith in the twelfth through fourteenth centuries. On Christmas Eve the ruin is decked out in thousands of *farolitos*, brown paper bags with a votive candle in them. On the grounds are a good visitor center, with displays and interpretive exhibitions, and a picnic ground.

Details: 1.5 miles north of the town of Aztec off NM 550; (505) 334-6174. Open daily Memorial Day through Labor Day 8–6; otherwise daily 8–5; closed Christmas through New Year's Day. Admission is $1 adults, 50 cents for kids under 16. (2 hours)

★★★ **Cumbres & Toltec Railroad**—Only a handful of coal-fired, steam-powered trains still run in the United States; this is one of the finer ones. The ride traverses a 64-mile route of tunnels, trestles, and great beauty—particularly in the fall, when the high mountain peaks and valleys shimmer in a golden suit of quaking aspen trees. It is the longest and highest (reaching an altitude of 10,015 feet) narrow-gauge rail line in the nation. The train runs between Chama, New Mexico, and Antonito, Colorado, and can be taken to the midday stop at Osier and back, or one way (a bus shuttles between Chama and Antonito). A snack bar is on board, and lunch can be had at Osier.

Details: (505) 756-2151, (719) 376-5483, or (888) 286-2737. Trains leave both depots daily May to mid-October at 10 a.m. Tickets are $32 for adults, $16 for children under 12 for midpoint turnaround excursions; $50 for adults, $26 for children for full-length trip and bus shuttle. (1 day)

★★★ **Jicarilla Apache Reservation**—The Jicarillas were once a nomadic people of two principal bands—the Hoyero, or "mountain people," and the Ollero, or "plains people." They roamed far and wide across northern New Mexico, southern Colorado, and onto the Great Plains but were restricted to this 742,000-acre central reservation in 1887. Recently they have purchased several major outlying ranches and have derived income from oil and gas wells.

Their lands straddle the Continental Divide and run from dry plains to lush mountains and thick pine forests crisscrossed by streams. Thus it's a popular place for hunters, who have taken many trophy mule deer here. Anglers enjoy **Stone Lake**, and birders head to **Stinking Lake** for waterfowl. Its principal trade and population center is the tribal capital of **Dulce** ("sweet," in Spanish). Here, tribal members and visitors gather for the big events of the year, the mid-September Go-Jii-Ya Feast Day and the Little Beaver Roundup and Indian rodeo in July. The reservation also has a small, full-spectrum casino, the **Apache Nugget**, (800) 294-2234.

Details: The main reservation is on US 64 some 35 miles west of Chama. For information on hunting, fishing, camping, or cross-country skiing, call (505) 759-3255. For general tourism information, call (505) 759-3442. Open year-round. Free. (30 minutes to several days)

✫✫ **Aztec**—This town of 7,000 has done a nice job of preserving its Victorian-era downtown ambiance, and for people who enjoy historic architecture it's a great stop. Aztec also provides convenient access to many of the area's attractions. Also in town is the **Aztec Museum and Pioneer Village**, with excellent Indian and pioneer exhibits, as well as a frontier village with a blacksmith shop, bank, old jail, and other buildings.

Details: 125 Main St.; (505) 334-9829. Open May 1 through Labor Day Monday through Saturday 9–5, Sunday 1–4; the rest of the year Monday through Saturday 10–4. Admission is $1. For additional information on Aztec, contact the Chamber of Commerce at (505) 334-9551. (1 hour)

✫✫ **Chama**—Tucked under the Colorado border and beneath one arm of the mighty San Juan Mountains and the Brazos Mountains, Chama is the greenest and wettest locale in northern New Mexico, receiving substantial winter and spring snows and summer thundershowers; thus it's a great place for outdoor sporting enthusiasts. Besides its outdoor attractions, a blocklong section of Chama's old railroad district and the rail depot itself are still largely intact. Even if you don't ride the train, a half-hour walk around the railyards will make you feel as if you've stepped into a time warp.

Details: Visit the New Mexico Welcome Center, at the intersection of NM 17 and US 84/64; or the Chamber of Commerce, 499 Main St.; (505) 756-2306 or (800) 477-0149. (1 to 2 hours)

★★ **Navajo Lake**—My pick for the state's most scenic lake, this man-made reservoir backs up many miles into slick-rock canyons and around majestic buttes—New Mexico's miniversion of Lake Powell. The lake holds trout, bass, crappie, catfish, and northern pike, and below the dam are the state's world-famous fly-fishing waters of the **San Juan River**. Located near the dam are **Navajo Lake State Park** and three developed recreation areas—Pine, San Juan, and Sims Mesa. Motor- and houseboat rentals are available.

Details: The lake is about 25 miles east of Aztec on the New Mexico/Colorado border. The state park visitor center is at the Pine facility, (505) 632-2278. Open year-round. $3 day-use fee. For details on fishing the San Juan River, call (505) 632-1770, or the N.M. Department of Game and Fish, (505) 827-7911. (1 hour to multiple days)

★ **Salmon Ruins**—This privately owned archeological site preserves a relatively small Anasazi settlement on the bank of the San Juan River, birthplace of the Anasazi culture. It includes a museum, and the **San Juan Archeological Research Center and Library**.

Details: 2 miles west of Bloomfield, just off US 64; (505) 632-2013. Open daily. Admission is $1 for adults, 50 cents for kids. (2 hours)

★ **Shiprock**—The Navajos call this jagged spire *Tse Bi Dahi*, Rock with Wings, and it does look like a shattered bird wing rising from the desert floor. This 2,000-foot peak is the remnant core of a volcano; the covering soil has eroded away. It's a prominent Four Corners-area landmark. On Navajo land, it is off-limits to climbers today.

Details: Southwest of the town of Shiprock. For a closer view, head south on US 666 some 6 miles to the Red Valley Road, and turn west. Interesting dirt roads lead to the formation. (1 to 3 hours)

★ **W.A. Humphries State Wildlife Area**—Here's a convenient place to spot some of the abundant wildlife in the region. Some 9,000 acres right on the Continental Divide protect elk, bear, cougar, a great variety of birds, and other critters in a setting of beautiful meadows carpeted with flowers and grasses.

Details: 9 miles west of Chama along US 64. Access via either a poorly marked dirt road on the right or just down the main highway on the left (parking lot in front) through the small gate next to the locked vehicle gate; (505) 756-2585 or (505) 841-8881. It is closed periodically, but entry is free. (1 hour to multiple days)

FITNESS AND RECREATION

There are ample chances for a broad range of outdoor activities in the Chama area. There's great trout fishing in the **Rio Brazos** and the **Rio Chama** (which flows right through town), and in many creeks, as well as at the lovely, 6,000-acre **Lake Heron**, (505) 588-7470, 23 miles south of town off NM 95. The latter is also popular for sailing.

This area is the state's snowmobile capital—you may run into the auto-racing Unser family on a trail—and its premier cross-country skiing spot. Quite popular is the **Community Trail**, 12.5 miles north of town on NM/CO 17. **Southwest Nordic**, (505) 758-4761, runs a series of hut-to-hut yurts (with guided and unguided day to multi-day trips), off **Cumbres Pass**, where the town also maintains a free trail. The same mountains also boast excellent summer hiking. You can rent horses in Chama at **Western Outdoor Adventures**, (800) 288-1386, or **Reed Hollo Enterprises**, (505) 756-2685.

The **Jicarilla Reservation** and **Navajo Lake** also present great outdoor sports opportunities, including boating and waterskiing.

FOOD

My first visit to Chama's **Elkhorn Café**, (505) 756-2229, 2663 S. US 84/64, was more than 30 years ago as a kid, when my family dropped in after we bailed out of a soggy, muddy camping trip. The waitress said, "Hon, you look like a wet dog. What do you want to eat?" The food is always satisfying, from burgers to New Mexican plates, and they still call patrons "hon." Another inexpensive in-town option is **Viva Vera's Mexican Kitchen**, 2209 S. US 84/64, (505) 756-2557, dishing up New Mexican and American food daily 7 a.m. to 8 p.m.

In Aztec, point yer feet toward the **Aztec Restaurant** for some very reasonably priced and decent New Mexican and American fare. Likewise, **Frank's**, 116 S. Main Ave., (505) 334-3882, is easy on the pocketbook with breakfast for $3 or so. In Dulce, on the Jicarilla Reservation, the **Jicarilla Inn**'s good dining room and bar serve mid-priced American fare.

LODGING

For outdoors lovers with deep pockets, a prime destination for the entire northern half of New Mexico is the **Lodge at Chama**, (505) 756-2133.

Encompassing 32,000 acres of mountain forests, valleys, rivers, and lakes, it offers premium hunting and fishing year-round. The cost is about $300 per person, including all meals.

Down a major notch in cost but still pricey is another sports-oriented retreat near Chama, **Corkin's Lodge**, (505) 588-7261 or (800) 548-7680. It features private fishing on the dependable Brazos River, some ponds for kids, and a small pool, at $110 for a two-person cabin. The **Elkhorn Lodge**, on the south edge of town on US 84, (505) 756-2105 or (800) 532-8874, has doubles for $45 and rooms with kitchenettes for $50–$70.

Chama also has some nice B&Bs. The **Jones House**, 311 Terrace at 3rd, (505) 756-2908, is a unique Tudor-style adobe built circa 1927 by the town's first banker. You can spot the steam train chugging past from the yard. Rates are $25–$50. Also in Chama is the **Gandy Dancer B&B**, (505) 756-2191, which is set in an antiques-filled Victorian home; each room has a private bath, with rates of $25–$50.

The brave might try a night at the **Foster Hotel**, opposite the train depot, (505) 756-2296), which was grand at its 1881 opening but has seen little change since. Rates are under $25. On the Jicarilla Reservation, there's the **Best Western Jicarilla Inn**, on US 64, (505) 759-3663 or (800) 742-1938, with the Hillcrest Restaurant and the Timber Lake Lounge, at $65 per room.

In Aztec, the **Enchantment Lodge**, 1800 W. Aztec Blvd., (505) 334-6143, offers 20 clean, modern rooms, a pool, playground, and laundry for $35–$45. The **Step Back Inn**, 103 W. Aztec, at the corner of NM 550 and NM 44, (505) 334-1200 or (800) 334-1255, has a Victorian theme and queen-size beds. Rates are $54–$68. There's also the 1907 brick **Miss Gail's Inn**, 330 S. Main St., (505) 224-3452, a B&B with ten rooms with private baths at $58 per night.

CAMPING

In the Chama area, **Heron Lake State Park**, 23 miles south of Chama via US 64 and NM 95, (505) 588-7470, provides sites (some with partial RV hookups) on the lakeshore, along with bathrooms and drinking water. At the north end of town, the **Rio Chama RV Campground**, a quarter-mile north of the train depot on NM 17, (505) 756-2303, provides tent sites for $8.50 and RV sites with hookups for $14, May through September.

On the Jicarilla Reservation, there is a tribal campground at
Stone Lake, (505) 759-3442, no RV hookups, $4. **Navajo State Park**,
(505) 632-2278, offers the Sims Mesa, San Juan River, and Pine units,
some with RV hookups. Sims is the least accessible and least crowded.
In Aztec, there's the **Aztec Ruins Road RV Park**, 312 Ruins Rd.,
(505) 334-3160, has 30 sites at $10 with hookup, $6 without.

7

SOUTHWESTERN COLORADO

For climate and scenic beauty, you can't get much better than Southwestern Colorado. At its back, to the north, rise the tremendous San Juan Mountains, feeding countless streams and rivers; at its feet lie the canyons and mesas of the Four Corners region—the best of both the temperate Rockies and the sunny Southwest.

It's no wonder, then, that this was the homeland of one of America's most advanced prehistoric cultures, the Anasazi, who eventually spread from the Dolores and San Juan River drainages throughout the entire Four Corners region. One of their most dramatic city-states—the cliff-dwelling structures of Mesa Verde National Park—continues to fascinate and amaze visitors from around the world, who come to see its delicate architecture and to walk in the footsteps of the "Ancient Ones." The area is also home to the only surviving Indian tribes of Colorado, the Ute Mountain Utes and the Southern Utes, making it the most culturally diverse part of the state.

To add to these attractions, the area's major city, Durango (population 13,500), is booming, fueled in large part by urban refugees drawn to the area's beauty, relatively unspoiled nature, and diverse range of outdoor recreational opportunities. It has a distinct character, part railroad frontier mixed with a lingering Victorian-era mining boomtown feel, spiced with artists and serious recreationalists bent on maximizing their fun on ski slopes, white water, and fat bicycle tires. In summer, tourists flock to ride its famous steam-powered train. ◼

SOUTHWESTERN COLORADO

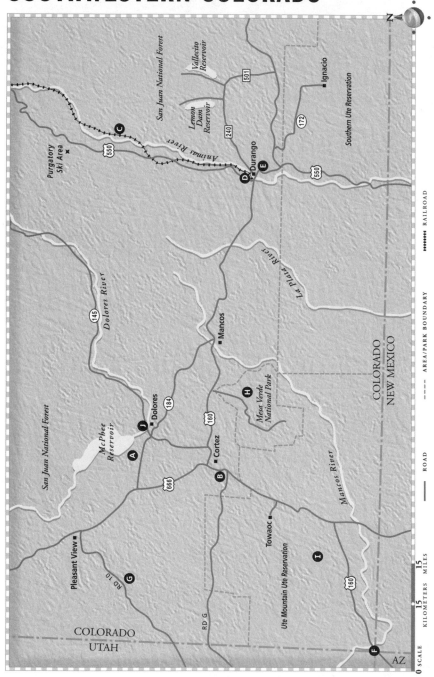

Sights

Ⓐ Anasazi Heritage Center

Ⓑ Cortez Center

Ⓒ Durango & Silverton
Narrow Gauge Railroad

Ⓓ Durango Fish Hatchery and
Wildlife Museum

Ⓔ Durango Historic Districts

Ⓕ Four Corners Monument

Ⓖ Lowry Ruins

Ⓗ Mesa Verde National Park

Ⓘ Ute Mountain Ute Reservation

Food

Ⓔ Ariano's

Ⓔ Carver Bakery Café and
Brewery

Ⓔ Durango Diner

Ⓗ Far View Terrace Café

Ⓔ Francisco's Restaurante and
Cantina

Ⓔ Henry's

Ⓗ Metate Room

Ⓑ Nashion's

Ⓑ Nero's

Ⓙ Old Germany Restaurant

Ⓔ Palace Grill

Ⓗ Spruce Tree Terrace

Note: Items with the same letter are located in the same town or area.

A PERFECT DAY IN SOUTHWESTERN COLORADO

To immerse yourself in Anasazi life, spend the entire day at Mesa
Verde National Park or at Ute Mountain Tribal Park. If you have kids
or are a train aficionado, ride the iron rails of the Durango & Silverton
Narrow Gauge Railroad. Spend the evening strolling the streets of
Cortez before dining at Nero's, or eat in Durango and spend the night
at the historic Strater Hotel.

SIGHTSEEING HIGHLIGHTS

✸✸✸ **Durango & Silverton Narrow Gauge Railroad**—In the late
1870s major gold and silver strikes were made in the San Juan Mountains of formerly isolated southwestern Colorado. Miners poured into
the area and began digging. Some of the richest strikes were made in
the Silverton area, but it was almost impossible to get supplies in and

ore out of the area. In 1881 the Denver & Rio Grande Railroad broke ground on a rail line into Silverton, using Durango, then just a collection of tents, as the base of operations. The line was completed in a year and has been in business ever since. Today, however, its income comes from hauling tourists.

I rode the line more than 35 years ago and recall the grandeur of the scenery and the thrill of the clackety-clacking rail cars, the wind in my face, and a coal cinder in my eye! The line clings at points to a narrow path blasted from the walls of the Animas River Gorge, with sheer drops to the jade-colored waters below, climbs high into alpine parks, and finally rolls into the time-warped enclave of Silverton.

The 90-mile round trip takes eight hours (three en route, a two-hour layover in Silverton, and three returning to Durango). If this is too much for you, you can arrange to return to Durango by bus or stay overnight in Silverton. Choose from both open and closed cars. First-class seating is available in the grand 1880s-era Alamosa parlor car (the only place liquor is served on the train). While occasional walk-up tickets are available, reservations are highly recommended.

Details: *For information or reservations, call (970) 247-2733. Trains run daily (leaving as early as 7:30 a.m. in peak season, mid-June through mid-August) from late April through October. A winter train runs a shorter excursion to Cascade Canyon from late November through early January (excluding December 24–25). Round-trip tickets cost $42.70 for adults, $21.45 for children under 12; cash only. (1 day)*

✮✮✮ **Mesa Verde National Park**—Established in 1906, this was the first national park dedicated to preservation of archeological resources. Today it has been elevated to a U.N. World Heritage Site, and for good reason. Mesa Verde protects one of the prime urban centers of the Southwest's greatest prehistoric civilization, the Anasazi (see Why Visit the American Southwest? for additional Anasazi history).

While Anasazi sites may cover more area, like Chaco; be set in even prettier locales, such as Canyon de Chelly; or have individual structures of even more sublime proportions, like Betatakin at Navajo National Monument; Mesa Verde is undoubtedly the capital of Anasaziland. As such, it also has the greatest number of visitors, especially in summer.

A paved scenic road runs 21 miles to the park headquarters, where a pair of optional 6-mile loop roads lead to many of the park's most acclaimed sites. Shortly after entering the park, a steep climb takes you up to the top of the great mesa, which erosion has carved into smaller submesas. Stop for a visual orientation of the area from **Park Point**, then proceed to the **Far View Visitors Center**, open May through September. Here you can view historic displays and contemporary Indian arts and crafts, and obtain information, books, and gasoline. Schedules of ranger-led walks are posted, and tickets for Cliff Palace and Balcony House, which can be visited only on guided outings, should be purchased here. (For those in a hurry or not up for a hike, dozens of overlooks of many of the major ruins exist.)

Proceed to the free, lovely, stone **Mesa Verde Museum**, open daily 8 a.m. to 6:30 p.m. in summer, where you'll find descriptive dioramas of the evolution of mesa civilization, and excellent collections of Anasazi pottery, jewelry, basketry, and weaving artifacts.

From here you can continue your explorations of some of the park's highlights found on **Chapin Mesa**, including **Cedar Tree Tower**, **Balcony House** and perhaps the finest site of all, **Cliff Palace**. The latter, with its 217 rooms and 23 kivas displaying superb masonry work, is reached via a half-mile hike requiring a 500-foot ascent, which takes at least an hour to complete. Writer Willa Cather described it in *The Professor's House* as "a little city of stone, asleep . . . as still as sculpture." Balcony House is popular with the young and athletic: it requires climbing a 32-foot ladder, crawling through a 12-foot tunnel, and negotiating hand and foot holes chopped into the cliff face.

Far fewer people chose to visit **Wetherill Mesa**, named after two Mancos, Colorado, cowboys who rediscovered Mesa Verde's central ruins in 1888. It is an 8-mile drive from the Farview Visitor Center to the parking lot on Wetherill Mesa, where you board trams. The trams make a 4-mile loop, with frequent stops allowing visitors to take self-guiding walking tours of various ruins. The mesa is home to a herd of wild horses, occasionally seen along this road. It also shelters the park's second largest site, **Long House**, and **Step House**. Here, too, and elsewhere in the park, are examples of even earlier human occupation, including rare Basketmaker pit houses.

Details: 10 miles east of Cortez off US 160, or 35 miles west of Durango, (970) 529-4461. The park is open year-round, but many services and some sections close between November and the end of April. Admission is $10 per vehicle. Visitors not camping in the park are required to park trailers just up the access road because of the park's narrow, sharply curved roadways. Expect hazardous ice to linger after storms on shaded, high-elevation road corners. (1 day)

✹✹✹ **Ute Mountain Ute Reservation**—Not much to look at from US 666—except for the arresting shape of Sleeping Ute Mountain—the large Ute Mountain Ute Reservation south of Cortez is much more than meets the casual eye. For openers, its 125,000-acre **Ute Mountain Tribal Park** is almost twice as large as Mesa Verde. It encompasses similar terrain and is packed with Anasazi ruins and Ute petroglyphs as well. Yet it receives a fraction of the national park's visitors. Only guided tours are allowed on the Ute land, which adds another dimension. Having Indians interpret and lead visitors to Indian ruins—what a concept.

You can also spend some time in the **Ute Mountain Ute Village**, next door to the **Ute Mountain Casino**. The village presents live entertainment, including Indian dancers, singers, and storytellers, Thursday through Sunday nights in summer, as well as daily craft demonstrations, such as the tribe's renowned beadwork. Also operating in the village in summer is a satellite branch of the tribe's Pottery Factory.

Details: Guided half-day, full-day or multi-day outings of the tribal park leave from the intersection of US 666 and US 160 20 miles south of Cortez; (970) 565-3751, ext. 382, or (800) 847-5485. It's open year-round, but call for schedules. Full-day tours are $25 for adults, $12.50 for college students, $7.50 for kids. The Ute Mountain Ute Village and Casino are located 11 miles south of Cortez on US 160/666. (1 day)

✹✹ **Anasazi Heritage Center**—When nearby McPhee Reservoir was being built, Anasazi ruins in its floodplain were excavated, and the found materials were turned over to this institution for study, storage, and display. The center is built in a lovely arch cupping a small ruin, **Dominguez**, and a paved, half-mile, handicapped-accessible self-guided trail takes you to another compact ruin, **Escalante**. There is also a reconstructed pit house. The center encourages hands-on activities, such as weaving, grinding corn with a *metate*, and handling Anasazi artifacts.

Details: 27501 CO 184, 3 miles northwest of Dolores; (970) 882-4811. Open year-round. Free. (2 hours)

✹✹ **Cortez Center**—This arts center presents dance performances, concerts, art exhibitions, lectures, cowboy poetry and other readings, traditional Indian arts and crafts demonstrations, and storytellers. In summer, events happen nightly except Sundays, but the center is open year-round. A highlight is the Octubre Fiesta in October.

Details: *25 N. Market; (970) 565-1151. Most events are free. (time varies with event)*

✯✯ **Durango Historic Districts**—Founded in September 1880, Durango flourished as money began to pour into town from the San Juan mining camps. Many of the town's great homes, public buildings, and hotels have been preserved and can be found in the Main Avenue district by the railroads and in the East Third Avenue residential district. The railyards include the original train station and provide daily tours of the functional train engine roundhouse.

Details: *Maps to self-guiding historic tours of the downtown core can be obtained from Durango Area Chamber Resort Association, 111 S. Camino del Rio: (303) 247-0312 or (800) 525-8855. (1 to 2 hours on foot)*

✯ **Durango Fish Hatchery and Wildlife Museum**—Opened in 1893, this is a historic as well as functional fish hatchery. See monster breeding trout, feed fish, and learn about fish hatchery operations.

Details: *151 E. 16th St.; (970) 247-4755. Visiting hours vary—call first. Free. (1 hour)*

✯ **Four Corners Monument**—A freak of mapmakers and a thrill for the young at heart is this sole point in the nation where four states touch. A granite, bronze, and colored concrete marker allows one to plant hands and feet in four different states.

Details: *One-quarter mile west of US 160, 40 miles southwest of Cortez; (520) 871-6647. Around its visitor center (open year-round) are Navajo vendors selling jewelry and other crafts. Free. Portable restrooms but no water. (30 minutes on site)*

✯ **Lowry Ruins**—This little-visited but compelling Anasazi site has one of the largest "great kivas" ever found. Its oldest section dates to the eighth century and reached three stories high by the twelfth century.

Details: *Drive 20 miles north of Cortez on US 666 to Pleasant View, where a small road goes west (left) 9 miles to the ruins. Open year-round. Admission is free. No water. (1 hour)*

KIDS' STUFF

Already mentioned above are ruins to visit and the D&RG Narrow Gauge Railroad. For details on Trimble Hot Springs, horseback and sleigh rides, skiing, and summer rides on the Alpine Slide at Purgatory Ski Area, see Fitness and Recreation, below. Other winners are the go-karts and minigolf at **Durango Park**, (970) 382-9090. Or take a stage-coach ride on the **Bartels Mancos Stage Line**, based in Mancos, (970) 533-9857 or (800) 365-3530.

FITNESS AND RECREATION

With more than 5 *million* acres of national parks, forests, state parks, and other public lands nearby, outdoor recreational opportunities are almost unlimited. Numerous hikes exist, from the long and tough to the short and simple. One of the more thrilling and unusual utilizes the narrow-gauge train to access remote country in the huge 492,000-acre **Weminuche Wilderness**, including beautiful **Chicago Basin**. Hikers and backpackers can be dropped off and picked up later. For details on hiking routes in the **San Juan National Forest**, contact the Animas Ranger District, 701 Camino del Rio, (970) 385-1286. Other local ranger district offices are in Dolores, 100 N. Fifth, (970) 882-7296, and in Mancos, 41595 E. CO 160, (970) 533-7716.

Because of its rich archeological resources, there are not many trails in Mesa Verde. However, the **Spruce Canyon Trail** runs 2.1 miles with a 700-foot change in elevation; and around the Morefield Campground, there's the 2.3-mile **Point Lookout Trail** and the 1.5-mile **Lookout Trail**. Hikers must register with park rangers at the Far View Visitors Center.

Durango vies with Moab for the title of mountain-biking capital of America. As with hiking, countless possibilities exist, including roads, trails, loops, flat tracks, and steeps. Check out the several specialized books on the subject. Rentals and guided tours are available from a number of sources in Durango. Information on appropriate trails is available at the district ranger offices noted above.

The Mesa Verde Museum rents bikes, providing a refreshing way to see the park without the hassles of dealing with a vehicle on summer-crowded roads.

Skiing is a major winter pastime. Downhillers head up US 550, 28 miles north of Durango, to **Purgatory Resort**, (970) 247-9000 or (800) 525-0892. Purgatory is a terrific, relatively compact (for Colorado!) ski area with good to great snowfall (300 inches average), lots of sunshine, and slopes that particularly favor intermediates and beginners. Its Legends section, however, presents a challenge.

Plenty of cross-country skiing routes exist as well. Opposite the Purgatory Resort entrance on US 550 is the **Purgatory Ski Touring Center**, (970) 247-9000, with more than 15 miles of groomed trails, instruction, and rentals. For something really different, try cross-countrying at Mesa Verde! The Cliff Palace and Balcony House loop road is closed to traffic for skiers and snowshoers in winter. Find rentals and information at a number of shops in Durango.

The snow melts from March to September, when it begins to accumulate again. This gives area anglers the opportunity for some outstanding fishing. Highlights include **McPhee Reservoir**, **Vallecitos Reservoir**, the **Animas River**, and the **Dolores River** (especially the tailwaters of McPhee Reservoir). **Duranglers Fly Shop**, 801B Main Ave., Durango, (970) 385-4081, can provide information, rentals, and guides. For regulations and licensing information, contact the Colorado Division of Wildlife, Denver, (303) 297-1192.

River running is also a major pursuit. Explorers from New Mexico probed these mountains in the 1700s, naming the river that flows right through Durango the *Rio de las Animas Perdidas*, or River of Lost Souls, a reference to some obscure old tragedy. Today there's only an occasional tragedy from overly ambitious kayakers in the **Animas River**'s upper rapids, but the tranquil waters close to town are fine for novices. Further afield are the rapids and shoreside Anasazi ruins of the isolated **Dolores River** and the **Piedra**.

Those with more sedate tastes can play golf at the highly touted **Tamarron Resort**, 18 miles north of Durango on US 550, (970) 259-2000, or at the **Hillcrest Course** just east of Durango, 2300 Rim Drive, (970) 247-1499.

After exercise, few experiences can beat a soak in a natural hot spring. Head over to **Trimble Hot Springs**, 6 miles north of Durango on US 550, (970) 247-0111, which has an Olympic-size outdoor pool, snack bar, bathhouse with lockers, landscaped park, two private tubs, and massage therapy. It's open daily. Admission is $7 for adults, $5 for children under 13.

FOOD

Within Mesa Verde, a very good meal at a reasonable price can be had at the **Metate Room** of the Far View Lodge, (970) 529-4421. Dinners include moderately priced shrimp, Mexican food, and steak, plus beverages in the lounge. Two inexpensive cafeterias are also in the park: the

Far View Terrace Café at the visitor center, and the **Spruce Tree Terrace**, adjoining park headquarters and the Mesa Verde Museum. Both offer budget breakfasts, lunches, and dinners.

Durango has more than 75 restaurants, with something for almost everyone's taste. Who can pass up the chance to eat in the gilded extravagance of **Henry's**, in the historic Strater Hotel? Seafood and steaks run $12–$20. The **Palace Grill**, next to the railroad station, (970) 247-2018, is another upscale Victorian-styled eatery with items like honey duck and brandy pepper steak. Another fine dining choice is **Ariano's**, 150 College Drive, (970) 247-8146, which specializes in northern Italian fare, including homemade pastas and ravioli, along with an extensive wine selection.

Francisco's Restaurante and Cantina, 619 Main Ave., (970) 247-4098, has been in business for more than 30 years, and is one of Durango's most popular establishments, serving consistently good, inexpensive New Mexico–style food and some American staples. The **Carver Bakery Café and Brewery**, 1022 Main Ave., (970) 259-2545, specializes in simple and modestly priced but well-prepared breakfasts, lunches, and dinners, including sandwiches, stews, and vegetarian burgers, as well as excellent coffee and homemade beer. Locals line the long counter of the **Durango Diner** for its tasty homemade hash browns served with green chile and cheese at breakfast. Open through lunch.

In Dolores, try the **Old Germany Restaurant**, on CO 145, (970) 882-7549, for fine Bavarian cooking, hearty, tasty dishes, homemade desserts, and German beers in the Ratskeller—all at reasonable prices.

Cortez has a few real surprises, too, including one of the best restaurants in southwestern Colorado, **Nero's**, 303 W. Main, (970) 565-7366, which has been serving fine Italian food since 1982, including pestos, grilled chicken in lime sauce, and beef tenderloin, with prices ranging from $11–$17. Dinner only, closed Sunday. Also popular is **Nashion's**, 1020 S. Broadway, (970) 565-1257, with delicious top sirloin for $11.25, and shrimp and scampi dishes at $17. Dinner only.

LODGING

Mesa Verde hosts one of the West's historic park hotels, the **Far View Lodge**, (800) 449-2288, near the visitor center, offering a good restaurant and magnificent views from private balconies. Open late April through late October. Rates are $83–$94.

Durango has many choices, from chain motels to one-of-a-kind

B&Bs. The handsome 1887 four-story **Strater Hotel**, 699 Main Ave., (970) 247-4431 or (800) 247-4431, houses the world's largest collection of antique walnut furniture and is a real treat. Rates are $110 in season. Its Old West Saloon is authentic, right down to its risqué waitress outfits.

Just a block away is the almost equally elegant, and expensive, **General Palmer House**, 567 Main Ave., (970) 247-4747, with lots of shiny brass and period furniture.

For a budget Victorian atmosphere bordering on frumpy, try the **Central Hotel and Hostel**, 975 Main Ave., (970) 247-0330, with dormitory accommodations and private rooms starting at $30.

Some of the many B&Bs in Durango include the **Apple Orchard Inn**, 7758 County Rd. 203, (970) 247-0751 or (800) 426-0751, an elegant country inn with cottages and award-winning gardens with ponds. Rates are $85–$150. The **Lightner Creek Inn**, 999 County Rd. 207, (970) 259-1226 or (800) 268-9804, is a romantic French country inn close to town, with ponds and a stream. Rates are $85–$150. In downtown Durango is the **Leland House**, 721 E. Second Ave., (970) 385-1920 or (800) 664-1920, a historic lodging with a Western theme; $95–$135. The **Gable House**, 805 E. Fifth Ave., (970) 247-4982, is a 1892 Queen Anne National Register of Historic Places–listed mansion within walking distance of downtown. Rates are $75–$85. Only 9 miles from Mesa Verde, Cortez's comfortable **Bed & Breakfast on Maple Street**, 102 S. Maple, (970) 565-3906, features four rooms and a hot tub for $60–$80.

CAMPING

Four miles into Mesa Verde off the main road is the **Morefield Campground**, with a laundromat, gasoline, snacks, supplies, coin-op showers, and restrooms. It has 117 tent and 300 RV sites, offered on a first-come, first-served basis; open May through mid-October. Cost runs $10–$17 for hookups, plus park admission.

Primitive camping along the Mancos River at Kiva Point, with a permit, is $10 a night at the **Ute Tribal Park**, (800) 847-5485.

Among the numerous campgrounds in both the San Juans and in the La Plata Mountains between Durango and Cortez are the **Mancos Lake State Park** (33 sites), plus several around **Lake Vallecitos**. Just 4 miles north of Durango is the 34-site **Junction Creek Campground** (head west on 25th Street). Many area campgrounds are open only

SOUTHWESTERN COLORADO

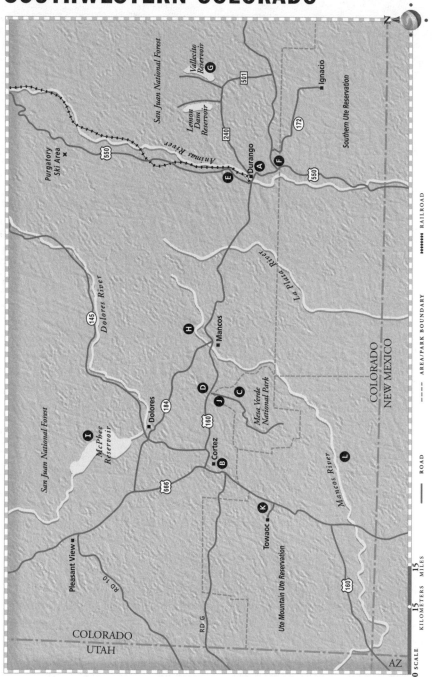

Lodging

- **A** Apple Orchard Inn
- **B** Bed & Breakfast on Maple Street
- **A** Central Hotel and Hostel
- **C** Far View Lodge
- **A** Gable House
- **A** General Palmer House
- **A** Leland House
- **A** Lightner Creek Inn
- **A** Strater Hotel

Camping

- **D** A & A Mesa Verde RV Park
- **E** Junction Creek Campground
- **F** KOA Campground
- **G** Lake Vallecitos
- **H** Mancos Lake State Park
- **I** McPhee Reservoir
- **J** Morefield Campground
- **K** Sleeping Ute RV Park
- **L** Ute Tribal Park

Note: Items with the same letter are located in the same town or area.

May through September. Contact the ranger districts noted in the Fitness and Recreation section under hiking for further information.

RVers have a number of choices, including the **KOA Campground**, 5 miles east of Durango's city limits at 30090 US 160, (970) 247-0783. On the shores of **McPhee Reservoir**, west of Dolores, (970) 882-2257, is a campground with several RV hookups at $8–$12. The **A & A Mesa Verde RV Park**, across US 160 from the park entrance, (970) 565-3517 or (800) 972-6620, has a playground, basketball courts, a heated pool, and horses for trail rides.

On the Ute Mt. Reservation is the **Sleeping Ute RV Park**, 11 miles south of Cortez on US 166/666, (800) 889-5072. The park rents 81 sites, 31 with full hookups, for only $12. On site are a laundry, convenience store, indoor pool, sauna, and showers.

NIGHTLIFE

With Ft. Lewis College, a steady flow of tourists, and a hardy band of local partyers, Durango doesn't roll up the sidewalks at dusk like many Southwestern towns. The staple for live rock 'n' roll, blues, reggae, and other music by local and small touring acts is **Farquahrts**, 725 Main

Ave., (970) 247-5440, serving excellent pizza and other light fare. The turn-of-the-century portrait of a nude woman over the bar sets the tone.

The **Diamond Circle Theater** in the Strater Hotel, 699 Main Ave., (970) 247-4431, presents dastardly evildoers and fair heroines in classic melodramas in a period setting. Cowboy songs, stories, and comedy are the staples of the **Bar-D Chuckwagon**, 9 miles north of Durango on County Road 250, (970) 247-5753, where you can also ride a miniature railroad, and browse shops in the pseudo–Old West street. The show starts after a frontier-style dinner of sliced roast beef, baked beans, biscuits, and applesauce, served at 7:30 p.m. Reservations are a must; $13 for adults, $6 for kids under 9. It's open nightly Memorial Day through Labor Day.

The General Palmer Hotel's **Muldoon Saloon**, 567 Main Ave., (970) 247-4747, is also a fun place to have a drink amidst its plush crushed velvet couches and long wooden bar.

8
SAN JUAN MOUNTAINS

The San Juan Mountains are one of the nation's largest and highest ranges, its 14 summits topping 14,000 feet in elevation. To describe them as spectacular is meek. Once the hunting grounds of the Ute Indians, they were occasionally visited by eighteenth-century New Mexicans, who named many of their prominent features. The San Juans later became the trapping grounds of lone mountain men and were not settled until the major gold and silver strikes of the 1870s. Literally overnight, boomtowns sprang up, with millions of dollars in ore extracted in just a few years from such places as Silverton.

Just as quickly as the mines played out, the towns folded up. But cattle ranching kept a hardy posse of people going, and a few towns held on and began a slow comeback in the 1960s, based on the new gold mine: tourism. The best towns here seem like time capsules—you can order a shot across the same Telluride bar that Butch Cassidy frequented (presumably before he robbed the local bank!). Or stroll down an Ouray street fronted by lovely brick and stone buildings with ornate overhanging cornices. Or drop a fishing line into a stream running through Ophir.

One of the nation's most scenic roads, the San Juan Skyway, threads through this region, hitting the major stops and providing access to even more remote areas. Interesting year-round, the region boasts excellent skiing in winter, bountiful wildflowers in spring, cool summers, and glorious aspen-lit autumns. It may not be the classic Southwest one imagines, but it's well worth seeing. ◼

SAN JUAN MOUNTAINS

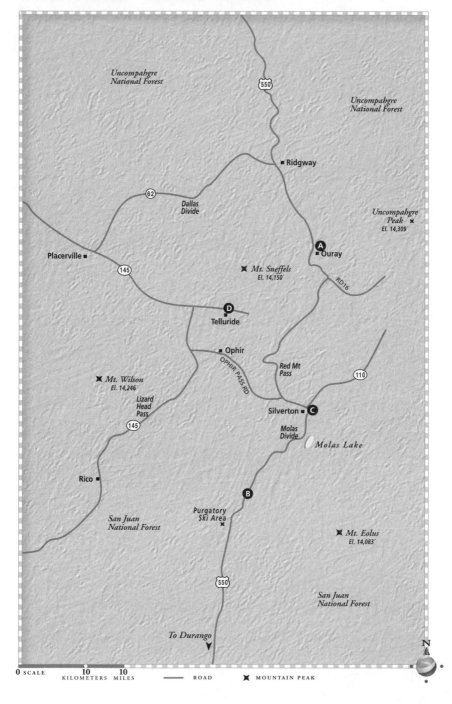

Uncompahgre
National Forest

Uncompahgre
National Forest

550

■ Ridgway

62

Dallas
Divide

Uncompahgre
Peak ✖
El. 14,309´

Ⓐ
■ Ouray

Placerville ■

145

✖ Mt. Sneffels
El. 14,150´

RD 16

Ⓓ
■
Telluride

■ Ophir

OPHIR PASS RD

Red Mt
Pass

110

✖ Mt. Wilson
El. 14,246´

Lizard
Head
Pass

Silverton ■ Ⓒ

145

Molas
Divide

Molas Lake

Rico ■

Ⓑ

San Juan
National Forest

Purgatory
Ski Area
✖

✖ Mt. Eolus
El. 14,083´

550

San Juan
National Forest

To Durango
▼

N

0 SCALE
10   10
KILOMETERS   MILES   ROAD   ✖ MOUNTAIN PEAK

Sights

Ⓐ Ouray

Ⓑ San Juan Skyway

Ⓒ Silverton

Ⓓ Telluride

Food

Ⓓ Baked in Telluride

Ⓐ Bon Ton

Ⓒ French Bakery Restaurant

Ⓓ Gregory's Bakery & Café

Food *(continued)*

Ⓓ Harmon's

Ⓓ Le Marmotte

Ⓓ Leimgrubers Bierstube & Restaurant

Ⓐ The Outlaw

Ⓒ Pickle Barrel

Ⓒ Silver Nugget Café

Ⓓ Sofio's

Ⓓ Sundance Restaurant

Note: Items with the same letter are located in the same town or area.

A PERFECT DAY IN THE SAN JUAN MOUNTAINS

It takes a good day just to drive the entire San Juan Skyway. If that's all the time you have for this area, consider it an introduction. Leave Durango early and have breakfast in Silverton at the French Bakery, lunch in Ourtay at the Bon Ton or The Outlaw, and dinner in Telluride, taking a walk through its historic streets. With more time, spend additional hours or days in Silverton, Ouray, or Telluride.

SIGHTSEEING HIGHLIGHTS

✯✯✯ **Ouray**—Called the "Switzerland of America," Ouray is tucked into a narrow valley of the **Uncompahgre River** and is ringed by towering peaks. It makes a fine point from which to explore the surrounding mountains and high alpine valleys. Another mining boom town, **Camp Bird**, produced more than $20 million in gold between 1896 and 1902. Its largely intact National Historic District, lined with sturdy, handsome buildings with wonderful flourishes, makes you wonder what's happened to modern American architecture. A deeper understanding of the area's past can be gleaned from a visit to the **Ouray County Historical Museum**, Fifth Street and Sixth Avenue,

(970) 325-4576. It's open daily 9–5 and charges a nominal fee. Pick up a walking-tour brochure here.

Details: Write P.O. Box 145, Ouray, CO 81427; (970) 325-4746 or (800) 228-1876. (1 hour to several days)

✩✩✩ **San Juan Skyway**—Running 236 miles in a loop, this paved two-lane road, a portion of which is also known as the "Million Dollar Highway," is both a national and state scenic highway. Most of its route winds through the majestic **San Juan Mountains**, past 13 peaks over 14,000 feet in elevation, and over three passes exceeding 10,000 feet. This is not a route for acrophobes! People poking along on a curvy mountain road are derisively referred to by locals as "flat-landers." And while the road is open year-round, snow can make travel impossible, occasionally for days at a time. Carry chains, and watch for snowplows blazing around corners. Spring comes late to the high country, with sporadic snowstorms even in May.

Beginning in Durango, the route heads due north up the lovely **Animas River Valley**, the river bordered initially by fields and narrow-leafed cottonwoods. Around mile 18, the highway climbs out of the valley and crosses the tracks of the **Durango & Silverton Narrow Gauge Railroad** (see Southwestern Colorado chapter). The first major height you scale is **Coal Bank Summit**, elevation 10,640, followed quickly by **Molas Pass**, elevation 10,910, where the great views are of the **Needle** and **Grenadier Mountains**, and, to the east, the Animas Gorge. You then drop into **Silverton**.

The next leg climbs **Red Mountain Pass**, the roughest in the San Juans, at 11,018 feet. Winter avalanches are so frequent here that the authorities no longer replace the ripped-out highway guardrails. Note the memorial plaque to two snowplow drivers, a reverend, and his two daughters, who died in Riverside Slide, a particularly nasty avalanche chute at mile marker 87. (The road here is now covered by a snow-shed.) You then reach **Ouray** (see above).

The route continues north to **Ridgeway**, an old railroad and ranching hub. Turn west (left) here onto CO 62, which climbs gentle Dallas Pass, offering tremendous views of **Mt. Sneffels** (14,150 feet) to the south. At the intersection of CO 145, turn south (left) toward **Telluride**, the world-famous festival center, ski town, and scenic retreat (see below for more information).

South of Telluride, the route continues on past the side road to the tiny former mining town of **Ophir**, over **Lizard Head Pass**

(10,222 feet), and past another still largely abandoned mining town, **Rico**. The road then rolls alongside the **Dolores River**. Past Stoner the valley broadens, and you pass through **Dolores**. CO 84 takes you back to US 160 at **Mancos**, west of Durango, or you can descend into Cortez on CO 145.

Details: Total distance from Durango to Cortez is 197 miles. You can do it in a day with only brief stops. (1 day minimum)

★★★ **Telluride**—The crown jewel of the San Juan's former mining boomtowns is today a booming destination of hardcore recreationalists, lone-eagle entrepreneurs, Hollywood celebs, and former hippies who "rediscovered" the town in the early 1970s. Telluride is truly a phenomenon. Set at the end of a box canyon encircled by 13,000-foot peaks and waterfalls, such as **Bridal Veil**, pouring out of hanging valleys, and bisected by the sparkling **San Miguel River**, it has a setting to die for.

Its style is noteworthy, with the downtown area a particularly fine National Historic District built in the town's heyday, when $60 million in gold and silver were pulled out of its nearby mountains between 1875 and 1905. Butch Cassidy and the Hole-in-the-Wall gang relieved them of $30,000 in 1889 by robbing the San Miguel Bank.

In 1891 Telluride boasted a population of more than 4,000, but by 1930, its citizenry had fallen to 500. Today it may have only 1,500 year-round residents, but it's home to one of the nation's more exciting ski resorts (see Fitness and Recreation, below) and is going great-guns again. If you owned real estate, even a shack, here 20 years ago, you're a millionaire today. Jet-setters have descended. Like many golden pockets of the intermountain West, the once-sleepy town is torn between residents desiring further growth and those who'd like to lock the gate.

One of its attractions is its deserved title as festival capital of the nation. This is particularly true in the warmer months, when it hosts the **Telluride Bluegrass Festival** in late June, the **Telluride Jazz Festival** in early August, and fall's **Brews & Blues Fest**, plus celebrations devoted to wildflowers, wild mushrooms, wild women, hang gliding, film, performing arts, and other topics.

Details: Maps to self-guiding historic district walking tours (including 160 homes, 16 businesses, six saloons, three hotels, and two schools) are available from the Telluride Visitor Center, located above Rose Victorian Food Mart, near the town entrance on your right. (1 hour to several days)

★★ **Silverton**—Perched at an elevation of 9,320 feet, Silverton is a classic Western mining town, from its exposed location to its historic main-street building facades. It's cold here: more than 300 inches of snow fall each winter, and frost-free summer days number as few as 12. Only the hardy survive. Those who do—some 500 strong—are a special breed who thrive on its raw beauty. The town is ringed by 13,000-foot peaks, thick forests, and cascading canyons.

Named after a miner who remarked, "We may not have gold here, but we have silver by the ton," the town at one point had 30 ore mills, two smelters, 37 saloons, copious card houses, opium dens, and the infamous Blair Street red-light district. Today its downtown core is a National Historic District in which you'll find the **San Juan County Historical Society Museum** and wonderful old hotels.

Details: The museum is next to the San Juan County Courthouse at the edge of Memorial Park, Reese Street at 16th Street. It's open June 1 to mid-September 9–5 daily, and to mid-October 10–3 daily. Admission is nominal. Silverton Chamber of Commerce, P.O. Box 565, Silverton, CO 81433; (970) 387-5654 or (800) 752-4494. (1 hour to 2 days)

FITNESS AND RECREATION

Did anyone mention awesome skiing? The San Juans are home to two major ski areas, **Purgatory Resort** (see Southwest Colorado chapter) and world-class **Telluride**, (970) 728-3856 or www.telski.com/pr. Though it was already an impressive area with a 3,125-foot vertical drop, Telluride recently gained Forest Service approval of a major expansion, which will provide it with the highest lift-served skiing in North America and more than 4,000 vertical feet. With good to great snowfall—300 inches average—the area holds terrain for all classes of skiers: extremes, exhausting bump runs like the famed Plunge, and huge swaths of beginner and intermediate slopes. Its 20-acre snowboard park has over 1,000 feet of vertical and a 49-foot halfpipe (opened in winter 1997–98). Stay in town and walk to lifts, or at the swank new **Mountain Village**, with its own lifts. A free $19-million gondola links the two, so you can park your car and still get around.

Nordic skiers have a plethora of possibilities. With the maze of jeep roads shut down in winter, skiers can fan out all over, but use extreme caution. Otherwise, stick to groomed trails at the **Purgatory Ski Touring Center** (see Southwestern Colorado chapter) or the **Telluride Nordic Center**, (907) 728-6900, which maintains 50 kilometers of track through aspen groves, meadows, and higher pine forests. Guides and rentals are also available in Telluride and Ouray.

Another thriving winter sport is ice-climbing. Ouray hosts an annual competitive and social gathering, where folks dangle off man-made ice flows hundreds of feet high. It looks insane, but if you're interested, there are instructors and rental equipment. You can also ice skate near Ouray for free at the **Box Canyon Falls Park**, (970) 325-4464. Rental skates are available.

Four-wheelers have a lot of terrain to poke around in here, such as the relatively easy route over **Ophir Pass**, at 11,750 feet. It's 10 miles one way, between US 550 and the small town of Ophir, off CO 145 south of Telluride. The exit off US 550 onto Forest Road 679 is 4.6 miles northwest of Silverton. Many tough routes also exist around Ouray. Former Mayor Bill Fries, otherwise known as country-western singer C.W. McCall, once remarked of the local landscape, "You can hike it if you got the legs, ride it if you've got the horse, and jeep it if you have the nerve." Notable are **Engineer Pass**, **Black Bear**, and **Imogene Pass**.

The area also provides, naturally, great hiking, mountain biking (Paragon Sports has rentals and info, 800-903-4525), and fishing. Trails begin right out your door, sometimes literally. One of the more grand, obvious hikes is to 365-foot **Bridal Veil Falls** in Telluride. This 2-mile round-trip hike overlooking town climbs to the top of the state's highest waterfall. The route is up a jeep road. You can also catch a chairlift up the Telluride ski area slopes in the summer and hike (or ride) down; (970) 728-3041. Also in the San Juans are the **Lizard Head Wilderness Area**, off CO 145 south of Telluride, and the **Mt. Sneffels Wilderness Area**, accessible from the Ridgeway area. For information on other hiking possibilities, biking, or fishing, contact local outdoor shops, visitor centers, or the U.S. Forest Service, Telluride area, (970) 327-4261.

Kids under 13 can dip a line at a reserved pond in the **Telluride Town Park**, while mom and dad head over to the **San Miguel**, the only major undammed river in Colorado. The San Juans also have a few commercial outdoor hot springs, including the **Ouray Hot Springs Pool**, at the north end of town on US 550, (970) 325-4638, and **Orvis Hot Springs**, 1585 Country Rd. 3, Ridgeway, (970) 626-5324. Watching the alpenglow on Ouray's summits as you bask in 104° water on a winter evening is a treat that makes life worthwhile.

The **Telluride Golf Club**, (907) 728-6366, is an 18-hole golf course at the Mountain Village. At this altitude, your balls carry 15 percent further! Weekend play is sometimes closed to the general public. Watch for elk. World-class fitness centers and other pampering places are available in Telluride, including **The Peaks at Telluride** and the **Telluride Athletic Club**.

FOOD

For a mountain range that was recently quite remote, the San Juans have developed some remarkably sophisticated taste buds. This is particularly apparent in Telluride. Some of the most inventive and delicious food I've ever eaten was at the **Sundance Restaurant**, at The Peaks in the Mountain Village, (970) 728-6800. The "Colorado Ranchlands" cuisine is an art form here, from preparation to presentation. **Le Marmotte**, 150 W. San Juan, (970) 728-6232, is a well-regarded country-style French restaurant with a wide selection of wines and a fine Sunday brunch.

Another Telluride spot, with varied prices, is **Leimgrubers Bierstube & Restaurant**, 573 W. Pacific, (970) 728-4663. Après ski you can hardly squeeze in the door for a draft beer, but when it soon clears out, you can enjoy some tasty, hearty German food—bratwurst, Wiener schnitzel, and smoked pork tenderloin.

Moderately priced restaurants do exist in Telluride. **Harmon's**, 300 S. Townsend, (970) 728-0100, is a lot of fun. Located in the nicely renovated historic Rio Grande Southern train depot, it features European food to accompany its microbrewed beer. **Sofio's**, 110 E. Colorado Ave., (970) 728-4882, has a huge range of $8–$12 Mexican dishes and good margaritas.

Telluride has a few low-end choices. **Baked in Telluride**, 127 S. Fir St., (970) 728-4775, offers a fine selection of croissants filled with fruit, meat, and cheese, plus deli sandwiches and pizza by the slice. **Gregory's Bakery & Café**, 217 E. Colorado, (970) 728-3334, serves worthy vegetarian cooking and baked goods.

In Ouray, the **Bon Ton**, 426 Main St., (970) 325-4951, in a cozy basement room in the St. Elmo Hotel, serves excellent northern Italian food, as well as beef and seafood, in a Victorian setting with cut-glass booth dividers and exposed brick. Dinners range from $11–$20. Reasonably priced Ouray restaurants include **The Outlaw**, 610 Main St., (970) 325-4366, which specializes in exceptional charbroiled steaks of aged Colorado beef, served with salad, rolls, baked potatoes, and vegetables. Red-checked tablecloths, local memorabilia on the walls—including John Wayne's hat—and a friendly staff give it a down-home feel. On the lower end but serving good food is the **Silver Nugget Café**, 940 Main St., (970) 325-4100. Generous portions, an old-fashioned counter, and a friendly staff make it a favorite with locals.

Of Silverton's modestly priced spots, those recommended include the **Pickle Barrel**, 1304 Greene St., (970) 387-5713, which prepares tasty sandwiches and burgers at lunch, and steaks and seafood for dinner, along with a good selection of beers. The **French Bakery Restaurant**, 1250 Greene St., (970) 387-5423, bakes its own delicious pastries, breads, and rolls, and also cooks good full meals.

LODGING

Telluride has many lodging options. At the top of the comfort ladder is **The Peaks**, in the Mountain Village, (970) 728-6800 or (800) 789-2220. This is the place to be pampered, from its covered entryway and sophisticated lobby to its premium spa facilities and sparkling dinning rooms. Rates are $175–$595.

Also in the expensive category is the **Skyline Guest Ranch**, outside Telluride, (970) 728-3757, a former working ranch sitting at 9,600 feet with views of a pair of 14,000-foot peaks. You can ride horses, fish ponds or streams, or try to count the wildflowers in a single square foot of meadow. It remains open in winter at slightly reduced rates.

Moderately priced accommodations in Telluride include the **New Sheridan Hotel**, 231 W. Colorado Ave., (970) 728-4351 or (800) 200-1891. This historic property, built in 1895 to rival the best hotels in Denver, has some rooms that shine, but others can be small and eight rooms do not have private bathrooms. Rates are $75–$250.

A good buy for families is the **Telluride Lodge**, 747 W. Pacific, (970) 728-4446 or (800) 662-8747, with full kitchens, telephones, cable TV, fireplaces, a steam room, and hot tubs. Rates are $175–$245.

Ouray has several excellent possibilities. I spent two nights in the historic **St. Elmo Hotel**, 426 Main St., (970) 325-0348, and enjoyed it immensely. Built at the turn of the century, it has an old-timey feel and decor but with modern amenities. Rates are $58–$150. Also in Ouray is one of the finest B&Bs I've ever visited, the **China Clipper**, 525 Second St., (970) 325-0565. Exquisite interior finishing and decor, fine service, a garden hot tub, and a comfortable, relaxed atmosphere add up to a high-quality experience. Rates start at over $100.

SAN JUAN MOUNTAINS

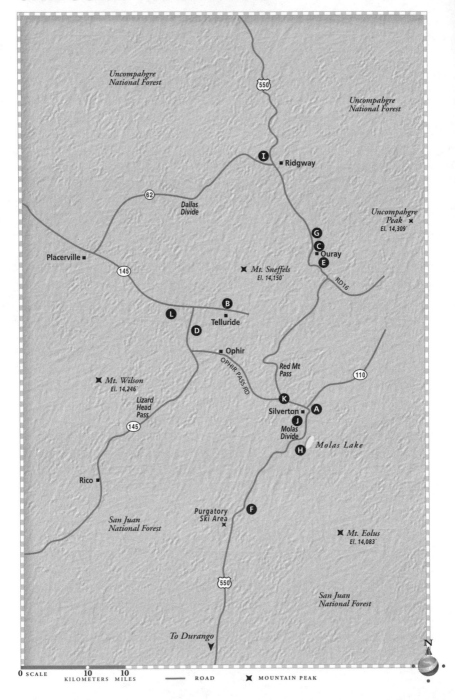

Uncompahgre
National Forest

Uncompahgre
National Forest

550

I ■ Ridgway

62

Dallas
Divide

Uncompahgre
Peak ✖
El. 14,309´

G

C
■ Ouray
E

Placerville ■

145

✖ Mt. Sneffels
El. 14,150´

RD16

B

L

■ Telluride

D

■ Ophir

Red Mt
Pass

110

OPHIR PASS RD

✖ Mt. Wilson
El. 14,246´

Lizard
Head
Pass

K

Silverton ■ **A**

145

J

Molas
Divide

H Molas Lake

Rico ■

San Juan
National Forest

Purgatory
Ski Area
✖

F

✖ Mt. Eolus
El. 14,083´

550

San Juan
National Forest

To Durango
▼

N

0 SCALE   10   10
KILOMETERS   MILES   —— ROAD   ✖ MOUNTAIN PEAK

Lodging

- **A** Alma House
- **B** Alpine Inn
- **B** Bear Creek
- **C** China Clipper
- **B** New Sheridan Hotel
- **B** The Peaks
- **C** St. Elmo Hotel
- **D** Skyline Guest Ranch
- **B** Telluride Lodge

Camping

- **E** Amphitheater
- **F** Chris Park
- **F** Haviland Lake
- **G** KOA Ouray
- **H** Molas Lake Park
- **F** Purgatory
- **I** Ridgeway State Park
- **J** Silverton Lakes Campground
- **K** South Mineral
- **L** Sunshine
- **B** Town Park Campground

Note: Items with the same letter are located in the same town or area.

Silverton also has a good B&B, **Alma House**, (970) 387-5336 or (800) 267-5336. The 1901 three-story small hotel is only two blocks from the railroad station, and has a free mineral and mining "museum" on the premises. Rates are $50–$80.

In Telluride, try the **Bear Creek**, 221 E. Colorado Ave., (970) 728-6681 or (800) 338-7064, with its cozy fireplace in the living room, sauna, steam room, and Jacuzzi on the roof deck, plus cable TV, telephones, and other attractions. Rates are $65–$180. The moderately priced **Alpine Inn**, 440 W. Colorado Ave., (970) 728-6282 or (800) 707-3344, built in 1907, is only steps from the lifts and downtown.

CAMPING

A handful of national forest campgrounds are found along the San Juan Skyway route, including **Amphitheater** (1 mile south of Ouray), **Chris Park**, **Haviland Lake**, **Purgatory** (across US 550 from the Purgatory ski area), **Sunshine** (8 miles southwest of Telluride on CO 145), and **South Mineral** (near Silverton). Five miles south of Silverton is the **Molas Lake Park** commercial recreation and camping center.

Telluride also has its popular and often full **Town Park Campground**, which has public restrooms and hot showers for $1.50. Primitive camping is also allowed in the **San Juan National Forest**. For details, contact ranger offices in Durango, 701 Camino del Rio, (970) 247-4874); or near Telluride, (970) 327-4261.

RVers can head over to the **Silverton Lakes Campground**, 2100 Kendall St., (970) 387-5721, open May through November with full hookups. **Ridgeway State Park**, (800) 678-CAMP, near Ridgeway, has 200 sites, many with hookups, as well as toilets, showers, and laundry. **KOA Ouray**, 4 miles north of Ouray on County Road 23, (970) 325-4736, offers hookups and tent sites, a store, and jeep rentals.

NIGHTLIFE

There's not much happening in the San Juans at night—people are too exhausted from playing, or working to support their play, to party much. However, in Telluride, try the **Fly Me to the Moon Saloon**, 132 S. Colorado Ave., (970) 728-6666, with occasional live music—generally rock, blues, or reggae, which have never waned in popularity here; and **Garfinkle's**, 101 E. Colorado, with its happenin' open mike night. For pool, darts, and suds with locals, head over to the **Last Dollar**, on the corner of Pine and Colorado Ave., (970) 728-4800. For a drink in elegance, drop into the **Sheridan Bar**, 200 E. Colorado Ave., (970)-728-3632, built at the turn of the century.

In the summer of 1997, the **Joffrey Ballet** began presenting annual performances in Telluride. In Silverton, partake of some unpretentious but highly entertaining live drama presented by **A Theater Group**, 1069 Greene St., (970) 387-5337 or (800) 752-4494, in the historic Miners Union Theater. Shows, including an annual George Bernard Shaw festival, generally run Wednesday through Sunday at 8 p.m. in the summer. Admission is $7.

9
SOUTHEASTERN UTAH

In 1879–80 Mormon pioneers pushed across the convoluted land-scape of Southeastern Utah in an amazing display of determination when blazing the Mormon Trail, lowering wagons over 100-foot cliffs with ropes. Over a century later, this is the last relatively "undiscovered" corner of southern Utah's famed canyon country. While millions of people troop annually to Zion and Bryce Canyon, and hundreds of thousands to nearby Canyonlands, the wonderful area around Blanding and Bluff receives only a fraction of this traffic—despite its arresting beauty and interesting history.

The Goosenecks of the San Juans rival any canyon complex in the American Southwest, and Grand Gulch contains world-class archeological ruins. The Abajo Mountains, poking their heads up over 11,000 feet in altitude, afford cool summer retreats and winter skiing. Some of the world's greatest natural stone arches are also found here, at Bridges National Monument. Another national monument, Hovenweep, in an isolated setting reminiscent of the pre-industrial world, contains remnants of the Anasazi culture that once flourished throughout the Four Corners area. Take a rafting trip down the San Juan River through thrilling rapids, past ruins and incredible vistas of rocks and more rocks. This region is sure to gain increasing renown in the years ahead. Come before the crowds do. ◪

SOUTHEASTERN UTAH

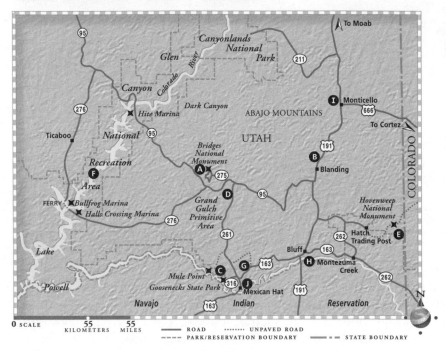

Sights

- **Ⓐ** Bridges National Monument
- **Ⓑ** Edge of the Cedars State Park
- **Ⓒ** Goosenecks State Park/ Muley Overlook
- **Ⓓ** Grand Gulch Primitive Area
- **Ⓔ** Hovenweep National Monument
- **Ⓕ** Upper Lake Powell
- **Ⓖ** Valley of the Gods

Food

- **Ⓗ** Dairy Café
- **Ⓘ** Lamplight Restaurant
- **Ⓘ** MD Ranch Cookhouse
- **Ⓙ** Valley of the Gods Inn & Restaurant

Note: Items with the same letter are located in the same town or area.

A PERFECT DAY IN SOUTHEASTERN UTAH

This destination covers a lot of ground, and one day can only encompass a partial look. Begin with a visit to Hovenweep National Monument, drive through the Valley of the Gods and up the Mokee Dugway to Muley Point for a grand vista, and end the day with a hike at Natural Bridges National Monument. Since large RVs are not recommended on the Mokee Dugway, RVers can swap Muley Point for a stop at the Goosenecks State Park and a longer but pretty route via US 191 and UT 95 to Bridges National Monument.

SIGHTSEEING HIGHLIGHTS

★★★ **Bridges National Monument**—While Arches to the north gets all the press, Bridges actually contains the second- and third-largest natural stone aches in the world. One can hardly believe the thin sweeping ribbon of stone called **Owachomo Bridge**, which runs 180 feet long at an average thickness of only 9 feet! Carved by water, wind, and the hot and cold cycles of nature, the park's three primary stone spans are a great testament to the astounding and creative hand of nature. A nice variety of foot trails allow you to approach the bridges (and a cliff dwelling) on both short (20 minutes to Owachomo) and long hikes.

A loop road provides vistas of each major bridge; the visitor center offers a short film and displays on area wildlife and geology.

Details: On UT 95, 31 miles west of US 191 and Blanding; (435) 692-1234. Open year-round. Day-use entry fee is $2 adults, $1 children. (2 to 4 hours)

★★★ **Goosenecks State Park/Muley Overlook**—Both of these spots provide dramatic, panoramic overviews of the entire southeastern corner of Utah, although Muley Point is higher, offering a larger picture. From Muley to the southwest, Navajo Mountain pokes up its prominent domed head, a landmark visible for much of the pending journey. On the southern horizon are the tops of Monument Valley spires. At your feet is the labyrinthian course of the San Juan River Goosenecks, which curves back and forth upon itself. To the southeast, plateaus and the distant Colorado San Juans faintly shimmer. Behind you rise the higher red slopes of the Red House Cliffs, Cedar Mesa, and the Abajo Mountains.

Details: At the end of paved UT 316, 4 miles off UT 261 just north of Mexican Hat; (435) 678-2238. The free park has a picnic area and out-houses, and camping is allowed. It is accessible year-round. Muley Point is reached via a good 5-mile gravel road from UT 261 north of Mexican Hat. At the top of the Mokee Dugway, turn west (left if heading north) onto the gravel road. If coming from the south, large RVs should be warned that the Mokee Dugway is not suitable for passage: it's narrow and quite steep, with sharp curves, dropping more than 1,000 feet. Muley Point has no facilities. It's open year-round, and is free. (1 to 2 hours)

★★ **Hovenweep National Monument**—While this would be a major attraction anywhere else, the rich archeological ruins of the Southwest overshadow this monument straddling the Utah-Colorado border. Little excavation or reconstruction has been done here, so many ruins are no more than piles of rubble. However, few people visit, lending a sense of the isolation that must have once pervaded the entire Anasazi homelands. The most accessible and best reconstructed ruins are located at **Square Tower**, including **Hovenweep Castle**. A visitor center at Square Tower contains exhibits, information, a bookstore, and rangers to answer questions.

Details: Southeast of Blanding off UT 262; (303) 529-4465. Access is also possible from the Cortez, Colorado, area (see a decent map). The visitor cen-ter is staffed 8–5 daily. Though open year-round, gravel roads approaching the monument can be impassable in winter or after heavy rains. (2 hours on site)

★★ **Lake Powell, Upper**—Immense Lake Powell, trapped behind Glen Canyon Dam near Page, Arizona, extends far up the Colorado River into Utah. **Hite**, **Hall's Crossing**, and **Bullfrog Marinas**, all within the confines of **Glen Canyon National Recreation Area** (see Lake Powell chapter), provide lodging, launch facilities, boat storage, rentals, and other services. Hite is the northernmost marina, contain-ing a National Park Service office in summer.

The lake's oddly green-tinted water laps at the base of thousand-foot cliffs and snakes up narrow side canyons, such as the 1,000-foot-deep **Dirty Devil River**, creating a dramatic panorama. Here the Colorado River enters the lake through **Narrow Canyon**, spanned by UT 95, on a dramatic steel bridge high above the river.

Lake Powell between Bullfrog and Hall's Crossing can be crossed only by ferry, (435) 684-7000/2261, a novel way to see the waterway and travel this section of the state. From May 15 through September

30, the ferry departs Hall's Crossing on even hours from 8 a.m.–6 p.m.; from Bullfrog, it departs on uneven hours, 9 a.m.–7 p.m. From October through May 14, the last departure from Hall's is at 3 p.m. Admission is $9 per vehicle. Rent motor- and houseboats at all three marinas, but make houseboat reservations well in advance, (800) 528-6154.

Details: *From southeastern Utah, take UT 95 at Hite, or UT 276 at Hall's Crossing. For Lake Powell National Recreation Area information, call (520) 608-6404. The lake and marinas are open year-round. (1 hour to several days)*

✸ **Edge of the Cedars State Park**—This park preserves the remains of a small Anasazi site, including kivas, occupied between A.D. 770 and 1200. A museum houses one of the region's premier pottery collections, artifacts, and displays; a gallery offers changing shows.

Details: *660 W. 400 North St., Blanding; (435) 678-2238. Open 9–5 daily. Admission is $1.50. (1 hour)*

✸ **Grand Gulch Primitive Area**—This canyon complex, a tributary of the San Juan River south of Bridges National Monument, shelters one of the largest concentrations of Anasazi ruins in the entire Southwest. The twisting canyons are quite beautiful in themselves, with tiny dripping springs, plunge pools perfect for swimming, and pockets of shady Fremont cottonwoods. Access is by foot only. Because of the archeological resources, hikers must register with the Bureau of Land Management, which oversees the area.

Details: *Accessible from UT 261 and UT 276; (435) 587-2141. (4 hours to several days)*

✸ **Valley of the Gods**—Elsewhere this would be a prime attraction; in southeastern Utah, it's just one of many. A 17-mile graded and gravel road winds through a gorgeous assembly of rock monoliths and spires reminscent of nearby, world-renowned Monument Valley.

Details: *The road leaves US 163 just northeast of Mexican Hat, and returns to pavement 11 miles north of Mexican Hat, on UT 261; (435) 587-2141. Not recommended in inclement weather. Admission is free. (1 hour)*

FITNESS AND RECREATION

As noted above, ample chances for hiking exist throughout the area, including trails at **Hovenweep**, **Grand Gulch**, and **Bridges**. If it's too

SOUTHEASTERN UTAH

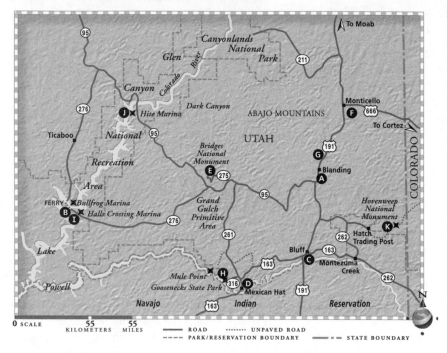

Lodging

Ⓐ Comfort Inn

Ⓑ Defiance House Lodge

Ⓐ Old Hotel B&B

Ⓒ Recapture Lodge

Ⓓ San Juan Inn

Ⓐ Sunset Inn

Camping

Ⓔ Bridges National Monument

Ⓕ Canyonlands KOA

Ⓖ Devil's Spring

Ⓗ Goosenecks State Park

Ⓘ Hall's Crossing RV Park

Ⓙ Hite RV

Ⓚ Hovenweep National Monument

Note: Items with the same letter are located in the same town or area.

hot, head into the **Abajo Mountains**, just north of Blanding or west of Monticello, where paved and primitive roads lead to foot trails, including hikes to the summit of 11,360-foot Abajo Peak.

In winter, these dirt roads offer excellent cross-country skiing. Near Monticello is the **Blue Mt. Ski Area**. For details, contact the **Manti-La Sal National Forest**, (435) 259-7125. Dropping out of the La Sals into canyon country is the **Dark Canyon Primitive Area** and the adjoining 45,000-acre **Dark Canyon Wilderness Area**, (435) 625-5306, for serious trampers.

The **San Juan River** provides wonderful white-water float trips. A common put-in is at **Sand Island Recreation Area**, just outside Bluff. You can reach Mexican Hat in a day or two, passing a slew of remote Anasazi cliff dwellings. Extended trips drift on into the Goosenecks, where the world is reduced to a ribbon of water pinched between never-ending and endlessly captivating rock walls more than 1,400 feet high. Permits are required on the San Juan. For details, contact the Bureau of Land Management, (435) 587-2144. Choose from among many river guide and outfitter companies here. For a complete list and the *Raft Utah* guide, call the Utah Travel Council, (800) 200-1160.

Southeast Utah has also been called the off-road capital of the nation. For four-wheelers, this is the place. A popular route is near Blanding, from the Abajos to Bridges National Monument and past the Bear's Ears. Most major towns have rental and guide services.

Golfers will enjoy the **Blue Mountain Golf Course**, in Monticello, (435) 587-2468, with rentals and a snack bar.

FOOD

In Monticello, "pardners" head on over to the **MD Ranch Cookhouse**, 380 S. Main St., (435) 587-3299, for some good out-West grub served up over live music. One of the fanciest places around is Monticello's **Lamplight Restaurant**, on US 666 E., (435) 587-2170, with prime rib, steaks, fish, soup, and a salad bar, plus a rare commodity in rural Utah: a liquor license. In Bluff, there is the **Dairy Café**, 6 W. Main St., (435) 672-2287, a basic but fulfilling road joint. In Mexican Hat, about the only game in town is the multifaceted **Valley of the Gods Inn & Restaurant**, with dining—including some Navajo dishes—accompanied by a motel, camping, general store, traditional hogan, laundry, and showers.

LODGING

The area has no large, outstanding resorts or inns, but plenty of other lodgings exist in Blanding, Monticello, Bluff, and even Mexican Hat. In Blanding, an inexpensive ($35) choice is the **Sunset Inn**, 88 W. Center, (435) 678-3323. Its off-highway location is quieter than most motels', and its amenities include a hot tub, cable TV, and laundry. Up a notch in price is the **Comfort Inn**, 711 S. Main St., (435) 678-3271, with a heated indoor pool, game room, and cable TV for $65. The **Old Hotel B&B**, 118 E. 300 St. South, (435) 678-2388, offers large, comfortable, nonsmoking rooms with private baths in a Victorian setting for $60.

At Bullfrog Marina, there's the **Defiance House Lodge**, (800) 528-6154. Rates are $99–$109. In Mexican Hat, perched on the edge of the San Juan River Canyon, is the basic but charming **San Juan Inn**, on UT 63, (800) 447-2022. Rates are $38–$62.

One of the most unique area accommodations is Bluff's **Recapture Lodge**, set back off US 191, (435) 672-2281. Its stone buildings, pool, hot tub, and restaurant are popular with San Juan boaters. Rates are $45.

CAMPING

In Monticello, there's the **Canyonlands KOA**, 6 miles east of town on US 666, (435) 587-2884, complete with a petting zoo and buffalo. The U.S. Forest Service, (435) 587-2041 for information or (800) 280-2267 for reservations, also runs a handful of campgrounds. Closest to Blanding, about 10 miles north of town, is **Devil's Spring**, set in a pretty ponderosa forest. Avoid the sites overlooking busy US 191.

Thirty-one individual (no group) sites await at **Hovenweep National Monument**, (303) 529-4465; while **Goosenecks State Park**, (435) 678-2238, offers primitive sites with outhouses. There is also a small, free campground at **Bridges National Monument**, with 13 sites and pit toilets. It's open year-round on a first-come, first-served basis. Dispersed, self-contained camping is also permitted along the shores of Lake Powell (see Lake Powell chapter), where there are also two RV camps, **Hall's Crossing RV Park** and **Hite RV**, both (800) 528-6154, the latter without hookups.

10

MOAB AREA—
CANYONLANDS AND ARCHES

Take two of the West's most powerful rivers—the Colorado and the Green—both cutting their own major canyons as they drop out of the Rocky Mountains and into the Colorado Plateau, and merge them. The result is immense Canyonlands National Park. Encompassing 337,000 acres, it's one of the most amazing, sprawling landscapes on Earth. In fact, it is so large and diverse that it's divided into three districts, each with its own character—The Maze, The Needles, and Islands in the Sky. And on its fringe is yet another geologic wonder, Arches National Park, containing the world's greatest concentration of stone arches.

The first to record impressions of the meeting of the mighty rivers area was explorer John Wesley Powell. In 1869 he wrote, "Wherever we look there is but a wilderness of rocks, deep gorges where the rivers are lost behind cliffs and towers and pinnacles . . ."

But fantastic rocks are not the sum of the area. It once was a haven for rustlers and outlaws, including Butch Cassidy and the Wild Bunch. Today its major town, Moab, has become the mecca of American mountain biking, and its rivers, including challenging Cataract Canyon of the Colorado, have become popular float trips. And, as if this gigantic hole in the ground had been inverted, the Abajo Mountains immediately to the east thrust out of the plateaus, reaching elevations of more than 12,000 feet. The juxtaposition of sun-blasted slickrock and snow-carpeted slopes is a sight you'll never forget. ◼

MOAB AREA

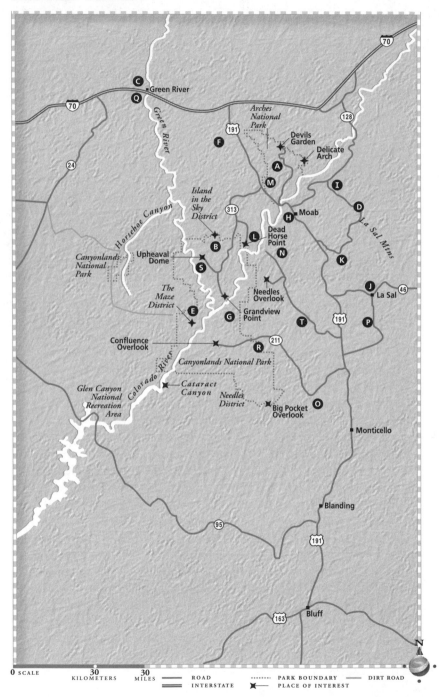

Sights

Ⓐ Arches National Park

Ⓑ Islands in the Sky

Ⓒ John Wesley Powell River History Museum

Ⓓ La Sal Mountain Loop

Ⓔ The Maze

Ⓕ Mill Canyon Dinosaur Trail

Ⓖ The Needles

Ⓗ O'Laurie Museum

Lodging

Ⓘ Castle Valley Inn

Ⓙ La Sal Mountain Guest Ranch

Ⓚ Pack Creek Ranch

Camping

Ⓛ Dead Horse Point State Park

Ⓜ Devil's Garden Campground

Ⓝ Hatch Point

Ⓞ Newspaper Rock

Ⓟ Oowah Lake Campground

Ⓠ Shady Acres RV Park

Ⓡ Squaw Flat Campground

Ⓟ Warner Campground

Ⓢ Willow Flats Campground

Ⓣ Wind Whistle

Note: Items with the same letter are located in the same area.

A PERFECT DAY IN THE MOAB AREA

Temperatures here can climb to more than 100 degrees in summer and dip to below freezing on winter nights, so come prepared—or visit in fall or spring. Pick one district in Canyonlands and explore it in the early morning, then tour Arches National Park in the late afternoon. Midday in summer, lay low or take in the O'Laurie Museum. Or visit either national park in the morning, then drive through the La Sal Mountains in the heat of the day. A third option is to take a daylong float trip on either the Colorado or the Green River. Have dinner at the Grand Old Ranch House.

SIGHTSEEING HIGHLIGHTS

★★★ **Arches National Park**—The world's greatest concentration of stone arches is within this 73,379-acre enclave—more than 2,000 have been found to date. A 48-mile-round-trip, self-guided, paved auto route winds into the park, providing easy access to most of its major features. Don't miss the spur road into the **Windows District**, where you can spot the unusual **Double Arch**. Short hiking trails bring you to several highlights, including **Double Arch**, **Landscape Arch** (one of the world's largest, spanning 306 feet), and **Delicate Arch**.

A dry environment, Arches has pockets of water and vegetation all the more beautiful for their scarcity. Ancient juniper trees, bonsai-like, twist directly out of rock crevices. Here and there are petroglyphs of the Fremont, Anasazi, and Ute Indians. You can see why writer Edward Abbey, who was once a ranger here, wrote his most lyrical work, *Desert Solitaire*, based on his Arches experiences.

Details: 5 miles northwest of Moab off US 191; (435) 259-8161. A visitor center near the entrance has a slide program, exhibits, and books. It is open year-round. Admission is $10 per vehicle. (2 hours minimum)

★★★ **Islands in the Sky**—This high plateau, suspended 2,000 feet above the confluence of the Green and Colorado Rivers, provides the single most impressive views of Canyonlands as a whole. **Grand View Point** is almost smack-dab in the geographic center of the huge park. It's well named: as you look south, the Colorado cleaves down on your left, with the Green on your right. Another stupendous view in the Islands district is from **Dead Horse Point State Park**, where a great meandering of the Colorado creates a massive horseshoe bend.

Stewart Udall, President Kennedy's visionary Secretary of the Interior, was flying over the area in a small plane surveying the proposed site of a Colorado River dam in 1962 when he exclaimed, "My God, that's a national park down there!" He was right, and in 1964 Canyonlands National Park was created.

Details: Both the turnoff to UT 313 and entrance to Islands in the Sky are on US 191 South, about 11 miles northwest of Moab, 6 miles past the turnoff to Arches. At mile 17 on UT 313 is a left fork that takes you to Dead Horse Point State Park. Its visitor center, (435) 259-2614, has spectacular viewpoints, restrooms, interpretive displays, snacks, and books. Proceed another 5 miles on the main road from the Dead Horse turnoff to the park boundary, then 7 more to Grand View Point, for a total of 29 miles from UT 191. The park's central number is (435) 259-7164. Open year-round. Admission is $10 per vehicle, good throughout the park for one week. (3 hours minimum)

✯✯✯ **The Needles**—Geologist John Strong Newberry, on the first
formal exploration of Canyonlands in 1859, wrote of its "battlemented
towers of colossal but often beautiful proportions, closely resembling
elaborate structures of art." This is nowhere more prevalent than in
this district, which is also full of rock art, arches, and ruins. **Horse
Canyon** is particularly rich in cultural resources, including **Tower**
and **Keyhole Ruins** and the powerful **Thirteen Faces** pictographs
made by the ancient Fremont people. Many of the sights can be
reached only by multi-day hikes or four-wheel-drive vehicles, though
a paved road does access more than enough sights for casual visitors,
including the huge pictograph panel with 1,000 years of artistry at
Newspaper Rock Recreation Area,12 miles along the district's main
road (UT 211).

*Details: The Needles District entrance is on US 191, 14 miles north of
Monticello or 41 miles south of Moab. A paved road, UT 211, heads west
into the park for 38 miles down Indian Creek Canyon to Squaw Flat, where
there is a visitor center; (435) 259-7164. Four-wheel roads fan out from here
and also enter the Needles from other directions. A small store at the Needles
Outpost near the campground stocks some limited supplies during peak season.
The district is open year-round. Admission is $10 per vehicle, good throughout
the park for one week. (4 hours minimum)*

✯✯ **La Sal Mountain Loop**—If it's hot in the canyons, head up into
the state's second-highest mountain range for a drive, a hike, or, in
winter, cross-country skiing. A 65-mile loop road takes you through a
popular film location, **Castle Valley**, into dense forests, and past
crystal-clear streams and lakes.

*Details: Drive north out of Moab on US 191 and turn east (right)
onto UT 128 just before crossing the Colorado. Continue along the river 16
miles to the Castle Valley road on the right, and begin your climb into the
mountains. Dirt side roads lead even higher, to more remote locales. The road
eventually returns to UT 191 just south of Moab. (3 to 4 hours)*

✯ **John Wesley Powell River History Museum**—This 20,000-
square-foot museum portrays the remarkable explorations of the
Colorado and Green Rivers by this Civil War veteran. In addition to a
20-minute video, displays, models, maps, and other materials are full-
scale reproductions of the small boats he used in his journeys. The
facility also includes the **Green River Visitor Center**, a bookstore,
and a gift shop.

Details: 885 E. Main St., Green River; (435) 564-3427. Open daily, summer 8–8, winter 9–5. (1 hour)

✦ **The Maze**—This is the most remote district of Canyonlands. Its roads range from improved gravel to white-knuckle, bone-jarring tracks over solid rock and the shifting dunes of the **San Rafael Desert**. Two-wheel traffic definitely ends at the **Flint Trail Overlook**. However, if you're well stocked with water and the right vehicle, continuing further into the Maze is a thrill. Its gooseneck canyons are pocketed with Fremont rock art and tiny springs supporting small deer herds. **Horseshoe Canyon** has one of North America's greatest pictograph sites, the 200-foot-long **Great Gallery**, with its life-sized, hollow-eyed humanoids.

Butch Cassidy and his boys, as well as rustlers, used to hightail it across the Maze and into the next canyon complex to the west, the Dirty Devil, losing their pursuers or jumping them in ambushes. **Robbers Roost Canyon** is named for them. It's outside Canyonlands itself on Bureau of Land Management lands; call (435) 542-3461 for information.

*Details: 40 miles from the town of Green River on UT 24. About 45 miles into the district is the **Hans Flats Ranger Station**, (435) 259-2652, staffed daily in spring, summer, and fall. The district is open year-round, but snow and mud increase the hazards. (8 hours to several days)*

✦ **Mill Canyon Dinosaur Trail**—Here's a chance to find dino bones and fossils in situ along a short self-guided trail and to view remains of the **Halfway Stage Station**, which served travelers between 1883 and 1904. This Bureau of Land Management site also has jeep and mountain-bike trails.

Details: 13 miles north of Moab off UT 191 West; exit onto a 2-mile dirt road; (435) 259-6111. It's accessible year-round. Admission is free. (1 to 2 hours)

✦ **O'Laurie Museum**—The museum features local geologic oddities, dinosaur fossils, and Indian, Spanish, and early pioneer artifacts.

Details: 118 E. Center St., Moab; (435) 259-7985. Open 1–4 and 7–9 p.m. in high season. Admission is free. (30 minutes)

FITNESS AND RECREATION

Except for the occasional oppressive heat of summer, hiking in Canyonlands and Arches can be a great experience. I once spent a

Thanksgiving hiking in Canyonlands, and had a fine outing. In the Islands in the Sky District, the **Mesa Arch Trail** is sweet. Only a half-mile round trip with an 80-foot ascent, it ends at a sandstone arch that frames the La Sal Mountains. The Needles District has the greatest number and length of trails in Canyonlands, including **Chesler Park Trail**, a 5-mile round trip ending at this great meadow, studded with spires and wrapped in a circular wall. In the Maze District, the 22-mile **Golden Stairs Trail** takes you into the Maze itself and out to the monolithic Doll House for a glimpse at Cataract Canyon far below.

In Arches, walk along the **Park Avenue Trail**, a 1-mile outing with parking at either end that traverses a maze of skyscraper-like sandstone fins; or the **Delicate Arch Trail**, a 3-mile round trip with a 500-foot ascent to perhaps the most beautiful of all the park's arches.

Canyonlands, and Moab, are ground zero for mountain biking. While biking within the national park is restricted to roads and jeep trails, that's a lot of terrain, and adjoining the park are immense Bureau of Land Management holdings called the **Canyon Rims Recreation Area**, (435) 259-6111, with more liberal biking regulations. Right at the edge of Moab is the scenic 10-mile **Slickrock Trail**. To reach it, travel 3 miles out of town on Sand Flats Road. Guides and rental operations abound in Moab.

The area is also terrific for river excursions. The Green River gently meanders 120 miles through **Labyrinth** and **Stillwater Canyons**, from the town of Green River to the confluence with the Colorado. The Colorado also flows placidly for 47 miles, from the put-in at Potash to the confluence. The combined rivers then plunge into **Cataract Canyon**, where the drop of 8 feet per mile exceeds that of the Grand Canyon. One section (not for amateurs) even descends 30 feet in 1 mile. In other words, hang on! Permits from the Bureau of Land Management, (435) 637-4584, and/or Canyonlands National Park, (435) 259-5277, are required for many stretches.

This is also prime four-wheeling country. All three Canyonlands districts feature miles of rough, sometimes frightening roads. I'll never forget the jolt down the Maze's **Flint Trail**—and that was 20 years ago! In Islands in the Sky, the **Shafer Trail** easily winds 100 miles along the White Rim through prime bighorn sheep habitat. At **Lathrop Canyon**, jeeps can reach the Colorado. In the Needles, a challenging route is the **Elephant Hill Trail**. Guides and rentals are available in Moab.

MOAB

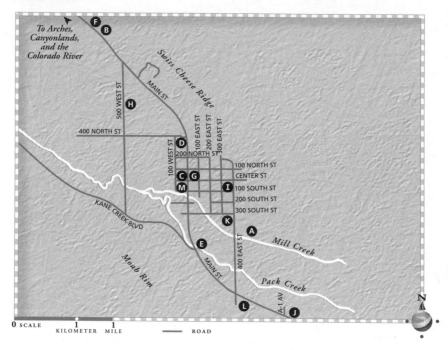

To Arches,
Canyonlands,
and the
Colorado River

Swiss Cheese Ridge

500 WEST ST

MAIN ST

400 NORTH ST

100 WEST ST

200 NORTH ST

100 EAST ST
200 EAST ST
300 EAST ST

100 NORTH ST
CENTER ST
100 SOUTH ST
200 SOUTH ST
300 SOUTH ST

KANE CREEK BLVD

Moab Rim

MAIN ST

400 EAST ST

Mill Creek

Pack Creek

A-1 AV

N

0 SCALE   1   1
KILOMETER MILE   ──── ROAD

Food

- **A** Bar M Chuckwagon Supper
- **B** Grand Old Ranch House
- **C** Honest Ozzie's Café
- **D** Westerner Grill

Camping

- **E** Canyonlands Campark
- **F** Slickrock Campground

Lodging

- **G** Best Western Canyonlands Inn
- **H** Canyon Country
- **I** Cedar Breaks Condos
- **J** Lazy Lizard
- **K** Old Hotel
- **L** Pioneer Spring
- **M** Ramada Inn–Moab

FOOD

In Moab, the **Westerner Grill**, 331 N. Main, has been a fixture since the 1950s uranium boom. Today it serves more than 16 kinds of modestly priced sandwiches, daily lunch and dinner specials, and breakfast any time. The **Bar M Chuckwagon Supper**, on the south edge of town off 400 East St., (435) 259-2276, presents open-air, ranch-style chuck-wagon dining on barbecued beef, followed by a cowboy serenade. **Honest Ozzie's Café**, 60 N. 100 West St., (435) 259-8442, is the saving grace for vegetarians in the area. It also serves natural, nonvegetarian dishes for breakfast, lunch, and dinner. One of the finer meals to be had locally is at the **Grand Old Ranch House**, 1266 UT 191 North, (435) 259-8442, which serves German cuisine. It's open for dinner only. The building is on the National Register of Historic Places. Dinners run $10–$20.

LODGING

In Moab, the **Best Western Canyonlands Inn**, 16 S. Main, (435) 259-2300, is a decent chain hotel with a restaurant, swimming pool, and hot tub. Rates are $75–$150. The **Ramada Inn–Moab**, 182 S. Main, (435) 259-7141, is similar. The **Cedar Breaks Condos**, Center Street and Fourth East, (435) 259-7830, offers deluxe accommodations, including kitchens, living rooms, and separate bedrooms, with a full breakfast, for $80.

The **Pack Creek Ranch**, on the La Sal Loop Road outside Moab, (435) 259-5505, is a nice place with 12 rooms. It has a liquor license, swimming, hot tub, sauna, and other amenities; $75–$150. Probably the prettiest setting in the area goes to the **Castle Valley Inn**, also on the La Sal Loop Road, (435) 259-6012. Collectibles decorate its eight guest rooms, and there's a hot tub. Rates are $95–$155. Outside of Moab, in La Sal, is the **La Sal Mountain Guest Ranch**, (435) 686-2223 or (800) 982-1540, with 11 homes with full kitchens. Rates are $70.

A handful of B&Bs in Moab include the **Old Hotel**, 118 E. 330 South St., (435) 678-2388, a country version of an old Victorian home, featuring large rooms with private baths and color TV for $55–$100; the **Canyon Country**, 590 N. 500 West, (435) 259-5262 or (800) 435-0284, with a hot tub and cable TV for $56–110; and the **Pioneer Spring**, 1275 S. Boulder, (435) 259-4663, with a pool, hot tub, and cable TV for $60–$120. About the cheapest digs are at the **Lazy Lizard**, 1 mile south of town behind A-1 Storage, (435) 259-6057, a hostel with a laundry, kitchen, and hot tub; doubles start at $17.

CAMPING

Arches National Monument features **Devil's Garden Campground**, (435) 259-4351, with 53 sites. It can accommodate RVs but has no hookups and operates on a first-come, first-served basis. No showers or water November through mid-March; $7 per night. Backcountry camping is possible in the monument as well, but a free permit is required.

In and adjoining Canyonlands are a number of options. **Dead Horse Point State Park**, (435) 259-2614 for information or (800) 322-3770 for reservations, in the Islands in the Sky District, has 21 $10 sites with tent pads, shelters, and restrooms. Also in Islands in the Sky is the National Park Service's **Willow Flats Campground**, near the Green River Overlook, with 13 primitive units but no water. Camping is free. Needles features **Squaw Flat Campground**, with drinking water, open from April through October (a $5 fee is charged only through September). The latter two sites operate on a first-come, first-served basis.

In Canyonlands, overnight backcountry permits for primitive camping by backpackers and four-wheel-drive parties are required. They're available on a first-come, first-served basis in the Needles and the Maze, but should be reserved well in advance for Islands in the Sky.

The Bureau of Land Management, (435) 259-6111, also runs a handful of local campgrounds on the fringes of Needles, including **Newspaper Rock** (no water), **Wind Whistle**, and **Hatch Point**. Newspaper Rock is open year-round; the latter two are open only April through October. Another nice option during the hottest times of the year are campgrounds in the nearby La Sal Mountains, including **Oowah Lake** and **Warner**, run by the U.S. Forest Service, (435) 259-7155 for information, (800) 280-2267 for reservations.

RV campgrounds include the **Shady Acres RV Park**, Green River, (435) 564-8290, with 92 hookups and 12 tent sites, showers, and laundry. Moab options include **Canyonlands Campark**, 555 S. Main, (435) 259-6848, with 70 hookups, 60 tent sites, showers, laundry, and a pool. **Slickrock Campground**, 1301½ N. UT 191, (435) 259-7660, has 120 complete hookups, with a dump station, pool, and laundry.

11

CAPITOL REEF NATIONAL PARK

M any people have never heard of this national park, but it is a gem. Like most of southern Utah, it is one immense chunk of modern art, with fantastically carved and cut rock and earthen formations of all colors, shapes, and sizes. A long, narrow, 242,000-acre preserve (the second largest in Utah) running along the sculpted face of a 100-mile upthrust fault, Capitol Reef has many areas that are seldom seen—especially the southern reaches. This is a place that you can visit many times and uncover something new every time.

The area has a variety of sights and activities available to people of all fitness levels. Paved roads and pullouts provide easy access and viewing for the least-mobile. Dirt roads up the adventure quotient a notch, while at least 27 maintained hiking trails run from the short and friendly to the strenuous and remote. And, unlike many of the region's parks, it has an interesting human story associated with its early Mormon settlers, who nicknamed the area for the physical barrier it presented travelers—like a reef to sailors. The park is also gateway to travels into neighboring lands, including the obscure Henry Mountains and the lovely, lush Aquarius Plateau. ◧

CAPITOL REEF NATIONAL PARK

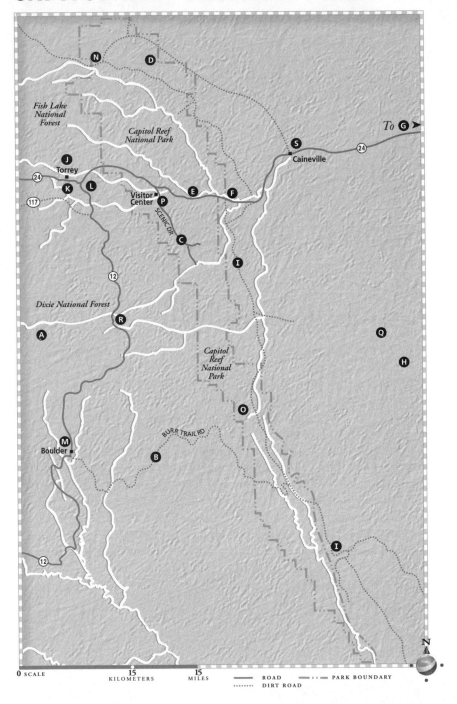

Sights

Ⓐ Aquarius Plateau

Ⓑ Burr Trail

Ⓒ Capitol Reef Scenic Drive

Ⓓ Cathedral Valley

Ⓔ Fruita

Ⓕ Fremont River Drive

Ⓖ Goblin Valley State Park

Ⓗ Henry Mountains

Ⓘ Notom/Bullfrog Road

Food

Ⓙ Café Diablo

Ⓙ Capitol Reef Inn

Ⓙ Sportsman Bar & Grill

Lodging

Ⓙ Best Western Capitol Reef
   Resort

Ⓚ Cactus Hill Motel

Ⓙ Capitol Reef Inn and Café

Ⓙ Desert Inn

Ⓛ SkyRidge B&B Inn

Camping

Ⓜ Boulder Mt. Homestead &
   RV Park

Ⓝ Cathedral Campground

Ⓞ Cedar Mesa Campground

Ⓙ Chuckwagon RV Park &
   Campground

Ⓟ Fruita Campground

Ⓖ Goblin Valley State Park

Ⓠ McMillan Springs and
   Lonesome Beaver Campgrounds

Ⓡ Singletree, Pleasant Creek,
   and Oak Creek Campgrounds

Ⓢ Sleepy Hollow Campground

Note: Items with the same letter are located in the same town or area.

A PERFECT DAY AT CAPITOL REEF NATIONAL PARK

Begin the day with a drive along the prehistoric and historic sites along the Fremont River and in the settlement of Fruita. Stop at the park visitor center to get an overview of this large reserve. Bring a picnic lunch to eat while you're on the park's scenic drive. In order to get a real feel for this striking landscape, get out and hike at some point. Camp at the lovely Fruita campground, or head west to Torrey for dinner and accommodations.

SIGHTSEEING HIGHLIGHTS

★★★ Capitol Reef Scenic Drive—The 25-mile-round-trip drive provides a great introduction to the park, though it traverses only a small slice of it. The paved road is suitable for all types of vehicles and leads to a handful of great hiking trails and a four-wheel-drive route. It winds south, rolling along the west face of a 100-mile fractured and bent uplift of the earth's crust, what pioneers called a "reef." Among the drive's highlights are **Grand Wash**, **Fern's Nipple**, the **Egyptian Throne**, and **Golden Throne**. It dead-ends at **Capitol Gorge** (see Fitness and Recreation, below). Here, **Pleasant Creek Road**, a dirt track suitable for high-clearance two-wheel vehicles in good weather, continues further south.

   Details: The drive begins at the Fruita visitor center, just off UT 24. The road is open daily year-round and rarely gets much snow. $4 per vehicle fee. (90 minutes minimum)

★★★ Fruita—Everywhere you look is a jumbled mass of rock, barren earth, more rock, and sun-scorched dirt. Then, mirage-like, before you opens a dazzlingly green valley. Fruit orchards, fields, and shade trees beckon—an oasis in the wilderness. This is Fruita, once a small but thriving Mormon colony set along the banks of the Fremont River and today the heart of the Capitol Reef National Park visitor facility. The pioneers no longer live here, but some of their historic structures have been preserved by the Park Service and are open for visiting, including the **Fruita Schoolhouse**. This tiny log cabin, circa 1895, built along UT 24, graduated its last class in 1941. It served as a center for community meetings, elections, and socializing until 1924.

   Also within this National Historic District is the **Gilford Homestead**, including a house, barns, rock-walled pastures, and smokehouse. The original home—typical of the spartan Mormon farmhouses—was built in 1908 and abandoned in 1969. Today one can purchase reproductions of the farm's original utensils, household tools, crafts, and toys. Craft-making demonstrations and other activities are held during summer. The farm is on Scenic Drive, 1 mile south of the park's visitor center. Admission is free. En route you'll also pass a blacksmith shop, open daily.

Right across from the farmhouse are Fruita's historic orchards, plump with cherries, apricots, peaches, apples, and pears. Visitors can pick fruit here in season (generally from early April through September). Fruit eaten on-site is free! The **Capitol Reef Visitor Center**, with a nice slide show, books, gifts, and information, is also in Fruita, just off UT 24.

Details: Fruita can be reached from the east or west on paved UT 24; (435) 425-3791. The visitor center is open 8:30–4:30 daily, later in summer. There is no fee to cross the park on UT 24. (1 to 2 hours)

✸✸ **Cathedral Valley**—This is the remote but relatively accessible northern portion of the park. It's reached via two linked roads, which can be used as a loop drive. Both roads require high-clearance vehicles but are passable to two-wheel-drive vehicles in good weather. The entire loop is almost 80 miles long, so don't embark on this route in questionable weather. I've seen flooding in Capitol Reef, and it's an awesome sight, with rivers of mud cascading off cliffs that were bone dry just moments before. Sights along the route include **Temple of the Sun**, **Gypsum Sinkhole**, **South Desert Overlook**, **Temple Rock**, and **Jailhouse Rock**, where Elvis has been spotted on occasion (just kidding).

Details: One access road begins on UT 24 in Cainville, 11 miles east of the park boundary; the other begins 3 miles east of the park boundary and involves fording the Fremont River. (4 hours)

✸✸ **Fremont River Drive**—The main road to the park, UT 24, winds through the Fremont River Canyon—named for John C. Fremont, the famous Western explorer. On the park's eastern edge, this road slices directly through the **Waterpocket Fold** (a huge bent and folded plane of earth) and provides a dramatic entry or exit to Capitol Reef. Driving from east to west, you pass (in order) the historic Mormon **Behunin Cabin**, the lower mouth of **Grand Wash**, the immense and striking **Capitol Dome**, and a collection of petroglyphs in Fruita. East of the park visitor center, UT 24 leaves the river canyon but continues past other major viewpoints, including the short access road to **Panorama Point**, outstanding geologic formations such as **Fluted Wall**, and trailheads like **Chimney Rock**.

Details: *UT 24 is open year-round. No fee. (1 hour)*

★★ **Notom/Bullfrog Road**—This dirt and gravel road runs south along the eastern edge of the **Waterpocket Fold**, leading to the tiny town of Notom and the park's seldom-visited southern realm—including **Muley Twist Canyon** and the amazing **Hall's Creek Narrows**, where experienced backcountry hikers are funneled through a sinuous 3-mile gorge notched with scalloped amphitheaters and deep pools. Hiking here once for five days in late fall, we saw no one. Some 29 miles south of its trailhead, it intersects the **Burr Trail** (see below), then passes a number of scenic viewpoints, including **Hall's Creek Overlook**, and **Bullfrog Creek Overlook**.

Details: *The road begins just east of the park's eastern boundary off UT 24, and intersects with UT 276 just north of Bullfrog Marina and its National Park Service visitor center on Lake Powell, (435) 684-2243—a total distance of 63 miles. (3 hours)*

★ **Aquarius Plateau**—Out of south-central Utah rises this surprisingly vast tabletop, towering over the surrounding canyons, plains, ruffles, and ridges. Its higher slopes, topping 11,000 feet, support huge quaking-aspen forests, lush meadows, lakes, and tinkling streams. In the heat of summer it's a lovely refuge from the dry air of the region's lowlands, which spread out before you like a dreamy picture. On its southern edge rise the Boulder Mountains.

Details: *It is easiest to view the plateau from paved, two-lane UT 12, which begins its long, loping run across south-central Utah just east of Capitol Reef National Park. Forest roads peel off UT 12 to higher and more remote areas. UT 12 is sometimes closed between Grover and Boulder during and following winter storms. The plateau is part of the Dixie National Forest, (435) 865-3700, and has several campgrounds (see Camping). (1 hour)*

★ **Burr Trail**—This is one of southern Utah's more famous off-pavement routes, and so has lost something of its pioneering character— but it's still quite an adventure for most folks. It runs 36 miles roughly east-west, across the park's southern section. It eventually exits the park on a paved 7-mile stretch through scenic **Long Canyon**, with its embedded arches and alcoves, and enters the town of **Boulder** (see next chapter). Its most impressive feature is that it's the only road to traverse the **Waterpocket Fold**.

Details: The trail's eastern terminus is on the Notom/Bullfrog Road (see entry above), just south of the Strike Valley Overlook. Its western end is on UT 12, in Boulder. It is open year-round. (3 hours minimum)

✩ **Goblin Valley State Park**—This isolated state park unit, located 61 miles northeast of Capitol Reef National Park's eastern edge, is noted for its bizarre rock formations, shaped like mushrooms, chess pieces, spooks, and goblins. A couple of 1- to 2-mile foot trails wind through the formations. The entry road also accesses the southern section of the huge, beautiful **San Rafael Swell**.

Details: Off UT 24; (435) 564-3633. Access it via a 12-mile dirt road 23 miles south of I-17 or 22 miles north of Hanksville. Five miles along this road, you'll intersect with another road heading north (right) into the San Rafael Swell. Turn south (left) at this intersection to reach the park. The park offers a campground and restrooms. It is open year-round; $3 day-use fee. (1 hour on site)

✩ **Henry Mountains**—This impressive mountain range is located outside of but adjoining Capitol Reef National Park. Its 11,000-foot-plus summits are said to comprise the last major mountain range explored in the lower 48 states—easy to believe, considering its isolation. It features incredible views of the surrounding terrain, small creeks, and several campgrounds. Over the range slugs the rugged, 68-mile **Bull Creek Pass Backcountry Byway**, climbing from low desert slopes to above 10,500 feet. The road, closed in winter, takes 6 to 7 hours to traverse.

Details: The range and byway can be reached from Notom/Bullfrog Road, or UT 276 and UT 95 south of Hanksville. For details, contact the Bureau of Land Management, Hanksville, (435) 542-3461. (3 hours minimum)

FITNESS AND RECREATION

The main activity in this area is hiking. Thirty miles of maintained trails and 120 miles of backcountry trails (sometimes unmarked) meander along UT 24 and the Scenic Drive around Fruita. One of the most dramatic of the former is the **Capitol Gorge Trail**, a rare cut through the Capitol Reef. For many years it contained the only paved roadway across southern Utah; until 1962, when UT 12 was carved into

Fremont Canyon. Even so, at one point its walls close down to what must have been a one-lane road! The 1-mile (one-way) trail starts at the end of the Scenic Drive. The route is fairly level, passing the Pioneer Register and the characteristic natural depressions, or water pockets, of the park's southern realm.

Another popular hike is the **Grand Wash Trail**. This 2.25-mile trail runs between UT 12 and the Scenic Drive, easing pickup and dropoff, through a drainage that narrows at one point to 16 feet wide and 600 feet deep. While normally dry, this and other park canyons can present life-threatening flood conditions, so keep a careful eye on weather before entering.

The **Fremont Gorge Trail** is more strenuous, climbing 1,000 feet in 2.25 miles to a great overlook of the Fremont River Canyon. From the Fruita campground, a short walk and mild climb on the self-guiding **Fremont River Trail** yields views of the river and orchards. Another route out of the campground is **Cohab Trail**, named after the Mormon cohabitationists who hid out here from U.S. marshals attempting to enforce federal laws against polygamy.

Hickman Bridge Trail, a 1-mile moderate climb on a self-guiding nature path past Fremont Indian ruins, leads to one of the park's uncommon natural bridges, 133 wide and 125 feet high, and close-up views of the park's namesake, the all-white Capitol Dome. Hikers intending to camp in the backcountry must obtain a free permit from the visitor center.

With only the scenic drive, UT 24 and parts of the Notom/ Bullfrog Road paved among the park's 140 miles of roads, it's obviously a good place for mountain biking as well. Bikes are permitted only on roads, and can be rented in nearby Torrey, at **Wild Hare Expeditions**, (888) 304-4273.

Having a sturdy, high-clearance two-wheel-drive or four-wheel-drive vehicle is great idea in Capitol Reef, where opportunities for four-wheeling abound. In addition to routes noted in Sightseeing Highlights, the **Pleasant Creek Road** is interesting. From its terminus in the park at the end of the paved Scenic Drive, it heads southwest to the creek, where it becomes a tough four-wheel route, emerging 19 miles later at the Pleasant Creek Campground along UT 12.

If you're interested in horseback riding, several commercial stables, such as **Capitol Reef Riding Stables**, (435) 425-3960, exist in nearby Torrey. A few tour companies, such as the **Hondoo River & Trails**, (435) 425-3519 or (800) 332-2696, run jeep tours of the area as well.

FOOD

Prepared meals can be found only outside of the park—mostly in Torrey, 11 miles west of the visitor center. For inexpensive Mexican fare with an inventive twist, visit **Café Diablo**, 599 W. Main St., (435) 425-3070. The **Capitol Reef Inn** is a surprise, with good salads, home-made soups, and rainbow trout. The **Sportsman Bar & Grill**, 288 W. Main St., (435) 425-3869, serves midpriced American food daily.

LODGING

No lodging exists inside the park. East of the park's visitor center 44 miles, Hanksville hosts the **Desert Inn**, 197 E. 100 North, (435) 542-3241 or (800) 894-3242, a small, simple motel. In Torrey, 11 miles west of the visitor center, there's the **Best Western Capitol Reef Resort**, 2600 E. UT 24, (435) 425-3761 or (800) 528-1234, a grandiose name for a nice hotel that contains 20 suites, a restaurant, heated outdoor pool, spa, tennis courts, and in-room movies. Rates are $49–$125. The **Capitol Reef Inn and Café**, 360 W. Main St., Torrey, (435) 425-3271, has in-room phones, satellite movies, and a restaurant.

Area bed and breakfasts include the **SkyRidge B&B Inn**, off UT 24 just east of its intersection with UT 12, (435) 425-3222, where all rooms have private baths and some have a private hot tub and decks. Rates are $72–$102. Near Teasdale, 13 miles west of the park, is the **Cactus Hill Motel**, (800) 50-RANCH, a 100-acre property featuring a fishing pond and lambs, five rooms built in 1994, and a cabin with two bedrooms, a living room, kitchen, and bathroom with shower. Rates are $45–$65.

CAMPING

Carpeted with bluegrass, the park's **Fruita Campground** is one of the nicest in the Southwest. Its 70 sites are side by side, with 63 designed for RVs (but no hookups). If you're tent camping, look for a more private site in the walk-in area. It's open year-round on a first-come, first-served basis; $7. In the park's northern sector, the free **Cathedral Campground** maintains five tent sites. In the southern section sits the free **Cedar Mesa Campground**. Backcountry, primitive camping is allowed with a free overnight permit obtained from the visitor center.

A handful of commercial campgrounds exist in nearby towns. In

Cainville, on UT 24 about 27 miles from the park's visitor center, the **Sleepy Hollow Campground**, (435) 456-9130, has showers and a store. Tent sites are $10; with electricity, $13.

In Torrey, the **Boulder Mt. Homestead & RV Park**, 4 miles south of UT 24 on UT 12, (435) 425-3374 or (800) 769-4644, with pull-through sites and hookups, is open March through November. Downtown is the **Chuckwagon RV Park & Campground**, 12 W. Main, Torrey,(435) 425-3335, with shady level sites, full hookups, showers, a laundry, market, bakery, large pool, and spa. It's open March through November.

The 21-site campground at **Goblin Valley State Park**, (435) 564-3633 for information, (800) 322-3770 for reservations, is open year-round; amenities include restrooms and showers. The Henry Mountains' three campgrounds include **McMillan Springs** and **Lonesome Beaver**, (435) 542-3461. They're open late spring through fall and charge a low-fee, but access requires at least a high-clearance vehicle.

The Aquarius Plateau has three campgrounds along UT 12 that are terrific in the heat of summer: **Singletree**, **Pleasant Creek**, and **Oak Creek**. Singletree, 17 miles south of Torrey, has 31 sites, including some RV hookups, and toilets. They are managed by the Dixie National Forest, Teasdale, (435) 425-3702.

NIGHTLIFE

There is life after dark, in the summer anyway, in the Torrey area. The **Casual Dinner Theater**, (435) 425-3219, presents drama and dinner at a reasonable price. **Wild West Wagon Rides and Horse Show**, in Torrey, (435) 425-3710, tosses in some entertainment as well. There's also the **Hale Summer Theater**, on UT 12 in Grover, (435) 425-3589. The Park Service conducts campfire activities and talks in the Fruita Campground on summer nights.

12

GRAND STAIRCASE–ESCALANTE NATIONAL MONUMENT

In the fall of 1996, President Clinton created the largest national monument in the lower 48 states, the immense Grand Staircase–Escalante National Monument. Spanning 1.7 million acres, it dwarfs any other national park or monument in the Southwest, running from the Dixie National Forest in the north to the Arizona state line in the south and from Bryce Canyon National Park in the west to Capitol Reef National Park in the east. The new monument derives its name from the series of cliffs rising in various hued bands 6,000 feet from the Colorado to Bryce Canyon (the Grand Staircase) and the Escalante River, which heads in the Boulder Mountains and flows through a complicated canyon complex to the Colorado.

Conservationists have been calling for a regional national park since the 1930s because of the area's incredible natural beauty. Thus, the move was cheered by environmentalists, though it was fiercely opposed by many people in southern Utah as a federal land-grab; towns were divided into camps of "agin-ers" versus "for-ers." The Utah Association of Counties even filed a lawsuit to overturn the executive action. However, it seems that the monument is here to stay, and in the long run it should prove more valuable to the area than mining or other extractive land uses. ◪

GRAND STAIRCASE–ESCALANTE NATIONAL MONUMENT

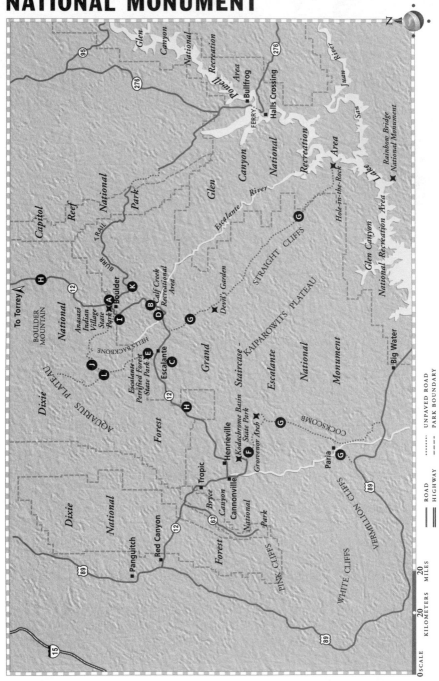

N

Glen Canyon National Recreation Area

Bullfrog

Halls Crossing

FERRY

Powell

San Juan River

Rainbow Bridge National Monument

Glen Canyon National Recreation Area

Escalante River

Glen Canyon

STRAIGHT CLIFFS

Devil's Garden

Hole-in-the-Rock

Capitol Reef National Park

BURR TRAIL National

To Torrey

BOULDER MOUNTAIN

Anasazi Indian Village State Park

Boulder

Calf Creek Recreational Area

KAIPAROWITS PLATEAU

Big Water

Dixie National Forest

HELLS BACKBONE

Escalante Petrified Forest State Park

Escalante

Grand

Staircase - Escalante

National Monument

COCKSCOMB

AQUARIUS PLATEAU

Kodachrome Basin State Park

Henrieville

Grosvenor Arch

Paria

Tropic

Cannonville

Bryce Canyon National Park

Panguitch

Red Canyon

Dixie National Forest

PINK CLIFFS

VERMILLION CLIFFS

WHITE CLIFFS

—— ROAD

········ UNPAVED ROAD

══ HIGHWAY

–––– PARK BOUNDARY

0 SCALE   20   20 MILES

20 KILOMETERS

Sights

Ⓐ Anasazi Indian Village State Park

Ⓑ Calf Creek Recreation Area

Ⓒ Daughters of the Escalante Pioneers Museum

Ⓓ Escalante Canyon

Ⓔ Escalante Petrified Forest State Park

Ⓕ Kodachrome Basin State Park

Ⓖ Scenic Backways

Ⓗ UT 12 Scenic Byway

Food

Ⓐ Burr Trail Trading Post

Ⓒ Canyon Country

Ⓒ Cowboy Blues Diner and Bakery

Ⓒ Escalante Outfitters

Ⓒ Golden Loop Café

Ⓐ Pole's Place

Lodging

Ⓘ Boulder Mt. Ranch

Ⓒ Circle D Motel

Ⓒ Padre Motel

Ⓐ Pole's Place

Ⓒ Prospector Inn

Ⓒ Quiet Falls Motel

Camping

Ⓙ Blue Spruce Campground

Ⓑ Calf Creek Recreation Area

Ⓚ Deer Creek

Ⓔ Escalante Petrified Forest State Park

Ⓕ Kodachrome Basin State Park

Ⓛ Posey Lake Campground

Ⓒ Triple S RV Park

Note: Items with the same letter are located in the same town or area.

A PERFECT DAY IN THE GRAND STAIRCASE

If you have only one day, travel UT 12 across the monument's northern edge. Stop at the Calf Creek Recreation area for a short hike, then take another brief walk at the Petrified Forest and end the day at Kodachrome Basin State Park. If you're traveling west to east, reverse this order. If you have additional time, walk into the Escalante Canyons or drive one of the scenic backways. Eat and rest in Escalante or Boulder.

SIGHTSEEING HIGHLIGHTS

★★★ **Calf Creek Recreation Area**—This creek and its canyon—a ribbon of green in a wilderness of rock—provide a great introduction to the white and tan sandstone slickrock terrain so prevalent in this region. One can wade in the creek at the recreation area, or better yet, hike the trail (2.2 miles one way) to **Lower Calf Creek Falls**, where you can swim under the 126-foot waterfall.

Details: 15 miles east of the town of Escalante right off UT 12. It is administered by the BLM, (435) 826-5499, and is open daily year-round. $2 day-use fee. (1–3 hours)

★★★ **Escalante Petrified Forest State Park**—An interpretive trail winds through this terrific park near Escalante, providing examinations of in situ 160-million-year-old petrified wood and fossilized dinosaur bones. A 1-mile hike is required to reach the prime sites, but specimens can easily be seen from the parking lot. The park's **Wide Hollow Reservoir** presents opportunities for boating, fishing, and swimming.

Details: 1 mile west of Escalante off UT 12; (435) 826-4466. Open daily year-round; day-use fee. (1–3 hours)

★★★ **Kodachrome Basin State Park**—This is one of the more appealing state parks ever, yet despite its relative proximity to Bryce Canyon National Park, it does not seem to be well known. In my last visit in August 1997, it was almost empty. The park protects a set of 67 or so geologic freaks called sandpipes, the stone columns, chimneys, and plug remnants of ancient mineral springs which once bubbled to the surface. The surrounding terrain has since eroded, leaving these hard spires, including "Big Stoney," behind. Encircling them is a cup of predominantly white, erodible earth hills several hundred feet high and banded in salmon-orange at the bottom. Elsewhere in the park are stone arches and other interesting landforms.

Details: 9 miles south of Cannonville, on the Cottonwood Canyon Scenic Backway, which is paved to the park; (435) 679-8562. Open daily year-round; $3 day-use fee. (1 to 2 hours on site)

★★★ **UT 12 Scenic Byway**—This is one of Grand Staircase–Escalante National Monument's two primary paved access roads, traversing its northern edge. Many of the monument's most popular attractions can be reached along this drive, which is a designated state scenic byway. It actually begins at Torrey and first traverses the beautiful, thickly forested **Aquarius Plateau** and the **Boulder Mountains**, before dropping down into the slickrock lowlands at the small town of **Boulder**, a pleasant farm and ranch community that is turning into one of the monument's primary gateway communities. It was the second-to-last town in the United States to receive mule-delivered mail—as late as 1935—reflecting its rock-aerie location. Here you intersect the **Burr Trail**, which cuts out of the monument and into adjoining Capitol Reef National Park.

Just west of Boulder, UT 12 slices into the first wave of an immense rock plateau of petrified sand dunes bisected by slashing slot canyons. Three miles west of Boulder, you encounter one end of the four-wheel-drive road known as **Hell's Backbone**. It makes a loop northward out of the monument, then curves back south to Escalante. The 44-mile route is one of the hairiest and most dramatic roads you'll ever cross, encircling the **Death Box Wilderness Area** on a narrow ridge with steep cliffs on both sides. It takes at least four hours to negotiate.

The main road continues west along its own exposed ridge, **The Hogback**, providing great views in all directions, then drops into Calf Creek, passing the **Calf Creek Recreation Area** (see above). Next up is a pullout and overlook of Mamie Creek, one of the many tributaries feeding into the huge, snaky **Escalante River Canyon** which bores southward from the Boulder Mountains to the Colorado River.

Next you'll see the worn-looking town of **Escalante**—or "Escalant," as the locals call it. Founded in 1876, today it's home to 850 people. You can stock up on supplies, gas, latte, and information from two visitor centers or visit the **DEP Museum** (see below). Just outside town is the **Escalante Petrified Forest State Park** (see above).

UT 12 then runs along the southern toe of the great **Aquarius Plateau,** with its pink and red **Powell Point** and **Escalante Mountains**, climbing slowly into pine forests. The road then dips southwest to the tidy green town of **Henrieville**, and **Cannonville**. The latter is becoming another major entryway for the Grand Staircase–Escalante National Monument.

The highway wraps north here, running through the prosperous tourism and farming town of **Tropic**, known for its unusually warm winter weather. Here it leaves the monument but continues to **Bryce Canyon National Park**, **Red Canyon**, and finally, its terminus near

Panguitch at US 89. It's quite a stretch of highway, one of the more scenic in the country.

Details: For additional information, contact the Interagency Information Office, 755 W. Main, Escalante,(435) 826-5499; or the Garfield County Travel Council, in the middle of Escalante, (800) 444-6689. The road is open year-round, although the stretch over the Aquarius Plateau sometimes closes temporarily. (4 to 5 hours with brief stops)

★★ **Anasazi Indian Village State Park**—This fine modern museum focuses on the history and lives of the remarkable Indian culture that occupied the northern half of the Southwest for centuries, the Anasazi (see Why Visit the American Southwest? for details). The park adjoins a Kayenta Anasazi village, the Coombs Site, abandoned circa A.D. 1200, which, with 87 rooms, is the largest Anasazi site yet found west of the Colorado River. A self-guiding walk, museum displays (including a diorama), and a life-size six-room replica structure give you a good sense of this long-departed civilization. A picnic area adjoins the site.

Details: On the north edge of town on UT 12; (435) 335-7308. Open May 16 through September 15 daily 8–6, September 16 through May 15 8–5. Admission is $2 for adults; $1 for kids 7–15. (1 to 2 hours)

★★ **Scenic Backways**—If the weather is good and you have the proper vehicle, the huge Grand Staircase–Escalante National Monument presents some of the best off-pavement driving in the nation. A slew of officially designated state scenic backways weave through great landscapes, including the following.

Hole-in-the-Rock Scenic Backway rolls southeast from the Escalante area along the eastern face of the **Kaiparowits Plateau** to overlooks of Lake Powell, roughly tracing the route Mormon pioneers blazed in their 1880 effort to settle southeast Utah. It ends at famous **Hole-in-the-Rock**, where the Mormons were forced to blast and hammer a wagon path through a slot canyon, then lower their wagons with ropes over otherwise impassable cliffs. (See Lake Powell chapter for further details.) The road also accesses the **Devil's Rock Garden**, close-up views of the **Straight Cliffs**, and other prominent landmarks. It begins 5 miles east of Escalante on UT 12 and runs 56 miles southeast, where it dead-ends. The last 5 miles require a high-clearance vehicle, but a passenger car can handle it up to there in good weather. A round trip takes six hours.

Cottonwood Canyon Scenic Backway plows 49 miles from Cannonville on the western border of the monument southward to US 89 west of Big Water. The first 9 miles to **Kodachrome Basin State Park** are paved; it then becomes a graded, dry-weather road. Along its course it passes a short spur road to the acclaimed **Grosvenor Arch**, which is named after *National Geographic*'s first full-time editor. It then climbs up and over **The Cockscomb**, skirting the edge of the fantastic **Paria River Canyon**. It takes two hours to traverse, one way.

Located along the southern fringe of the monument, the 5-mile **Paria River Valley Scenic Backway** accesses some interesting historical sites: the ghost town of **Pahreah**, and the Paria movie set, where Wayne, Eastwood, and Peck once worked. The graded road dead-ends at Pahreah, and can be negotiated by a passenger car in good weather. It leaves US 89 just east of Sand Gulch where the highway makes a huge horseshoe bend, 30 miles east of Kanab. It's administered by the BLM, Kanab, (435) 644-2672.

Details: Current weather information and other traveler assistance is available from the Escalante Interagency Office, 755 W. Main, in Escalante; (435) 826-5499. These scenic backways are open year-round, weather permitting. Carry water. (2 hours minimum)

✯ **Canyons of the Escalante**—Several drainages funnel the waters of the Aquarius Plateau's southern flanks and huge expanses of exposed rock at its base into the Escalante River, creating a major canyon complex that drops toward the Colorado River some 90 miles away. A pullout on UT 12 overlooking **Mamie Creek**, 14 miles east of the town of Escalante, offers a great view of the upper canyon. The Hole-in-the-Rock Scenic Backway (see above) provides more remote access to the lower canyon sections, where arches, Anasazi ruins, and petroglyphs are found.

Details: Park to the sides of the bridge on UT 12 over the Escalante River, and hike up or down the canyon. Free. (2 hours minimum)

✯ **Daughters of the Escalante Pioneers (DEP) Museum**—This small museum may interest history and sociology fans of pioneer gear, photos, personal memorabilia, and other materials related to Escalante's Mormon settlers.

Details: 102 W. Main, Escalante; (435) 826-4448. Open by appointment only. (30 minutes)

FITNESS AND RECREATION

Many horseback-riding opportunities exist here. Stables and guides (and stagecoach rides!) are located in **Kodachrome Basin State Park**, (435) 679-8536, and in the towns of Escalante and Boulder. The **Boulder Mt. Ranch**, (435) 335-7480, offers a "no-pansy daylong outing" with lunch for $125. Kodachrome is also noted for its mountain-biking terrain, but the monument's many dirt and gravel roads also create terrific biking possibilities areawide. Snowmobiling is popular in the high elevations, north of Boulder and Escalante. This is also prime terrain for cross-country skiing and fishing—particularly popular is **Posey Lake**.

Hiking is the major pastime among visitors. The favorite hiking locales, though still often vacant, are the **Canyons of the Escalante**. Hikers can access them from 15 miles east of Escalante, at the Calf Creek Recreation Area and bridge-crossing on UT 12. The canyon can also be reached from several other points along the Hole-in-the-Rock Scenic Backway (see Sightseeing Highlights). It's open year-round but extremely hot in summer and subject to flash flooding. Because the "trail" in the main canyon often is submerged by the waterway, some canyoneers carry inflatable air mattresses to ferry their packs across deep water. Plenty of terrain exists for off-trail hiking along the monument's scenic backways, if you know what you're doing. Overnight hiking permits are required. For details, call (435) 826-5499.

FOOD

Bring your frying pan, since the dining choices are on the thin side in the monument. In Escalante, **Cowboy Blues Diner and Bakery**, 530 W. Main St., (435) 826-4251, prepares decent meals and baked goods. There's also the simple but adequate **Golden Loop Café**, 39 W. Main St., (435) 826-4433. **Canyon Country**, on UT 12, (435) 826-4259, open daily 6 a.m.–10 p.m., has hot dogs, pizza, coffee, soft ice cream, and grocery items. **Escalante Outfitters**, 310 W. Main, (435) 826-4266, has some surprisingly good pizza, cold draft beer, latte, and coffee—as well as a state liquor outlet, camping supplies, and showers.

Boulder also has a few possibilities. Last time through, we had some tasty cheeseburgers, sandwiches, real lemonade, soft-serve ice cream, and good onion rings at **Pole's Place**, across from the Anasazi State Park, on UT 12 on the north side of town, (435) 335-7422. The

Burr Trail Trading Post, at the intersection of UT 12 and the Burr Trail, has a good café that opens early and closes fairly late.

LODGING

Few options exist in or near the vast monument. In Escalante, there's the modest **Quiet Falls Motel**, 75 S. 100 West, (435) 826-4250, with some kitchenettes, $35; the **Padre Motel**, 20 E. Main St., (435) 826-4276, $38; and the **Circle D Motel**, 475 W. Main St, (435) 826-4297, which has 29 rooms with cable TV and AC at $45, plus a restaurant serving three squares a day.

A bit higher up the comfort chain is the **Prospector Inn**, 380 W. Main St., (435) 826-4653, with room service from a nearby diner and a free Continental breakfast. Rates are $55.

In Boulder, **Pole's Place**, across UT 12 from Anasazi State Park, (435) 335-7422, has a handful of clean, relatively new motel rooms and a gift shop. Rates are $40–$50. The **Boulder Mt. Ranch**, 7 miles from Boulder on Hell's Backbone Road, (435) 335-7460 or (800) 556-3446, offers seclusion and a fabulous setting. Its 20 units, including a suite, range from $70–$135. Its restaurant, Hell's Backbone Grill, is open for breakfast and dinner.

CAMPING

The Escalante area has many choices for camping, among them **Escalante Petrified Forest State Park**, 1 mile west of town off UT 12, (435) 826-4466 for information, (800) 322-3770 for reservations. It's open year-round with 22 sites (no hookups), a visitor center, restrooms with hot pay showers, fishing, and swimming; $9. The **Calf Creek Recreation Area**, 15 miles east of Escalante along UT 12, has 13 $5 sites with water but no showers, on a first-come, first-served basis. Nearby, off the Burr Trail, is **Deer Creek**, with only four sites. Both are run by the BLM, (435) 826-5499, and open March 1 through October 30.

In the heat of summer, retreat to ground in the mountains north of Escalante, including **Posey Lake Campground**, with 23 sites for $5; and **Blue Spruce Campground**, with six sites at $5. Both are run by the Dixie National Forest, (435) 826-5499.

Kodachrome Basin State Park maintains a nice campground 9 miles south of Cannonville on Cottonwood Canyon Scenic Backway road (paved to park); (435) 679-8562 for information, (800) 322-3770 for reservations. Open all year, it has 24 $9 sites (#21 is prime, #21A is good), with drinking water, pay hot showers, and firewood.

You can also camp primitively throughout most of the monument if you follow certain regulations. For details, contact the Interagency Information Office, (435) 826-5499. RVs can head to the **Triple S RV Park**, 495 W. Main St., Escalante, (435) 826-4959, with showers, laundry, and 30 sites ranging $10–$14.

NIGHTLIFE

Howling coyotes.

13

BRYCE CANYON AREA

Scottish immigrant Ebenezer Bryce and his family homesteaded in a canyon feeding into the Paria Valley in 1875. He was one of the first to explore the area now named after him, Bryce Canyon, one of the most popular national parks in the Southwest. A practical man, he assessed the incredible maze of odd earthen and rock formations that the park is so famous for by saying, "It's a hell of a place to lose a cow."

Visitors today don't have to be concerned about such mundane details and can instead appreciate Bryce's unique geologic splendors, which have been protected as national parkland since 1924. The canyon's name, however, is something of a misnomer: it is actually the eroding edge of the Paunsaugunt Plateau, and its bowl shape is technically a 56-square-mile amphitheater that drops to the Paria Valley to the east. My son Travis says it looks like the insides of an ant pile.

The canyon's easily accessible rim, paralleled by a paved road, provides wonderful bird's-eye views of its hundreds of thousands of multicolored spires and columns, or hoodoos, standing like an army of sentinels awaiting their marching orders. While rim views are terrific, even a brief walk down one of the many trails into the formations will greatly enrich your visit—and remove you from the traffic jams that clog the major viewpoint parking areas. And while most folks speed in and out of Bryce and onto other destinations, nearby are a few other notable attractions that receive a fraction of national park visitors' attention. ◣

BRYCE CANYON AREA

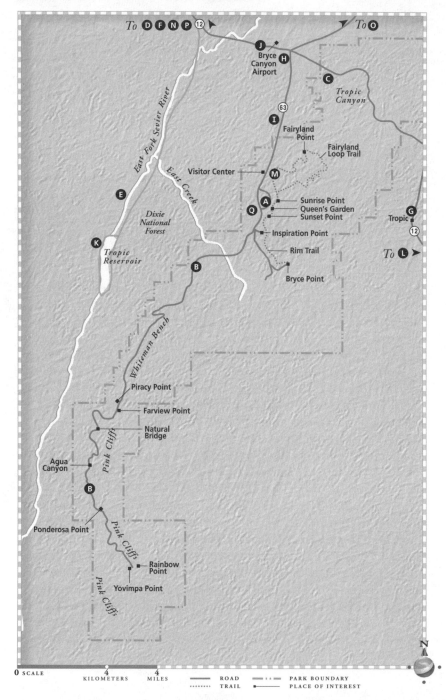

To **D** **F** **N** **P** ⑫

To **O**

J Bryce Canyon Airport **H**

C

Tropic Canyon

East Fork Sevier River

63

I Fairland Point

Fairyland Loop Trail

Visitor Center **M**

East Creek

E

Dixie National Forest

Q **A** ■ Sunrise Point
■ Queen's Garden
■ Sunset Point

G ■ *Tropic*

⑫

K *Tropic Reservoir*

■ Inspiration Point

■ Rim Trail

To **L**

B

■ Bryce Point

Whiteman Bench

■ Piracy Point

■ Farview Point

■ Natural Bridge

Pink Cliffs

Agua Canyon ■

B

■ Ponderosa Point

Pink Cliffs

■ Rainbow Point

Pink Cliffs

■ Yovimpa Point

Pink Cliffs

N

0 SCALE   4   4
        KILOMETERS   MILES

—— ROAD   ▪ ▪ ▪ PARK BOUNDARY
········· TRAIL   ■—■ PLACE OF INTEREST

Sights

Ⓐ Bryce Canyon Lodge

Ⓑ Bryce Canyon National Park Rim Drive

Ⓒ Mossy Cave and Waterfall

Ⓓ Red Canyon

Ⓔ Sevier Backcountry Byway

Food

Ⓐ Bryce Canyon Lodge

Ⓕ Cowboy's Smoke House Café

Ⓖ Doug's

Ⓗ Foster's Motel and Restaurant

Ⓖ Hungry Coyote

Ⓘ Ruby's Inn Restaurant and Steakhouse

Lodging

Ⓐ Bryce Canyon Lodge

Ⓖ Bryce Valley Inn

Lodging (continued)

Ⓖ Doug's

Ⓖ Francisco's B&B

Ⓘ Ruby's Inn

Camping

Ⓙ Bryce Canyon Pines

Ⓚ King Creek Campground

Ⓛ Kodachrome Basin State Park

Ⓜ North Campground

Ⓝ Panguitch Lake

Ⓞ Pine Lake Campground

Ⓓ Red Canyon Campground

Ⓗ Red Canyon RV Park

Ⓟ Riverside Motel and Campground

Ⓘ Ruby's Inn

Ⓠ Sunset Campground

Ⓝ White Bridge

Note: Items with the same letter are located in the same town or area.

A PERFECT DAY IN THE BRYCE CANYON AREA

Begin the day cruising the canyon's Rim Drive, stopping at various scenic points to differing views of its scupted face. If you don't take a picnic, have lunch at the Bryce Canyon Lodge. Take at least a short hike on a trail beneath the rim, such as the Navajo Loop Trail to the Wall Street formation. End the day with some time in Red Rock Canyon or a drive on the Sevier Backcountry Byway. For a good dinner outside the park, try Cowboy's Smoke House.

SIGHTSEEING HIGHLIGHTS

★★★ **Bryce Canyon Rim Drive**—This paved road runs from one end of the 36,010-acre park to the other parallel to the edge of the plateau. It provides easy access to 13 major viewpoints, each offering a different perspective on the dazzling eroded formations lying beneath the rim.

Consider driving as far south as you desire on the Rim Drive, then turning around and beginning to make stops. This way all the viewpoints are on your right, avoiding turns across the busy road.

Many visitors pass by **Fairyland Point**, the northernmost rim viewpoint, as its access road is just inside the park's boundary. However, its views rival any in the park, and are highlighted by the **Sinking Ship** formation as well as the distant Aquarius Plateau and, on clear days, Navajo Mountain.

Sunrise, **Sunset**, **Inspiration**, and **Bryce Points** (listed from north to south) edge the park's largest single amphitheater, offering the classic views of the park. Many of the park's more well-traveled hiking trails begin at these points (see Fitness and Recreation, below).

Continuing south the plateau climbs slowly, and by **Farview Point** you are surrounded by spruce-and-fir forest. In clear weather you can see the **Kaibab Plateau**, 90 miles away on the north rim of the Grand Canyon. At the very end of the road lie **Yovimpa** and **Rainbow Points**, with more hoodoos and distant vistas, and trailheads for several other backcountry excursions, including a short walk to an ancient bristlecone pine forest containing trees more than 1,700 years old.

Details: Just south of UT 12, 7.6 miles west of Tropic, and 13.5 miles east of US 89. Its access road is UT 63, which becomes the scenic Rim Drive. The park is open daily year-round. Its visitor center is on UT 63, at the north end of the park. Open daily 8:30–4:30, with extended summer hours, it has a nice museum, a running slide show, a bookstore, and a gift shop. Day visitors cannot take trailers beyond Sunset Campground; they must be parked at the visitor center or Sunset Point parking lot.

Because of its high elevation—more than 9,000 feet at points—Bryce is cooler than many of the Southwest's national parks, though it can record temperatures in the 90s in July and August. Winter brings beautiful snowfalls. Day-use entry fee is $10 per vehicle. (3 to 8 hours)

★★ **Mossy Cave and Waterfall**—Approaching Bryce from the east along UT 12, the first of its fantastic earthen and rock formations

© Daniel B. Gibson

Bryce Canyon National Park

appears at the foot of the Paunsaugunt Plateau at this site. In a reverse of the usual Bryce experience, you walk *uphill* to view this canyon's attractions, which include the well-named Mossy Cave and a waterfall. You'll rarely encounter anyone here, a bonus to its lovely setting.

Details: The trailhead is located alongside UT 12, at a marked site 3 miles east of the UT 63/UT 12 juncture, 4.5 miles northwest of Tropic; (435) 834-5322. Open daily year-round. Free. (1 hour)

★★ **Red Canyon**—I hadn't heard of this spot until a recent trip, yet it is as interesting and lovely as the Southwest's other renowned attractions. Its vermilion rock formations dotted with stands of stately ponderosa pines are exceptionally scenic. UT 12 runs right through its primary canyon and a tunnel or two, but side roads and trails provide a much better look. **Birds Eye Trail**, less than 1 mile, is a good start, and 3-mile **Losee Canyon Trail** offers a more in-depth view.

Details: On either side of UT 12 midway between US 89 and UT 63, the entrance roadto Bryce. Its trails are open daily year-round. A visitor center is open daily from Memorial Day to Labor Day. Free. (2 hours minimum)

★ **Bryce Canyon Lodge**—This handsome stone-and-timber multistory structure was built in 1924 by Gilbert Stanley Underwood. It's a classic example of National Park–style architecture, like the El Tovar, the Grand Canyon Lodge, and the lodges at Yellowstone and Yosemite. This National Historic Landmark is surrounded by a cluster of attractive stone-and-log guest cabins. Nonpaying visitors can stroll through the building or have a meal and a drink here.

Details: Near Sunset Point, off the Rim Drive just south of the visitor center; (435) 834-5361. (15 minutes)

★ **Sevier Scenic Backcountry Byway**—This scenic byway runs 30 miles south along the west face of the Paunsaugunt Plateau—the east face Bryce Canyon is slowly eroding. Thus, the terrain greatly resembles Bryce's—without the crowds. The gravel road, suitable for passenger cars in good weather, reaches **Tropic Reservoir** after 7 miles. Abundant wildlife is often spotted along its path, including pronghorn antelope, elk, mule deer, and prairie dogs.

Details: The head of the road is on UT 12, about 4 miles west of its intersection with the Bryce access road, UT 63. (2 to 3 hours minimum)

FITNESS AND RECREATION

Bryce has more than 60 miles of maintained hiking trails, from simple and short to multi-day outing routes. With hundreds of thousands of people congregating on the rim, even a short walk to get down among the striking formations is highly recommended. Remember, though, on all but the Rim Trail, you begin by going down. Don't exhaust yourself; you'll have to climb up at the end!

Here are some hiking options. Most popular is the **Rim Trail**, which traces a path along the dramatic edge of the amphitheaters. Its total distance is 11 miles, with an altitude gain of 550 feet, but it can be accessed at a number of viewpoints, allowing for even shorter strolls. The section between Sunset and Sunrise Points is paved and fairly level. **Queen's Garden Trail** is considered the easiest route for descending below the rim. The 1.8-mile round trip drops 320 feet, passing wind- and erosion-carved portals in various rock formations that frame views of Queen Victoria and her "garden."

My choice for a quick dip below the rim is **Navajo Loop**. Dropping over the rim at Sunset Point, it switchbacks down a steep incline through a fantastic cleft named **Wall Street**, where a lone pine tree struggles upward toward the faint light above. You don't have to complete the entire 1.4-mile and 521-foot descent loop trail, but can instead retrace your route after the 15-minute walk to Wall Street. The loop also provides close-up views of **Thor's Hammer**, one of the park's signature formations.

At the south end of the Rim Drive, at Rainbow Point, is **Bristlecone Pine Trail**. The 1-mile round-trip route descends 100 feet to an exposed cliff where ancient bristlecone pines cling to survival. For those seeking longer hikes, the 23-mile **Under-the-Rim Trail** runs from Bryce Point to Rainbow Point. Overnight backcountry hiking requires a $5 permit, issued at the visitor center until two hours before sunset.

Horseback and trail rides are popular at Bryce, including two-hour, half-day and full-day outings, conducted April through October. For details, contact **Canyon Trail Rides**, (435) 834-5500 or (435) 679-8665 for advance reservations. Biking is restricted to paved roads, but is allowed on the extensive trail system at nearby **Red Canyon** (435) 676-2690. There is no fishing within Bryce, but it's available at the **Tropic Reservoir** (see Sightseeing Highlights), on the Markagunt Plateau's **Panguitch Lake** (west of the town of Panguitch on UT 143), and at points along the **Sevier River** and its headwaters.

The park area is also becoming an increasingly popular winter destination. Cross-country skiing along the park rim becomes dramatic when the formations are draped in snow, accentuating their already fantastic forms. Skiers also enjoy the mile-long spur road to **Fairyland Point**, which is not plowed in winter. Cross-country rental equipment is available at the **Ruby's Inn** complex just outside the park, (435) 834-5341. Nordic skiers and snowmobilers also enjoy the Forest Service roads to the north of UT 12, the many trails of **Red Canyon**, and the Sevier Backcountry Byway near Tropic Reservoir.

Off-road vehicles and four-wheelers also have room to roam in the area, though not in the national park. Red Canyon's **Castro Canyon Trail** is designated for ORV use, and forest roads off the Sevier Scenic Byway are also suitable, as is the 50-mile **Fremont Trail** from Circleville to Tropic Reservoir. For details on all area recreation opportunities, call the Garfield Country Travel Office, (800) 444-6689.

FOOD

The **Bryce Canyon Lodge** serves three meals a day in its rustic and wonderful old quarters, off the Rim Drive by Sunset Point, (435) 834-5361. It also houses a bar—rare in these parts. Just outside the park entrance is **Ruby's Inn Restaurant and Steakhouse**, (435) 834-5341, with breakfast, lunch, and dinner, plus a deli. **Foster's Motel and Restaurant**, on UT 12 a few miles east of the park entrance, (435) 834-5227, is another option.

In Tropic, try **Doug's**, 141 Main, (435) 679-8633, with good homemade soups and pies, salad bar, daily specials, trout, and char-broiled steaks. Also in Tropic is the **Hungry Coyote**, at the Bryce Valley Inn on Main Street, (435) 679-8811, with modestly priced American and Mexican food. Some 24 miles to the west of the park, in Panguitch, is a notable joint, **Cowboy's Smoke House Café**, 95 N. Main St., (435) 676-8030, which slow-smokes ribs, chicken, brisket, and turkey over pecan, oak, hickory, and mesquite woods for some delicious eatin'. It's closed in January and February and on Sunday year-round.

LODGING

By far the choicest lodging (in fact, the only lodging) within the park is the classic **Bryce Canyon Lodge**, just off the rim drive near the visitor center and Sunset Point; (435) 834-5361 for information, (303) 297-2757 for reservations. It's open April through October. The handsome structure dates to 1924. It is surrounded by stone-and-log guest cabins that rent for $70–$120.

Ruby's Inn, (435) 834-5341, about a mile south of the park entrance, is an assembly-line hotel, campground, restaurant, and souvenir-laden "Western" town. Summer rates are in the $80s; family suites, $120.

Ten miles from the park entrance in Tropic is the **Bryce Valley Inn** on Main Street, (435) 679-8811 or (800) 442-1890, with 65 rooms at $64–$89 and a restaurant with a liquor license. Also in Tropic is **Doug's**, 141 N. Main, (435) 679-8600 or (800) 993-6847, with 28 motel rooms at $25, a hot tub, and AC; and **Francisco's B&B**, (435) 679-8721, with three rooms on a working farm owned by Charlie Francisco, a retired horse wrangler at Bryce. Rates are $50–$75.

CAMPING

The park maintains **Sunset** and **North Campgrounds**, with a total of 216 $10 sites (none have hookups), drinking water, and restrooms. They're open year-round on a first-come, first-served basis. The General Store, near the Sunrise Point parking lot, has a laundry and showers.

Overnight backcountry camping along the Under-the-Rim and Riggs Spring Trails is allowed in designated sites but requires a $5 permit, issued at the visitor center up to two hours before sunset. Backcountry campfires are not permitted.

Outside of the park are a number of options. My pick (except in the worst heat of summer) is **Kodachrome Basin State Park** (see previous chapter), a 30-minute drive away. A bit closer is **Red Canyon Campground**, on UT 12 west of the park, in Red Canyon, (435) 676-2690, which has showers and a playground; it's open March through October. Just outside the park entrance is the **Ruby's Inn** complex, (435) 834-5341, which includes 200 campsites open April through October; $14.

Summer options at higher elevations include **King Creek Campground**, on the western shore of Tropic Reservoir (see Sightseeing Highlights), and **Pine Lake Campground**, 20 miles north of the park (take Forest Road 16 at the intersection of UT 63 and UT 12 to Forest Road 132, a gravel and dirt road). About an hour away are campgrounds in the Markagunt Plateau off UT 143, including one at **White Bridge** and two at **Panguitch Lake**. Campgrounds listed in this paragraph are supervised by the Dixie National Forest, (435) 676-8815, with fees from $5–$7.

RVers have a couple of handy choices. Just outside the park entrance is **Bryce Canyon Pines**, on UT 12 only six minutes east of the park entrance, (435) 834-5411 or (800) 88-BRYCE, with RV and tent camping and a motel, open April through October; $9–$15. Just east of the intersection of US 89 and UT 12 is **Red Canyon RV Park**, (435) 676-2690, with hot showers, full hookups, a convenience store, and some cabins. South on UT 89, 24 miles from Bryce, is the **Riverside Motel and Campground**, on UT 89 a mile north of Hatch. Amenities include full hookups for $15, tent sites for $12, hot showers, a playground, pool, laundry, game room, eight nice motel rooms, and a restaurant open 8 a.m.–10 p.m.

NIGHTLIFE

Slide shows and talks are held nightly during summer at the campground amphitheaters and visitor center. Occasionally, astronomers lead stargazing with telescopes, as well. Summer also brings the nightly **Bryce Canyon Country Rodeo**, held at the Ruby's Inn compound, just outside the park entrance.

14

ZION NATIONAL PARK AREA

When Mormon pioneer Isaac Behunin laid eyes on the 2,000- to 3,000-foot-high polished rock walls surrounding the North Fork of the Virgin River, he was moved to write, "These great mountains are natural temples of God. We can worship here as well as in the manmade temples." He compared it to the Heavenly City of God, or Zion, and thus this awesome realm of rock was named. Others followed him and were also moved by the area, which became Utah's first national monument in 1909, one year after the Grand Canyon received national monument status.

Today Utah's most-visited park encompasses 147,035 acres but most see it as a drive-by, since paved roads wend close to many of its most spectacular features. In summer, you will run into traffic jams near popular points and maxed-out parking lots. A bike is a great idea here, as is hiking. With a short walk you'll leave behind 98 percent of the other visitors—2.5 million strong in 1996!—and open entirely new vistas not seen from the bottoms of the park's deep canyons.

The southern gates of Zion mark a major transition from the Colorado Plateau. West lies the tough Great Basin Desert and southwest the desolate Mohave Desert—the lowest and hottest sector of this region. History buffs should check out the attractive winter house of Mormon leader Brigham Young in Georgetown and walk the streets of Silver Reef, a ghost town. While tourists are not common outside Zion, some visitors have discovered the area's attractions; its major city, Georgetown, is Utah's fastest-growing community. ◣

ZION NATIONAL PARK AREA

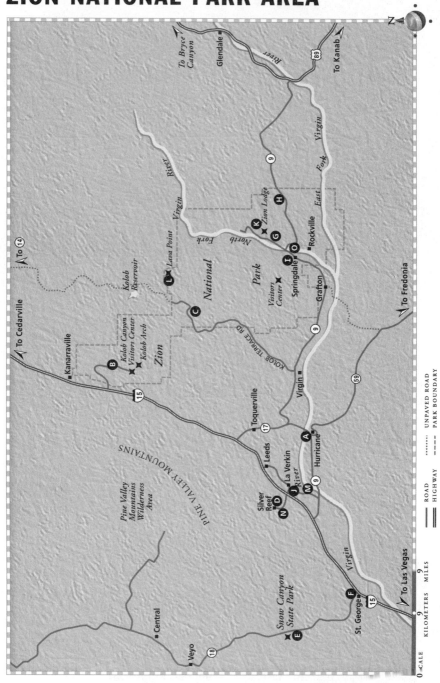

Sights

Ⓐ Hurricane

Ⓑ Kolob Canyons Road

Ⓒ Kolob Terrace Road

Ⓓ Silver Reef Ghost Town

Ⓔ Snow Canyon State Park

Ⓕ St. George

Ⓖ Zion Canyon Scenic Drive

Ⓗ Zion–Mt. Carmel Highway

Food

Ⓘ Bit and Spur Saloon

Ⓕ Ernesto's

Ⓐ Grandma Bishop's

Ⓙ Los Gringos

Ⓕ Pizza Noodle

Ⓚ Zion Lodge

Lodging

Ⓘ Cliffrose Lodge

Ⓕ Dixie Palm Motel

Ⓘ Harvest House

Lodging (continued)

Ⓘ O'Toole's

Ⓘ Pioneer Lodge

Ⓕ Seven Wives Inn

Ⓘ Snow Family Guest Ranch

Ⓘ Under the Eaves Guest House

Ⓚ Zion Lodge

Ⓘ Zion Park Inn

Camping

Ⓐ Canyons RV Resort

Ⓛ Lava Point

Ⓜ Quail Creek State Park Campground

Ⓝ Red Cliffs Campground

Ⓕ St. George Campground & RV Park

Ⓕ Settlers RV Park

Ⓔ Snow Canyon State Park Campground

Ⓞ South Campground

Ⓞ Watchman Campground

Ⓘ Zion Canyon Campground

Note: Items with the same letter are located in the same town or area.

A PERFECT DAY IN THE ZION NATIONAL PARK AREA

With summer temperatures occasionally hitting 110, Zion is at its best in fall and spring. If you only have a day, spend it all in Zion National Park. If possible, enter through the East Highway (UT 9), which makes for a dramatic arrival. Head up the park's scenic drive along the Virgin River. Have lunch at the Zion Lodge or in nearby Springdale. At some point, take a walk—early in the day during summer! Or if you seek more solitude, drive the Kolob Terrace Road and do some hiking. Stay in one Springdale's excellent bed-and-breakfasts.

SIGHTSEEING HIGHLIGHTS

✮✮✮ **Zion Canyon Scenic Drive**—This is what most people see of Zion, craning their necks in their cars as they roll by to get a peek at some of the world's most stupendous cliffs, pinnacles, buttresses, and stone columns. The dead-end 6-mile road parallels the North Fork of the Virgin River, which, over the course of 13 million years, has dissected a massive stone plateau into an astounding array of colossal forms. Light filters through the cottonwood, willow, and velvet ash trees lining the waterway's banks, providing shaded walking, picnicking, or wading. Pullouts and parking areas allow you to stop and savor the views or embark on short (or long) hikes.

The only way to enter the canyon is from the south. The scenic drive heads due north, crosses the river, and passes the **Court of the Patriarchs**—Abraham, Isaac, and Jacob—and **Mountains of the Sun**. A parking area and 200-yard trail provide excellent views of them. Next up is the **Zion Lodge**, center of many organized park activities. In a canyon across the river from the lodge is the lovely **Emerald Pools**, where water pours off a lip into a green oasis. A few minutes up the road is one of the park's most famous landmarks, the **Great White Throne**, but you'll have a better view of it on the return drive.

Approaching the end of the road, you pass another popular and beautiful spot, **Weeping Rock**, where water seeps and drips off a huge ledge, creating a greenhouse effect. The last site is the **Temple of Sinawava**, from which the road has a turnaround loop. Here, hikers depart on the demanding but rewarding outing up **The Narrows** river section. Heading back down, you'll spot incredible formations that were hidden on your way up, such as the beautiful **Angel's Landing**, perhaps my favorite among the pantheon of possibilities.

With some 2,000 vehicles a day on this road, vying for the 400 designated parking spots can be exasperating. However, authorities are planning to implement a park-and-shuttle system in 1999, run from the town of Springdale and the visitor center at the park's south entrance. A commercial shuttle service within the park already exists (see Details).

Details: The park is open daily all year. The main visitor center is located at the South Entrance to the park, on UT 9, Springdale; (435) 772-3256. It is open daily—in summer 8–9, in spring and fall 8–7, and in winter 9–5. Bus and RV parking (vehicles more than 21 feet long) is not allowed at Weeping Rock or the Temple of Sinawava during peak periods. Shuttle service to these and other Scenic Drive points ($3 adults, $2 children under 12) operates out of the Zion Lodge, (435) 772-3213, every hour on the hour in summer. Park admission, collected at either the South or East Entrance, is $10 per vehicle. (1 to 2 hours)

★★★ **Zion–Mt. Carmel Highway (UT 9)**—This road makes a most dramatic entry to the park from the east. Huge sheets of petrified sand dunes now cut by clefts and waterways into classic slickrock terrain set the initial scene, including one of the park's more renowned landmarks, **Checkerboard Mesa**, with its crosshatched surface. Next the road cuts into a short tunnel, only to emerge briefly before diving back into a remarkable 1.1-mile tunnel blasted and chipped out of solid rock in the 1930s. To avoid hauling the broken rock all the way out the tunnel, five holes were cut in one side over deep Pine Creek Canyon, where it was dumped. These "windows" provide incredibly tantalizing glimpses (stopping in the tunnel is forbidden) of the wonderful rock-peak panoramas that lie ahead in Zion's central district. Emerging from the tunnel, one is immediately taken by the grand form of the **Great Arch**, which is really an arch in the making. The road then switchbacks down a 6-percent grade into Zion Canyon, where it intersects with the Zion Canyon Scenic Drive.

Details: Vehicles more than 94 inches in width or 132 inches high (including those bikes on the roof) are subject to traffic regulation at the Zion-Mt. Carmel Tunnel. From November to mid-March, such vehicles must arrange a park escort in advance at the East or South Entrance Stations, or by calling (435) 772-3256. From mid-March to October, escorts are available at the tunnel 8–8 daily. There is a fee of at least $10. (30 minutes' drive time)

★★ **Kolob Canyons Road**—Located to the northwest of the park's major attraction is another beautiful park section that sees a fraction of the visitors found along the Scenic Drive. Deep red canyons that radiate like fingers of a hand and the park's huge **Kolob Arch**, measuring 310 feet in length, are highlights.

Details: A 5-mile-long paved road winds into this area, reached via I-15 at Exit 40, 13 miles north of the juncture of UT 17 and I-15. There is a visitor center and bookstore on the Kolob Canyons Road; (435) 586-9548. It is open year-round, issuing overnight hiking permits and providing information, maps, and other services. (1 hour to several days)

★★ **St. George**—The leading city of southwestern Utah—home to Dixie College, the Washington County seat, a major medical center, a symphony orchestra, seven golf courses, and a booming retirement community—has an interesting history. In the 1860s Brigham Young, Mormon prophet and leader, sent settlers into this corner of Utah to grow cotton and other essential food stocks for the budding Mormon empire. Its balmy climate and southern locale led to the area's nickname of "Dixie." Young named the small colony after one of his most faithful followers, George A. Smith, whose good works included delivering fresh potatoes to hungry Mormon parties traveling across Utah.

Among the highlights of its three-block historic district is the **Brigham Young Winter Home**, 89 W. 200 North, (435) 673-2517, a simple but fairly large, attractive, and comfortable house built from 1869–1873, where he went to alleviate his rheumatism. Free tours are conducted daily 9 a.m. to dusk. Just a few blocks away is **St. George Temple**, 440 S. 300 East, (435) 673-5181, the oldest Mormon temple in use today. Although ground was broken on it in 1871, the site proved difficult, and it took 13 years to complete, with the foundations sinking on three corners. Undaunted, Young ordered his men to stabilize it by blasting rock into the muddy earth with a 1,000-pound cannon —which had been used, incidentally, by Napoleon in his siege of Moscow. The cannon is on display in the temple gardens. You can't tour the temple's interior, but its interesting visitor center is open daily 9 to 9.

Also in the area is the **Pioneer Museum**, 135 N. 100 East, (435) 628-7274, housed in an attractive brick building erected in 1938. It houses frontier-era relics, including a dress made of locally produced silk. The historic district also features a jail, an opera house, lovely old homes, the county courthouse, two schools, and some stores.

Details: The historic district is located around St. George Boulevard to the west of I-15. A walking map is available from the Pioneer Museum. Not all sites are open to the public. (1 to 3 hours)

✴ **Hurricane**—This pretty, quiet farming and fruit-growing community 25 miles southwest of Zion has a lot going for it. Its 6,500 residents are friendly, the climate is good, and the pace is easy. Visitors might enjoy a stop at its **Hurricane Valley Pioneer Heritage Park and Museum**, 35 W. State St., (435) 635-3245. In this handsome, WPA-built, sandstone building, you can look over artifacts and documents related to the construction of an amazing irrigation canal built by all-volunteer labor between 1893 and 1906, which brought prosperity to the area. The museum is chock-full of photos and odds and ends of early life in the valley, with one room devoted to Southwestern Indian relics. Outside, a nice park features wagons, farming tools, and other materials. Across the street is an annex containing a re-created pioneer doctor's office, a restored barn and corral, and a blacksmith's shop.

Details: The museum is open in winter Monday through Saturday 10–5, and in summer 10–6. Admission is by donation. (1 hour)

✴ **Kolob Terrace Road**—Another beautiful drive to a more remote northwestern section of the park overlooks the white and salmon-colored cliffs of the Left and Right Forks of North Creek. Stands of aspen, fir, and pine are found atop **Lava Point**. The 21.5-mile road to Lava Point is paved most of the way, with a short stretch of gravel. It then turns to dirt as it continues north out of the park to a distant junction with UT 14 near Cedar City. Passenger cars should turn around at this point.

Details: Off UT 9 in the town of Virgin, about 18 miles from the Visitor Center. Snows often close this road from late November through April. Admission is free. (1 to 2 hours)

✴ **Silver Reef Ghost Town**—This was once a rip-roaring mining town with a population of more than 1,500. Its original Wells Fargo building has been restored and houses a small museum and art gallery.

Details: 17 miles northeast of St. George. Take I-15, exit at Leeds, and drive west 2 miles on a forest service road toward the Pine Valley Mountains. (1 hour)

✴ **Snow Canyon State Park**—Blackened remnants of ancient lava flows squeeze between red and white sandstone formations at this little-known but outstanding state park 11 miles northwest of St. George. A paved road winds 7 miles through its gorgeous terrain, sand dunes where dune buggiers boogie, lava tube caves, creek bottoms, and an old set where scenes from *Butch Cassidy and the Sundance Kid* were filmed. The canyon was named after a family, not typical weather conditions; it's extremely hot here in summer, and even in winter snow is rare.

Details: 9 miles northwest of St. George, the park is reached via UT 18; (435) 628-2255. Open year-round; $3 day-use fee. (1 to 3 hours)

KIDS' STUFF

Zion National Park runs a **Junior Rangers** program in summer for children 6–12 out of the Nature Center in the South Campground. Registration is $2. Kids also enjoy tubing, horseback rides, and short hikes (see Fitness and Recreation), and the **Zion Canyon Cinemax** (see Nightlife).

FITNESS AND RECREATION

Zion's true beauty is realized on foot. Some 13 trails cover more than 165 miles and range from short walks to multi-day outings. All distances listed are for round trips. One of the most popular hikes is up to, or through, **The Narrows**. The route begins at the Temple of Sinawava with the paved 2-mile **Riverside Walk** alongside the Virgin River. The canyon walls then pinch in, closing at times to only 24 feet wide but 1,000 feet deep!

This section of the Narrows often requires hiking in the river itself. It should not be attempted in inclement weather because of the danger of flash flooding, or by children shorter than 56 inches. The entire journey is 16 miles long—a strenuous day hike. Hikers on the Riverside Walk do not need a permit, but if you continue on into the Narrows itself, a $5 day-hiking permit is required. Permits are issued by the visitor center the day before your planned hike, beginning at 8:30 a.m.

Another very pretty short hike is the **Lower Emerald Pools Trail**, a 1.2-mile paved route with interpretive signage, which brings you to a series of three waterfalls. The **Watchman Trail**, 2 miles, heads out of the Watchman Campground, climbing to viewpoints of lower Zion Canyon. In summer, do this one early or late in the day. Along Zion–Mt. Carmel Highway is the 1-mile interpretive **Canyon**

Overlook Trail, which provides terrific views of lower Zion Canyon, Pine Canyon, and East Temple. In the Kolob Canyons area, **Taylor Creek Trail** runs 5 miles from the paved road to the Double Arch Alcove.

Shuttles to remote trailheads can be arranged, for a fee, from Zion Lodge. Call (435) 772-3213 for details. Permits ($5 per person per day) are available at the visitor centers at the South Entrance and Kolob Canyons, and are required for all backcountry hiking and camping.

Inner-tubing on the Virgin River is a popular pastime here. Several businesses near the park's South Entrance in Springdale rent tubes. Horseback riding is also available in the park, through the Zion Lodge. Bicycling is permitted only on established roads and the 1.8-mile (one-way) **Pa'rus Trail**, which runs from the Watchman Campground amphitheater parking lot to the Scenic Drive junction with UT 9. Riding through the Zion–Mt. Carmel Tunnel is prohibited.

Outside the park the 10,300-foot **Pine Valley Mountains** and the **Pine Valley Wilderness Area** afford opportunities for fishing, cool mountain biking, cross-country skiing, hiking, and other pursuits. For general details, call the Dixie National Forest, (435) 652-3100 or (435) 673-3431. For a booklet outlining area mountain biking trails, contact Utah Color Country, (800) 233-8824. Seven major golf courses are in and around St. George, including the **St. George Golf Club** (435) 634-5854, **Green Spring** (435) 673-7888, and **Dixie Red Hills** (435) 634-5852.

FOOD

The **Zion Lodge**, on the Zion Canyon Scenic Drive, (435) 772-3213, serves three good meals a day, with something for everyone's budget, in an informal but gracious setting. Reservations are almost mandatory in summer. With at least eight hours' advance notice, you can order box lunches. There's also a convenience counter with sandwiches, ice cream, and drinks.

Just outside the park, in Springdale, are a number of options. One of the better places is the **Bit and Spur Saloon**, 1212 Zion Park Blvd., (435) 772-3036, with an old-timey Western look but good, contemporary Southwestern and Mexican food. It's open for somewhat pricey breakfast and dinner.

St. George has another one of the area's better restaurants, **Ernesto's**, 929 W. Sunset Blvd., (435) 674-2767. Though situated in a strip mall, it has lovely views of red-rock cliffs. But better yet is its Mexican food, including homemade refried beans. It's open for lunch and dinner Monday through Saturday. **Pizza Noodle**, in town center, (435) 772-3815, has funny-named but tasty pizzas, like the Tree Hugger and the Cholesterol Hiker, as well as calzones, salads, good desserts, espresso, and capuccino.

In Hurricane, drop into **Grandma Bishop's**, 270 W. State, (435) 635-4856. You'll love her amazingly inexpensive but wholesome cooking, including daily lunch and dinner specials and homemade pies. Tiny La Verkin, near Hurricane, has a good Mexican restaurant, **Los Gringos**, 160 S. State, (435) 635-8045, with a liquor license.

LODGING

Zion once had another magnificent lodge built by Gilbert Stanley Underwood. It burned down in 1966, and its replacement, while nice, does not match other great national park lodges. **Zion Lodge**, on the Zion Canyon Scenic Drive, (303) 297-2757 for reservations or (435) 772-3213 for information, has motel rooms, cabins with gas fireplaces, and suites, with rates of $75–$95. It's open year-round.

Just outside the park in Springdale is a slew of choices. At the high end is **Cliffrose Lodge**, 281 Zion Park Blvd., (435) 772-3234 or (800) 243-UTAH, set on the Virgin River. It has 5 acres of attractive, landscaped grounds with a pool, and its rooms come with phones, TV, and AC for $60–$145. The **Zion Park Inn**, 1215 Zion Park Blvd., (435) 772-3200 or (800) 934-7275, has 120 rooms with cable TV, phones, and AC. On site is the Switchback Grille, laundry, gift shop, pool, and hot tub. Rates are $58–$89. At the lower end of the scale is **Pioneer Lodge**, 838 Zion Park Blvd., (435) 772-3233, with doubles for $40–$60. Amenities include a restaurant.

For a bed-and-breakfast, try **Snow Family Guest Ranch**, 633 E. UT 9, Springdale, (800) 308-7669, a scenic site including nine rooms ($60–$120) furnished with cowboy decor. Its Sundowner Room has particularly noteworthy views. Another option in Springdale is **O'Toole's**, 980 Zion Park Blvd., (435) 772-3457, with wonderful views of Zion Canyon, a comfortable front porch frequented by hummingbirds, and rooms in either an English-style cottage or a log cabin relocated from the park. Some rooms share baths; $60–$125.

A third choice is **Harvest House**, 29 Canyon View Dr., (435) 772-3880, Its four rooms have private decks overlooking Zion Canyon and private baths. An impressive cactus garden in front contradicts the myth that desert vegetation is ugly. Rates are $75–$90. **Under the Eaves Guest House**, 980 Zion Park Blvd., (435) 772-3457, built of local sandstone in the 1930s, has two small but quaint rooms that share a bath, a larger suite with private bath, and two cabin bedrooms ($55–$90). A spa is also on site.

St. George has more than 2,000 hotel and motel rooms, running from the inexpensive to the luxurious. At the low end ($35) is **Dixie Palm Motel**, 185 E. St. George St., (435) 673-3531, with clean rooms and pool privileges next door. A midpriced bed-and-breakfast ($55–$100), the **Seven Wives Inn**, 217 N. 100 West, (435) 628-3737, in the historic district, is named after the polygamist who once loved here. All rooms have private baths and antique furnishings, some with fireplaces. There is also a pool.

CAMPING

Two camping options exist in Zion National Park: **Watchman** and **South Campgrounds**. Both are located at the South Entrance along UT 9. At least one is open year-round. Their 369 sites rent for $10 on a first-come, first-served basis, with restrooms and drinking water but no hookups. There are also six free primitive sites at **Lava Point**, open June through November.

In Springdale, just outside the park, **Zion Canyon Campground**, 479 Zion Park Blvd., (435) 772-3237, has 200+ sites with hookups, a pizza parlor, store, laundry, and playground. Further afield are a number of interesting possibilities. Some 11 miles northwest of St. George is **Snow Canyon State Park Campground**, (435) 628-2255 for information, (800) 322-3770 for reservations, with 35 sites (electric hookups), restrooms, and hot showers.

Quail Creek State Park Campground, off UT 9 between Hurricane and I-15, (435) 879-2378 for information, (800) 322-3770 for reservations, has 23 sites and restrooms. Open year-round, its adjoining reservoir offers fishing, swimming, and boating. The BLM runs the **Red Cliffs Campground** at the foot of the Pine Valley Mountains, off I-15 about 4.5 miles south of Leeds, (435) 673-4654.

The campgrounds in Zion do not have hookups, but **Canyons RV Resort**, in Hurricane on UT 9, (435) 635-0200, has 160 sites in the first phase of a huge development that will eventually include 1,300 sites, a 12,000-square-foot clubhouse, sauna, year-round pool, tennis courts, and other amenities. The handful of RV parks in St. George include **St. George Campground & RV Park**, 2100 E. Middleton Dr., (435) 673-2970, with a pool, toilets, showers, and laundry, for $12–$16; and **Settlers RV Park**, 1333 East 100 South, (435) 628-1624, with a pool, spa, and game area, for $13–$17.

NIGHTLIFE

The national park conducts free programs on summer evenings. Schedules are posted in the visitor centers. The **Zion Canyon Cinemax** in Springdale, (435) 772 2400, boasts one of the world's largest movie screens—six stories high and 80 feet wide—where a six-track Dolby sound system and IMAX projection system transports audiences hither and yon with hourly screenings year-round of the movie *Treasure of the Gods*.

Near St. George and Snow Canyon State Park is **Tuacahn Amphitheater**, (435) 674-0012 or (800) SHOW-UTAH, where nightly productions of a multimedia stage show called *Utah!* are presented nightly in summer. The performance focuses on the history of Utah's southwestern Dixie area, from Anasazi Indians to explorers and Mormon pioneers. St. George also has a modern performance and music venue, the **Dixie Center**, (435) 628-7003, where rock and country concerts, symphony, ballet, and opera are presented.

15
LAS VEGAS

Las Vegas stands in stark contrast to the rest of the Southwest, where the landscape dominates and the major attractions are of the natural variety. There's nothing natural about Vegas, but that's also its charm. It's an entirely artificial construct, where fantasy, illusion, and carefully choreographed facades are the rule of the day—or the night, more properly. When the lights begin to blink on and the party animals rise from slumber, a weird, fascinating, novel scene begins to unfold around its historic downtown core and the newer, glitzier Strip. Never will you see more money change hands faster among more people than here, the city comedian Milton Berle tagged "Lost Wages."

Seen in the harsh daylight of the Mohave Desert, Las Vegas does not shine. That's not to say that Las Vegas is entirely a night city. Home to more than a million people, it is one of the nation's fastest-growing cities. It has a beautiful baseball park, a university, and nice residential areas. If you live to shop, you've found nirvana. The city is also becoming a major family destination.

But most of its 30 million visitors (in 1997) came to enjoy, or at least observe, its wild nightlife, to visit its larger-than-life modern theme hotels, to take in a show, to gamble, to drink, to eat. The stream of people from around the world—it's the largest U.S. destination for the Japanese—has led to its status today as Earth's greatest entertainment center, drawing more visitors than all of America's theme parks combined. You'd think the Vegas phenomenon would run out of gas—or at least water—but I wouldn't bet on it happening any time soon. ∎

LAS VEGAS

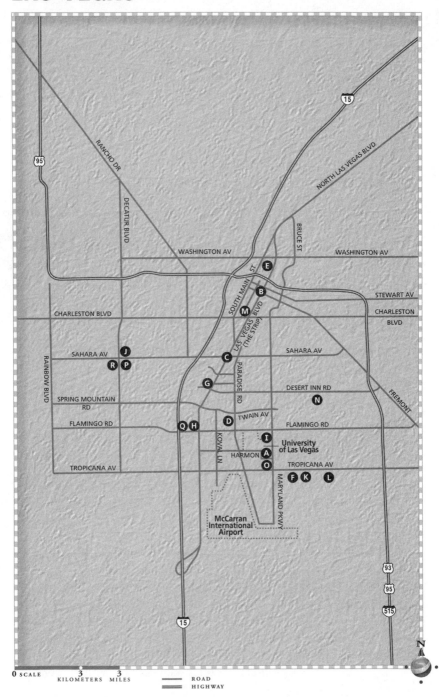

RANCHO DR

DECATUR BLVD

95

15

NORTH LAS VEGAS BLVD

BRUCE ST

WASHINGTON AV   WASHINGTON AV

SOUTH MAIN ST

E

B   STEWART AV

CHARLESTON BLVD   M   CHARLESTON BLVD

LAS VEGAS BLVD (THE STRIP)

SAHARA AV   J   C   SAHARA AV

RAINBOW BLVD

R P

PARADISE RD

G   DESERT INN RD   FREMONT

SPRING MOUNTAIN RD   N

FLAMINGO RD   Q H   D TWAIN AV   FLAMINGO RD

KOVAL LN

I   University
A   of Las Vegas

TROPICANA AV   HARMON   O

TROPICANA AV

F K   L

MARYLAND PKWY

McCarran
International
Airport

93

95

515

15

N

0 SCALE   3   3
     KILOMETERS MILES   ROAD
                                HIGHWAY

Sights

Ⓐ Barrick Museum of Natural History

Ⓑ Downtown

Ⓒ Guinness World of Records Museum

Ⓓ Imperial Palace Auto Collection

Ⓔ Las Vegas Natural History Museum

Ⓕ Liberace Museum

Ⓖ The Strip

Food

Ⓑ Andre's

Ⓗ Bacchanal

Food *(continued)*

Ⓑ Binion's Horseshoe Hotel

Ⓘ Café Michell

Ⓙ Café Nicole

Ⓚ Carluccio's

Ⓛ Cipriani

Ⓜ Doña Maria's

Ⓝ Gates and Sons Bar-B-Q

Ⓞ Mamouia

Ⓟ Mayflower

Ⓗ Palace Court Restaurant

Ⓠ Rio Suite Hotel and Casino

Ⓡ Shalimar

Ⓗ Spago's

Note: Items with the same letter are located in the same place or area.

A PERFECT DAY (AND NIGHT) IN LAS VEGAS

It's impossible to take in Vegas in one day. Ideally you'd have at least two nights: one to spend taking in a show or performance of some kind followed by some gaming, a morning to recover, a visit to one of the museums or daytime attractions, a nap, and then another evening on the town—checking out the amazing neon and lights downtown and several of the huge hotel/casinos along The Strip.

SIGHTSEEING HIGHLIGHTS

★★★ **Downtown**—This is what people used to think of when they thought of Vegas. Also known as "Glitter Gulch," it contains the world's most eye-dazzling array of neon and lights, including Vegas icons like 50-foot-tall **Old Vic** (the waving cowboy puffing on a cig), at 25 E. Fremont St., outside the **Pioneer Club**; his counterpart, **Vegas**

Vickie (a neon cowgal advertising one of the city's more popular strip clubs, the Girls of Glitter Gulch), at 26 E. Fremont St.; and the **Golden Nugget Hotel**'s awesome yellow facade, at 129 E. Fremont St.

Downtown flourished in the 1930s, '40s, and '50s during Las Vegas' first major boom, but the growth of The Strip led to a slow slide into a honky-tonk ambiance, and a reputation as a place for low-rollers and street hustlers. But what it lacks in taste it compensates for with bargains—some of the city's best lodging and dining deals are found here.

In 1995 the downtown hotels and casinos initiated a major counteroffensive, pouring $70 million into covering five blocks along **Fremont Street** with a 90-foot-high canopy (providing daytime shade) and coming alive at night with a dazzling light show powered by 2.1 million light bulbs and a 540,000-watt sound system.

Several of the major downtown joints continue to draw loyal followings today, and a visit to Vegas without seeing Glitter Gulch is hardly complete. The **Golden Nugget**, 129 E. Fremont St., (702) 385-7111, is downtown's largest and fanciest lodging and casino. Its lobby displays gold nuggets, including a 61-pound lunker—the world's largest—found in Australia. Its casino attracts downtown's high-rollers.

One of Vegas' most infamous "old guards" was Benny Binion, a Cadillac cowboy, bootlegger, and gambler originally from Dallas, who made no bones about having "eliminated" enemies from time to time. A statue of him on a horse is found at the corner of Ogden and First Streets. He made his mark in Vegas with his **Binion's Horseshoe Hotel and Casino**, 128 E. Fremont St., (702) 382-1600. A wall display of a hundred $10,000 bills is found in its old wing—a popular spot for a photo. In its newer west wing you'll find one of the city's busiest poker pits, as well as craps tables where $1-million bets are often dropped.

***Details**: See Food and Lodging sections for additional details on Downtown venues. (3 hours)*

☆☆☆ **The Strip**—Running 5 miles—from Sahara Boulevard south to Hacienda Avenue—this stretch of Las Vegas Boulevard is the heart of the Vegas experience today. It's hard to grasp its size, the amount of money that trades hands here, or the ambitions of its fantasy-pandering creative movers and shakers. I recently tried to walk it all in one night, stopping in briefly at its major hotel and casino complexes, but it's impossible. Any one of its dozen or more major destinations could occupy a tourist for nights on end—and that doesn't even include partaking in what used to be Vegas' sole draw, its gambling.

The Strip was launched in 1941 when Thomas Hull opened his El Rancho Vegas just beyond city limits. Its 100-room Spanish Mission decor and, more importantly, a swimming pool were an immediate hit with travelers entering the dusty town from Los Angeles. Soon movie mogul D.W. Griffith joined Hull with his Last Frontier Hotel, followed by Benjamin "Bugsy" Siegel, who created the road's first grand hotel, the Fabulous Flamingo. In 1955 the Riviera Hotel opened, adding an even more luxurious tone to the accommodations, and the modern hotel/casino wars began, with each new facility trying to top its predecessors.

Today the string of properties lie along The Strip like pearls on a necklace—some showing signs of wear, others highly polished and gleaming. All of the newer ones come with a theme. Pick your time frame—middle ages, modern, or space age; your culture—Egyptian, Roman, or buccaneer; your experience—uptown New York, the world of movies, or a circus. It's all here.

Highlights running north to south include the following.

Circus Circus, 2880 Las Vegas Blvd. S., (702) 734-0410 or (800) 634-3450, was the first casino to lure families with its carnival atmosphere at its 1968 opening. The blazing portico topped by the neon Lucky the Clown says it all—lots of flash but little substance. However, it does present free circus shows from 11 a.m. to midnight under its pink-and-white striped **Big Top** near the front entrance, with trapeze and high-wire acts, jugglers, and dancing poodles. Surrounding the stage area is a cluster of carnival games at which you can win stuffed animals.

The $300-million **Treasure Island**, 3300 Las Vegas Blvd. S. (at Spring Mt. Rd.), (702) 894-7111 or (800) 944-7444, elevated free, public entertainment to a new level when it launched its streetside sea battles between a life-size pirate vessel and a Royal British frigate. The Royals go down in a blaze of fire and smoke, only to re-emerge from the lagoon 15 minutes later for the next show. The show packs the sidewalks in front of the hotel with a crowd that then funnels into the hotel—a brilliant get-'em-in-the-door idea. The battles are held every hour and a half nightly, from 3:30 p.m. to 10 p.m.

Probably the nicest complex on The Strip is **The Mirage**, 3400 Las Vegas Blvd. S. (between Spring Mt. Road and W. Flamingo), (702) 791-7111 or (800) 627-6667, even though it's getting old, for Vegas (having opened in 1989). Rather than entering into a clangin', bangin' casino, The Mirage entrance is through a ten-story atrium filled with living palm tress, flowering bushes, and waterfalls. Good signage and wide walkways help steer you to attractive bars, the front desk with its 200,000 gallon aquarium, and further back, the glass-fronted display area of the resort's famous white tigers, where you can observe these magnificent beasts for free. The tigers are part of the act of the resort's famous illusionists, **Siegfried and Roy**, who perform five nights a week (see Nightlife). Oh, and at the front of the resort, don't forget to check out the 54-foot waterfalls, which at night are lit on fire to create an erupting volcano effect.

 Caesar's Palace, 3570 Las Vegas Blvd. S., (702) 731-7110 or (800) 634-6661, is another remarkable Vegas resort, with perhaps the perfect theme for the city's barely contained decadence. It sits so far off The Strip that they've installed tunnellike moving sidewalks to whisk possibly interested patrons into the inner sanctum. As you roll forward, side panels entertain you with a $2-million holographic projection of **The World of Caesar**, portraying a miniature Rome. Inside you'll wander past a full-size reproduction of Michelangelo's *David*, **Cleopatra's Barge** (a boat bar surrounded by water), the 1,200-seat **Circus Maximus**, the **Olympiad Sports Book** room, the **Omnimax Theater** (a dome-shaped space featuring 70-mm super-sensory films shown daily afternoons and evenings; 702-731-7901), the upscale 390,000-square-foot **Forum Shops** (where the statues come alive every half-hour and the "sky" dims as night falls), **Planet Hollywood**, and two huge casinos flanked by open lounges, where some decent R&B acts belt out their stuff. You could get lost in here and never be seen again. Outside are the **Gardens of the Gods** (with replicas of the baths of Pompeii), and the **Brahma Shrine**, a Thai import sitting on the north lawn that is popular with Oriental gamblers.

 New York-New York, 3790 Las Vegas Blvd. S., (702) 740-6969 or (800) NY-FOR-ME, is another phenomenal sight. The $300-million complex re-creates the New York City skyline in miniature, with two-room towers in the form of the Empire State Building and the lovely Chrysler Building, a Statue of Liberty, and other landmarks. A monster roller coaster loops around the exterior of the buildings. Inside, the shopping arcades look like typical NYC streetscapes, including a Little Italy. Where am I?

 The **MGM Grand**, 3799 Las Vegas Blvd. S., (702) 891-1111 or (800) 929-1112, certainly is grand—it's the largest hotel in the world, with more than 5,000 guest rooms. Here the theme is film, with the main carpet pathways done in the form of unraveling film stock. Over there is the Land of Oz, over here a museum of film and movie material. It also houses shopping arcades, a 33-acre amusement park, and some fine restaurants, but in a brief foray I couldn't find a way out of the endless (171,000-square-foot) casino that greets you at the door.

Ye gods! Merlin the Magician has been turned into a pitchman at the **Excalibur**, 3850 Las Vegas Blvd. S., (702) 597-7777 or (800) 937-7777, where a Knights of the Round Table theme rules. Merlin's voice greets you to "The Realm" over loudspeakers as you enter, and he pops up everywhere. Too bad you can't employ his magic in the Arthurian casino! Kids enjoy its **Fantasy Faire**, featuring the Great Racing Knights, William Tell Darts, the Flagon Toss, and other gussied-up games. A real gem, though, is **Merlin's Magic Motion Machines**, where the theater benches move in time with a wild film.

Finally, at the end—for now—of The Strip's row of amazing massive entertainment-and-accommodations palaces sits one of its ultimate statements, the **Luxor**, 3900 Las Vegas Blvd. S., (702) 262-4000 or (800) 288-1000. Here we enter the land of the Pharaohs, pyramids, and Egyptian mysticism. The 30-story, $300-million tetrahedron with the "world's most powerful" beam of laser light shooting out its top, is a modern wonder, if not one of the classical Seven Wonders. A reproduction of the River Nile runs through the building—guests are transported from the front desk to the elevators via Nile boats—and there is an exact replica of the **Tomb of King Tutankhamen** ($2 entry, 9–11 daily). Also inside the resort is the **IMAX Theater**, (702) 262-4555, with a seven-story screen, 15,000-watt sound system and two films— one designed to be viewed with super-realism-inducing 3-D goggles.

*Details: While a casino may look just a short stroll away, the size of the buildings often fools you. The **Las Vegas Strip Trolley** runs up and down Las Vegas Boulevard from 9:30 a.m.–1:30 a.m. For $1.30, it stops at all the major casinos. However, you can walk, since the streets are safe and people are out in numbers until 3 a.m. or later. Taxis are readily available at casino entrances, and there is also a public bus system. (several nights)*

★☆ **Liberace Museum**—Where else but Vegas would you find a museum dedicated to this endearing oddball, known affectionately in town as Mr. Showmanship? On display are samples of his glittering wardrobe, furs, and the world's largest rhinestones, as well as a rare miniature piano collection and his Rolls-Royce limo.

Details: 1775 E. Tropicana; (702) 798-5595. Open Monday through Saturday 10–5, Sunday 1–5. Admission is $7 for adults, $4.50 for teens, $3.50 for children under 13. (1 to 2 hours)

☆ **Barrick Museum of Natural History**—Exhibits of Southwestern and Mohave Desert archeology, anthropology, and natural history, plus a traveling exhibition gallery, make this a small but fine institution.

Details: 4505 S. Maryland Pkwy. on the campus of the University of Nevada at Las Vegas; (702) 895-3381. Open Monday through Friday 8–4:45, Saturday 10–2. Free. (1 to 2 hours)

☆ **Guinness World of Records Museum**—The Bible of odd and official records of all kinds comes to life in this museum through the use of displays, video, computer animation and information, as well as full-scale replicas of things like the world's tallest man.

Details: 2780 Las Vegas Blvd. S. (next to Circus Circus behind Arby's); (702) 792-0640. Admission is $5 for adults, $4 for teens, $3 for kids under 13. (1 to 2 hours)

☆ **Imperial Palace Auto Collection**—More than 250 antique, classic, and special-interest autos define this attraction, including a 1947 Tucker, Duesenbergs, Benito Mussolini's 1939 Alfa Romeo, and Ike's 1952 Chrysler Imperial limo.

Details: 3535 Las Vegas Blvd. S., Imperial Palace Hotel and Casino's parking structure, fifth story; (702) 794-3174. Open daily 9:30 a.m.– 11:30 p.m. Admission is $7 adults, $3 children under 13. (1 to 2 hours)

☆ **Las Vegas Natural History Museum**—Nevada's wildlife includes a collection of rattlesnakes; stuffed critters are the primary strength of this facility, plus a live shark tank and children's hands-on activities.

Details: It's located at 900 Las Vegas Blvd. North; (702) 384-3466; and is open daily 9–4. Admission is $5 adults, $4 for teens and seniors, $2.50 for ages 4–12. (1 to 2 hours)

KIDS' STUFF

The **Lied Discovery Children's Museum**, 833 Las Vegas Blvd. N., (702) 382-3445, is one of the nation's largest children's museums. It's open daily year-round. Admission is $5 for adults, $4 for ages 12–17, and $3 for ages 3–11. The **Magic and Movie Hall of Fame**, 3555 Las Vegas Blvd. S. (in O'Shea's Hilton Casino), (702) 737-1343, presents movie special effects, ventriloquism, and a live magic act. It's open Tuesday through Saturday 1–6 year-round. Admission is $10 for adults, $3 for children under 13.

Circus Circus has a 5-acre amusement arcade, **Grand Slam Canyon**, (702) 734-0410, describing how parents feel upon exiting. It features a great roller coaster—the Canyon Blaster—that performs two loop-the-loops and a couple of corkscrews, a log flume, and less vertiginous attractions for younger children. Surrounded by arcade games, it's located at the farthest edge of the sprawling Circus Circus complex. It's open 11 a.m.–midnight. Its $19 daylong ticket is a good deal.

Many other major resorts also have extensive activities for kids, particularly the 33-acre **MGM Grand's Theme Park**, with a single-ticket admission price of $19 for adults, $16 for kids. Some of the evening shows are suitable for kids (see Nightlife), as are some outdoor activities (see Fitness and Recreation), especially the Wet 'n' Wild waterpark.

FITNESS AND RECREATION

Golf is probably the major recreational activity in Vegas—besides wrestlin' one-armed bandits and doing 12-ounce curls. Many public and resort courses exist in the city. Right on The Strip is the **Desert Inn** championship course, 3145 Las Vegas Blvd. S., (702) 733-4444 or (800) 634-6906. Also on The Strip is the 18-hole course at the **Sheraton Desert Inn**, 3145 Las Vegas Blvd. S., (702) 733-4444 or (800) 634-6906. The **Angel Park Golf Course**, 100 S. Rampart Blvd., (702) 254-4653, has two 18-holers designed by Arnold Palmer.

Considering the heat—often over 100 degrees in the summer— one can understand the popularity of another recreation destination, the **Wet 'n' Wild** waterpark, 2601 Las Vegas Blvd., (702) 734-0088. The variety of its slides—from hairy to manageable for 4- and 5-year-olds—plus the Lazy River, wave pool, snack bars, locker rooms, grass picnic areas, and shade trees do make for a fun outing. You pay extra for inner tubes (required for some attractions), lockers, etc., etc. Admission is $22 for adults, $16 for kids ages 3 to 9. It's open daily May through September.

Another way to beat the hellish summer afternoon heat is to visit the **Santa Fe Hotel and Casino Ice Arena**, 4949 N. Rancho Dr. between Lone Mt. Road and I-95, (702) 658-4993. It normally schedules two public sessions a day ($5 adults, $4 children). You'll find plenty of tennis courts (play early in the day or in winter), and lots of swimming spots (the **Tropicana**'s is one of the town's nicest pool complexes, on more than 5 acres). There's also abundant hiking, boating, swimming, and even skiing just outside of Las Vegas (see next chapter).

Finally, if you've overdone it, a number of hotels operate spas and fitness programs, including **Bally's**, (702) 739-4111; **Caesar's**, (702) 731-7110; and the **Imperial Palace**, (702) 732-5111.

SPECTATOR SPORTS

Las Vegas has one of the nicest minor-league baseball parks in the country, the **Cashman Field Center**, 850 Las Vegas Blvd. N., between E. Harris and E. Washington Aves., (702) 386-7200 for information or (702) 474-4000 for tickets, home of San Diego Padres' farm team the **Las Vegas Stars**. Games are played April through Labor Day. The city is home to the **Runnin' Rebels** of the **University of Nevada Las Vegas**, who play basketball in the 19,000-seat **Thomas and Mack Center**, (702) 895-3900. The city also hosts the **Las Vegas Senior Classic** and the **Las Vegas Invitational** Golf Tournaments (contact the Las Vagas Information Center, 800-332-5333); the **Las Vegas Cup Hydroplane and Formula 1 Racing** event on Lake Mead in September, (702) 390-5439; and the **National Finals Rodeo** in December, (702) 895-3900.

Las Vegas now has a multiuse car-racing facility with more than 20 different racetracks, the **Las Vegas Motor Speedway**, 7000 Las Vegas Blvd. N., (702) 644-444 for information, (702) 644-4443 for tickets, with weekly NHRA and NASCAR programs.

FOOD

Las Vegas was once known primarily as the place for plenty of cheap food, subsidized by the casinos' gambling profits and supplemented by a handful of good restaurants. While one can still find real deals, including the ubiquitous casino buffets and a plethora of fast-food franchises, the sophistication meter has kicked in and today you can eat as well here as in most other major cities.

At the high end ($20–$50 per person) downtown is **Andre's**, 401 S. Sixth St. (between Bridger and Leis Avenues), (702) 385-5016. Its intimate rooms in a former residence are comfortable, and the French cuisine, including scallops in the shell, beef, veal, and lamb dishes, is outstanding. It also has an extensive wine cellar; open for dinner daily.

For some good, cheap Mexican food downtown, head over to **Doña Maria's**, 1000 E. Charleston Blvd. (at Las Vegas Blvd. S.), (702)

382-6538. It serves terrific tamales, tasty a la carte tacos, and other South of the Border fare for breakfast, lunch, and dinner. Also downtown, **Binion's Horseshoe Hotel**, 128 E. Fremont, (702) 382-1600, has been a popular draw for decades for its relatively inexpensive good food. In fact, between 10 p.m. and 5 a.m. you can score a steak dinner here for $2!

On The Strip, few places impress like the **Palace Court Restaurant**, in Caesar's Palace, (702) 731-7547, with excellent French dining—including truffled goose liver and salmon smoked on-site. Equally impressive, and expensive, in Caesar's Palace is **Bacchanal**, (702) 731-7525, where a seven-course fixed-price meal is served with belly dancers shimmying, "vestal virgins" pouring wine, and two nightly appearances by Caesar and Cleopatra. Dinners only, jackets required. **Spago's**, in the Forum Shops at Caesar's Palace, (702) 369-6300, is a popular place for upscale lunches, where celebrity chef Wolfgang Puck (of L.A. renown) serves up creative world cuisine such as lobster pizza.

Off The Strip are a number of other fine choices ranging widely in cost. A somewhat pricey popular brunch and lunch spot that chic locals frequent is **Café Michell**, 1350 E. Flamingo Rd (at South Maryland Parkway), (702) 735-8686.

As might be expected, Vegas hosts some excellent Italian restaurants. One of the best is **Cipriani**, 2790 E. Flamingo Rd. (between Topaz Street and McLeod), (702) 369-6711, with elegant decor and such finely prepared northern Italian food as *cioppino* (shellfish and fish in a tomato sauce), steamed clams in shallots and herbs, and delicious fresh pasta. It's fairly expensive but well worth it. Open for lunch and dinner; closed Sunday. **Carluccio's**, 1775 E. Tropicana Ave. (at Spencer Street in Liberace Plaza), (702) 795-3236, serves good, modestly priced Italian dishes, such as veal Florentine, and other specialties like crab-stuffed shrimp.

Café Nicole, 4760 Sahara Ave (at Decatur Blvd.), (702) 870-7675, prepares pricey but excellent Greek, American, and Italian food, but you can also find tasty salmon cakes, egg dishes, and other varied fare. Its nice outdoor patio is heated in winter and misted in summer. Lunch and dinner daily, Saturdays dinner only.

Among the ethnic options are **Mamouia**, 4632 S. Maryland Pkwy. (between East Harmon and East Tropicana), (702) 597-0092, with delicious Moroccan dining and a great room (dinner nightly); **Mayflower**, 4750 W. Sahara Ave., (702) 870-8432, serving contemporary

LAS VEGAS

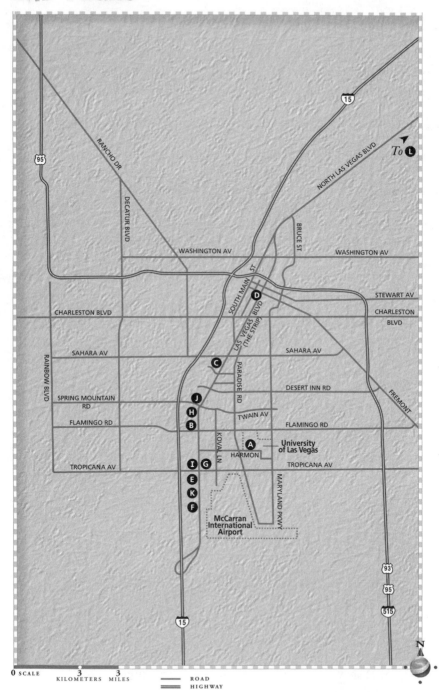

Lodging

Ⓐ Alexis Park Resort Inn

Ⓑ Caesar's Palace

Ⓒ Circus Circus

Ⓓ El Cortez Hotel

Ⓔ Excalibur

Ⓓ Golden Nugget

Ⓕ Luxor

Ⓖ MGM Grand

Ⓗ The Mirage

Lodging *(continued)*

Ⓘ New York-New York

Ⓙ Treasure Island

Camping

Ⓙ Bond Trailer Lodge

Ⓒ Circusland RV Park

Ⓚ Good Sam–Hitchin' Post Camper Park

Ⓛ Sam's Town

Note: Items with the same letter are located in the same area.

California-style Chinese cuisine using only fresh ingredients and no MSG; **Shalimar**, 2605 S. Decatur Blvd. (at W. Sahara Blvd.), (702) 252-8320, with good, modestly priced East Indian food, including many curry dishes and vegetarian fare; and **Gates and Sons Bar-B-Q**, 2710 E. Desert Inn Rd. (between Eastern Avenue and Pecos Road), (702) 369-8010, which smokes up some fine BBQ at excellent prices.

Among the buffets served by all the major casinos, the **Rio Suite Hotel and Casino**, 3700 W. Flamingo Rd., (702) 252-7777, is renowned for its Carnival World Buffet, a roundup of international foods at a modest price. It's open for all three meals, closing down at 3:30 a.m. on weekends.

LODGING

Las Vegas has more than 100,000 hotel and motel rooms, but can— and often does!—fill up on weekends; reservations are important.

Downtown is not the lodging destination that The Strip is today, but it still offers options at both high and low ends of the scale. One of the best downtown budget hotels is the **El Cortez Hotel**, 600 E. Fremont St., (702) 385-5200 or (800) 634-6703, with rooms under $30. Once owned and run by "Bugsy" Siegel, it's received little updating since the 1950s, with perhaps the oldest casino in the city, but it has some unusually large rooms at reasonable rates.

The **Golden Nugget**, 129 E. Fremont St., (702) 385-7111 or (800) 634-3454, $59–$229, is downtown's largest, fanciest lodging and casino, with polished white marble, gold fixtures, and etched glass doors.

On The Strip are a huge number of choices, detailed in the Sightseeing Highlights section. From north to south, there's the carnival atmosphere of **Circus Circus**, 2880 Las Vegas Blvd. S., (702) 734-0410 or (800) 634-3450, $29–$200. The $300-million **Treasure Island**, 3300 Las Vegas Blvd. S. (at Spring Mt. Rd.), (702) 894-7111 or (800) 944-7444, $59–$269, shows some creative touches in its buccaneer-themed resort. My choice on The Strip, money aside, is **The Mirage**, 3400 Las Vegas Blvd. S. (between Spring Mt. Road and W. Flamingo), (702) 791-7111 or (800) 627-6667, $79–$390. It has a huge casino, but gambling doesn't dominate the atmosphere.

Caesar's Palace, 3570 Las Vegas Blvd. S., (702) 731-7110 or (800) 634-6661, $100–$300, is a sprawling, lavish resort that set the standard for excellence on The Strip for many years.

New York-New York, 3790 Las Vegas Blvd. S., (702) 740-6969 or (800) NY-FOR-ME, $89–$129, is another impressive newcomer built at a cost of $300 million. The **MGM Grand**, 3799 Las Vegas Blvd. S., (702) 891-7777 or (800) 929-1112, $69–$269, is the largest hotel in the world, with more than 5,000 guest rooms.

The **Excalibur**, 3850 Las Vegas Blvd. S., (702) 597-7777 or (800) 937-7777, $59–$125, is the relentlessly themed realm of Arthur and Merlin. At the end of The Strip's huge resort facilities is the Egyptian-styled **Luxor**, 3900 Las Vegas Blvd. S., (702) 262-4000 or (800) 288-1000, $59–$189, with eight restaurants and 4,474 rooms (including 484 suites), plus a 120,000-square-foot casino.

There is also a good nongaming hotel here, the **Alexis Park Resort Inn**, 375 E. Harmon Ave., (702) 796-3300, with health club, spa, putting green, tennis courts, and three pools, starting at $135.

CAMPING

I'd suggest tent camping out of town (see next chapter), though RVers do have a number of choices. Right on The Strip, next to Circus Circus, is **Circusland RV Park**, corner of Sahara Blvd. and Las Vegas Blvd. S., (702) 794-3757, a 35-acre plot for 421 RVs, along with a laundry, two pools, grocery store, sauna, and Jacuzzi.

Other in-town RV options include **Bond Trailer Lodge**, 284 E. Tropicana Ave., (702) 736-1550, just off The Strip; **Sam's Town**, 4040 S. Nellis Blvd., (702) 454-8055 or (800) 634-6371, with 500 spaces next to a casino, swimming pools, and laundry; and **Good Sam–Hitchin' Post Camper Park**, 3640 N. Las Vegas Blvd. N., (702) 644-1043.

NIGHTLIFE

Since the late 1940s days of "Bugsy" Siegel, who brought in stars like Jimmy Durante and Lena Horne, celebrity performers have been a staple in Vegas. Elvis. Frank. Sammy. Dino. Liza. Wayne. Engelbert. Everyone's on a first-name basis here, baby. Big shows, with big stars— the flashier the better. What's surprising today is that Vegas is more than just a bright spotlight for brand-name performers, lounge lizards, glitzy production acts, and shows with lots of feathers and skin. On a given night you can catch comedians like George Carlin and Dennis Miller, rock shows ranging from the Neville Brothers to David Byrne, R&B stars like James Brown and Grace Jones, classic soul groups like the Temptations, country crooners like Travis Tritt and Patty Loveless, and retro rockers like Dion and Fabian.

The **Hard Rock Hotel**, 4475 Paradise Rd. (at E. Harmon Ave.), (702) 798-1111 or (800) 300-7389, hosts some excellent live shows by major acts in its 1,200-seat theater, **The Joint**. It also houses a $2-million collection of rock 'n' roll and movie memorabilia you can check out even if you don't take in a show.

On the East Side of town is the **Western Dance Hall at Sam's Club**, 5111 Boulder Highway, (702) 456-7777, a favorite of locals, who two-step to live country tunes every night.

At the **MGM Grand** is the pull-out-all-the-stops production *EFX*, starring David Cassidy, presented in the 1,700-seat Grand Theater. It runs nightly Tuesday through Saturday. Call (702) 891-7777 or (800) 929-1111 for information. The **Stardust**'s primary claim to fame these days is its popular show *Enter the Night*, which successfully mixes such diverse elements as tap dancing, laser effects, erotic dance, skating, and gymnastics in a portrayal of the passions unleashed by darkness. Nightly performances are $27 plus tax. For information, call (702) 732-6111.

Cirque du Soleil, presented at Treasure Island, is one of the city's performance highlights, combining acrobatics, dance, comedy, music, and mime into an energetic show that packs 'em in night after night.

Performances nightly at 7:30 p.m. and 10:30 p.m. Call (702) 894-7722 for tickets, which are $65 for adults, $32 for kids under 12.

Even more popular, with tickets double to triple the price of most shows in town, is the act of illusionists **Siegfried and Roy**, who perform to a dramatic operatic score on a custom stage featuring a fearsome dragon Friday through Tuesday evenings at 7:30 p.m. and 11 p.m. in **The Mirage**. They are working on a $57-million, five-year contract—the grandest ever signed in entertainment history. If you're not a guest here, your best shot at getting one of the $90 tickets (which includes two drinks) is to line up at 6:30 a.m. at the resort's box office three days prior to the show you hope to see.

Other leading shows include *Legends in Concert* (celebrity impersonators), at the **Imperial Palace**; *Starlight Express* (Andrew Lloyd Webber's 90-minute pop musical), at the **Las Vegas Hilton**; *Splash II* (featuring synchronized swimmers, mermaids, high divers, and laser-light effects), at the **Riviera**; *Jubilee!* (a pastiche of high-tech effects, 100 splendidly costumed—and uncostumed—dancers, singers, and variety acts that's great fun), at **Bally's Casino Resort**; *Conga*, one of the few dinner shows left, with the meal choreographed to the story, at the **Rio Suite Hotel**; and the **Folies Bergère** (The Strip's longest-running production show, with its traditional but well-done skin, feathers, and mass choreographed numbers), at the **Tropicana**.

Tickets may be reserved for some shows; others still require you to show up and wait for available tickets. For current entertainment information, call (702) 225-5554.

16
OUTSIDE LAS VEGAS

Most people fly into Las Vegas, head to a hotel resort, blow a bunch of dough, return to the airport, and jet out. However, if you get there and the casino thing is wearing a bit thin, there's actually a lot to see and do in southern Nevada outside of Vegas. Most surprising is the great range in elevation nearby, which means cool forests and streams in summer and even skiing in winter. In the other direction is immense Lake Mead, and further south on the Colorado, Lake Mohave. Surrounding both is the massive Lake Mead National Recreation Area, with endless boating, waterskiing, fishing, camping, and hiking opportunities.

Primarily because of these water bodies, and some astute marketing, nearby you'll find the state's third most-popular vacation spot today—the booming resort community of Laughlin, on the Colorado River at the Arizona state line. A short distance away, plugging up the Colorado, is the graceful Hoover Dam, the world's tallest. The Las Vegas area also has desert walks, some historic museums, petroglyphs, and trail rides. I'll bet you'll like it. If not, The Strip is rarely more than an hour away. ◼

OUTSIDE LAS VEGAS

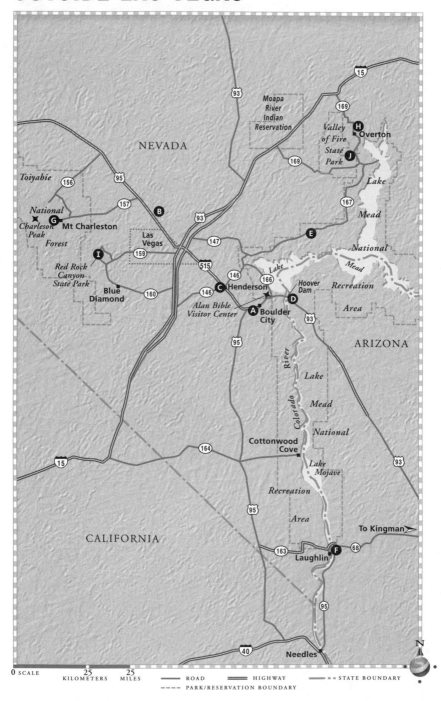

Sights

Ⓐ Boulder

Ⓑ Floyd R. Lamb State Park

Ⓒ Henderson

Ⓓ Hoover Dam

Ⓔ Lake Mead Scenic Drive

Ⓕ Laughlin

Ⓖ Mt. Charleston

Ⓗ Overton

Ⓘ Red Rock Canyon

Ⓙ Valley of Fire State Park

Food

Ⓐ Boulder Dam Hotel

Ⓖ Mt. Charleston Lodge

Lodging

Ⓕ Avi Resort

Ⓐ Boulder Dam Hotel

Ⓕ Harrah's Laughlin

Ⓕ Flamingo Hilton

Ⓖ Mt. Charleston Inn

Ⓖ Mt. Charleston Lodge

Ⓕ Pioneer

Ⓕ Riverside Resort Hotel and Casino

Camping

Ⓕ Avi RV Park

Ⓕ Riverside Resort Hotel and Casino

Ⓙ Valley of Fire State Park

Note: Items with the same letter are located in the same town or area.

A PERFECT DAY OUTSIDE LAS VEGAS

Depending on the weather, a visit to Red Rocks State Park and Mt. Charleston west of Las Vegas is the prime call for a day of hiking, photography, scenic driving, or skiing, with lunch at the Mt. Charleston Lodge or from a picnic basket. Another option is to head in the opposite direction and tour Boulder City and Hoover Dam, then drive Lake Mead's scenic shoreline to Valley of Fire State Park, where you'll find petroglyphs and seared landscapes.

SIGHTSEEING HIGHLIGHTS

★★★ **Hoover Dam**—Not only a stunning engineering feat, Hoover Dam also possesses a rare elegance, even beauty, especially at night when it is bathed in light. Gone are the days when they made dams with winged sculptures and art deco flourishes. The first dam to span the mighty Colorado was dedicated in 1935, and today the graceful, 726-foot marvel is a National Historic Landmark. A recently rebuilt visitor center on the dam's edge overlooks **Black Canyon** on one side and **Lake Mead** on the other.

Details: 34 miles south of Las Vegas on US 93. Take the Boulder Highway (US 93) from Charleston Ave. south through Henderson, or the faster US 95 to the Old Boulder Hwy. Exhibitions and a movie about the dam and its construction can be viewed in the visitor center, which also conducts guided dam tours daily 8:30–5:30 for $3; (702) 294-3515. A parking structure is available on the Nevada side. (1 to 2 hours on site)

☆☆☆ **Mt. Charleston**—On a spring day you can be doing a slow early-season broil in Las Vegas, while an hour away, other people— lucky people—are skiing. It seems impossible, but in the Southwest, elevation (and water) mean everything. While Vegas sits at 2,165 feet, Mt. Charleston clears 11,918 feet, which means much greater moisture and much lower temperatures. On the drive approaching the peak, you begin surrounded by Joshua tree, yucca, and cactus; rise through piñon and juniper country, and top out in thick quaking aspen, fir, and spruce forests. It's a remarkable, beautiful transition not found outside of the Mohave region.

In winter, the attractions here include horse-drawn sleigh rides, sledding, and cross-country and downhill skiing at **Las Vegas Ski and Snowboard Resort**, formerly Lee Canyon Ski Area, (702) 872-5408. The resort runs a ski shuttle from Las Vegas. For information, call (702) 386-2SKI. In warm weather there's hiking, mountain biking, and other activities, with summer providing access to the **Mt. Charleston Wilderness Area**.

Details: Travel north on US 95 about 25 miles to NV 156 and head west 16 miles to the ski area. It's about an hour from Las Vegas. You can also access Mt. Charleston by heading north on US 95 about 11 miles to NV 157 and heading west 19 miles into the mountains. UT 158 links UT 157 and UT 156, a pretty alpine loop drive. For further information, call the Lee Canyon Ranger Station, (702) 872-5453, or the Kyle Canyon Ranger Station, (702) 872-5486. (3 hours minimum)

☆☆☆ **Red Rock Canyon**—This National Conservation Area is Vegas' quick-getaway secret, where people go to unwind, take a walk, climb rocks, ride bikes, or view wildlife. If you visit after a rainstorm, you'll find waterfalls cascading over cliffs at the end of Lost Spring, Oak Creek, and Icebox Canyon trails. A 13-mile scenic drive loop road winds through the park, including one stretch beside rust-colored cliffs frequented by climbers. In summer, go early or late in the day, since midday temperatures soar above 100 degrees.

Just past the Scenic Drive is **Spring Mountain State Park**, a historic ranch once owned by Howard Hughes and managed today by the state, providing picnic grounds, evening theater performances, and a glimpse into working-ranch life. Guided tours leave Monday and Friday at 1 and 2 p.m.; on weekends at noon, 1, 2, and 3 p.m.

Details: Take Charleston Blvd. west from The Strip about 20 miles until it becomes NV 159. The conservation area, managed by the Bureau of Land Management, has a visitor center, (702) 363-1921 open daily year-round. The loop road is always open. The state park, (702) 875-4141, is open daily 8 a.m. to dusk, with extended evening hours in summer. It charges a day-use fee. (2 hours on site)

⭐⭐ **Boulder City**—One of the nation's first planned communities, built to house the engineers and construction crews that built Hoover Dam (originally named Boulder Dam), this orderly oasis of shady parks—the state's only community in which gambling is outlawed—has a few attractions for visitors beyond its general tranquillity. Antique stores, unique retail shops and galleries, and quaint restaurants seem thousands of miles and decades from Vegas. The **Hoover Dam Museum**, 444 Hotel Plaza, (702) 294-1988, runs a movie and exhibits artifacts, documents, and displays relating to Hoover Dam construction. It's open daily. Admission is by donation.

Details: Take Boulder Hwy. (US 93) about 25 miles from Charleston Ave. south through Henderson, or the faster US 95 to the Old Boulder Hwy. (1 to 2 hours)

⭐⭐ **Lake Mead Scenic Drive**—Wrapping around Lake Mead's Nevada shores are two state highways that form a 46-mile scenic drive through a portion of the 1.4-million-acre **Lake Mead National Recreation Area**. The drive accesses a number of unpaved backcountry roads and wonderful recreational possibilities, including hiking, sailing, boating, swimming, soaking in natural hot springs, and photography (see Fitness and Recreation for details).

The route can be taken from either north to south or south to north. The southern terminus is found along US 93 between Boulder

City and Hoover Dam, at the **Alan Bible Visitor Center**. Here you can tour a lovely outdoor botanical garden of local plant life and pick up maps and detailed information about the national recreation area and the Scenic Drive. The route passes numerous lake access points, viewpoints, and developed recreation sites, as well as the northernmost leg of **Valley of Fire State Park**.

*Details: The first part of the route is on NV 166, **Lakeshore Scenic Drive**, which runs north from the visitor center to NV 167. The second, northern leg, NV 167, also known as the **North Shore Scenic Drive**, ends at its intersection with NV 169, just outside Valley of Fire State Park. It can be split in half if time is short. For additional information on the Scenic Drive or the Lake Mead National Recreation Area, stop at the Alan Bible Visitor Center, on US 93 between Boulder City and Hoover Dam, (702) 293-8990. It's open 8:30–4:30 daily. (2 to 4 hours)*

★★ **Laughlin**—Set on the banks of the Colorado River, this modern boom town has suddenly become Nevada's third most-popular vacation destination—after Vegas and Reno. I rank this striving miniature Las Vegas as a secondary attraction because it's not my cup of tea but obviously appeals to plenty of others. The town was founded in the 1960s by Don Laughlin, a Midwestern entrepreneur who worked in Vegas until he squirreled away enough dough to buy 6 sagebrush acres along a deserted patch of Colorado riverfront called Sandy Beach, today the community boasts at least a dozen large hotel/casinos strung along the waterfront for 2.5 miles.

Take the **Riverwalk** boardwalk that links many of these resorts, or hail a water taxi to zip around. The resorts also provide easy opportunities for Jet Skiing, waterskiing, swimming, fishing, and boating.

Details: From Vegas, take I-95 south to NV 163 and head east into town, a total of 90 miles. (1 hour minimum)

★★ **Valley of Fire State Park**—This 36,000-acre natural reserve was established as Nevada's first state park, and deservedly so. A lunarlike landscape that appears scorched on first glance, it is a convoluted complex of eroded red sandstone formations offset by contrasting rocks and cut by small canyons sheltering many Indian petroglyphs, pieces of petrified wood, and historic sites, such as **Mouse's Tank**, home to a small band of Indians who raided nearby homesteads for 11 years while the U.S. Cavalry searched in vain for their hideout. The 4-mile **White Domes Road** branches off the main park route, providing close-up views of some of the park's premiere sights from **Rainbow Vista**. If it's been a wet winter and early spring, expect great outbursts of desert wildflowers. Summer can be brutal here; visit early or late in the day.

Details: From Vegas, take I-15 north 33 miles to exit 75 onto NV 169. The park is 55 miles away. A visitor center, (702) 397-2088, in the middle of the park on NV 169, presents exhibits on geology, ecology, prehistory, and park area history; drinking water and restrooms; open daily 8:30–4:30. Information centers at the park's east and west entrances provide maps and advice on what to see. There's a $3 day-use fee. (1 to 2 hours)

✪ **Floyd R. Lamb State Park**—This natural oasis has excellent grounds for bird watching, picnicking, horseback riding, and fishing on a 7-acre lake.

Details: 15 miles north of Las Vegas on US 95; (702) 486-5413. Open daily 8–8. There's a nominal day-use fee. (1 hour)

✪ **Henderson**—The inventor of the Mars Bar and M&Ms, the late Mr. Ethel Mars, retired to this industrial town just outside Vegas to create gourmet chocolates. Chocolate-lovers from around the world clamor for the goods produced in his small **Ethel M Chocolate Factory**, 2 Cactus Garden Dr., (702) 433-2500 or (800) 225-3792. A self-guided free tour reveals how the delicious chocolates are made, and there's a shop—of course. What do you do with chocolates in 100-degree weather? Eat 'em! Outside is a beautiful cactus garden with 350 different species spread over 2.5 acres.

Also in Henderson is the **Clark County Heritage Museum**, 1830 S. Boulder Hwy., (702) 455-7955, which contains examples of vintage Las Vegas architecture, railroad artifacts, and remarkable relics of early Indian and pioneer dwellings. It's open daily 9–4:30.

Details: 15 minutes south of Las Vegas via the Boulder Hwy. (UT 93) or US 95. (2 hours)

✪ **Overton**—Founded by Mormons sent by Brigham Young to colonize southern Nevada in 1865, this small farming and budding retirement town is also home to the diminutive but excellent **Lost City Museum of Archeology**. The institution displays materials collected from Pueblo Grande de Nevada, also known as Lost City—the state's largest Anasazi settlement. Baskets, pottery, weapons, food, and several reconstructed dwellings are collected here, along with materials on the local Paiute people.

Details: *721 S. Moapa Valley Blvd., Overton, (702) 397-2193, about 60 miles northeast of Las Vegas. Take I-15 north to NV 169 and head south through Logandale. Open daily 8:30–4:30. (1 hour)*

KIDS' STUFF

Bonnie Springs, Old Nevada, just off NV 159, (702) 875-4400, is a private ranch west of Las Vegas near Red Rock Canyon that converted from running cattle to running tourists decades ago. It operates a large petting zoo with farm animals, conducts trail rides, and stages daily gun battles and other entertainment. Features include a historic "stamping mill" for crushing ore, a miniature train that leaves the station only on weekends and holidays, a dining room, and a saloon. It's open daily year-round.

FITNESS AND RECREATION

Outside of Las Vegas is a world of recreation opportunities. For mountain diversions, head west of the city to **Mt. Charleston** (see Sightseeing Highlights), where you'll find downhill skiing at the **Las Vegas Ski and Snowboard Resort** (702) 593-9500, or Nordic skiing on Forest Service roads and trails. The small but growing ski area can be very difficult to access during or after storms. Instead, take a shuttle from Las Vegas. This alpine enclave is part of the larger Spring Mountain Range of the **Toiyabe National Forest**, where you can hike, lie under waterfalls, bird watch, mountain bike, or rock climb. Commercial guide services abound in Las Vegas.

The vast 1.4-million-acre **Lake Mead National Recreation Area**, which surrounds Lakes Mead and Mohave, offers numerous possibilities. With a combined shoreline of more than 700 miles, the two lakes are popular for their many water sports options, including sailing, windsurfing, motorboating, houseboating, waterskiing, Jet Skiing, and kayaking. Permits are required for launching canoes or kayaks below Hoover Dam. Call (702) 293-8204 for details.

Fishing—for largemouth and striped bass, rainbow trout, channel catfish, black crappie, and bluegill—is also popular. Nine marinas around the two lakes allow you to launch and rent boats, and obtain fishing licenses and supplies. For boat rentals, call **Forever Resorts**, (800) 255-5561, or **Seven Crown Resorts**, (800) 752-9669. Local commercial guiding and water sport companies are also available.

Commercial river-running and excursion-boat outings are other possibilities. The *Desert Princess*, (702) 293-6180, for instance, is a popular paddle wheeler that plies Lake Mead. The boat cruises the lake year-round on morning, lunch, and evening dinner trips. Prices for the midday excursion are $16 for adults, $6 for children. Several companies, such as **Black Canyon Raft Tours**, (702) 293-3776 or (800) 696-7238, also guide three-hour rafting trips down a 12-mile, easygoing section of the Colorado's **Black Canyon**, between Lakes Mead and Mohave.

Both lakes are clear and clean, and with the heat, swimming is a natural here. Water temperature averages 78 degrees in fall, summer, and spring, except for exceptionally cold waters in the north end of Lake Mohave. Some areas, including **Boulder Beach** on Lake Mead and Telephone Cove on Lake Mohave, are designated swimming beaches marked with buoys to keep out boats.

Few developed trails exist in the Lake Mead National Recreation Area, but off-trail hiking is allowed. Don't try it unless you are good at backcountry orientation and carry lots of water. The **Wetlands Trail**, off North Shore Drive, runs 1.2 miles (round-trip) to a perennial stream frequented by lots of birds. Information on maintained trails is available at the visitor center. Off-road driving is forbidden; a map of unpaved roads approved for driving is available at either the visitor center or the developed marinas.

Laughlin's few golf courses include the tough **Emerald River Course**, (702) 279-4653, and the 18-hole **Avi Course**, (702) 535-5555 or (800) AVI-2WIN, owned by the Fort Mohave Tribe. Courses can also be found in Overton, Boulder City (including a pretty 18-hole course), and other locales outside Las Vegas.

FOOD

The **Mt. Charleston Lodge**, (702) 386-6899, on the flanks of Mt. Charleston west of Las Vegas, serves filling and delicious breakfasts and wild game for dinner, at prices ranging $13–$20. The **Boulder Dam Hotel**, 1305 Arizona St., Boulder, (702) 293-1808, has wholesome food at modest prices. Food service is available at most of the nine developed marinas around Lake Mead and Lake Mohave, from snack bars to restaurants with lounges. Laughlin's casinos and resorts, like their Vegas counterparts, offer relatively inexpensive food, from snack bars and bar service to full-service, fancy dining.

LODGING

In the Mt. Charleston area, the **Mt. Charleston Inn**, on NV 157, (702) 872-5500, offers fine accommodations, as well as horseback riding, hayrides, and winter sleigh rides, for $60–$90 per night. At the end of UT 157 is the **Mt. Charleston Lodge**, (702) 386-6899, a rustic log structure surrounded by comfortable cabins with log furniture, dining tables, and fireplaces.

The **Boulder Dam Hotel**, 1305 Arizona St., Boulder, (702) 293-1808, is an interesting, reasonably priced hotel built in the 1930s that's been renovated periodically over the years.

Laughlin boasts of more than 11,000 affordable guest beds clustered along Casino Drive. Among the options are **Riverside Resort Hotel and Casino**, (702) 298-2535 or (800) 227-3849, owned and operated by community founder Don Laughlin; **Harrah's Laughlin**, (702) 298-4600 or (800) 447-8700; the **Flamingo Hilton**, (702) 298-5111 or (800) FLAMINGO; and the **Pioneer**, (702) 298-2442 or (800) 634-3469. For something a bit different in casino accommodations, try the **Avi Resort**, just south of Laughlin on the Colorado River, (702) 535-5555 or (800) AVI-2WIN, operated by the Fort Mohave Tribe. The 300-room hotel has a pool, spa, and fitness center, video arcade, and a palm tree–dotted beach on the river of the 4,000-acre development.

CAMPING

There are a number of developed campgrounds in the Mt. Charleston area off NV 156, NV 157, and NV 158, operated by the **Toiyabe National Forest** and open from May 1 through September 1. For details, call the Lee Canyon Ranger Station (702) 872-5453, or the Kyle Canyon Ranger Station, (702) 872-5486 or (702) 331-6444. Most of the developed marinas around Lake Mead and Lake Mohave have campgrounds for tent campers and RV sites with hookups. Most of these also have a convenience store, laundry, and hot pay showers. For details, call Forever Resorts, (800) 255-5561, or Seven Crown Resorts, (800) 752-9669.

Valley of Fire State Park has two campgrounds near the west end of the park, with 51 sites, restrooms, shaded tables, and drinking water ($8 a night). Camping is allowed only in designated areas. Laughlin has several large RV parks, including the **Riverside Resort**

Hotel and Casino, (800) 227-3849, and the brand-new **Avi RV Park**, (800) 284-2946, with full hookups, including electricity, cable TV, limited phone service, and sewer, in addition to laundry, showers, and a convenience store.

NIGHTLIFE

Like its big brother up the road, the budding casino and resort community of Laughlin revs up at night. All the casinos offer entertainment of some kind, from variety and production acts to live music. Noteworthy are the **Flamingo Hilton**, (800) 435-8469, which pulls in stars like Shania Twain; Harrah's **Rio Vista Amphitheater**, (800) 447-8700; and **Gold River**, (800) 835-7904.

John Steinbeck forever immortalized old U.S. Route 66 in his book *Grapes of Wrath* as America's "Mother Road," a tribute to its importance in the migration of residents and visitors from the Midwest to the West in the early part of the twentieth century. Poetry, books, and songs were penned in its honor, including Bobby Troup's famous tune "Route 66": "If you ever plan to motor west/Travel my way, take the highway that's best/Get your kicks on Route 66." Today most of the old roadway is obliterated, replaced by modern I-40. However, a long stretch still remains on Arizona's western edge, where a trip will spin you down memory lane.

The route begins on I-40 at Topock, down among the reeds, tamarisks, and birdlife of the lower Colorado River Valley—including white pelicans, egrets, night herons, kingfishers, ducks, snow geese, osprey, and bald eagles—on the fringes of the **Havasu National Wildlife Refuge**, (760) 326-3853. Head north on AZ 95 for 4 miles to the tiny community of Golden Shores, where you intersect a narrow, crumbling asphalt ribbon on the right: Route 66. It's hard to believe that this was once the only significant highway to Southern California!

Route 66 continues north for another 23 miles before reaching **Oatman**. Founded around 1906, it is a classic boom-and-bust mining town, which produced nearly $30 million in gold from nearby mines between 1914 and 1934, peaking with a population of more than 10,000. After mining was halted, it was nearly deserted for many years. Artists, iconoclasts, and entrepreneurs slowly filtered in during the 1960s and 1970s, and today it is a ramshackle collection of old buildings, tourist shops, and restaurants. Its streets are lined by boardwalks, and on weekends, mock gunfights are staged. Wandering its streets are wild burros, descendants of the stock once used by miners. (Oatman can also be reached more directly from Bullhead City via South Oatman Road, which runs 14 miles from AZ 95 south of Bullhead City to Oatman.)

The route then winds and jolts 6 miles up and over 3,610-foot-high **Sitgreaves Pass**, where views of California, Nevada, and Arizona open up. On the east side of the pass you'll see the remnants of **Ed's Camp**, once a popular stop for cross-country travelers, who would dig in the adjoining fields for fire agates. On the left you'll pass an information kiosk for the **Thimble Mountain Back Country Byway**, which heads north through the rugged Black Mountains.

The road rolls on into **Kingman**, where you can visit the **Mohave Museum of History and Arts**, 400 W. Beale St., (520) 753-3195, which has a terrific turquoise collection, as well as displays on regional history, a Mohave Indian village diorama, and memorabilia of former Kingman native and Western actor Andy Devine. Admission is $2 for adults, 50 cents for kids under 12. It's open daily.

This first leg of Route 66 covers about 48 miles. It continues between Kingman and Seligman for an additional 93 miles, on better pavement.

This second leg heads northeast out of Kingman across the Hualapai Valley, through the villages of Hackberry, Valentine, and Truxton to **Peach Springs**. The latter community was a thriving spot in Route 66's heyday, and manages to eke out an existence today as headquarters of the **Hualapai Indian Nation**'s tribal council. Here you'll find the **Hualapai Lodge**, 900 N. Hwy. 66, (502) 769-2230 or (888) 216-0076, with 60 rooms, a restaurant serving three squares a day, and a gift shop.

ROUTE 66

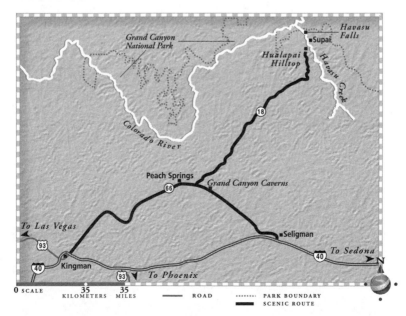

Grand Canyon National Park
Havasu Falls
Supai
Hualapai Hilltop
Havasu Creek
18
Colorado River
Peach Springs
66
Grand Canyon Caverns
To Las Vegas
93
Seligman
To Sedona
40
40
Kingman
93
To Phoenix
N

0 SCALE   35   35
KILOMETERS   MILES   —— ROAD   ········ PARK BOUNDARY
                              ▬▬▬ SCENIC ROUTE

The lodge also serves as headquarters for the Hualapai River Runners, which conducts raft trips on the Colorado River in the western stretch of the Grand Canyon and guides sightseeing trips to the canyon rim. One can also drive to seldom-visited parts of the Grand Canyon's western rim, and/or reach the river itself at **Diamond Creek**, on dirt and gravel roads running 90 miles north from Route 66. For details, call (602) 277-7225 or (888) 216-8456.

Seven miles east of Peach Springs is the turnoff to **Supai**, an optional detour heading northeast for 62 miles on a paved road, then another 11 miles on dirt to Hualapai Hilltop. Here, hikers can descend into the Grand Canyon on foot, down an 8-mile trail dropping 2,000 feet into the remote Indian village of Supai—the only human settlement inside the Grand Canyon—then further down to gorgeous Havasu Falls and the Colorado River. You can camp along Havasu Creek or stay in a lodge in Supai ($55–$80). Reservations are essential, even for camping. For details contact Havasupai Tourist Enterprise, Supai, AZ 86435, (520) 448-2121.

Back on Route 66, a few miles past the Supai turnoff, is the entrance to **Grand Canyon Caverns**, a beautiful limestone cave complex some 210 feet beneath the surface. Visitors descend in an elevator and are led on a 45-minute walking tour on paved, well-lit trails. A motel, lounge, and minimarket are on the premises. The cave is open daily, 8–6 in summer, 10–5 other seasons. The tour costs $8.50 for adults, $5.75 for kids ages 4–12. For details, call (520) 422-3223. Seligman is another 27 miles southeast. As you see, you can still get some kicks on Route 66. ◼

17
SEDONA AREA

Over the past two decades, the impressive crimson-colored rock formations around Sedona have become the poster children of the Southwest, almost as famous and as photographed as the Grand Canyon. Some 2.5 million people visit here annually, a triumph of marketing as much as of geology. Yet there is no denying the uncommon beauty of this area, where the Colorado plateau drops off into the southern deserts in a remarkable complex of canyons, valleys, buttes, and domes.

But there is more than scenic beauty here. Nearby Jerome has a fascinating history as a mining boomtown. Flanking it are Prescott, the former territorial capital, and Tuzigoot National Monument, a breathtaking cliff dwelling built 800 years ago by the obscure Sinagua Indian culture. A short drive brings you to another facet of Arizona's rich historical tableau, Fort Verde State Historic Park, where the Apache Indians' nemesis, General George Crook, once headquartered.

No longer a quiet corner of Arizona, the Sedona area has become a mecca for artists, retirees, and resort vacationers drawn by its temperate year-round climate and for New Age pilgrims drawn by its mystical and powerful "energy vortices." ◼

SEDONA AREA

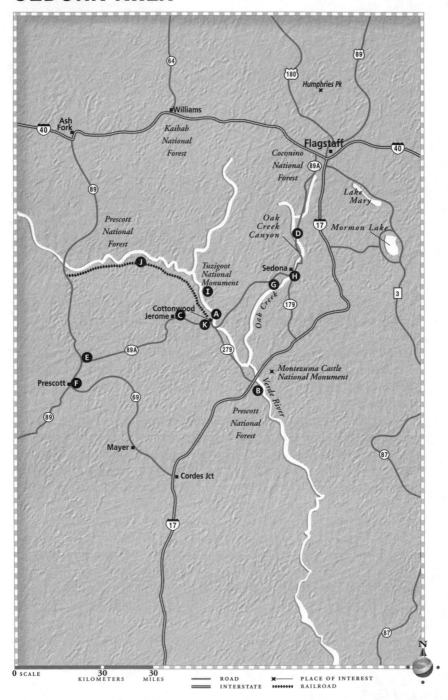

Sights

Ⓐ Dead Horse Ranch State Park

Ⓑ Ft. Verde State Historic Park

Ⓒ Jerome

Ⓓ Oak Creek Canyon

Ⓔ Phippen Museum of Western Art

Ⓕ Prescott

Ⓖ Red Rock State Park

Ⓗ Sedona

Ⓘ Tuzigoot National Monument

Ⓙ Verde River Canyon Railroad

Food

Ⓚ Chanelle's

Ⓗ Coffeepot

Ⓕ Dinner Bell Café

Ⓒ English Kitchen

Ⓕ Greens and Things

Ⓗ Heartline Café

Ⓗ L'Auberge de Sedona

Ⓕ Peacock Room

Ⓗ Rene at Tlaquepaque

Ⓗ Shugrue's

Ⓗ Yavapai Dining Room

Note: Items with the same letter are located in the same town or area.

A PERFECT DAY IN THE SEDONA AREA

Start the day with a drive through Oak Creek Canyon; explore some of the out-of-the-way red-rock country corners on short walks. Then head west, stopping at Tuzigoot National Monument or Dead Horse Ranch State Park, and have lunch at the English Kitchen in Jerome. Spend the rest of the day poking around museums, shops, and other attractions in Jerome and Prescott. If you like trains, hitch a ride on the Verde River Canyon Railroad. Finish the day with dinner at one of Sedona's fine restaurants or at the Peacock Room in Prescott.

SIGHTSEEING HIGHLIGHTS

★★★ **Jerome**—It's hard to fathom, but over the course of 72 years, the mines in, under, and around tiny Jerome produced more than $900 million in mineral wealth—mostly copper. It was a place, said local historian James Brewer, "of hard rock, hard work, hard liquor, and hard play." In the 1920s roughly 15,000 people—Americans, Mexicans, Croatians, Irish, Italians, and Chinese—lived in the rip-roaring town perched on a slope called Cleopatra's Hill. Then the ore played out, and by the late 1950s, only 50 or so people remained.

Sections of the business district began sliding into the open pit mines that had eaten to the town's edges, with the former jail straying 225 feet from its original location. In the 1960s it was rediscovered by the counterculture, urban dropouts, artists, and craftspeople, who slowly began to stabilize and restore it. Today it's one of Arizona's more charming small towns, declared a National Historic Landmark in 1976. Its collage of small galleries, restaurants, and rock shops clinging to a steep slope are lots of fun to poke around in, and the Chamber of Commerce has walking-tour maps of its historic residences and buildings.

Also in town is the **Jerome State Historic Park Museum**. The handsome museum building was once the adobe mansion home of James S. Douglas, otherwise known as Rawhide Jimmy. The restored building is now filled with local historical materials, mining tools, photos, and displays.

Details: *The town and museum are midway between Prescott and Sedona, on AZ 89A; (520) 634-5564. The museum is open 8–5 daily. Admission is $2 for adults, $1 for kids 12–17. (2 hours minimum)*

✸✸✸ **Oak Creek Canyon**—Views along this road are what most people have in mind when they arrive in the Sedona area, having seen photographs of this lovely stream-fed canyon and its surrounding crimson, orange, and white domes, buttes, and walls. A good two-lane road, AZ 89A, parallels the canyon for 16 miles through forests of ponderosa pine and Douglas fir, offering wonderful but brief views of the countryside and the nearby creek shaded by maple, oaks, cottonwoods, sycamores, oak, and cedars. It's as pretty a drive as you will find anywhere in America. A particularly fine spot to stop and admire the view is **Oak Creek Scenic Viewpoint**, 16 miles north of Sedona, where the road drops off the edge of the Colorado Plateau down to the fringe of the Sonoran Desert.

The Oak Creek Canyon road also accesses 43-acre **Slide Rocks State Park**, where the creek has polished the sandstone so finely that its gentle current pushes you down its curved trough, or you can stretch out on the sandstone shelves stepping down to the water's edge. On summer holidays and weekends, this place is understandably popular. Picnic grounds, restrooms, drinking water, and fishing exist, but camping is not allowed.

Details: *8 miles north of Sedona; (520) 282-3034. Open daily 8–6. Admission is $5 per vehicle. (1 to 3 hours)*

☆☆☆ **Prescott**—While there no longer are 40 saloons along Prescott's Montezuma Street, you can still quench your thirst on "Whiskey Row." This is but one aspect of this colorful community—a mix of a ranch town, Yavapai County seat, college town, and artist outpost—which served as the first territorial capital of Arizona from 1864 to 1867. A proliferation of stately Victorian homes, antique shops, and the historic grand Hassayampa Inn are further reminders of its prominent role in Arizona history. Prescott becomes especially lively during its annual Frontier Days, celebrated the second weekend in June.

The **Sharlot Hall Museum** is perhaps the state's finest Territorial-era historical institution. Its 3-acre grounds include a dozen nineteenth-century buildings moved here from other parts of Arizona, including two former governors' quarters. Indoors are a remarkable glass-plate photo collection, ranch antiques, Indian artifacts, and many stage-coaches and wagons. Located at 415 W. Gurley St., (520) 445-3122, the museum is open Tuesday through Saturday, in April through October 1–5 p.m. and November through March 1–4 p.m. Donations are welcome.

Also in Prescott is the **Bead Museum**, 140 S. Montezuma, (520) 445-2431, which exhibits one of the world's largest collection of old and new beads and explains their many uses throughout time. It's open Monday through Saturday 9:30–4:30. Donations are welcome.

Details: *61 miles southwest of Sedona; (520) 445-2000 or (800) 266-7534. (2 to 4 hours)*

☆☆ **Ft. Verde State Historic Park**—In 1865 a U.S. Cavalry fort was established at the infant community of Verde River to protect its early farmers and ranchers from the local Yavapai and Tonto Apache Indians. Famed Indian-fighter General George Crook was stationed here to wage war on these tribes, who surrendered to him in 1873. Today four of the fort's original 18 buildings have been restored. Along with the parade grounds, foundations, and interpretive and historical displays, you can get an inkling of life in this frontier military outpost. Visit on the second Saturday in October, when the site hosts Ft. Verde Day.

Details: *Just east of I-17 exit 287, Verde Valley; (520) 567-3275. Open 8–5 daily. Admission is $2 for adults, $1 for kids 12–17. (1 hour)*

★★ Sedona—While greater Sedona includes several of the attractions noted elsewhere in this section and is a base for exploring the entire area, there isn't much to the town itself, which underwent an explosive and not-too-attractive 1980s growth spurt. For decades before then there was hardly a thing here, but in 1950 surrealist painter Max Ernst settled in, forming the nucleus of an art colony. In 1965 local artists Joe Beeler, Charlie Dye, John Hampton, and George Phippen organized the Cowboy Artists of America, now an important art organization. Today Sedona continues to grow in stature and size as a regional art center. Currently housing 40+ art galleries and sponsoring art markets and events, the community devotes significant attention to the arts.

Sedona's **Tlaquepaque**, on AZ 179 near its intersection with AZ 89A, is patterned after an old arts-and-crafts community near Guadalajara, Mexico. The attractive development of courtyards and fountains was built around some pretty sycamore trees alongside Oak Creek and is quite charming. It's packed with art galleries, craft shops, other unique retail stores, and a few good restaurants, all open 10–5 daily.

Another popular site is the **Chapel of the Holy Cross**, on Chapel Road off AZ 179, about 3 miles south of its intersection with

© Option G

Sedona, Arizona

AZ 89A, (520) 282-4069. Open to the public for nondenominational meditation or prayer from 9 a.m. to 5 p.m., this chapel is a modernistic structure built into a cleft in a red rock outcropping in 1952.

Also worth inspecting is this town's flourishing New Age culture. For details, contact the **New Age Center**, 2445 W. AZ 89A (in the Village West Plaza), (520) 282-1949; or the **Center for the New Age**, 341 AZ 179, (520) 282-2085, where you can attend angelic healing sessions on Tuesday and Thursday from 1 to 4 p.m. Be on time—the angels have a tight schedule!

> **Details**: *30 miles south of Flagstaff via AZ 89A. (1 hour)*

✵✵ **Tuzigoot National Monument**—This Sinagua pueblo, on an exposed hillside overlooking the Verde River, was occupied from A.D. 1125 to a relatively late 1425. Once housing about 200 people, the two-story structure was excavated in the 1930s by University of Arizona students, and some of what they found is on display in its visitor center. Its name is Apache for "Crooked River."

> **Details**: *The 43-acre preserve is 2 miles north of the town of Cottonwood, between Jerome and Sedona. Look for the signs on AZ 89A, or from town, follow North Tenth Street north through Dead Horse State Park; (520) 634-5564. Open Memorial Day through Labor Day 8–7, the rest of the year daily 8–5. Admission is $2 for adults. (1 hour)*

✵✵ **Verde River Canyon Railroad**—Restored diesel locomotives from the New York Metro Line power four-hour round-trip rail excursions into the rugged Verde River Canyon, skirting the edge of the beautiful **Sycamore Canyon Wilderness Area**. Open-air observation cars and enclosed cabins provide great views of the terrain, and occasional glimpses of bald eagles, blue herons, and deer.

> **Details**: *All trains depart from 300 N. Broadway, Clarkdale (continue on North Main from Cottonwood); (520) 639-0010 or (800) 293-7245. Trains run year-round: June through August Wednesday through Sunday at 10 a.m., the rest of the year at 11 a.m. Tickets cost $35 for adults, $20 for kids under 12, $31 for seniors over 65. First-class seats are $53. (4 hours)*

✵ **Dead Horse Ranch State Park**—This 320-acre park sits along a picturesque section of the Verde River on the north edge of Cottonwood, and contains some of Arizona's finest cottonwood and willow riparian forests. Its mix of desert, water, and healthy riparian cover provide excellent birding terrain. Other activities include hiking, fishing, biking, and horseback riding. Facilities include a visitor center, restrooms, drinking water, and a campground. About 1.5 miles away is **Tavasci Marsh**, a 20-acre wetland with active beaver dams.

Details: Access is from North 5th Street; (520) 634-5283. Open daily. There's a small day-use fee. (1 to 3 hours)

✴ **Phippen Museum of Western Art**—Named after George Phippen, one of the founders of the Cowboy Artists of America, this museum near Prescott holds a number of his works, plus paintings, bronzes, and some photography by other contemporary Western artists.

Details: 4701 N. AZ 89 (6 miles north of Prescott at the intersection of AZ 89 and AZ 89A); (520) 778-1385. Open March through December Monday and Wednesday through Saturday 10–4, Sunday 1–4. January through February 1–4 daily; closed Tuesday. Admission is $2 for adults,$1 for children and students. (2 hours)

✴ **Red Rock State Park**—This 286-acre park serves as a natural classroom, with signed and self-guided interpretive trails winding about its striking red rock formations, sycamore trees, and cottonwoods. More than 150 species of birds—including bald eagles in the winter—and 450 types of plants have been found here. A visitor center holds additional displays, a picnic area, drinking water, and restrooms.

Details: Travel about 4 miles west of Sedona on AZ 89A, turn left onto Lower Red Rock Loop Road, and proceed 3 miles; (520) 282-6907. Open daily 8–5, in summer 8–6. Admission is $5 per vehicle. (2 hours)

KIDS' STUFF

Youngsters, and many adults, often enjoy fish hatcheries. The **Page Springs Fish Hatchery**, (520) 634-4805, has an excellent visitor center with interpretive displays, nature trails with handicap access, trout production facilities, and natural springs that produce 15 million gallons of fresh water a day. To get there, head west out of Sedona about 10 miles and turn south (left) onto Page Springs Road, then proceed a few miles to Oak Creek. Admission is free.

If your kids would rather catch fish than look at them, visit the **Rainbow Trout Farm**, 3.5 miles north of Sedona on AZ 89A, (520) 282-5799, where they are guaranteed to catch artesian spring–raised trout. State licenses are not required.

The **Blazin' M Ranch**, in Cottonwood, (520) 634-0334 or (800)

WEST-643, features an Old West streetscape where you can ride ponies, pitch horseshoes, visit with farm animals, or take in a dinner meal followed by a cowboy concert. Also of interest to kids are a number of sites already mentioned in this chapter, including **Slide Rocks State Park** in Oak Creek Canyon, **Ft. Verde Historical State Park**, the many Indian ruins, and the **Verde River Canyon Railroad**. Most kids also enjoy jeep excursions—the rougher the better!

FITNESS AND RECREATION

One of the most popular activities in the entire area is wading and swimming at **Slide Rocks State Park** (see Sightseeing Highlights) and other spots along Oak Creek, just off AZ 89A.

Hiking and biking around Sedona are outstanding. One of the most deservedly popular local hikes is through **Boynton Canyon**, which harbors cliff dwellings not mentioned in most visitor literature, and, say the New Agers, a wealth of energy vortices. To get there, turn north onto Dry Creek Road just west of Sedona off AZ 89A and proceed more than 2 miles to Long Canyon Road, then turn west (left) and proceed another 1.5 miles to the canyon mouth. The road to this point is rough but passable for a two-wheel vehicle. Proceed up the canyon on foot.

Another outstanding hike is the 5.6-mile **Wilson Mt. Trail**, which enters the **Red Rock-Secret Mt. Wilderness Area**. It climbs 2,300 feet from Oak Creek's Muley Bridge. Oak Creek's **West Fork** can be crowded but is a spectacular route winding through a deep canyon cut by the stream. After 3 miles, it pinches down to a slot, turning hikers into waders.

Anglers will enjoy ample opportunities in this area. Oak Creek is stocked with fish but is also heavily used, so the fishing at Slide Rock State Park is not outstanding. However, more remote lakes—such as **Lynx Lake**, just south of Prescott—can be quite good. For details, contact ranger stations in Sedona, (520) 282-4119, Prescott, or Camp Verde (see listings below).

Prescott is almost entirely surrounded by the **Prescott National Forest**, offering opportunities for hiking, camping, and hunting. Popular Prescott hikes include routes through the **Granite Dells** (along AZ 89 and around **Watkins Lake**), and to the summit of **Thumb Butte**, which overlooks the town from a vantage point 1,000 feet higher. To get to the butte, drive 3 miles along Gurley and Thumb

Butte Roads and park at the picnic area. A 1.2-mile loop trail leads to the summit. The last 200 feet are impassable to most casual hikers. For details, contact the Bradshaw Ranger Station, 2230 E. AZ 69, (520) 445-7253, open daily year-round, except Sunday.

Some limited but excellent river-running water flows on the **Verde River**, which can be canoed, kayaked, or rafted. The section from Clarkdale to Camp Verde is fairly calm and suitable for beginners. The 60-mile stretch from Camp Verde to Horseshoe Reservoir, however, is much wilder. The **Verde Ranger Station**, on AZ 260 southeast of town, (520) 567-4121, can provide maps and additional information, or consult the rental and guide companies in Verde River.

The region also contains the 56,000-acre **Sycamore Canyon Wilderness Area** north of Clarkdale, the 10,000-acre **Granite Mt. Wilderness Area** northwest of Prescott (the southwest face of Granite Peak is popular with climbers), and the 5,700-acre **Woodchute Mt. Wilderness Area**, just north of Jerome (phone all three at 520-445-7253); the **Beaver Creek Wilderness Area**, (520) 567-4501, east of Camp Verde; and the **Red Rock–Secret Mt. Wilderness Area**, just north of Sedona, (520) 282-4119. All have great hiking and backcountry camping potential. Sycamore Canyon, for instance, cuts through 25 miles of the Coconino Plateau, from the heights of Williams to the lowlands of Clarkdale.

Scenic jeep drives are also popular around Sedona, and a number of companies provide rentals or guided outings. You can also take a hot-air balloon trip in Sedona or ride horses. **El Rojo Grande Ranch**, (520) 282-1898 or (800) 36COWBOY, 7 miles outside of town, conducts guided trail rides and stagecoach excursions.

For more sedate recreation, there are several local golf courses, including one of the state's nicer, older courses at **Antelope Hills**, (520) 776-7888 or (800) 972-6818, 8 miles north of Prescott on AZ 89. Near Sedona, try the **Oak Creek Country Club**, (520) 284-1660, an 18-hole course.

FOOD

Sedona is one of the better locales in the Southwest for fine food, with a wide range of options in all price categories. Expensive ($18–$25 for entrees) establishments include **Rene at Tlaquepaque**, in the commercial complex of the same name on AZ 69 at Oak Creek, (520) 282-9225, historically one of the town's best establishments, serving

Continental cuisine and lamb specialties. The **Yavapai Dining Room**, at the Enchantment Resort, (520) 282-2900, has superb, creative Southwestern dining, remarkable dining room views, and a great Sunday brunch. The restaurant at **L'Auberge de Sedona**, (520) 282-1667, features rich French dining and an elegant room—it's one of the few places in Arizona that require men to wear jackets at dinner.

For modestly priced dining, try **Shugrue's**, 2250 W. AZ 89A, (520) 282-2943, with good American fare at all meals. The **Coffeepot**, 2050 W. AZ 89A, (520) 282-6626, has been packing 'em in for years with a huge menu and good food; breakfast is served all day, along with burgers and Mexican food for lunch and dinner. Another lower-priced option is the **Heartline Café**, 1610 W. AZ 89A, (520) 282-0785, with fine fresh and healthy Southwestern foods and a patio.

Cottonwood offers some good American food at the rustic (but not heavy-handed) **Chanelle's**, 2181 E. AZ 89A, (520) 634-0505. In Jerome, stop into the **English Kitchen**, 119 Jerome Ave., (520) 634-2132. Said to be Arizona's oldest restaurant, opened in 1899, it has inexpensive breakfasts, as well as burgers, sandwiches, and soups for lunch. In Prescott, **Greens and Things**, 106 E. Gurley, (520) 445-3234, is well regarded for its breakfasts and lunches—omelets, homemade soups, and salads. The inexpensive **Dinner Bell Café**, 321 W. Gurley St., Prescott, (520) 445-9888, is one of central Arizona's most popular restaurants. Perhaps the town's most attractive restaurant, with good food as well, is the **Peacock Room**, in the Hassayampa Inn, Prescott, (520) 778-9434.

LODGING

Sedona is a very popular weekend getaway for Phoenix residents, and prices often jump on Friday and Saturday nights. The upside of its popularity is lots of choices. One of the finest accommodations is the **L'Auberge de Sedona**, 301 L'Auberge Ln., (520) 282-1661 or (800) 272-6777. This French country-style stone and wood lodging includes secluded cottages along Oak Creek and great views, a pool, and spa. Rooms have fireplaces but no TVs. Rates are $170–$325.

Just outside town, in beautiful and secluded Boynton Canyon, is the **Enchantment Resort**, (520) 282-2900 or (800) 826-4180. All rooms, which start at $200, have private balconies with great views. Four pools accompany tennis courts, croquet, and a fitness center with massage and sauna. Another upscale resort is **Los Abrigados**, 160

SEDONA AREA

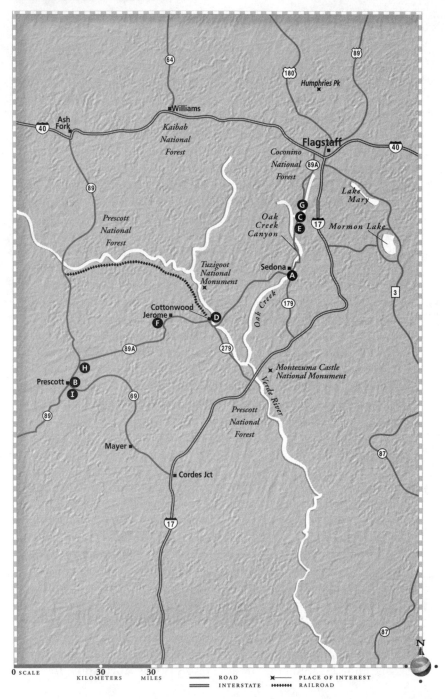

Lodging

A Apple Orchard Inn

A Briar Patch Inn

A Canyon Portal Motel

A Country Gardens B&B

A Enchantment Resort

A Graham Inn

B Hassayampa Inn

B Highland Hotel

B Hotel St. Michael

B Hotel Vendome

A L'Auberge de Sedona

A Los Abrigados

B Marks House Inn

A Prescott Pines Inn

B Quail Ridge Resort

A Saddle Rock Ranch

A Southwest Inn at Sedona

Camping

C Cave Springs Campground

D Dead Horse Ranch State Park

A Hawkeye Red Rock RV Park

E Manzanita Campground

F Mingus Mt. Campground

G Pine Flat Campground

H Point of Rocks RV Park

A Rancho Sedona RV Park

D Rio Verde RV Park

A Sedona RV Resort

B Waston Lake Park

I White Spar Campground

I Willow Lake RV Park

Note: Items with the same letter are located in the same town or area.

Portal Ln., (520) 282-1777 or (800) 521-3131, an attractive Mexican-style facility in the heart of town next to Tlaquepaque (see Sedona Sightseeing Highlight). Rooms begin around $210.

The **Southwest Inn at Sedona**, 3250 W. AZ 89A, (520) 282-3344 or (800) 483-7422, is a cross between a small hotel and a B&B. Terrific views of the area's famed rock formations are had from its hillside location. The inn also features a pool and spa, and every room has a fireplace, phone, modem jack, refrigerator, and large TV; $115–$195.

Families on a budget might appreciate the **Quail Ridge Resort**, 120 Canyon Circle Dr., (520) 284-9327, with its two-bedroom chalets and efficiency suites with full kitchens for $69–$100. On site are a pool, tennis courts, and a spa. Another affordable choice is **Canyon Portal Motel**, 280 N. AZ 89A, (520) 282-7125 or (800) 542-8484. Rates are $49–$130.

Sedona has many fine bed-and-breakfasts. For further details, visit the Website bb.sedona.net. Some of the better include the following—all (but one) priced between $100 and $199 per night. The **Apple Orchard Inn**, 656 Jordan Rd., (520) 282-5328 or (800) 663-6968, occupies a beautifully restored red rock home, featuring wonderful views and out-the-door hiking. The **Briar Patch Inn**, 3190 N. AZ 89A, (520) 282-2342, is set on 8½ acres along Oak Creek. Sixteen private cottages are furnished in Southwestern and Indian-style decor.

Quiet and tiny **Country Gardens Bed and Breakast**, 170 Country Ln., (520) 282-1343 or (800) 570-0102, with only two rooms and two cottages, is set in a secluded forest with mountain views and nearby hiking trails. The **Graham Inn**, 150 Canyon Rd., (520) 284-2340 or (800) 579-2340, is a luxury bed and breakfast with waterfall showers, bathroom fireplaces, a pool, and spa; $100–over $200. The **Saddle Rock Ranch**, 255 Rock Ridge, (520) 282-7640, is a historic hillside estate with fabulous views, lush gardens, a pool and spa, and fireplaces in its three rooms.

Prescott has a unique accommodation, the **Hotel Vendome**, 230 S. Cortez St., (520) 776-0900. This Clarion Carriage House property is one of the state's finest historic lodgings. Built in 1917, it has a great wooden bar downstairs, and rooms with private baths and limited room service for $60–$100 per night. Another grand, historic lodging in Prescott is the **Hassayampa Inn**, 122 E. Gurley St., (520) 778-9434. Originally built in 1927, it was carefully renovated in 1985. Accommodations include a full breakfast and an evening drink; rooms begin around $100.

Prescott bed-and-breakfasts include the 1902 Victorian-style **Prescott Pines Inn**, 901 White Spar Rd., (520) 445-7270 ($55–$85), and the two-story 1894 Queen Anne–style **Marks House Inn**, 203 E. Union, (520) 778-4632 ($60–$90). For budget digs, head over to the **Hotel St. Michael**, 205 W. Gurley St., (520) 776-1999, with rooms starting at $44; or the **Highland Hotel**, 154 S. Montezuma St., (520) 445-9059, with doubles for $23—the bathroom is down the hall.

CAMPING

Prescott and Coconino National Forests have many campgrounds. **Pine Flat Campground** contains 58 sites, 13 miles north of Sedona off US 89A, right alongside Oak Creek. **Cave Springs Campground**, with 78 sites, is 12 miles from Sedona off AZ 89A. **Manzanita Campground**, also off AZ 89A, is only 6 miles from town. All three are open from May through September, charge $10 a night, and are extremely popular. Call (520) 282-4119 for information, (800) 280-2267 for reservations.

    White Spar Campground, (520) 445-7253, has 62 sites with toilets and drinking water. It's open all year, charges $8 a night, and is located 2.5 miles south of Prescott on AZ 89. The free **Mingus Mt. Campground**, (520) 567-4121, is particularly noteworthy for its abundant wildlife, including mule deer, Merriam's turkey, and tassel-earred Abert squirrels. It has 27 sites open May through November and pit toilets. It's located 16 miles west of Jerome off AZ 89A. Take Forest Road 104 3 miles to the site. **Dead Horse Ranch State Park**, (520) 634-5283, adjacent to Cottonwood, has a campground with 45 sites (some with electric hookups), showers, and a dump station ($8 a night).

    RVers have lots of options. Near Sedona, the **Sedona RV Resort**, 6701 W. AZ 89A, (520) 282-6640 or (800) 547-8727, has 196 RV sites with partial and full hookups running $18–$26, a restaurant, pool, spa, laundry, showers, playground, and minigolf. Other year-round RV options include **Rancho Sedona RV Park**, (520) 282-7255, and **Hawkeye Red Rock RV Park**, (520) 282-2222.

    In the Prescott area, try the **Point of Rocks RV Park**, 3025 N. AZ 89 (4 miles north of town in the Granite Dells), (520) 445-9018, which has 100 RV-only sites for $15.25. **Watson Lake Park**, (520) 778-4338, has cheaper RV and tent sites, along with showers. **Willow Lake RV Park**, (520) 445-6311, has RV sites with hookups for $18 and tent sites for $13, along with a pool, showers, playground, and laundry.

In Cottonwood, head over to the **Rio Verde RV Park**, 3420 AZ 89A, (520) 634-5990, with showers, laundry, and more than 60 sites; $9 for tents, $17 for hookups.

NIGHTLIFE

This isn't much nightlife in the area, but Sedona is renowned for its **Jazz on the Rocks** series, launched in 1981. Held the last weekend in September, it features mainstream jazz artists in shows that usually sell out. The **Sedona Arts Center**, on the corner of AZ 89A and Art Barn Road, (520) 282-3809, presents cultural events from time to time. **Skunker's Red Rock 'n' Blues**, 1730 W. AZ 89A, (520) 282-1655, has live music, pool, and dancing. The **Sedona Cabaret**, Safeway Sedona Plaza, (520) 204-9979, presents varied entertainment in a nonsmoking environment nightly after dinner.

In Prescott, the **Yavapai College Performance Hall**, (520) 776-2015, occasionally stages live music, dance, or drama. Along Whiskey Row, some of the saloons harken back to rowdier days once in a while with a country-western band. The **Yavapai Indian Reservation**, on Prescott's northeastern edge on AZ 69, (520) 445-8790, offers card games, slots, and Bingo 24 hours a day.

18
FLAGSTAFF AREA

The largest city in northern Arizona (population 54,000), Flagstaff makes a perfect hub for exploring this fascinating and scenic portion of the state. Rising gracefully over the town are the splendid San Francisco Peaks—including the state's highest summit, Mount Humphreys, at 12,670 feet. The peaks form an ever-changing panorama of light, color, and form, and offer terrific outdoor recreation activity, including excellent downhill skiing. Close at hand are many prehistoric Indian sites, an immense volcanic field that's been active within the past 800 years, and a huge crater left from the impact of an ancient meteor. And, of course, the Grand Canyon is just an hour and a half away.

But what many visitors fail to note about Flag, as it's often called by residents, is that the town itself is so pleasant. Located at 7,000 feet, it has a great four-season climate. It is also home to a major university and several important cultural institutions, an interesting and architecturally important downtown core as well as a slice of historic Route 66, and a diverse cross-section of people. Though growing, it still retains a small-town feel, and people may greet you on the street with a "howdy" and a smile. ◼

FLAGSTAFF

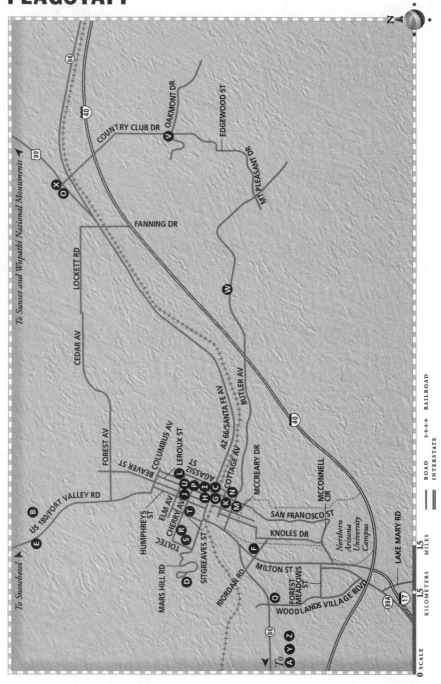

Sights

Ⓐ Arboretum at Flagstaff

Ⓑ Coconino Center for the Arts

Ⓒ Flagstaff Core

Ⓓ Lowell Observatory

Ⓔ Museum of Northern Arizona

Ⓕ Riordan Mansion State
   Historic Park

Food

Ⓖ Beaver St. Brewery

Ⓗ Café Express

Ⓘ Charlie's Pub and Grill

Ⓙ Chez Marc Bistro

Ⓚ Cottage Place

Ⓛ Down Under New Zealand

Ⓜ El Charro

Ⓝ Hassib's

Ⓞ Horseman Lodge Restaurant

Ⓖ Macy's European Coffeehouse
   and Bakery

Ⓟ Pasto

Ⓠ Sakura

Ⓠ Woodlands Café

Lodging

Ⓞ Best Western Woodlands Plaza

Ⓡ Birch Tree Inn

Ⓢ Comfi Cottages

Ⓣ Dierker House

Ⓤ Inn at 410

Ⓥ Residence Inn by Marriott

Ⓙ Weatherford Hotel

Camping

Ⓦ Black Bart's

Ⓧ Flagstaff KOA

Ⓨ Kit Carson RV Park

Ⓩ Woody Mt. Campground

Note: Items with the same letter are located in the same town or area.

A PERFECT DAY IN THE FLAGSTAFF AREA

Split the day between visiting some of the sights outside of town and wandering around Flagstaff itself. Spend half the day visiting the San Francisco Peaks (best in the warmer months unless you're planning to ski), or Sunset Crater and Wupatki National Monuments, or Walnut Canyon National Monument and Meteor Crater. Have lunch in town at Charlie's Pub and Grill. Then explore the town's museums and shops. If it's open, visit the Lowell Observatory at night.

SIGHTSEEING HIGHLIGHTS

★★★ **Flagstaff Core**—In 1876 a group of New England settlers in what is now Flagstaff chose a tall pine tree, trimmed off its branches, and attached a flag to its top to mark the nation's centennial, and so a budding town was named. In 1882 the Atlantic & Pacific Railroad arrived and so did boom times, fed by the city's role as a regional center for timber harvesting, ranching, and other trade. Many of the town's finest old buildings survive downtown today, including the **McMillan Building** (erected in 1888), the **Babbitt Brothers Trading Co.** (circa 1888—current U.S. Secretary of the Interior Bruce Babbitt is a family descendant), and the **Weatherford Hotel**, built in 1889, all serving new roles today as thriving restaurants, galleries, bars, and specialty shops.

Just a few blocks away is the storied **Route 66**, with many of its original buildings intact. Since the town gave it back its original name (it had been called Santa Fe Avenue for some time), the district is undergoing a renaissance partly fueled by the legions of Route 66 fans from around the world who trace its path.

Details: Maps of Flagstaff's historic district, with more than 40 sites, are available from the Flagstaff Visitor Center, in the 1926-era Santa Fe Railway Depot, 1 E. Rt. 66, (520) 774-9541. (walking tour 1 hour)

★★★ **Museum of Northern Arizona**—If you are interested in the Indian arts and culture, or the natural history of the Colorado Plateau, this is a terrific institution. Founded in 1928, it houses permanent exhibitions and changing displays that explore anthropology, biology, geology, and fine arts. Particular attention is given to Hopi customs and history, with a rare Hopi kiva display. Outside the attractive stone building is a half-mile nature trail with a lovely and thorough collection of local plant life. Kids will love the life-size skeletal model of carnivorous *dilophosaurus*, a dino once found exclusively in northern Arizona. There is also a shop with an excellent selection of Indian arts and, in summer, live artist demonstrations and Indian dances.

Details: *3001 N. Fort Valley Rd. (on the north side of town off US 180); (520) 774-5211. Open daily 9–5. Admission is $4, for adults, $2 for students and children. (2 hours)*

✯✯✯ **Wupatki National Monument**—This 35,253-acre park preserves the remains of what was once, apparently, a prehistoric cultural melting pot. When nearby volcanoes erupted at what is now Sunset Crater National Monument local inhabitants fled, but when the eruption ceased, these Sinaguans discovered the volcanic ash had dramatically improved the soil's fertility, and they were soon joined by people from the Anasazi culture to the north and east, the Hohokam culture from the Phoenix area, the Cohonina from the west, and other peoples, creating a city-state unlike anything else in the Southwest.

At **Wupatki Ruin** you'll find the northernmost example of a "ball court," a sunken, oval-shaped structure used to play a ball game (the oldest known game to use a rubber ball) imported from central and southern Mexico. Side roads and short self-guided trails provide access to three other pueblos, marked by freestanding sandstone masonry walls.

Next to **Wukoki Ruin**, you'll find a fascinating blowhole, which responds to changing atmospheric pressure by sucking in air or blowing it out—a phenomenon Indians attribute to the Earth breathing, and home to the Hopi's wind god. Several beautiful cinder craters also exist at the monument. You can hike up **Doney Crater**—an experience denied visitors at nearby Sunset Crater National Monument. The monument also contains the **Strawberry Crater Wilderness Area**, which can only be reached on foot.

Details: *Head north out of Flagstaff on US 89 some 26 miles to the monument's entrance road, Forest Service Road 545, which is paved throughout the park. This road also accesses nearby Sunset Crater Volcano National Monument. A visitor center is located 14 miles from US 89; (520) 556-7040. Open daily 8–5 and 8–6 in summer, with natural and human history displays. Admission is $5 per vehicle. (3 hours)*

✯✯ **Lowell Observatory**—This is one of the nation's oldest and foremost astronomical observatories, established by Bostonian Percival Lowell in 1894. With the powerful telescope he mounted on a hill above town, he was the first to describe the immense water-carved canyons—mistakenly identified as "canals"—on Mars. Photos shot through this scope were also used in the discovery of Pluto, and work here led to the concept of the expanding universe.

Today you can attend lectures and tour displays in a visitor center, and star-gaze through the historic 24-inch Clark telescope in the original observatory dome several nights a week in summer.

Details: 1400 W. Mars Hill Rd.; (520) 774-2096. A donation is suggested. (1 to 2 hours)

★★ **Meteor Crater**—While this site that looks like an immense round hole in the ground is nothing special in its scenic appeal or novelty, it's highly recommended as a demonstration of the incredible power of moving objects. About 50,000 years ago a meteor 80 to 200 feet in diameter and weighing some 300,000 tons slammed into the Earth here, blowing a hole 600 feet deep and almost a mile across. A 3.5-mile rim trail circles the top edge, but you cannot descend into the crater itself, which is the world's largest and most recent meteor pit.

Details: Head east from Flagstaff on I-40 and take exit 233 3 miles to the crater; (520) 289-2362. It's open in summer 8–6, the rest of the year 8–5. Admission is $7 for adults, $4 for students, $2 for ages 6–12. (1 hour)

★★ **San Francisco Peaks**—These mountains are northern Arizona's most prominent landmark, with **Mt. Humphreys** soaring to an elevation of 12,643 feet—the highest point in Arizona. Snowcapped much of the year, they are a white beacon clothed in a mantle of thick pine and aspen forests. It is no wonder they are revered by the nearby Hopi people as the home of their kachina gods. To protect their shrines from vandals, one of the higher peaks, Agassiz, is off-limits to hikers. The highest 1,200 acres include the only tundra zone in the state, home to plants found nowhere else on Earth. Much of this terrain lies within the 19,000-acre **Kachina Peaks Wilderness**, and is accessible only on foot or horseback.

However, a number of Forest Service roads exist at the mountain's base, and you can completely circumnavigate by car on the **Peaks Loop Drive**. Another much shorter but lovely drive along **Schultz Pass Road** leads you around the southern foot of the peaks.

Details: Contact the Coconino National Forest Peaks Ranger Station, 5075 N. US 89, 86004; (520) 526-0866. Open Monday through Friday 7:30–4:30, plus Saturday in summer. (1 to 6 hours)

✯✯ **Sunset Crater Volcano National Monument**—In A.D. 1064, just a blink ago in geologic time, the Earth ripped open at a point just northeast of Flagstaff and an explosive mixture of gas, volcanic magma, rocks, and cinders erupted into the calm of the Colorado Plateau. Eventually the activity grew to become a mountain more than 1,000 feet tall, today called **Sunset Crater**. It is actually just one of 600 to 800 volcanic cones and meandering lava flows created in the area over the past 6 million years, called the **San Francisco Volcanic Field**.

Sunset Crater is one of the most beautiful cones, a graceful pimple of red, yellow, purple, green, and black ash. A 1-mile self-guided hiking route, **Lava Flow Trail**, follows the base of the cone, but access to the rim is no longer allowed. It begins about a mile past the visitor center.

From Sunset, you can return to US 89 and Flagstaff, or continue northeast on the monument road another 15 miles to enter Wupatki National Monument, and in another 20 miles intersect US 89 again. In between Sunset and Wupatki is the **Painted Desert Vista** and picnic area. A round trip combined visit to Sunset and Wupatki totals about 80 miles from Flagstaff.

Details: Head north from Flagstaff on US 89 and proceed 12 miles to the turnoff, AZ 545. A visitor center, (520) 556-7134, has local geology displays and a seismograph recording new volcanic activity. Open daily 8:30–5. Admission is $5 per vehicle, which also includes entrance to Wupatki. (1 hour at Sunset Crater)

✯✯ **Walnut Canyon National Monument**—This monument conserves the remnants of yet another Sinagua site, abandoned some 800 years ago. A 1-mile (round-trip) asphalt foot trail descends 185 feet into Walnut Canyon, from which it wraps around a limestone outcropping pocketed with shallow overhanging ledges into which the Sinaguans tucked about 300 small living, storage, and ritual structures. A rim trail offers views of the ruins from above. The small 3.5-square-mile monument shelters wildly diverse plants and animals, which certainly drew prehistoric inhabitants to this isolated, beautiful spot.

Details: Take I-40 east 7 miles from Flagstaff to exit 204, and drive south on the access road into the monument grounds. There's a picnic ground and visitor center on the canyon rim; (520) 526-3367. Open daily from Memorial Day to Labor Day 7–6, the rest of the year 8–5. Admission is $5 per vehicle. (1 to 2 hours on site)

☆☆ **Williams**—Billing itself at the turn of the century as "The Gateway to the Grand Canyon," this small town of 2,700 people west of Flagstaff fell onto hard times when its economic link to the canyon—a railroad—shut down in 1968, its sawmills closed, and other businesses collapsed. However, the railroad was reborn in 1989 as a scenic train, the **Grand Canyon Railroad**, and the charming and historic downtown core along Route 66 was carefully restored. This stretch of "America's Main Street" was the last to be bypassed by I-40, in 1984, and looks much as it did in its heyday. In 1984 it was designated as a National Historic District.

The railroad departs from Williams on daylong, round-trip excursions to the Grand Canyon's South Rim, rolling 65 miles through forests, open plains, and small canyons. Strolling musicians and a stickup by an "armed gang" entertain travelers en route. A 3½-hour layover at the rim provides an opportunity to view the Grand Canyon on your own or via a guided motorcoach tour. All the rolling stock has been faithfully and beautifully restored to its original condition, including its steam and diesel locomotives. Trains come and go from the original 1908 depot (which houses a train museum).

Just south of town is the **Williams Ski Area**, (520) 635-9330, (see Fitness and Recreation for details), with beautiful lakes and forests. Every Memorial Day weekend the town hosts modern-day buckskinners and Rendezvous Days, with parades, craft demonstrations, tall-tale trading, music, and black-powder shooting.

Details: 30 miles west of Flagstaff on I-40. To reach the depot, take I-40 exit 163 then proceed a ½-mile south on Grand Canyon Blvd.; (800) 843-8724. Trains depart daily at 9:30 a.m. and return at 5:30 p.m. There are five classes of service, from coach to chief, with prices ranging from $50 to $115 for adults, $20 to $85 for kids under 17. Coconino class provides access to the train's glass-roofed dome car. Packages including an overnight stay on the rim are also available. Reservations are highly recommended. (1 hour town visit)

☆ **Arboretum at Flagstaff**—If you're interested in the native plant life of the Colorado Plateau, this is the place to go. This highest-elevation botanical research institute in the nation boasts a wide variety of gardens, a riparian area, meadows, and greenhouses.

Details: 4 miles south on Woody Mt. Rd., off Rt. 66 just west of town; (520) 774-1441. It's open Monday through Friday 10–3, and also on Saturday in summer. Admission is free. (1 to 2 hours)

✷ **Coconino Center for the Arts**—This attractive, modern, performing and special events center hosts a year-round schedule of significant happenings—everything from music concerts, art exhibitions, and drama and dance performances to literary readings and the annual Festival of Native American Arts. Each May the Trappings of the American West show rolls in.

Details: 2300 N. Ft. Valley Rd., (520) 779-2984. Open year-round. Admission fees vary. (1 hour minimum)

✷ **Riordan Mansion State Historic Park**—This odd but endearing 13,000-square-foot building was designed by the architect of the grand El Tovar Hotel, Charles Whittlesey. He erected a stone building in the American Craftsman style, fronted by a facade of split logs and shingles. It is open today for guided tours and is decked out in its original furnishings, including Tiffany windows, a 1884 billiard table, and a 1904 Steinway piano. Facilities include a visitor center and picnic grounds.

Details: 1300 Riordan Ranch St.; (520) 779-4395. Open mid-May to mid-September 8–5, the rest of the year 12:30–5. Admission is $3 for adults, $2 for children ages 12–17. (1 hour)

KIDS' STUFF

Kids will love the **Lowell Observatory**, especially during its nighttime public viewing sessions, hiking in **Walnut Canyon National Monument**, and riding the **Grand Canyon Railway** from Williams, and may also enjoy the **Pioneer Museum** (see Sightseeing Highlights for details). In winter, they'll have a blast skiing at **Arizona Snowbowl** or sledding (see Fitness and Recreation section).

Another popular attraction is the **Deer Farm**, a petting zoo with Pygmy, Nigerian, and Angora goats, as well as the 60 to 80 fallow deer, mule deer, sika deer, axis deer and reindeer, pronghorn antelope, wallabies, monkeys, chickens, turkeys, peacocks, and a buffalo. Open daily, the farm is 8 miles east of Williams, off I-40 on Deer Farm Rd. For details, call (520) 635-4073 or (800) 929-3337.

FITNESS AND RECREATION

Boasting the state's highest mountains, as well as a slice of the world's largest ponderosa forest, a volcanic field, and the Mogollon Rim, greater Flagstaff has a lot to offer recreationalists.

Most hikers head into the nearby **San Francisco Peaks**, laced with a network of trails and home to the **Kachina Peaks Wilderness Area**. The **Kachina Trail** is a mildly strenuous 8-mile round-trip hike across the south face of the peaks through aspen, old-growth pine, and small meadows. It starts from the first parking lot at Arizona Snowbowl (see below for directions). Ideal for families, the **Veit Spring Trail** is a short hike passing through lush vegetation and ending at an old cabin. To get there, travel 4.5 miles up the Arizona Snowbowl ski area road and onto a short access road on the right, where the trailhead is marked.

Much more ambitious, daylong hikes lead to the summit of the state's highest peak, **Mt. Humphreys**. The shortest route, 5 miles one way, is the **Humphreys Trail**. It also starts at the base of the ski area, and climbs through thick woods of corkbark fir, Engelmann spruce, and aspen, their roots dotted with yellow columbines, ferns, and other wildflowers. At the edge of the tundra zone, tough bristlecone pines cling to a harsh existence. Adjoining the San Francisco Peaks to the northwest is the much-less-visited **Kendrick Mountain Wilderness Area**. For maps and details on either destination, contact the Coconino National Forest, (520) 526-0866.

When winter puts a stop to high-altitude hiking, drop down to trails in **Wupatki** and **Sunset Crater** National Monuments. Between Wupatki and Sunset Crater is **Strawberry Crater Wilderness Area**, ideal for late spring and fall outings. For details, contact the monuments (see Sightseeing Highlights). Or head into the fantastic and little visited **Sycamore Canyon Wilderness Area**, (520) 635-4061, accessible via Forest Service roads south of Williams in the South Kaibab National Forest.

Adjoining Sunset Crater National Monument is the **Cinder Hills Recreation Area**, a 13,500-acre playground for off-road athletes, where four-wheeling and ORV use is encouraged. The area is also popular with hang gliders and parasailers, who receive tremendous thermal lift off the black ash fields. For details, contact the Coconino National Forest, (520) 526-0866.

The mountains, Forest Service roads, and lowlands provide almost limitless possibilities for mountain biking. For details, contact the Coconino National Forest, (520) 526-0866, or the many local sporting goods shops. These shops also provide rental equipment for backpacking, biking, and other outdoor sports.

Flagstaff has one of the nation's premier urban trail systems,

FUTS for short, linking all parts of town and outlying areas. The 12 miles of aggregate-surfaced trails are used by joggers, walkers, and bikers. The visitor center has detailed maps.

Fishing is another option, either in the seven lakes near Williams, (520) 635-4061, or those southeast of Flagstaff along Forest Service Highway 3, including **Upper Mary Lake**, **Lower Mary Lake**, and, a bit further off in the same direction, **Mormon Lake**. For details, contact the Arizona Game and Fish Department, (520) 774-5045, or the Mormon Lake Ranger District, (520) 526-4119.

The Flagstaff region also hosts two downhill ski areas. **Arizona Snowbowl**, (520) 779-1951, has a high base elevation of 9,200 feet that generally ensures adequate to great snowfall, averaging 260 inches. A chair on Agassiz Peak climbs to 11,500 feet, providing a 2,300-foot vertical drop. There are two day lodges with hot food, rental services, and instruction programs. The Snowbowl is generally open from December to mid-April. It's 7 miles northwest from Flagstaff on North Valley Road (US 80), then right another 7 miles up the paved ski area access road. During winter storms, chains are recommended.

Just south of Williams is **Williams Ski Area**, (520) 635-9330, a small family-oriented place with a handful of surface lifts and a 750-foot vertical drop. A small base lodge serves hot food, and lift tickets are cheap. It is generally open mid-December through March.

Cross-country skiing is another possibility. The **Flagstaff Nordic Center**, (520) 779-1951, on US 180 north of town, maintains 25 miles of groomed trails for beginner, intermediate, and advanced skiers, and also can provide lessons, rentals, and guided tours.

This cool climate is also great for golf. In Flagstaff, check out the 18-hole **Elden Hills Course**, (520) 527-7999. Williams boasts of the **Elephant Rocks Course**, (520) 635-4935, bordered by ponderosa pines. The *Arizona Republic* once rated it the state's best nine-holer, yet it's inexpensive and, on weekdays, almost empty.

Flagstaff is also home to a high-altitude training site for Olympic swimmers and divers, at the **Wall Aquatic Center**, Northern Arizona University, (520) 523-7170.

FOOD

Flagstaff has a good range and large number—over 100—of places to eat, most at very reasonable prices. One of its premier dining establishments is **Woodlands Café**, 1175 W. Rt. 66 (in the Best Western

FLAGSTAFF AREA

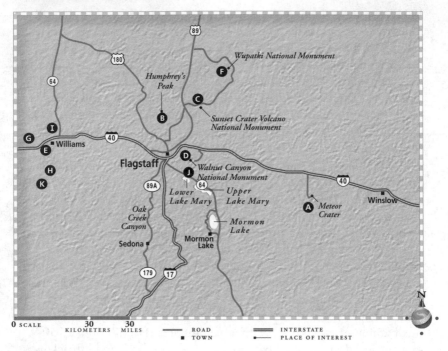

Sights

- **A** Meteor Crater
- **B** San Francisco Peaks
- **C** Sunset Crater Volcano National Monument
- **D** Walnut Canyon National Monument
- **E** Williams
- **F** Wupatki National Monument

Food

- **E** Old 66 Coffee House and Deli
- **E** Old Smokey's
- **E** Rod's Steakhouse
- **E** Spencer's

Lodging

- **E** Fray Marcos Hotel
- **E** Red Garter Bed & Bakery

Camping

- **C** Bonito Campground
- **G** Cataract Campground
- **C** Cinder Hills Recreation Area
- **E** Circle Pines KOA
- **H** Dogtown Lake Campground
- **E** Grand Canyon KOA
- **I** Kaibab Lake Campground
- **J** Lake View Campground
- **A** Meteor Crater RV Park
- **E** Railside RV Ranch
- **K** White Horse Lake Campground

Note: Items with the same letter are located in the same town or area.

Woodlands Plaza), (520) 773-9118, with its international menu and
attractive atmosphere of traditional Navajo and modern Southwestern
decor. Entrees run $10–$24. Other contenders for "finest in Flag" are
Chez Marc Bistro, 503 N. Humphreys St., (520) 774-1343; and
Cottage Place, 126 W. Cottage Ave., (520) 774-8431. Both have intimate environments and excellent wine lists. Chez Marc is classic
French, serving lamb, duck, beef, and seafood; Cottage Place has a varied Continental menu. For big, old-fashioned delicious steaks, check
out the **Horseman Lodge Restaurant**, 8500 N. US 89 (3 miles out of
town), (520) 526-2655.

Coming down to moderately priced possibilities, try the **Beaver
St. Brewery**, 11 S. Beaver St., (520) 779-0079, with wood-fired pizza,
sandwiches, soups, and salads; **Charlie's Pub and Grill**, 23 N. Leroux
St. (in the Weatherford Hotel), (520) 779-1919, cooking inventive
Southwestern dishes, along with breads, soups, and delicious pies; or
the **Down Under New Zealand**, 413 N. San Francisco St., (520) 774-
6677, where you can dine on lamb and imbibe Australian wines.

A handful of ethnic options include **Hassib's**, 211 S. San
Francisco St., (520) 774-1037, for Lebanese food; **Pasto**, 19 E. Aspen
St., (520) 779-1937, for creative Italian; **Sakura**, 1175 W. Rt. 66 (in the
Woodlands Plaza), (520) 773-8888, for sushi and other Japanese fare;
and **El Charro**, 409 S. San Francisco St., (520) 779-0552, for Mexican
food and mariachi music on weekends.

For excellent breakfasts and light fare throughout the day—
including vegetarian dishes—visit **Macy's European Coffeehouse and
Bakery**, 14 S. Beaver St., (520) 774-2243, a longtime local favorite.
Another option is **Café Express**, 16 N. San Francisco St., (520) 774-
0541, with vegetarian and natural-food specialties, beer and wine, fresh
juices, and pastries.

In Williams, head over to **Spencer's**, on Railroad Avenue in the
attractive new Fray Marcos Hotel, (520) 635-4010, for casual dinner
fare and cocktails in its English bar built in 1887. Nostalgia buffs
should drop into the **Old 66 Coffee House and Deli**, 246 W. Rt. 66,
(520) 635-0047, for espresso, salads, homemade soups, daily specials,
and Route 66 memorabilia. **Rod's Steakhouse**, 301 E. Bill Williams
Ave., (520) 635-2671, has been in business for more than 50 years,
offering tasty steaks at good prices as well as cheaper chicken and fish
options. For breakfast, slide into **Old Smokey's**, 624 W. Bill Williams
Ave., (520) 635-2091, which prepares more than 14 kinds of fresh
breads as well as cinnamon rolls, eggs dishes, and pancakes.

LODGING

Flag boasts more than 65 motels and hotels, yet rates can more than double on summer weekends, and vacancies can be hard to come by. One of the nicest, and most expensive, places is the **Best Western Woodlands Plaza**, 1175 W. Rt. 66, (520) 773-8888 or (800) 972-8886, with a pool, spa, sauna, the Sakura Restaurant, a coffee shop, and room service. Rooms are large and well decorated; $120 per night. Another high-end option is **Residence Inn by Marriott**, 3440 N. Country Club Rd., (520) 526-5555 or (800) 331-3131, with an outdoor pool and hot tub; $150 per night. Neither is near downtown.

A plethora of modestly priced chain motels and hotels lines the intersection of I-17 and I-40, and edges the east and west legs of Route 66 For inexpensive digs, head to one of the many motels that back up to the railroad tracks (not recommended for light sleepers!), or better yet, try the **Weatherford Hotel**, 23 N. Leroux St., (520) 774-2731, in the heart of downtown. In 1897 it was northern Arizona's finest hotel; today it functions as a HI/AYA hostel, with $10 dorm beds for members. Its few private rooms rent for $25 and up.

Of the more than 16 B&Bs in Flag, the following are recommended. The **Birch Tree Inn**, 824 W. Birch Ave., (520) 774-1042 or (888) 774-1042, is set in an attractive 1917 home with a billiard room in a quiet residential area. Three rooms feature private baths for $69–$109. The **Comfi Cottages**, 1612 N. Aztec St., (520) 774-0731 or (888) 774-0731, was once selected by the *Arizona Republic* as a "Best Weekend Getaway" for its six charming cottages featuring fireplaces, color cable TV, fully stocked kitchens (prepare your own breakfasts), and bikes, for $95. The **Dierker House**, 423 W. Cherry, (520) 774-3249, is a small downtown B&B with private entrances, king beds, and antiques that's well priced at $50 per night.

Perhaps the town's cushiest bed-and-breakfast is the **Inn at 410**, 410 N. Leroux St., (520) 774-0088 or (800) 774-2008, a charming 1907 home with eight spacious suites—all with refrigerators and some with fireplaces and Jacuzzi tubs; $95–$140.

If you're staying in Williams to catch the Grand Canyon Railway in the morning, spring for the **Fray Marcos Hotel**, (520) 635-4010 or (800) 843-8724. Opened in 1995, it echoes the architectural style of the adjoining 1908 train depot; $120 per night. The **Red Garter Bed & Bakery**, 137 W. Railroad Ave., (520) 635-1484 or (800) 328-1484, a restored bordello with private baths, is a modest, colorful alternative.

CAMPING

The Coconino National Forest operates a number of campgrounds in the forest southeast of Flagstaff, with drinking water but no RV hookups or showers. The fee is generally about $7 a night. The grounds are open May through September and operate on a first-come, first-served basis. The closest to town is **Lake View Campground**, 16 miles down Forest Service Highway 3 by Lower Lake Mary. For additional details, call the Mormon Lake Ranger District, (520) 527-3650.

Just outside the entrance to Sunset Crater Volcano National Monument is the **Bonito Campground**, (520) 526-0866, with 44 RV and tent sites (no hookups) and drinking water but no showers. It's open May through September on a first-come, first-served basis and often fills early. Nearby, primitive camping is allowed in the **Cinder Hills Recreation Area**.

At least six commercial campgrounds in Flag include **Black Bart's**, 2760 E. Butler, (520) 774-1912, with 110 RV sites and 12 tent spaces; **Flagstaff KOA**, 5803 N. AZ 89, (520) 526-9926, with 200 RV spaces and 80 tent sites; **Kit Carson RV Park**, 2101 W. Rt. 66, (520) 774-6993, with 265 RV slots and six tent spaces; and **Woody Mt. Campground**, 2727 W. Rt. 66, (520) 774-7727 or (800) 732-7986, with 118 RV sites and 28 tent spots. All have full hookups and are open all year, except Woody Mt.

At Meteor Crater is the **Meteor Crater RV Park**, (520) 289-4002, with 72 full hookup sites, showers, laundry, and playground. No tents.

The numerous lakes with campgrounds north and south of Williams in the Kaibab National Forest include **Kaibab Lake**, **Dogtown Lake**, **Cataract**, and **White Horse Lake Campground**— the latter with 85 sites. To reach the forest, drive 9 miles south on Fourth Street, then left about 8 miles on Forest Service Road 110, then 3 more miles on Forest Service Road 109. The fee is $10. Primitive camping is also allowed throughout the forest. For additional details, call (520) 635-4061.

Williams also has four RV parks in or just outside town, including the **Circle Pines KOA**, exit 167 off I-40, 1000 Pines Rd., (520) 635-4545 or (800) 732-0537; the **Grand Canyon KOA**, US 64 north of I-40, (520) 635-2307 or (800) KOA-5771; and the **Railside RV Ranch**, 877 N. Rodeo Rd., (520) 635-4077.

NIGHTLIFE

Befitting its role as northern Arizona's largest city and a college town, Flagstaff doesn't roll up the sidewalks at night. In fact, one of the more lively music venues in the Southwest is here. The **Museum Club**, 3404 E. Rt. 66, (520) 526-9434, was born as a Depression-era roadhouse along Route 66 and is still rocking today—mainly to local country-western bands. Said to be the region's largest log cabin, the two-story rambling structure first housed a taxidermy business. When it metamorphosed into a nightclub, the stuffed animals on the walls stayed, leading to its nickname, "The Zoo."

A popular music event is the town's **Jazz, Rhythm & Blues Festival**, (800) 520-1646, held every July with local, regional, and national artists. You can also catch fine classical and pops concerts presented by the **Flagstaff Symphony Orchestra**, (520) 774-5107, founded in 1949. The 85-member group performs 11 shows a year, from October through February in Ardrey Auditorium at Northern Arizona University. For details on NAU's own performance and musical events, call (520) 523-3731. In summer 1998 the **Arizona Opera**, (602) 266-7464, will premiere its ambitious presentation of Richard Wagner's complex *Der Ring des Nibelungen* at the Ardrey Auditorium.

Another highly acclaimed cultural asset is **Theatrikos**, (520) 774-1662, a community theater group founded in 1972 that puts on six plays and some 78 performances a year in the Flagstaff Playhouse, including comedy, historical works, satire, and drama. The **Coconino Center for the Arts**, (520) 779-6921, presents a variety of evening performance events, including folk, ethnic, jazz, and classical music, plus dance and drama, in its 200-seat amphitheater. Launched in 1966, the **Flagstaff Festival of the Arts**, (520) 774-7750 or (800) 266-7740, continues to grow every year with a wide array of activities.

In an entirely different vein, but in keeping with Flag's history as a ranching center, is the **Pine Country Pro Rodeo**, (520) 526-9926, held each June at the Coconino County Fairgrounds. More than 250 contestants compete in bareback ridin', saddle bronco ridin', bull ridin', calf ropin', team tyin', barrel racin', and steer rustlin'.

In Williams, the **Sultana Bar**, 301 W. Bill Williams Ave., (520) 635-2021, occupies a building with a rich and colorful history, often hosting live music on weekends. Just a few steps away is the **Sultana Theater**, where the Rt. 66 Players perform '50s music four nights a week in summer and on fall and spring weekends.

19

GRAND CANYON: SOUTH RIM

The Grand Canyon is one of those rare places that exceeds your expectations, despite the thousands of photos you may have seen. The world's greatest single-canyon complex on earth, its scale is almost incomprehensible. It varies between 2 and 18 miles wide, running 279 miles from Lee's Ferry to Lake Mead and linking up at either end with still more canyons. At one point it is more than 6,000 feet deep. Put all of mankind's earth-moving machinery to work for a century and it could not begin to carve out even one of the canyon's smallest corners.

Several fine trails drop off the South Rim to the canyon floor, and even a short walk down one of them gives you a sense of the Grand's immense scope. Isolated from its rims are a fantastically convoluted conglomeration of buttresses, pinnacles, domes, spires, nipples, and conical buttes. Side canyons burrow into its north and south rims, carving coves, amphitheaters, and huge cliffs; far below, the Colorado River writhes and roars.

Of course, you can remain "above the rim" and enjoy many spectacular and convenient viewpoints from the two scenic drives, as well as the lovely and important historic structures dotting the canyon's edge. Or you can really escape the crowds by heading to the North Rim. The visitor center there is only 10 miles from the South Rim visitor center as the raven flies, but 215 miles by car. That tells you something of the scope of this remarkable gash, which reveals some 2 billion years of geology in its multicolored bands of rock dropping, dropping, dropping to the river far below. ◼

GRAND CANYON: SOUTH RIM

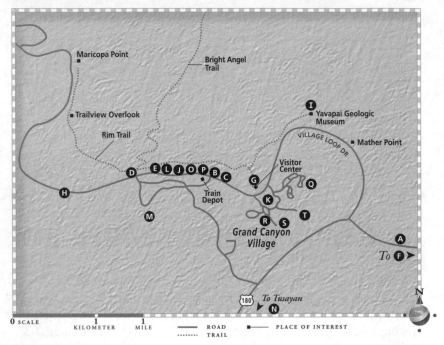

Maricopa Point

Bright Angel Trail

Trailview Overlook

Rim Trail

Yavapai Geologic Museum

VILLAGE LOOP DR

Mather Point

Visitor Center

Train Depot

Grand Canyon Village

To Tusayan

To

N

| 0 SCALE | 1 KILOMETER | 1 MILE | —— ROAD | ■ PLACE OF INTEREST |
| | | | ········ TRAIL | |

Sights

- **A** East Rim Drive
- **B** El Tovar
- **C** Hopi House
- **D** Kolb Studio
- **E** Lookout Studio
- **F** Tusayan Museum
- **G** Visitor Center
- **H** West Rim Drive
- **I** Yavapai Observation Station

Food

- **J** Arizona Steakhouse
- **K** Babbitt's Deli
- **L** Bright Angel Fountain
- **L** Bright Angel Dining Room
- **B** El Tovar
- **M** Maswik Cafeteria
- **N** Tusayan
- **Q** Yavapai Cafeteria and Grill

Lodging

- **N** Best Western Grand Canyon Squire Inn
- **L** Bright Angel Lodge
- **B** El Tovar
- **O** Kachina Lodge
- **M** Maswik Lodge
- **N** Moqui Lodge
- **N** Quality Inn
- **N** Red Feather Lodge
- **N** Seven Mile Lodge
- **P** Thunderbird Lodge
- **Q** Yavapai Lodge

Camping

- **R** Fred Harvey Trailer Village
- **N** Grand Canyon Camper Village
- **S** Mather Campground
- **T** Trailer Village

Note: Items with the same letter are located in the same place or area.

A PERFECT DAY ON THE SOUTH RIM
OF THE GRAND CANYON

Approach the South Rim early in the morning from the park's South Entrance, on US 180, which provides a mind-blowing, abrupt arrival at The Edge at Mather Point. Stop at the main visitor center to get an overview of the canyon's natural and human history, then meander along the East Rim Drive and pause at a few viewpoints. At Yaki Point, descend the South Kaibab Trail for an hour or more to get immersed in the canyon itself, then continue on to the Watchtower at Desert View. Return to the West Rim Drive and pick a spot for watching the sun go down. Finish the day off with a stop in the El Tovar Hotel for dinner; if you can, stay the night at this historic lodge.

SIGHTSEEING HIGHLIGHTS

✻✻✻ **East Rim Drive**—This paved, two-lane road runs along the edge of the South Rim eastward 26 miles from the main visitor center in Grand Canyon Village to the eastern boundary of the park near Desert View. It is one of two rim drives: the other, Western Rim Drive, is closed to private vehicles from mid-April to mid-October, making this the park's prime scenic self-guiding auto route. Expect congestion in peak periods.

East Rim Drive passes, in order, **Yavapai Observation Station** (see separate entry), **Mather Point** (named after the first director of the National Park Service, this is often the first jaw-dropping stop for East Entrance entrants), **Yaki Point** (where the South Kaibab Trail begins), **Grandview Point**, **Moran Point** (named after the famed artist Thomas Moran, whose paintings did much to popularize the canyon's beauty near the turn of the century), and **Zuni Point**.

A few miles further on are the **Tusayan Indian Ruin and Museum** (see separate entry), followed by **Lipan Point** (an excellent vantage point for the eastern canyon), and **Desert View** (see separate entry). A few miles further east, the road curves out of the park. This is the official end of East Rim Drive, but AZ 64 rolls southeast off the Coconino Plateau down to the edge of the **Little Colorado River Gorge**, another spectacular sight. Several short spur roads afford vistas into its depths of more than 1,000 feet in places.

Details: East Rim Drive is open year-round. (Although private car access to Yaki Point is barred from mid-April to mid-October, a free shuttle bus runs every 15 minutes from the Yavapai Lodge and the Backcountry Reservation Office to Yaki.) Winter can bring occasional snow and ice, but the road is plowed. (2 to 3 hours)

★★★ **Visitor Center**—This is an important stop for first-time tourists. Here you can catch a continual slide show and view exhibits on the geology, ecology, and human history of the park. National Park Service rangers also answer questions and lead activities and guided tours. Guidebooks, maps, brochures, and other literature—including the helpful and free *Grand Canyon Guide* and the *Trip Planner*—are available. Bulletins boards post the latest information on special activities, guided hikes, trail conditions, and so forth. Check here first for news, as getting to a ranger can be difficult. Free shuttle buses depart from here for the West Rim Drive every 15 minutes mid-April through mid-October.

Details: In Grand Canyon Village on Village Loop Drive, 6 miles north of the South Entrance on US 180; (520) 638-7888. It is open daily 8–6, with extended peak-season hours. Admission is free.

Admission to Grand Canyon National Park—at either the South Entrance on US 180 or the East Entrance on AZ 64—is $20 per vehicle, $10 per person for pedestrians or bicyclists. The fee is good for seven days on both rims. (30 minutes)

★★★ **West Rim Drive**—This is the South Rim's other main scenic auto route. The two-lane, paved road begins at Grand Canyon Village and runs west along the canyon's edge for 8 miles, where it dead-ends. Along its course are half a dozen main points that provide terrific views into the canyon. One passes, in order, **Maricopa Point**, **Powell Point and Memorial** (a tribute to the leader of the first organized river-running expedition through the Grand Canyon, the amazing John Wesley Powell), the spectacular 90-mile east-west canyon views of **Hopi Point**, **The Abyss** (where the great Mojave Wall drops away 3,000 feet and the distant Colorado can be glimpsed), **Pima Point** (where the sounds of Granite Rapids float up occasionally), and **Hermit's Rest**—the end of the line.

At this last site you will find restrooms, snacks, souvenirs, and Indian arts and crafts, sold in the rough-hewn but beautifully conceived limestone National Historic Landmark built in 1914 by renowned park architect Mary Elizabeth Jane Colter.

Details: Because of summer crowds, West Rim Drive is closed to private

Grand Canyon

vehicles from mid-April through mid-October. During this time, free shuttle buses run its length every 15 minutes. The Hermit's Rest facility is open 9–5 in winter and 8–7 in peak seasons; (520) 638-2351. (2 to 4 hours)

★★ **Desert View**—This is the final stopping point on **East Rim Drive** (see above), and offers a grand goodbye or introduction to the park. The point displays some of the best views on the South Rim: the Colorado River takes a sharp bend to the north here through **Marble Gorge**, and you can see directly into its length. Here you'll find the 70-foot-high stone **Watchtower**, perhaps the park's most remarkable manmade structure. It was designed by Mary Elizabeth Jane Colter after the form of Anasazi towers, and was built in 1932. Its ceremonial kivalike room has wall murals painted by the great Hopi artist Fred Kaboti. It is the highest point on the South Rim, and interior stairs and panoramic windows at its top afford great views on a clear day: the Painted Desert to the east, the Vermillion Cliffs on the Utah border to the north, and the canyon itself.

Also here is a park information center that carries maps, informational brochures, and books, and has a gallery. Adjacent to the Watchtower is the **Desert View Trading Post**, with snack bar, gas station, Navajo rugs, Pueblo pottery, and traditional Grand Canyon souvenirs. The post is open 9–5 in winter, 8–8 in peak seasons; (520) 638-2360.

Details: At the eastern end of East Rim Drive, a few miles inside the park's East Entrance on AZ 64; (520) 638-7893. In peak seasons the visitor center is staffed by rangers daily 9–5. There's a nominal fee to climb the tower. (1 hour)

★★ **El Tovar**—This fantastic building, only 560 feet from the rim at one point, did much to institutionalize the "rustic" architectural style found in our national parks. The cavernous three- and four-story structure was built of massive Oregon pine timbers and local stone in 1905 by the Fred Harvey Company, whose railroad hotels played a major role in "civilizing" the West. El Tovar served as *the* gateway lodging for the canyon in the early days of tourism, and though architect Charles Whittlesey modeled it after European hunting lodges, it is distinctly American. It has a fine Indian arts and crafts gift shop, and is certainly worth a look around, if not a drink, meal, or special night's stay.

Details: In Grand Canyon Village, just off Village Loop Road; (520) 638-2631/2401. It's open year-round. (30 minutes)

★★ Hopi House—Designed by Mary Elizabeth Jane Colter in 1904, this building reveals her early fascination with and appreciation of Indian architecture. Now a National Historic Landmark, the beautiful canyon-rim structure was modeled after one at Oraibi on the Hopi Mesas and built with the help of Hopi craftsmen. The first curio shop/trading post at the park, it is still one of the region's best. In 1995 the building was entirely renovated, and its second-floor **Fred Harvey Waddell Gallery** was reopened.

Details: In Grand Canyon Village next to the El Tovar, (520) 638-2631, ext. 6383. It's open winter 9–5, peak seasons 8–8. Free. (30 minutes)

★ Kolb Studio—The first river-runners through the Grand seen in motion pictures were the brothers Kolb. In 1904 Emery and Ellsworth Kolb built a South Rim studio for processing film and photos. Today a National Historic Landmark, it is a bookstore and photo gallery.

Details: In Grand Canyon Village at the head of the Bright Angel Trail. Open daily 8–7 in summer, 9–5 in winter. (15 minutes)

★ Lookout Studio—Mary Elizabeth Jane Colter created this structure as a curio shop and sheltered viewing station. Today it carries rock and fossil specimens, photographic prints, and traditional souvenirs.

Details: In Grand Canyon Village next to Bright Angel Lodge; (520) 638-2631, ext. 6087. It's open winter 9–5, peak seasons 8–7. (15 minutes)

★ Tusayan Museum—The story of the canyon's early Indian settlement is best experienced at this site on East Rim Drive. This was the location of the largest Anasazi village found in or along the canyon. It is believed to have harbored 30 people, circa 1185, who farmed nearby and most likely traded with or were an extension of the Anasazis who periodically occupied the Unkar Delta site on the canyon floor. There is a self-guiding tour through the ruins. An adjoining museum provides additional displays of Anasazi, pre-Anasazi (including some delightful twig animal figures found in canyon caves), and Hopi materials. In peak seasons park rangers are also stationed here.

Details: 23 miles east of Grand Canyon Village on East Rim Drive and 4 miles west of Desert View; (520) 638-2305. Open all year; hours change seasonally. Free. (30 minutes to 2 hours)

★ Yavapai Observation Station—Set on the canyon's edge, this building has glassed interior observation points that are handy in inclement weather (with views clear to the canyon floor), as well as the park's best geology exhibits. It is also a park contact station, with literature and, in the peak seasons, on-site rangers.

Details: *In Grand Canyon Village on Village Loop Road, ½-mile east of the visitor center. It's open year-round, but hours change seasonally. Free. (15 minutes to 2 hours)*

KIDS' STUFF

While it's not right on the South Rim, **Flintstones Bedrock City** is a sure draw for kids. There is a tiny train rolling through "an active volcano," the Flintstones' and Rubbles' houses, and minigolf, as well as shops selling Fred T-shirts, Wilma mugs, and Barney hats. Sample their theme foods for breakfasts, lunch, and Dino . . . . On the junction of US 180 and US 64, 28 miles south of the South Entrance; (520) 635-2600. Admission is $4 for adults, $2 for kids.

In addition, kids enjoy the **Tusayan Museum** ruins (see Sight-seeing Highlights), the mule rides (or even watching them prepare for daily departures at 8 a.m. from the stone corrals at the Bright Angel trailhead), any of the over-the-rim hiking trails (see Fitness and Recreation), or the **IMAX Theater** (see Nightlife).

FITNESS AND RECREATION

Few people tread on more than a few of the park's 1.2 million acres, which is a grand shame. It's really the only way to respect its immense scope and to note its tiny details—and if more people got out of their cars, congestion wouldn't be such a problem. Those that do choose to walk or hike have quite a few options.

The most popular route is the **Rim Trail**, which runs right along the edge of the canyon. The section closest to Grand Canyon Village, from Yavapai Point to Maricopa Point, is both paved and wheelchair accessible. Unpaved legs extend further in both directions, to Mather Point and Hermit's Rest. The trail offers great views, and walking brochures accompany its interpretive signs. Bikes are not allowed.

A number of trails drop off the rim and head toward the canyon floor. Even short walks down these trails provide a much firmer contact with the nature of this amazing place. However, a few words of caution. Every year several people fall off cliffs in the canyon and are killed: stay away from drops and steep slopes! Many rescues are also undertaken for those suffering from heat stroke or crippling thirst. The canyon floor in summer is often 20 degrees hotter than the South Rim. Remember, this is a mountain upside-down: you start off fresh heading down, and when you're tired and ready to return, you have to hike up. Ascending generally takes twice as long as descending. Carry at least a gallon of water per person per day (there is almost no drinking water under the rim), and drink it! Also, several of the trails are also used by mule caravans—they have the right of way. When you encounter mules, step to the uphill side of the trail and let them pass.

That said, don't be afraid to try an under-the-rim trail as a day hiker. They are all open year-round, though their top stretches can be icy or snowy in winter. The two most popular, and the only ones maintained by the park, are Bright Angel and South Kaibab.

Bright Angel Trail, the first designed for tourists—in the 1890s!—starts in Grand Canyon Village near Bright Angel Lodge. At 1½ and 3 miles down the trail are rest shelters that have water in the summer. At the first short tunnel, note the Havasupai Indian pictographs on the left above the ledge. The trail continues on, dropping 3,100 feet more in the 4.6 miles to **Indian Gardens**, where you'll find fresh water, restrooms, a ranger station, and campgrounds. For most folks, a day hike to and from Indian Gardens is a very strenuous outing. The river is yet another 1,350 feet below and almost 5 miles (one way) further by trail.

South Kaibab Trail starts from Yaki Point, about 4.5 miles east of Grand Canyon Village off East Rim Drive. In summer, you can take a free shuttle to the trailhead from the Yavapai Lodge or the Backcountry Reservation Office. In other seasons, you can park nearby. It drops 4,800 feet over a 6.7-mile course to the river. Attempting to hike down and back up in a day is nuts, but a very nice hike running several hours to a half-day (depending on your speed) takes you 1,300 feet down 1.5 miles to Cedar Ridge. This walk provides dramatic views of **Zoroaster Temple**, **Brahma Temple**, and **Pipe Creek Canyon**.

The unmaintained trails should be left to experienced hikers. Of these, the easiest to negotiate are **Hermit Trail** and **Grandview Trail**. Though not required for day hikes, permits are necessary for overnight camping within the canyon and are very difficult to obtain. (For additional details on obtaining backcountry permits, see Camping.)

Hiking from the South to North Rims takes several days, covers 21 miles via the North and South Kaibab Trails, and requires a permit. One-way free shuttles are available. For additional details on hiking the

Grand Canyon's hundreds of trail miles, look to detailed guidebooks, and/or talk with park rangers. Those who cannot obtain an overnight camping permit may wish to consider **Phantom Ranch**, a commercial operation on the canyon floor (see Lodging).

Another popular Grand Canyon activity is mule rides down Bright Angel Trail. Even the great naturalist John Muir hitched canyon rides on these easygoing beasts of burden; it's a time-honored tradition. Don't be surprised, however, to be met with glares by exhausted hikers when you come plodding up the trails from the canyon floor. And if you're not used to riding, you'll be discovering leg, hip, and back muscles you never knew about for days afterward! Year-round outings include daylong trips that almost reach the river, to overnighters at Phantom Ranch and multi-day trips. Day outings run about $120. For details, call (303) 297-2757.

Just outside the park, **Apache Stables**, (520) 638-2891, offers horseback riding in both the park and the adjoining Kaibab National Forest for one, two, or four hours.

River-running is another obvious recreational activity here, but few white-water trips actually begin below the South Rim. Most boats put in at **Lee's Ferry** (see Chapter 21) for the run through "the Big Ditch," as boaters affectionately call the Grand Canyon.

Running the Grand is the big kahuna of river boating. You can run a lot of white water, but this is graduation time. The volume of water, especially in spring when the distant Rocky Mountain headwaters bloat with snowmelt, and the riverbed's periodic drops and constrictions create some of Earth's hairiest rapids, including **Crystal**, **Hance**, **Granite**, and **Lava**. It is also intensely sublime and mindbending, due to the terrain and the often lengthy passages. The world is reduced to water, narrow bands of beach and boulders, cliffs, and sky. It is both a thrilling and ultimately relaxing endeavor.

It's also not something amateur boaters should attempt. Permits are required and are extremely difficult to secure. Most of the 20,000 or so people who run the Grand each year today do so with commercial guide companies. Prices run $200 or so per day per person, with trips running from three to 16 days. A complete list of licensed commercial guides is available in the park's free publications *The Guide* or *Trip Planner*, which can be obtained by writing to the visitor center (see Visitor Center entry in Sightseeing Highlights).

There aren't a lot of opportunities for bicycling in the park. All the trails are off-limits to bikes, but they can be very handy for cruising out West Rim Drive in peak season when it's closed to cars. Biking is allowed in the adjoining Kaibab National Forest, (520) 638-2443.

The Colorado River and some of its tributaries have very good fishing, with large trout flourishing in the super-chilled water released from Lake Powell. Licenses and tackle can be purchased in the general store in Grand Canyon Village.

As hot as it is on the South Rim most of the year, people are surprised that one can occasionally engage in some decent cross-country skiing here. While the higher North Rim offers better skiing, the Kaibab National Forest, (520) 638-2443, maintains 18 miles of easy to difficult trails near the park's East Entrance on AZ 64. There is an information kiosk describing routes about a half-mile into the access trail. Nordic rental gear is available at Babbitt's General Store in the village.

FOOD

One of the rewards of a Grand Canyon hiking trip is to climb out of the Big Ditch, clean up, and sit down to an elegant dinner at **El Tovar**, the historic hotel right on the canyon's edge in Grand Canyon Village, (520) 638-2631/2401. White linen, antique chandeliers, fine china, attentive waiters, a bar and fine wine list, and good to excellent food add up to a memorable experience—whether or not it follows an outing. It's open 6:30 a.m.–2 p.m. and 5–10 p.m. Continental dinner entrees run $15–$25. Reservations are essential in peak seasons.

More modestly priced American menus are featured in the other Grand Canyon Village hotels, including the **Bright Angel Dining Room**, the self-service **Maswik Cafeteria**, and the **Yavapai Cafeteria & Grill** (open only March through December). Also in the village is the **Arizona Steakhouse** (next to Bright Angel Lodge, open March through December, with seafood as well), the **Bright Angel Fountain** (near the Bright Angel trailhead, with sandwiches and snacks), and **Babbitt's Deli** (in the shopping center opposite the visitor center, with both a dining area and carry-out, including some vegetarian fare and chicken dinners).

Hermit's Rest Snack Bar, at the end of West Rim Drive, is open daily year-round, as is the **Desert View Cafeteria**, near the East Entrance on East Rim Drive. Dining is also available on the canyon floor at **Phantom Ranch**, (303) 297-2757, for overnight guest and passing hikers and rafters by reservation (breakfast $12, dinner

GRAND CANYON

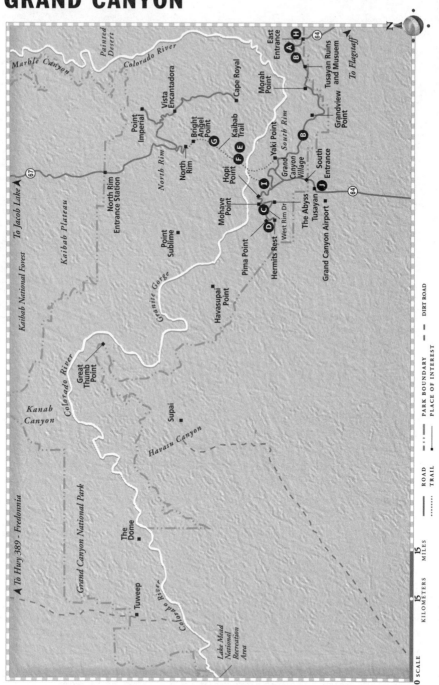

Sights

Ⓐ Desert View

Ⓑ East Rim Drive

Ⓒ West Rim Drive

Food

Ⓐ Desert View Cafeteria

Ⓓ Hermit's Rest Snack Bar

Ⓔ Phantom Ranch

Lodging

Ⓔ Phantom Ranch

Camping

Ⓕ Bright Angel Campground

Ⓖ Cottonwood Campground

Ⓗ Desert View Campground

Ⓘ Indian Hollow Campground

Ⓙ Ten-X Campground

Note: Items with the same letter are located in the same town or area.

$17–$27). Snacks, *cold beer*, and other refreshments are available on a walk-up basis from its cantina. **Tusayan**, the service center just outside the park's South Entrance on US 180, has hotels with dining rooms, as well as a McDonald's, Denny's, pizza joint, and steak house.

LODGING

Longstanding Grand Canyon concessionaire the Fred Harvey Company oversees about 1,000 rooms on the South Rim. Lodging is almost impossible to obtain without reservations during peak seasons. In fact, reservations can be made up to 23 months in advance, and often are. To reserve at any of the Fred Harvey properties, call (303) 297-2757, or write AmFar Parks & Resorts, 14001 E. Iliff, Aurora, CO 80014. There are occasional cancellations. For same-day opportunities, call (520) 638-2631.

The nicest accommodations are at **El Tovar**, nestled right on the rim. Built in 1905, it has been renovated periodically and is still in fine shape. All rooms have a full bath, TV, phones, and room service. Some suites offer magnificent views into the canyon. Rates are $120–$285.

Another historic property on the rim is **Bright Angel Lodge**. Designed of native stone and logs by Mary Elizabeth Jane Colter, it opened in 1935. The large lobby fireplace contains stones from each of the canyon's major geologic formations placed on top of each other in geologic-time sequence. Inside the lodge is the **Fred Harvey Museum**. Some cabins feature fireplaces; rates range $55–$120.

Other Fred Harvey options include the neighboring contemporary **Kachina Lodge** and **Thunderbird Lodge** ($98–$108), the **Yavapai Lodge** (motel accommodations set in the forest, $82–$96), and the **Maswik Lodge** (a short walk from the rim, $55–$105).

Another real treat (again operated by Fred Harvey Co.) is **Phantom Ranch**, the only lodging available on the canyon floor. It's located on the North Kaibab Trail, near its juncture with the Bright Angel and South Kaibab Trails. Construction of its rustic cabins of uncut river stone was directed by Mary Elizabeth Jane Colter in 1922. The cabins sleep four to ten people in bunk beds, with separate shower facilities; $22 per person. Outstanding meals are served as well. A cantina also sells snacks, cold beer, and souvenirs to passing hikers and rafters.

You'll find a handful of accommodations in Tusayan, just outside the park's South Entrance on US 180. Reservations are advised, especially in peak season. Options (from cheapest to expensive) include the **Seven Mile Lodge**, (520) 638-2291 ($80); the **Moqui Lodge**, (520) 638-2424 ($85); the **Red Feather Lodge**, (520) 638-2414 or (800) 538-2345 ($95); the **Best Western Grand Canyon Squire Inn**, (520) 638-2681 or (800) 622-6966 ($110); and the **Quality Inn**, (520) 638-2673 or (800) 221-2222 ($130). The latter two feature pools.

Many other options exist in Williams (60 miles south on AZ 64) and Flagstaff (80 miles south via US 180).

CAMPING

There are three campgrounds within the park on the South Rim. **Mather Campground** in Grand Canyon Village has 320 sites for tents and RVs (no hookups) year-round. From March through November you can—and should!—make reservations up to five months in advance with DESTINET, (800) 365-2267, or P.O. Box 85705, San Diego, CA 92186-5705. Sites (maximum of six occupants and two vehicles) go for $15 June through August; $12 September through May. From December through February it operates on a first-come, first-served basis. Pay showers and laundry facilities are available near the Backcountry Reservation Office.

Next to it is **Trailer Village**, with 84 RV sites (with hookups), pay showers, and a nearby dump station for $18; open all year. For reservations, call (303) 297-2757. Also in the village is **Fred Harvey Trailer Village**, (520) 638-2401, with 84 RV sites (with hookups) for $18; open year-round.

Near the east end of East Rim Drive, 26 miles from Grand Canyon Village on AZ 64, is **Desert View Campground**. It has 50 sites (no RV hookups), with water but no showers, available on a first-come, first-served basis only for $10. It is open mid-May to mid-October.

Outside the park are a number of possibilities. The Forest Service operates **Ten-X Campground** 3 miles south of Tusayan on US 180 from May through September. It has 70 sites (no RV hookups or showers) and water, available on a first-come, first-served basis for $10. Tusayan's several commercial options include **Grand Canyon Camper Village**, (520) 638-2887, with 300 sites, showers, and a playground; open all year. RV sites with full hookups cost $22; tent sites are $15.

Free primitive camping is also allowed in the **Kaibab National Forest** if you camp at least ¼-mile off paved roads. A number of dirt Forest Service roads intersect US 180 south of Tusayan; USFS FR 686 (1 mile south of the Ten X Campground) is usually open year-round. Call the Tusayan Ranger District at (520) 638-2443 for details.

There is also extremely limited camping in the canyon, and it is regulated by permits which are very difficult to obtain. Camping without them will likely result in a fine. They are issued by the Backcountry Reservation Office, based on the number of camping sites available in the three in-canyon campgrounds: **Indian Hollow**, **Bright Angel**, and **Cottonwood**. Spring and fall are particularly favored because of the cool temperatures. Permits cost $20, plus $4 per person per night. Information is available by phone, but reservations must be made in writing. Applications are accepted for the current month and the next four—if you hope for an overnight hiking trip in October, you should apply in June. Occasional cancellations can be had by showing up in person at the Backcountry Reservation Office in Grand Canyon Village, open 8–7 in peak seasons and 8–5 otherwise. Its mailing address is P.O. Box 129, Grand Canyon, AZ 86023; (520) 638-7875.

NIGHTLIFE

There is isn't much to do on the South Rim at night, except look at the magnificent stars. **El Tovar** has a piano bar, and there's live music Wednesday through Sunday at **Bright Angel Lodge**. The **Maswik**

Lodge in Grand Canyon Village has a sports bar. Look for the **Grand Canyon Chamber Music Festival**, (520) 638-9215), every September.

The National Park Service also conducts nightly lectures, slide programs, and other events during the peak season in Mather Auditorium, Grand Canyon Village—check the bulletin board at the main visitor center or *The Guide*, or call (520) 638-7888 for details.

In Tusayan, the small commercial center just outside the South Entrance, some hotels feature live entertainment. Tusayan's **IMAX Theater**, (520) 638-2203, airs the movie *Grand Canyon: The Hidden Secret* daily all year every hour on the half-hour (in summer 8:30 a.m.–8:30 p.m., in winter 10:30 a.m.–6:30 p.m.) on a screen 82 feet wide and six stories high, with six-track Dolby SurroundSound. The movie, produced by Academy Award talents, traces the ancient and modern history of the canyon via historic re-enactments and wonderful photography. Admission is $8 for adults, $4 for kids ages 4–11.

20

GRAND CANYON: NORTH RIM

A lmost 90 percent of the Grand Canyon's 5 million yearly visitors see it from its South Rim. The North Rim, in contrast, is the canyon of yesteryear: a place where one can find solitude while over-looking one of the world's greatest natural wonders. Though they are separated by only 10 miles of canyon air, the North Rim feels far removed from its southern counterpart, in part because of its thick, lush forests. At an elevation of more than 8,000 feet—roughly 1,000 feet higher than the South Rim—the North Rim is cooler and captures much more moisture; in fact, it's closed from December through mid-May because heavy snows bury its access road.

Visitor facilities are extremely limited on and near the North Rim. If you hope to stay in the wonderful old Grand Canyon Lodge right on the rim, book way in advance. Even camping spots inside the park are hard to obtain, and the closest private facilities are a long drive away. While inconvenient, these lodging limitations help reduce the number of people here, providing an experience that must echo the trips enjoyed by visitors long ago.

Getting here takes some doing—it's 215 miles by car from South Rim to North Rim visitor centers. Consider taking a few extra days to explore a handful of other interesting destinations in the isolated patch between the Grand Canyon and the Utah line known as the Arizona Strip. ◨

GRAND CANYON

Marble Canyon
Painted Desert
Colorado River
Vista Encantadora
Point Imperial
Cape Royal
Morah Point
East Entrance
Tusayan Ruins and Museum
To Flagstaff

Bright Angel Point
Kaibab Trail
Grandview Point
North Rim
Yaki Point
Grand South Rim

To B E I J
Hopi Point
Grand Canyon Village
South Entrance

67
K
F H
North Rim Entrance Station
North Rim
Mohave Point
West Rim Dr
The Abyss
Tusayan
64
To Jacob Lake

Kaibab National Forest
Kaibab Plateau
Point Sublime
Pima Point
Hermits Rest
Grand Canyon Airport

Granite Gorge
Havasupai Point

Great Thumb Point
Colorado River

Kanab Canyon
Supai
Havasu Canyon

Grand Canyon National Park
The Dome

To Hwy 389 · Fredonia
Tuweep
D
Colorado River

Lake Mead National Recreation Area

0 SCALE
5 KILOMETERS
5 MILES

PARK BOUNDARY
PLACE OF INTEREST
ROAD
TRAIL
DIRT ROAD

Sights

Ⓐ North Rim Center

Ⓑ Pipe Spring National
Monument

Ⓒ Point Imperial/
Cape Royal Drive

Ⓓ Toroweap Overlook

Food

Ⓐ Grand Canyon Lodge

Ⓔ Jacob Lake Inn

Ⓕ Kaibab Lodge

Lodging

Ⓐ Grand Canyon Lodge

Ⓔ Jacob Lake Inn

Ⓕ Kaibab Lodge

Camping

Ⓖ Cottonwood Campground

Ⓗ DeMotte Park Campground

Ⓘ Heart Canyon RV Campground

Ⓙ Jacob Lake Campground

Ⓚ Kaibab Camper Village

Ⓛ North Rim Campground

Note: Items with the same letter are located in the same town or area.

A PERFECT DAY ON THE NORTH RIM OF THE GRAND CANYON

If possible, camp out the night before and awaken to daybreak on the canyon's edge. Take a short morning walk on the Bright Angel Point Trail. On the way back visit the historic Grand Canyon Lodge, perched on the rim. After a picnic lunch, take a longer walk down the North Kaibab Trail to immerse yourself in the canyon; or, if it's hot, cruise through the shady, cool forest along the Windfoss Trail. End the day with a wonderful drive, and watch a spectacular sunset from Point Royal. Be sure to have made reservations ahead of time for dinner at the Grand Canyon Lodge.

SIGHTSEEING HIGHLIGHTS

★★★ **North Rim Center**—This is the heart of the services and facilities on this side of the canyon. It's also where you'll run into crowds, but they aren't oppressive. From the parking lots, head first toward the rim, where you'll find the **Bright Angel Point Trail**. This ¼-mile paved trail provides some of the North Rim's best views. The trail rolls out onto a ridge with tremendous drops on either side, descending 200 vertical feet past wind-gnarled junipers and weathered rocks to an observation deck ringed by a handrail. On windless days you can sometimes hear an odd sound: the water of Roaring Springs gushing out of solid rock walls some 3,800 feet down a side canyon. This spring provides all the park's drinking water—it's even piped down the canyon, across the Colorado River, and up the opposite wall to the South Rim. Here you can gaze out on the magnificent **Deva**, **Brahma**, and **Zoroaster Temples**, and the depths of the inner gorge that hide the river itself.

Back on the rim, drop into the **Grand Canyon Lodge**. While the original building, designed by Gilbert Stanley Underwood and built by the Union Pacific Railway in 1926, burned down immediately after opening, it was promptly rebuilt. Today the native stone and timber structure is a wonderful example of rustic architecture. You can grab a chair and sit on its outdoor patio sipping a drink while looking out over the canyon, or, in inclement weather, sit inside in a glass-enclosed Sun Room backed by a large fireplace. In the Sun Room you'll find a bronze, life-size statue of Brighty, a beloved burro that ferried people to the canyon floor for many years.

Just a few steps away is the **North Rim Visitor Center**, offering current news on trails, weather conditions, and special events, as well as the informative free publication *The Guide*. The center has a small bookstore, free literature, and park rangers who can answer questions. Drinking water and restrooms are also available.

Details: At the end of AZ 67, 44 miles from its juncture with US 89A at Jacob Lake and 14 miles north of the park boundary; (520) 638-7864. Open May 15 through October 15. Services and facilities on the North Rim shut down after Oct. 15, though the campground remains open until December 1, barring heavy snowfall, and park entry remains open year-round to cross-country skiers or hikers with a backcountry permit (see Fitness and Recreation for details). Admission is $20 per vehicle, $4 for hikers/bikers, and is good for a week at both rims. (1 to 2 hours)

★★★ **Point Imperial/Cape Royal Drive**—This paved, two-lane road is a perfect microcosm of everything special about the North Rim. Forking off of the park's main access road, it climbs through beautiful, thick, flourishing stands of quaking aspen, spruce, and pine pocketed by small meadows bursting with wildflowers and lush grasses—a perfect picnic setting. Wild Merriman's turkeys wander out of the forests, and other game abounds in this portion of the **Kaibab Plateau**, which Indians once called "The Mountain Lying Down," because of its almost imperceptible slope upward from hot lowlands to a moist summit on the North Rim.

Eleven miles from the visitor center is **Point Imperial**, the highest overlook on either rim. Great views open here, particularly to the east of the park and north toward Utah.

You then pass a series of observation points, including **Vista Encantadora**, **Roosevelt Point**, and **Walhalla**. A short trail from Walhalla leads to a small Anasazi ruin. This road also provides a glimpse of the Colorado River, largely hidden from view on the North Rim, at **Unkar Delta**, once the shelter of a small Anasazi settlement on the canyon floor.

The road ends at **Cape Royal**, which offers the best views of any single point in the park. The cape juts out into the central canyon, and the river makes a huge sweeping curve around it, almost surrounding you with plunging walls, buttes, conical temples, and other majestic formations that erosion has isolated from the canyon rim. A short, self-guiding, asphalt nature trail winds from the parking lot to the point through beautiful trees, shrubs, and ground cover. Along the way is **Angel's Window**, a rare (for the Grand Canyon) natural arch.

Details: The 28-mile stretch begins about 3 miles north of the North Rim visitor center along AZ 67. It is open to vehicles from May 15 to October 15 and is free with park admission. (2 to 3 hours)

✯✯ **Pipe Spring National Monument**—Outside Grand Canyon National Park is the isolated area known as the **Arizona Strip**. Cut off from the rest of Arizona by the Grand Canyon, deep tributary canyons, cliffs, and mountains to the west and east, and the Utah border to the north, this area was actually settled by Utah Mormon pioneers in the 1860s—and continued to harbor polygamists long after they'd been rooted out of most other places. It would most likely have been incorporated into Utah's borders but for the work of writer Sharlot Hall, who mounted an expedition across "The Strip" and the Kaibab forests in 1910, then lectured on its attributes to fellow Arizonans. When Arizona was granted statehood in 1912, it included The Strip within its territory.

Pipe Springs was one of the more successful ranching outposts established by the Mormons here, at the site of one of its few permanent water sources. In 1923 the National Park Service bought the 40-acre ranch, to maintain it as an example of early local ranching.

People in period clothing demonstrate weaving, quilting, and other pioneer crafts in its antique-furnished buildings and in an adobe fort built as protection against the local Paiute Indians, who didn't appreciate the loss of this precious water hole.

Details: On AZ 389, 14 miles west of Fredonia. A visitor center, (520) 643-7105, open 8–4 daily, has a bookstore and snacks. Admission is $2 for adults, $1 for children. (1 to 3 hours)

☆ **Toroweap Overlook**—This would be a three-star destination if it were easier to reach. But intrepid travelers with enough time and the proper vehicle will treasure this overlook of the Grand Canyon's far northwestern realm because of its isolation. To get here you must leave the park, cut across the Arizona Strip on the dirt Sunshine Road, and then reenter the park. The road crosses the desolate Antelope Valley, an extension of the Great Basin Desert to the northwest.

Some 47 miles into the drive you'll pass a side road to Mt. Trumbull, a prominent high peak that rises out of the bleak desert floor and harbors the state's most remote wilderness, the 7,900-acre **Mt. Trumbull Wilderness Area**. This side road also provides access to the 14,600-acre **Mount Logan Wilderness Area**. At mile 54 you'll reach the **Tuweep Ranger Station**, near the park boundary, which is staffed year-round. It is then another 5 miles to the overlook, which dishes up a spectacular unbroken 3,200-foot drop to the river—not a spot for acrophobes! If the weather is calm, you can sometimes hear the roar of Lava Falls wafting up from below. There's a primitive campground with 11 sites a mile back from the rim. If you go, be sure to take lots of water. No gas or other services are available en route.

Details: The graded roads leading to the ranger station are in pretty good shape and passable to ordinary vehicles in good weather, but the last 5 miles can be more difficult. The total distance to the rim is 60 miles. Head 6 miles east of Fredonia on AZ 389, and turn south (left) onto an unpaved road. You'll come to several forks, some unmarked: stay on the southwest route. There is also another 97-mile route to Toroweap via graded dirt roads from St. George, Utah. (2 hours drive time one way from Fredonia)

FITNESS AND RECREATION

As with the South Rim, the primary activity on the North Rim is hiking, with both pleasant, easygoing trails along the forested rim and strenuous options into the canyon itself.

A great introduction to North Rim hiking is the **Bright Angel Point Trail** (see Sightseeing Highlights). Another easily accessible route is the **Transept Trail**, which runs 1.5 miles along the rim between the North Rim Campground and the Grand Canyon Lodge.

Another mellow hike is on the **Windforss Trail**, which travels lovely forests of white fir, Englemann and blue spruce, aspen, and ponderosa pine as it winds along the rim. Here you may run across the Kaibab squirrel (native only to the Kaibab Plateau on the Grand Canyon's north side), a large, dark critter with tufted ears and a bushy white tail. The trail totals 10 miles round-trip, but you can go as far out as you like and then turn back. A half-hour stroll brings you through the woods to a canyon view point. To get to the trailhead, go north on AZ 67, the park road from Jacob's Lake, some 3 miles from the visitor center and look for the dirt road on the left. It drops into a pretty meadow and a parking lot, and is passable for all vehicles.

The **North Kaibab Trail** is the only maintained trail into the canyon from the North Rim. From the trailhead it will take you 14 miles to reach the Colorado River and you'll descend almost 6,000 feet—this is not a day hike! However, even brief forays down the trail and back up provide a taste of hiking "below the rim." **Coconino Overlook** is .75 mile down, the **Supai Tunnel** is 2 miles down, and **Roaring Springs** is 4.7 miles and 3,000 feet down. The latter is a popular destination for day hikers, who can cool off with a swim in the pools below the springs. It is the limit for most day hikers; people who proceed beyond this point in summer are often the ones requiring medical assistance. . . . The total distance across the canyon, from rim to rim, is 21 miles via the North and South Kaibab Trails, and is usually done in three days.

Day hikers are not required to get a permit, but hikers planning to overnight in the backcountry must obtain one—very difficult to do. Permits are occasionally available on a walk-up basis from the Backcountry Office in the North Rim Visitor Center. (For more on backcountry permits, see Camping, South Rim chapter.)

Outside the park are other opportunities for hiking. Just north of the park is the **Saddle Mt. Wilderness**, accessed via a road that branches off AZ 67 near the Kaibab Lodge. For details, contact the Kaibab National Forest, (520) 643-7298. Further afield are the **Kanab Creek Wilderness Area** (which protects the largest tributary canyon on the north side of the Grand Canyon, which is more than 3,000 feet deep at points), **Mt. Trumbull Wilderness Area**, and **Mt. Logan**

Wilderness Area. For details on these three, contact the BLM in
Kanab, Utah, at (801) 644-2672.

Biking on the North Rim is restricted to paved and dirt roads but
is allowed in the **Kaibab National Forest**, just outside the park's
boundaries. Maps and information on the Kaibab is available at the
North Rim Visitor Center, or at the ranger visitor center in Jacob
Lake, (520) 643-7298.

Dirt roads of the Kaibab National Forest, and BLM roads in the
remote backcountry of the Arizona Strip, offer fantastic four-wheel drives. For details, contact the BLM in Kanab, (801) 644-2672 or the
Kaibab National Forest.

River-running on the Colorado is an obvious recreational activity
here. For details, see the South Rim chapter.

Mule rides are also popular on the North Rim. Outings run from
an hour ($15) to all day ($85). For details, call (520) 638-2292 in season, (801) 679-8665 off season, or ask at the Grand Canyon Lodge.

The North Rim is also a remote but increasingly popular cross-
country skiing destination, receiving an average of 140 inches of snow
a year. The park is legally open for visitation in winter, but all facilities
and services are shut down and the access road from Jacob Lake is
closed, requiring a 52-mile ski-in. Another option is to book a visit
with the **North Rim Nordic Center**, run out of the Kaibab Lodge on
AZ 67, about 25 miles south of Jacob Lake. The center transports
skiers to the Kaibab Lodge in specially equipped snow vans from late
December to mid-March (depending on snowfall). There are 25 miles
of groomed trails and numerous ungroomed trails around the lodge,
and snow van transportation to the North Rim allows unforgettable
skiing on the edge of the snow-blanketed Great Abyss. Note, however,
that there is talk of shutting down this facility as this book goes to
press. For details, call (520) 526-0924.

FOOD

Dining options on and around the North Rim are sparse. On the rim,
the **Grand Canyon Lodge**, (520) 638-2612, is open for breakfast,
lunch, and dinner. The formal dinning room has terrific views. The
menu is limited, but the food is quite good and reasonably priced.
Dinner and breakfast reservations are essential in summer. The lodge
cafeteria serves all meals. The North Rim Campground's general store
provides sandwiches and a few other hot snacks.

The next closest dining possibility is the **Kaibab Lodge**, (520) 638-2389, outside the park on AZ 67. It serves a breakfast buffet, lunch, and dinner to guests and the general public. The next option is in Jacob Lake, some 44 miles from the North Rim, at the **Jacob Lake Inn**, (520) 643-7232, which has both a quick-serve counter and a very nice wood-paneled dining room filled with Indian arts and crafts. It's staffed by pleasant young women, many of whom have been working here for years. The food is good and well priced. The inn is open intermittently throughout the winter.

Still further away, almost 80 miles from the North Rim, in Fredonia, are a number of restaurants, and even more options another 7 miles north in Kanab, Utah.

LODGING

As with dining, lodging choices on and around the North Rim are very limited. In fact, the only accommodations right on the rim are the cabins and rooms of the **Grand Canyon Lodge**, (303) 297-2757 for reservations, (520) 638-2612 for the lodge itself. Like other North Rim facilities, it shuts down from mid-October through mid-May. The lodge is another of the classic "rustic-style" rock-and-timber structures that grace some of our national parks. In this case, the original structure was designed by Gilbert Stanley Underwood and built by the Union Pacific Railway in 1926. However, it burned down soon after opening, and this version followed. The basic rooms and cabins all have private baths and some have canyon views. All adjoin the main lodge, but accommodations in the lodge itself are no longer offered. Amenities include a bar—The Saloon, open 11–10 daily—a large gift shop, and a good dining room, at rates from $56–$95.

The closest accommodation outside the park is the charming 1926 **Kaibab Lodge**, (about a half-hour drive from the North Rim on AZ 67, (520) 638-2389 or (800) 525-0924. Its rooms have private baths in cabins for up to five people. Rates are $65–$95. The lodge also contains a dining room and a store selling the only diesel fuel on the North Rim. It's open from mid-May to mid-October, and again in winter for cross-country skiers.

Further down AZ 67, about 45 miles from the North Rim, is the **Jacob Lake Inn**, (520) 643-7232. Its simple cabins are clean and have showers. The inn maintains a decent dining room, a well-stocked Indian arts and crafts shop, and a gas station. It's open mid-May to mid-October, and sporadically otherwise; $75 per night. Additional lodging exists in Fredonia, almost 80 miles from the North Rim, and another 7 miles north, in Kanab, Utah.

CAMPING

Few lodgings exist on and around the North Rim, and camping options are limited as well. The **North Rim Campground**, operated by the Park Service, has only 83 sites (no hookups), at $15 a night, with a seven-night maximum stay. It sits under a canopy of stately ponderosa pines a few minutes' walk from the rim and its Transcept Trail, 1.5 miles north of the Grand Canyon Lodge and visitor center. The campground has drinking water and restrooms, with nearby showers, a laundry, and a general store/snack bar. Reservations can (and should be!) made up to eight weeks in advance, by calling (800) 365-2267. Quieter sites numbers 39–46 are reserved for tent campers. Sites 5–38 are on the outside perimeter, with forest on one side.

Five miles north of the park boundary in the Kaibab National Forest is **DeMotte Park Campground**, with 23 pull-through sites (no hookups), $10 each, on a first-come, first-served basis. Further north, 45 miles from the North Rim, is **Jacob Lake Campground**, with 56 sites (no hookups), water, and restrooms at $10. Reservations at the latter can be made at (303) 297-2757. Both are open late May to late October.

You may also camp at undeveloped sites within the **Kaibab National Forest**, as long as you are at least ¼-mile away from paved roads and/or water. A number of decent dirt roads intersect AZ 67. For details, contact the ranger visitor center in Jacob Lake next to the Jacob Lake Inn, or call (520) 643-7298.

Cottonwood is the only campground accessible from the North Rim. However, a permit is required to overnight here (see Camping, South Rim chapter).

For RVers, only one option for hookups exists: **Kaibab Camper Village**, ¼-mile south of Jacob Lake on AZ 67, (520) 643-7804, with 60 sites with hookups as well as 50 tent sites.

Another more distant possibility that generally has space when all other roadside spots are taken is **Heart Canyon RV Campground**, on the Kaibab-Paiute Indian Reservation ½-mile east of Pipe Springs National Monument, on AZ 389 west of Fredonia, (520) 643-7245, with 45 sites ($8 for tents, $12 for RVs with hookups), a laundry, and pay showers.

21

LAKE POWELL AREA

One of America's greatest water playgrounds, Lake Powell receives close to 3 million visitors a year, in a region that probably saw a few thousand tourists 30 years ago. What's different? Glen Canyon Dam.

Dedicated by Lady Bird Johnson in 1966, this massive concrete plug in the Colorado River eventually created a pool running almost 200 miles upstream and a shoreline 1,960 miles long in its intricately carved side canyons—more than the entire west coast of the United States! Add sunshine and the spectacular rock scenery previously only visible to hardy explorers, and you have one of the nation's premium outdoor recreation sites.

The dam's construction also drowned one of the nation's most beautiful places, Glen Canyon, a loss that helped spark the modern environmental movement. The canyon was named by John Wesley Powell, who led the first expedition down the Colorado River by boat. He wrote of this spot as "a curious ensemble of wonderful features—carved walls, royal arches, glens, alcove gulches, mounds and monuments. . . . We decided to call it Glen Canyon." Much of its beauty still remains above water, making it a paradise for boaters.

Around the lake is the million-acre-plus Glen Canyon National Recreation Area, containing excellent opportunities for hiking, four-wheel drives, and other pursuits. Small Anasazi ruins and other sites make for fascinating historical visits, while Lee's Ferry alternates between a sleepy historical outpost and a bustling put-in point for most Grand Canyon river-running expeditions. ◼

LAKE POWELL AREA

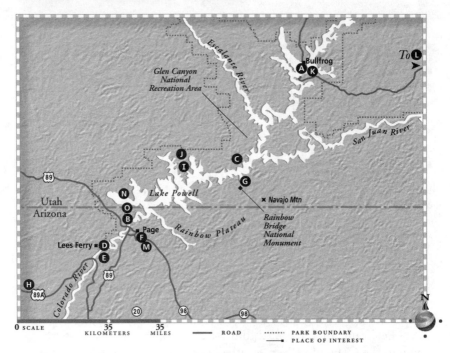

Sights

- **A** Bullfrog Visitor Center
- **B** Glen Canyon Dam
- **C** Hole-in-the-Rock
- **D** Lee's Ferry
- **E** Navajo Bridge
- **F** Powell Museum
- **G** Rainbow Bridge National Monument
- **H** San Bartolome Historic Site

Camping

- **A** Bullfrog Bay Campground
- **A** Bullfrog Marina Campground
- **I** Canyon Campground
- **J** Farley Canyon Campground
- **K** Halls Crossing Campground
- **L** Hite Campground
- **M** Lake Powell Campground
- **D** Lee's Ferry Campground
- **N** Lone Rock Beach Campground
- **O** Wahweap Campground

Note: Items with the same letter are located in the same town or area.

A PERFECT DAY IN THE LAKE POWELL AREA

Begin the day with a stop at the Carl Hayden Visitors Center atop Glen Canyon Dam for a look at its innards. If you're not here to boat, visit the Powell Museum in Page before heading down river to check out the river-runners at Lee's Ferry. Stop en-route at Navajo Bridge and have lunch at Lee's Ferry Lodge. Or, if you're lucky enough to snag a houseboat or powerboat, head off onto the lake and visit Rainbow Bridge. Spend the evening dining on the Canyon King paddle wheeler or at the Rainbow Room overlooking the lake.

SIGHTSEEING HIGHLIGHTS

★★★ **Glen Canyon Dam**—Called the last great dam on the Colorado, this $187 million engineering marvel acts like a faucet for the Grand Canyon, shunting the water of Lake Powell trapped behind it 186 miles upstream into southeastern Utah. The nation's second-largest artificial water body, the lake flooded one of the Colorado's most splendid sections, Glen Canyon. This event helped spark the modern environmental movement.

But positive attributes of the dam are often overlooked: daily generation of enough electricity to power a city of 1.5 million people, storage of 27 million acre-feet of water for downstream irrigation, and, perhaps most important, flood control. The old Colorado was a wild beast, with periodic bucking floods and raging spring runoffs that wreaked havoc along its banks year after year. This dam tamed it, for better or worse. Even opponents who'd like to see it torn down have to be impressed by it.

The area holds several notable attractions. To build the dam, construction crews needed to cross the canyon easily; thus, the first thing built was **Glen Canyon Bridge**. Opened in 1959, at 700 feet above the river, it is the second-highest steel arch bridge in the world. You can walk out on it for some cheap thrills and amazing views of the dam just upstream.

Perched right on the edge of the canyon's north side and one end of the 583-foot-high dam is the **Carl Hayden Visitor Center**. Here you can see a film on the dam's construction, a large-scale relief map of the entire Colorado Plateau, and other displays, and pick up information on Glen Canyon National Recreation Area. Free guided tours of the dam start at the crest and descend via elevators into the dam, which

is always a cool 50 degrees. You'll learn how the "buckets" used to haul
cement carried 24 tons a scoop, and how the concrete was cured by a
network of tiny aluminum tubes filled with ice water.

*Details: On US 89 at the Colorado River, just north of Page, Arizona;
(520) 608-6404. The visitor center is open daily from Memorial Day
through Labor Day from 7–7; the rest of the year 8–5. Admission is free.
Guided tours are conducted April through October and run every hour on the
half-hour. They last about an hour, but you can also take a (faster) self-guided
tour throughout the year (1 to 2 hours)*

★★★ **Lee's Ferry**—This historic site played a key role in the settlement and trade of the Four Corners area. In 1871 John D. Lee was
sent here to operate a ferry service across the Colorado that would
enable Mormon colonization south of the great river. He was executed
in 1877 for participating in the Mountain Meadows Massacre, when
Mormons attacked a non-Mormon wagon train. The ferry, though,
remained in business until 1929.

Today a small stone fort and a trading post mark the remains,
which can be toured on a self-guiding trail. Just a stone's throw away is
the primary put-in point for white-water expeditions through the
Grand Canyon, and almost any day of the year you'll find experienced
boaters loading up their rafts and kayaks, while enthusiastic, trembling
passengers wave farewell as their rafts swing into the river's powerful
grip. Nearby, in the Paria River Valley, is the **Lonely Dell Ranch
Historic District**, overseen by the Park Service.

*Details: Lee's Ferry is just 15 miles as the fish swims downriver from
Glen Canyon Dam, but it's 46 miles via US 89, US 89A, and the Lee's
Ferry access road from Marble Gorge. En route is a great scenic viewpoint at
US 89 mile marker 527 atop the Echo Cliffs. A ranger station at Lee's Ferry
is staffed periodically; (520) 355-2234. The river launch site and historic
properties are accessible year-round. Access is free. (1 to 3 hours)*

★★ **Rainbow Bridge National Monument**—Navajos knew this huge
rock span long before whites did, calling it *Nonnoshoshi*, the "Rainbow
Turned to Stone." Believed to be a door to the afterlife, it is the world's
largest natural bridge: 275 feet long, arching 290 feet above its original
streambed. A 160-acre national monument was created in 1910, but
access was very difficult, requiring a week or so of rough travel on horse
or foot. Lake Powell solved that problem, backing its waters right to the
bridge's base, and today you can boat in 50 miles from Wahweap.

Details: The site is accessible year-round, and visits are free. For information on tour boat excursions, see the Fitness and Recreation section. You can also approach it on foot or horseback via a 14-mile trail across the Navajo Reservation. For the required permit, write to: P.O. Box 308, Window Rock, AZ 86515, or call (520) 871-6647. (6 hours by boat from Wahweap)

⭐ **Bullfrog Visitor Center**—Located far up-lake from Glen Canyon Dam in Utah, this facility has a good museum on the area's natural and human history, including an interesting scale model of a slot canyon. Boaters can also obtain current weather and lake conditions here.

Details: On the north shore of Lake Powell in Utah, opposite Hall's Crossing. Reach it via a ferry from Hall's Crossing or from the north on Utah 276; (435) 684-7400. Open daily April through early October 8–5; March and November 8–5 weekends only; closed otherwise. (For additional details on the Bullfrog area, see Burr Trail and Notom/Bullfrog Road entries in the Capitol Reef chapter.) (1 hour)

⭐ **Hole-in-the-Rock**—This isolated spot on the north shore of Lake Powell marks one of the most impressive, or crazed, efforts ever undertaken by the Mormon pioneers. In 1879 the church formed the San Juan Mission and sent it off to colonize southeastern Utah. More than 200 people, 400 horses, and 1,000 cattle hit the road, which they had to blaze as they went. Crossing canyon after canyon, they managed only 1.7 miles a day but finally found themselves at the brink of the Colorado River. Here they had to blast, chop, and hack a trail more than a 1,000-foot precipice, lowering the wagons by rope at one point. This fissure was nicknamed Hole-in-the-Rock.

Details: If you have a four-wheel-drive vehicle, access the site via a 55-mile dirt road from Escalante, Utah (see Grand Staircase–Escalante chapter). Otherwise, a much longer route originates from Big Water, Utah and US 89. It can also be approached from Lake Powell. (3 hours minimum)

⭐ **Navajo Bridge**—The first and, for many years, the only bridge to span the Colorado River between Green River, Utah, and California is now a National Historic Landmark closed to vehicular traffic. It's a great place to get out of your car and stretch your legs on a walk over the upper reach of **Marble Canyon**, the head canyon of the Grand Canyon. The graceful steel bridge aches over the jade-colored river 467 feet below and makes a great vantage point for watching river-runners heading into the Grand. The south end of the bridge is on the

Navajo Reservation, and Navajo vendors sell jewelry, rugs, and other arts and crafts here.

Details: The bridge is located just to the side of US 89A. It's open daily year-round, and walking on it is free. About a mile north on US 89A in Marble Gorge is the Navajo Bridge Interpretive Center, which has displays on area history, as well as a restaurant, service station, and store. Open daily April through October 9–5. Free. (30 minutes)

✩ **Powell Museum**—This small museum tells the story of John Wesley Powell, who led the first organized expedition down the Colorado River in 1869. It also contains displays on the area's geology and Indian history.

Details: 6 N. Lake Powell Blvd., Page; (520) 645-9496. Open in summer, Monday through Saturday 8–6:30 and Sunday 10-6:30, with shorter hours in fall and spring; closed in winter. Free. (30 minutes)

✩ **San Bartolome Historic Site**—The fellows who named this spot were well versed in the geography covered by this book. On July 29, 1776, two New Mexican Catholic priests and their followers set out from Santa Fe to find an overland route to the missions of Monterey, California, because they believed they were only a few months' walk away—at the most. After struggling across Utah's rugged southern canyons, they barely made it back to the Hopi and Zuni missions before winter. They camped near this site one night.

Details: This small site is easy to pass by on US 89A; look carefully for roadside markers about 17 miles west of Marble Canyon village. Open year-round. Admission is free. (15 minutes)

FITNESS AND RECREATION

With a surface area of 161,390 acres when full, water sports such as waterskiing, sailing, kayaking, houseboating, swimming, and Jet Skiing are the primary attraction at Lake Powell.

The lake's thousands of side canyons, which twist and wind back into slickrock country, are a delight to explore, providing isolated out-ings even when tens of thousands of people are on the lake. As winters here can be quite cold, and the lake is recharged with snowmelt in the spring, midsummer to midfall are ideal times for water sports. Sailing is best in the large bays, including Wahweap, Padre, and Bullfrog.

Lake Powell Resorts & Marinas maintains a rental fleet of 330 houseboats, 275 powerboats ranging from 16- to 19-foot models, and personal watercraft including Jet Skis ($200 a day), kneeboards, ski tubes, and water skis ($19 a day). Other than houseboats, rentals can also be arranged by the hour.

Houseboating is a huge draw here, and one can rent units with air conditioning, dual bathrooms, and other cushy amenities, as well as simpler models. Reservations should be made months—even a year!—ahead of time. A minimum of two days is required for rentals from October through mid-May, three days otherwise. Rates for three days run from $611–$2,073. For details, call (800) 528-6154 or the individual marinas listed below.

A handful of marinas operate year-round on the lakeshore and are accessible by car. All have launch ramps, boat rentals, lodging, fuel, fishing gear, groceries, and other supplies. The largest, **Wahweap Marina**, (520) 645-2433, is just 6 miles from Page, next to Glen Canyon Dam. Next to it, on the Arizona/Utah border, is **Stateline Marina**, (520) 645-6381. **Bullfrog Marina**, (435) 684-3000, is in Utah near midlake, accessed via UT 276. **Halls Crossing Marina**, (435) 684-7000, is opposite Bullfrog, also accessed via UT 276. **Hite Marina**, (435) 684-2278, is the northernmost facility, at the end of the lake just off UT 95. **Dangling Rope**, about 7 miles southwest of the canyon leading to Rainbow Bridge, is 40 miles up-lake from Wahweap. Accessible only by boat, it stocks ice, fuel, fresh water, and basic food supplies.

In 1997–1998, new entrance fees for recreational activities (not applied to stops at visitor centers) were instituted within the Glen Canyon National Recreation Area. Rates (good for one to seven days) are now $3 per individual, $5 per vehicle, and $10 for boating.

Lake Powell offers guided boat tours and charter boat services to Rainbow Bridge, fishing, skiing, and other activities, ranging from one-hour trips to day outings. The *Canyon King,* an authentic 95-foot paddlewheeler operated by Lake Powell Resorts & Marinas, offers one-hour cruises and evening dinner trips in Wahweap Bay; call (800) 528-6154 for details. For other commercial lake boating services, contact the Page Chamber of Commerce (520) 645-2741.

River-rafting on the Colorado is another possibility, though you can't just plop down and take off. Tranquil, flat-water trips from the base of Glen Canyon Dam (accessed via a 2-mile tunnel that emerges at the water's edge) downstream to Lee's Ferry through the remnant of Glen Canyon is one option available from commercial guide services, many based in Page. Half- and full-day outings are possible, with prices (including lunch) for the latter around $70 for adults and $60 for kids. Lee's Ferry is the put-in point for Grand Canyon trips, but these are by permit only and take years for private boaters to secure. Your best opportunity is with a commercial operation. For details, see Fitness and Recreation in the South Rim chapter.

Lake fishing is also popular, in particular for largemouth and striped bass, black crappie, bluegill, and walleye. With the lake overlapping two states, licenses are required from Arizona and/or Utah, depending on your destination. They are available at the lake's marinas or in nearby communities.

In addition to lake angling, Glen Canyon Dam has created some of North America's premium trout-fishing waters in the Colorado River below the dam. Access is from Lee's Ferry.

While water sports are the main draw in the Lake Powell area, that's not the only game in town. Some of the world's premiere rugged canyoneering country is found in the **Paria Canyon/Vermilion Cliffs Wilderness Area** near Lee's Ferry. The narrow, twisting **Buckskin Gulch** arm of the Paria is particular amazing, as is the **Corkscrew** slot section of **Antelope Canyon**. However, a flash flood in Antelope Canyon took the lives of nine people in the summer of 1997; both Paria and Antelope should only be tackled by experienced canyoneers. The best seasons for exploration are spring and late fall. The Vermilion Cliffs also shelter 12 super-rare California condors. The world's largest birds, they were released a few years ago in an experimental program. For details on the Vermilion Cliffs/Paria area, contact the Bureau of Land Management, Kanab, Utah, (435) 644-2672. For details on Antelope, contact the Navajo Nation Parks and Recreation Department, (520) 698-3360/3347.

You'll find many tamer hiking routes as well. The canyons of the Escalante River and its tributaries provide some dramatic terrain. A free backcountry hiking permit is required for overnights here. Call (435) 826-5499 for details.

This is also prime four-wheel-drive country, particularly the spectacular **Smoky Mountain Road**, **Romana Mesa Road**, and **Grand Bench Road** at the western end of Lake Powell (accessed off US 89 at Big Water), and the **Wilson Mesa Road**. The latter, forking off UT 276 near Halls Crossing, is truly a gnarly route and should be undertaken only by experienced backcountry drivers.

Golfers should check out the nice-looking new 18-hole course in

Page, **Lake Powell National**, (520) 645-2023, overlooking the lake. It has a clubhouse, practice ranges, pro shop, and restaurant/lounge.

FOOD

The most impressive dining facility on Lake Powell is probably the **Rainbow Room** at Wahweap Lodge, (520) 645-2433, with its panoramic views of Wahweap Bay and Gunsight Butte. It is open for all meals and serves liquor. The food is good, but you pay for the view. Reservations are not taken.

All of the marinas have food service of some kind. In Wahweap there's **ITZA Pizza** (open May through September); in Bullfrog the **Anasazi Restaurant** adjoins the Defiance House Lodge, (435) 684-3000, providing lovely views, bar service, and all meals year-round. Marina convenience stores at Halls Crossing, Hite, and Dangling Rope also carry sandwiches, snacks, and drinks.

Page has dozens of options, including the following good and extremely well-priced possibilities: The **Bella Napoli**, 810 N. Navajo, (520) 645-2706, boasts fine Italian fare for lunch and dinner. The **Dam Bar & Grill**, in Tower Plaza, 644 N. Navajo, (520) 645-2161, offers steaks, seafood, pasta, a sports bar, and nightly live music in its Gunsmoke Saloon (closed Sunday). **Padre Bay Café & Grill**, on Elm across from the Safeway, (520) 645-9058, serves lunch and dinner with ribs, seafood, great hamburgers, Mexican fare, a sport bar, and microbrews. **Mandarin Gourmet**, next to Basha's in Gateway Plaza on US 89, (520) 645-5516, cooks fresh Oriental dishes for daily lunch and dinner. For breakfast, try **Denny's**, US 89, (529) 645-3999.

The lodges around Lee's Ferry and Marble Gorge also have modest but acceptable restaurants (see Lodging, below).

LODGING

The poshest digs on the lake are at **Wahweap Lodge**, (520) 645-2433 or (800) 528-6154, with a heated outdoor pool overlooking the lake, the Rainbow Room restaurant, satellite TV, and room service, all for $65–$105.

Four miles from the dam on a bluff overlooking the lake is **Lake Powell Motel**, with prices ranging $30–$70. Up-lake at Bullfrog is **Defiance House Lodge**, with a restaurant, lounge, and satellite TV. Under the same management are basic three-bedroom condos at **Halls**

LAKE POWELL AREA

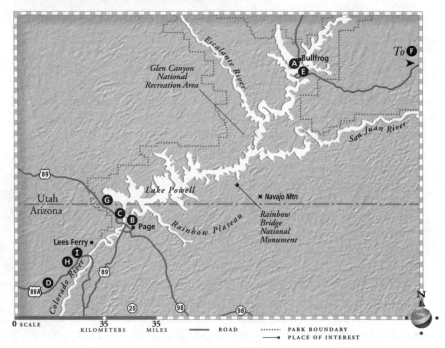

Food

- Ⓐ Anasazi Restaurant
- Ⓑ Bella Napoli
- Ⓑ Dam Bar & Grill
- Ⓑ Denny's
- Ⓒ ITZA Pizza
- Ⓑ Mandarin Gourmet
- Ⓑ Padre Bay Café & Grill
- Ⓒ Rainbow Room

Lodging

- Ⓑ Best Western Arizonian/
  Weston Inn & Suites
- Ⓐ Bullfrog Marina
- Ⓓ Cliff Dweller Lodge
- Ⓑ Courtyard by Marriott
- Ⓐ Defiance House Lodge
- Ⓔ Halls Crossing Marina
- Ⓕ Hite Marina
- Ⓖ Lake Powell Motel
- Ⓗ Lee's Ferry Lodge
- Ⓘ Marble Canyon Lodge
- Ⓑ Navajo Trail Motel
- Ⓒ Wahweap Lodge

Note: Items with the same letter are located in the same town or area.

Crossing, Hite, and **Bullfrog Marinas**. One can also stay on the company's houseboats on the lake (see Fitness and Recreation). For details or reservations for any of the above, call (800) 528-6154.

A boomtown created from scratch by the dam construction and subsequent tourism, Page has a slew of accommodations, including most of the chains. The **Best Western Arizonian/Weston Inn & Suites** (just up the hill from US 89 on Powell Blvd., 800-826-2718) has rooms for $75–$105. The **Courtyard by Marriott**, 600 Clubhouse Drive, (520) 645-5000 or (800) 851-3855, has a heated outdoor pool, Pepper's Restaurant, and an adjoining golf course for $69–$149. A much cheaper option is the **Navajo Trail Motel**, 800 Bureau Rd., (520) 645-9508, with rates of under $30.

In a different vein, offering history and color but not convenient lake access, are the accommodations near Lee's Ferry, which are popular with anglers plying the Colorado River below Glen Canyon Dam. **Marble Canyon Lodge**, US 89A a half-mile west of Navajo Bridge, (520) 355-2225 or (800) 726-1789, has 60 rooms ($65) and a few condos, plus a restaurant, laundry, and bar. **Lee's Ferry Lodge**, on US 89A 3 miles west of Navajo Bridge, (520) 355-2231, was built of local stone in 1929. It has about ten rooms opening onto a small garden patio ($48), a very good restaurant, and a bar serving more than 150 varieties of ice-cold beer. **Cliff Dweller Lodge**, on US 89A 9 miles west of Navajo Bridge, under the Vermilion Cliffs, (520) 355-2228 or (800) 433-2543, was built in 1949 and has 20 updated motel rooms ($60–$70), a restaurant, and bar.

CAMPING

Lakeshore and boat camping are permitted throughout the Glen Canyon National Recreation Area, except within developed areas or the Rainbow Bridge National Monument. Camping is limited to 14 consecutive days. Strict rules govern human waste disposal, and anyone camping within ¼-mile of Lake Powell must use a portable toilet, available from marinas and local camping stores.

Primitive campgrounds also exist at **Lone Rock Beach** (popular with local partying teens), **Hite, Bullfrog Bay, Farley Canyon**, and **Canyon**. They are free and have portable toilets but no water.

Commercial RV/tent campgrounds are run by Lake Powell Resorts & Marinas at **Wahweap, Bullfrog**, and **Halls Crossing**. All sites have water, sewer, and electrical service. For details, call

(800) 528-6254. The commercial **Lake Powell Campground**, on AZ 98 less than 1 mile south of Page, has tent sites for $17 and RV sites with hookups for $20, plus showers.

The National Park campground at **Lee's Ferry**, (520) 355-2234 for the local ranger, has 54 $8 sites on a first-come, first-served basis. They have water but no showers or hookups.

22

INDIAN COUNTRY— HOPI AND NAVAJO LANDS

T his chapter bites off a lot—almost the entire northeast corner of Arizona, which harbors the traditional homelands of the Hopi and Navajo Indians. A few spots are popular with tourists—particularly the stupendous stone monoliths of Monument Valley and Canyon de Chelly's cliff dwellings, as well as the fantastically well-preserved ruins of Navajo National Monument and the odd and fascinating sights of Petrified Forest National Park. Here you find North America's oldest inhabited locale, Hopiland, and the Third World-ish capital of the immense Navajo Nation, Window Rock, with its unique tribal council chambers, its zoo, and the famous landmark from which it derives its name.

However, much of the area remains *tierra incognita* to visitors, and even to modern life as most know it. Whether you are on dirt roads, atop the immense Black Mesa, on the isolated fingers of the Hopi Mesas, or in the cozy room of a trading post warmed by a cedar fire on a snowy winter day, the twentieth century and Main Street U.S.A. seem years and continents away.

This is a land that begs for slow exploration, for taking time to get to know another breed of American, for savoring mutton stew cooked over a wood fire, and for rolling down an endless strip of black-top in a pickup truck as huge clouds boil overhead, lightning zigzags to earth, and the thunderbird's cry echoes over the rocky mesas and plateaus. ◼

INDIAN COUNTRY

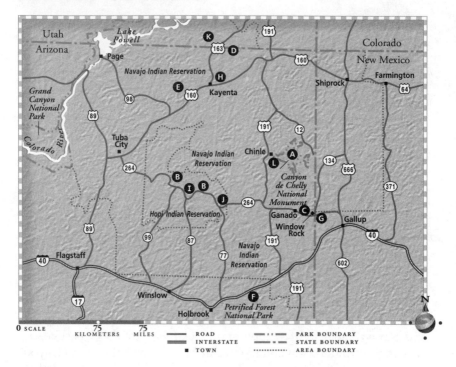

Sights

Ⓐ Canyon de Chelly
National Monument

Ⓑ Hopi Mesas

Ⓒ Hubbell Trading Post
National Historic Site

Ⓓ Monument Valley
Navajo Tribal Park

Ⓔ Navajo National Monument

Ⓕ Petrified Forest National Park

Ⓖ Window Rock

Food

Ⓗ Amigo Café

Ⓗ Basha's Deli

Food (continued)

Ⓗ Blue Coffee Pot

Ⓓ Haskeneini Restaurant

Ⓘ Hopi Cultural Center
Restaurant

Ⓙ Keams Canyon
Motel Restaurant

Ⓖ Los Verdes

Ⓖ Navajo Nation Inn
Dining Room

Ⓘ Nova'ki

Ⓗ Pizza Edge

Ⓚ Stagecoach Dining Room

Ⓛ Thunderbird Lodge

Note: Items with the same letter are located in the same town or area.

A PERFECT DAY IN INDIAN COUNTRY

This is a huge area, far too large to see in one day, or even several. Some good one-day itineraries include a day on the Hopi Mesas; a morning at Navajo National Monument and evening at Monument Valley; a morning at Monument Valley and afternoon at Canyon de Chelly; a day at Canyon de Chelly; a morning at Canyon de Chelly and a drive to Tsaile and down the Chuska Mountains to a late afternoon in Window Rock; or a morning at Petrified Forest National Park, a stop at the Hubbell Trading Post, and an afternoon in Window Rock. Picnicking and camping are the ways to go, though modest food and lodging establishments are available throughout the area.

SIGHTSEEING HIGHLIGHTS

★★★ **Canyon de Chelly National Monument**—Since my first visit when I was 10 years old, I have never forgotten either the beauty of its serpentine sandstone canyons flanked by fall's golden cottonwoods, or the awesome sight of the abandoned cliff dwellings tucked into alcoves along its walls. This was when I realized I lived in a region people had occupied for a very long time. A recent visit revealed that while growing up diminishes some things, others—like Canyon de Chelly—continue to impress.

The 83,340-acre monument is owned by the Navajo Nation but managed by the National Park Service, a novel collaboration that gives it an unusual character. Navajo families continue to live and farm on the canyon floor, watering fields and peach orchards with the thin trickle of water coursing down the central canyon, and Navajo guides lead tours into these rock retreats.

The canyon has sheltered people off and on over the past 2,000 years, beginning with the Basketmaker culture. The Anasazi left behind the park's most prominent ruins, the remarkably intact multistory cliff dwellings, which have been protected from weather by their alcove locations above the canyon floor. They abandoned the canyon around 1300. In the seventeenth century Navajos began to enter and settle in the canyon, and they have been here ever since—excepting the 1864–1868 period, when the U.S. military interred them at distant Bosque Redondo.

At the mouth of the canyon, just outside the Navajo community of Tsaile, is the park's visitor center. Here you can watch a fine film about the natural and human history of Canyon de Chelly (pronounced "deh-SHAY"), watch daily Navajo silversmithing demonstrations, view some excellent exhibits of artifacts, obtain free printed information, and browse a bookstore and gift shop. Outside is a replica of a traditional female Navajo hogan, the round, domed dwelling of logs and earth, with its door facing the rising sun.

The canyons can only be entered in the company of Navajo guides, on foot, on horseback, or in vehicles (see Fitness and Recreation section, below). Otherwise, you may see many of the sites from above via two rim-road drives, both starting from the visitor center. The first stop on the **South Rim Drive** is **Tsegi Overlook**, where you can see patches of green fields on the canyon floor below. Off in the distance, across the highway a half-mile away, are sand dunes just like the ones that were buried, petrified, and later exposed throughout the canyon walls. The dunes can be reached via a side dirt road. At 5.7 miles from the visitor center, you reach the short side road to **White House Overlook**. Be sure to make this stop. It provides a great view of one of the canyon's largest ruins at the foot of a huge cliff adorned with desert varnish and etched into a cleft above. At the parking lot is the trailhead for the only footpath into the canyon visitors may hike without a guide. The beautiful 1.25-mile **White House Ruin Trail** drops more than 600 feet to the ruin.

At mile 21.8 from the center is **Spider Rock Overlook**. This spire is one of the park's most photogenic features, delicately climbing 800 feet straight up from the canyon floor. Navajo mythology says it is the home of Spider Woman, who brought the art of weaving to them. A rougher road continues eastward, but this is the end of the South Rim Drive; backtrack to the visitor center.

The **North Rim Drive** begins at the visitor center. First up are tiny **Ledge Ruin** and **Antelope House**. Near the latter site was found the **Tomb of the Weaver**, so finely constructed that archeologists who opened it in 1920 found a white cotton blanket that looked freshly woven wrapped around the well-preserved body of a man. At 17.5 miles from the visitor center is the side road to **Mummy Cave** and **Massacre Cave**. Believed to have been occupied for 1,000 years, Mummy Cave's striking three-story tower displays fine masonry and architecture similar to structures at Mesa Verde, Colorado. This is the final North Rim stop. You can backtrack to the visitor center, or continue east along this road, Navajo Road 64, to **Tsaile** and the **Chuska Mountains**.

Details: *Off US 191, just east of Chinle. The visitor center is on Navajo Road 7 at the canyon mouth; (520) 674-5500. Open daily in summer 8–6, otherwise. 8–5. Free. (2 hours for each round-trip drive)*

★★★ **Hopi Mesas**—Archeologists and the Hopis believe that these isolated, treeless, rugged mesas comprise the oldest continually occupied spot in the United States. Tree-ring dating of roof vigas in Old Oraibi village show that some trees were cut down around A.D. 1150. The stone and mortar pueblos clinging precariously to the high mesa edges certainly *seem* ancient.

Standing on a dirt rooftop overlooking a small dusty plaza, one watches as the colorfully dressed butterfly dancers slowly file out of a kiva, wind through the narrow lanes, and assemble below. A drummer begins to beat out a rhythm, and the body of men surrounding him begin a chant. The dancers lift their feet with a jangling of rattles and bells, raise and drop their hands clutching feather fans, and begin a steady shuffle. Far in the distance the sun begins to drop behind the San Francisco Peaks, and a chill wind stirs. The spectators pull their blankets around them a bit tighter, immersed in the spectacle and living prayer before them. It could be A.D. 1300, or 1998. In fact, it is 1998, and you are watching the age-old but ever-new and renewed ceremonial cycle of the Hopis.

While much of the Southwest deals with remnants, fragments, and ruins of ancient life, Hopi offers a rare opportunity to observe an ancient and spiritually centered life in a contemporary context. Direct descendants of the Anasazi and other cultures that occupied the region for thousands of years, the Hopi are probably the most traditional of all American Indian groups.

Renowned as tremendous potters, silversmiths, and wood-carvers of images representing their gods—the kachinas who periodically come to Earth to visit them during their many dance ceremonies—the Hopi are truly a remarkable people. But they don't reveal themselves or their rich spiritual and artistic heritage easily.

I would recommend the following itinerary. First, call ahead and obtain a schedule of upcoming dances open to the public (generally those held in the fall), and time your visit to include at least a half-day at a dance. Also make a visit to the **Hopi Cultural Center and Museum**, located on Second Mesa at mile marker 379.5, just off AZ 264, the main highway through Hopiland, (520) 734-6650. It contains a small museum, a gift shop, and restaurant. It is open year-round,

weekdays 8–5 and on summer weekends 9–4. Admission is $3 for
adults, $1 for kids under 14. Another good stop is the **Hopi
Cooperative Guild**, located on Second Mesa at mile marker 375 on
AZ 264. More than 300 artists display their work here, and Hopi silversmiths work on-site. It's open 8–5 every day.

One may also drive through the villages, park, and walk around,
except at the spectacularly sited Walpi, which requires a guide. Many
artisans sell pottery, jewelry, and other works from their homes. However, do not enter villages that are closed due to nonpublic dances,
never walk into anyone's home without being invited, and do not enter
kivas or other restricted areas. Photography, audio- or videotaping, and
sketching are strictly prohibited.

*Details: The Hopi Reservation is surrounded by the much larger
Navajo reservation. It straddles AZ 264, 62 miles east of Tuba City and 93
miles west of Window Rock. AZ 264 is open year-round, but the two-lane
blacktop can be nasty in winter storms. Tours of Walpi village on First Mesa
can be arranged through Ponsi Hall, (520) 737-2262, and other tours can be
set up through Hopi Polewyma Travel & Tours, (520) 525-9490. (1 day)*

✸✸✸ **Petrified Forest National Park**—One is not immediately
impressed by this national park. Speeding along I-40, there is little or
nothing visually outstanding that breaks the barren landscape. But get
off the highway, and slow down, and the natural and scenic wealth of
this odd place begins to emerge.

Since the park's name includes the word *forest*, your first question
may well be, "Where are all the trees?" They lie in pockets here and
there on the ground, or protruding from the multicolored earth, where
they fell some 200 million years ago and were turned into fantastically
colored stone. In fact, this park preserves the largest known concentration of petrified woods in the world, despite the fact that thousands of
tons of it were hauled off by commercial gatherers in the early twentieth century and that visitors today continue to pocket illegally some 12
tons a year. In 1906 President Theodore Roosevelt signed legislation
creating the park's core. Two wilderness areas were added in 1970; they
were the first wilderness designations within a national park.

In addition to the stone wood, the park encompasses a portion of
the vast **Painted Desert**, a wonderfully-colored "badlands" of rounded
hills, gullies, small buttes, and plains that have a unique beauty of their
own. It also harbors some 300 archeological sites, including standing
Anasazi ruins and petroglyphs; in the 1980s several important and pre-

viously unknown dinosaur fossils turned up. A 27-mile (one way) paved road cruises the length of the park, providing excellent views of its major features and access to short walks among the petrified forests and ruins.

The drive begins at I-40, where you'll find the **Painted Desert Visitor Center**. Close-by is **Kachina Point** and the Spanish Colonial and Pueblo Revival–styled **Painted Desert Museum**, built in the 1920s by Mary Elizabeth Jane Colter, with interior murals painted by the great Hopi artist Fred Kabotie.

A mile past **Puerco Indian Ruins**, a small Anasazi Pueblo, is a great assembly of petroglyphs at **Newspaper Rock** (best seen with binoculars). Past this point one enters the oldest section of the park, containing concentrations of petrified forests at stops including **Blue Mesa**, **Agate Bridge** (where a petrified log more than 100 feet long hangs over an arroyo), **Jasper Forest**, and **Crystal Forest**. There is even a ruin constructed of the beautiful wood-turned-to stone **Agate House**. At the southern end of the drive is the **Rainbow Forest Museum**, where the complex process that created the petrified wood is explained.

Details: The park straddles I-40 to the north and south. Its primary entrance is off I-40 about 27 miles east of Holbrook. It can also be entered from the south off US 180. Its main visitor center is located just off I-40; (520) 524-6228. Along with displays, it has a bookstore and rangers to answer questions and issue backcountry camping permits. The park is open daily in summer 7–7, the rest of the year 8–5. During winter snows, the scenic drive may be closed. There are no developed campgrounds, but wilderness camping is allowed with a permit. A restaurant sits near the visitor center. Admission is $10 per vehicle. (3 hours minimum)

✩✩ **Monument Valley Navajo Tribal Park**—Its visitor center patio at sunset is a global happening: to the beat of a big drum and the drone of Navajo chanting, you catch glimpses of German, French, Italian, and Japanese tourists as they shoot photos of the musicians and the glowing, stupendous towers of stone that rise up all around like a prehistoric Gotham City. Novelist Willa Cather wrote, "From the flat red seas of sand rose great rock mesas, generally Gothic in outline . . . This plain might once have been an enormous city, all the smaller quarters destroyed by time, only the public buildings left."

It is, in fact, one of the favored must-sees in the Southwest— due in no small measure to the many Western films shot on location including a handful by John Ford and John Wayne, such as *Stagecoach*.

But the soaring rock formations are best seen in early light or at sunset, and in between it can be a long, hot day. Many visitors here fill the time between driving the dusty 17-mile loop road, which brings one to the feet of some of the landmarks, or by taking a horseback ride. These are the only way to see it more closely; unsupervised hiking is not allowed. Located on the Navajo Reservation and managed by the tribe, Monument Valley provides a unique experience, especially if you spend the night at its ridgetop campground—where you awaken, look around, and say amen.

On the way to the park, just north of Kayenta, you also pass **Agathla Peak**, the stump of a massive volcanic neck that resembles a smaller cousin of famous Shiprock. It thrusts up 1,200 feet off the valley floor.

Details: On the Arizona/Utah border, north of Kayenta, Arizona. Head north on US 163 for 24 miles to the paved park entrance road on the right (Navajo Road 42B), which runs 4 miles to the visitor center; (801) 727-3353. Here you can register to camp, have a meal in the cafeteria, or browse a gift shop. Its parking lot is filled with Navajo vendors selling horse rides, guided tours, arts and crafts, and food. You are not allowed to drive, bike, or hike any of the park's roads other than the one designated 17-mile loop route from the visitor center. This road, though rough, is passable for normal cars in dry weather. The park is open daily May through September 7–7 and October through April 8–5 (the campground, however, is always accessible). Admission is $2.50 for adults, $1 for seniors, and free for kids under 6. (3 hours minimum)

★★ **Navajo National Monument**—In 1895 Richard Wetherill, who "discovered" many of the primary ruins at Mesa Verde, Colorado, was led by Navajo guides into an isolated canyon to the north of Navajo Mountain in northeastern Arizona. He thus became the first recorded non-Indian to gaze upon a masterpiece of its long-departed Kayenta Anasazi architects: the extraordinarily well-preserved 150-room **Keet Seel**. In 1909 Navajos led him to another nearby site, **Betatakin Ruin**, a 135-room complex nestled into a gorgeous 425-foot-high salmon-colored alcove. Later he would lead others to the ruins, including author Zane Grey. Today both ruins and other, smaller sites are protected in the 336-acre Navajo National Monument.

A visitor center contains artifacts recovered from the ruins and other displays. Just out the door is **Sandal Trail**, a self-guiding, 1-mile, round-trip route that leads to an overlook of Betatakin Ruin. From May 31 through August 31 at 9 a.m. and noon, rangers lead groups of 25 hikers to Betatakin. In fall and May, one tour a day leaves at 10 a.m. The 5-mile round-trip hike takes five to six hours, climbing 700 vertical feet to the bottom of a canyon, then back out. Tickets are free but can only be obtained in person on the morning of your proposed hike; no reservations are taken.

Keet Seel is even more remote, requiring a daylong horseback outing covering 16 miles and a canyon descent of more than 1,000 feet. Kids under 12 aren't allowed. The trip costs $55, and is conducted from May 31 through August 31. Reservations should be made at least two months in advance; (520) 672-2366. Limited backcountry hiking permits are issued for Keet Seel on summer weekends.

Details: Head west on US 160 32 miles from Kayenta or 50 miles east from Tuba City, turn onto AZ 564, and proceed almost 10 miles on this paved road to the visitor center; (520) 672-2366/2367 or (520) 727-3287. Open daily in summer 8–6, early September to mid-December 8–5, and mid-December to May 8–4:30. Admission is free. (2 hours to full day)

★★ **Window Rock**—The capital of the immense Navajo Nation (some 16 million acres, larger than Connecticut, Massachusetts, and New Hampshire combined) looks like an impoverished Third World town, perhaps in Mexico. But the Navajos are the nation's largest Indian tribe, and a visit here is eye-opening.

They settled in the region in the fourteenth and fifteenth centuries. As a hunting and gathering culture not averse to occasional raiding when times got tough, they were often at odds with the Pueblo Indians of New Mexico and the Hopi of Arizona, as well as the Spanish and, later, the Americans. In 1864 they were finally conquered by a U.S. military campaign, led by Kit Carson, and packed off to Bosque Redondo on the Pecos River. Four years later they were allowed to return to the Four Corners area. In the 1930s administrative functions were centralized at Window Rock, and about 4,000 residents live here today.

A first stop for visitors is often the red sandstone arch, **Window Rock**, after which the town is named, located on the northeast side of town, a half-mile north of AZ 264 on Navajo Road 12. A small park at its foot has some short trails, restrooms, drinking water, and picnic tables. It's open during daylight hours.

In August 1997 the tribe dedicated its new **Navajo Nation Museum** in Window Rock, AZ 264, (520) 871-6673/75. The 58,000-square-foot facility features historical and contemporary artwork of tribal members.

A small zoo and botanic garden with fauna and flora native to the reservation sits along AZ 264 on the east side of town, (520) 871-6573, and is open daily. Admission is by donation.

Another interesting possibility is a visit to the **Navajo Nation Council Chambers**, where you can watch tribal politics—featuring the largest Indian legislative body in the nation—in action. The chambers, set in a beautiful building constructed in 1923, are located just below the Window Rock arch.

Special events in Window Rock include the world's largest Indian get-together—the **Navajo Nation Fair**, held over Labor Day weekend, with an intertribal powwow, all-Indian rodeo, live concerts, a midway, and livestock and farming competitions.

When touring the Navajo reservation, keep in mind that livestock is often not fenced and can be encountered on highways. I hit a cow once, and while it eventually got up, my car was trashed! Be aware that the Navajo Nation observes daylight savings time (one hour ahead) in summer, unlike the rest of Arizona. Also, it's fun to tune into the reservation's main radio station, KTTN (AM 660), which mixes country-western tunes with Indian music, and features Navajo DJs who speak a hybrid Navglish.

Details: 24 miles northwest of Gallup, New Mexico. For information on tribal parks, camping, hunting, and fishing, contact the Navajo Parks and Recreation Department, P.O. Box 9000, Window Rock, AZ 86515; (520) 871-6647/6636. (2 to 4 hours)

☆ **Hubbell Trading Post National Historic Site**—John Lorenzo Hubbell was an important and greatly respected figure in Arizona and on the Navajo reservation in the late nineteenth and early twentieth centuries. He helped to popularize Navajo weaving with the Ganado Red style (a red background with a diamond or cross pattern in the center) and his promotion of Navajo weavings as rugs (traditionally they were used primarily as blankets). This effort continues to pay dividends today for the many Navajos who make their living through weaving.

The trading post is now overseen by the U.S. Park Service. It sells general goods and a terrific selection of regional Indian arts and crafts, including New Mexico Pueblo and Hopi pottery, Hopi kachinas and jewelry, and Navajo weavings. An adjoining visitor center is filled with interesting displays and area artifacts; weavers and jewelers demonstrate their work daily. Guided tours of the Hubbell home, filled with period furniture and an incredible rug collection, are also given.

Details: Just off AZ 264 west of Ganado, 30 miles west of Window Rock; (520) 755-3475. Open in the summer 8–6, and the rest of the year 8–5. Admission is free. (2 hours)

FITNESS AND RECREATION

None of the national monuments in this chapter have extensive hiking trails (some details are provided under Sightseeing Highlights), nor is biking much of an option except on paved and dirt roads. Water for fishing is limited to the Chuska Mountains, where you can angle (with a permit from the Navajo Game and Fish Department, see Window Rock Sightseeing Highlight) at **Tsaile**, **Assayi**, **Wheatfields** and **Whiskey Lakes**, among others.

The best hiking is found at **Petrified Forest National Park**, which has two wilderness areas—one in the northern district on the **Painted Desert**, the other in the southern district. With no major canyons, cliffs, or waterways, you can basically wander in any direction. Free backcountry permits (required), can be obtained until 4 p.m. daily at the visitor center off I-40.

Tours of Canyon de Chelly led by Navajo guides are a popular activity at this national monument; in fact, they are the only way to see the cliff dwellings up close, except for the White House Ruin Trail (see Sightseeing Highlights). Walking or four-wheel-drive tours in your own vehicle, at $10 an hour (three-hour minimum), can be arranged from **Tsegi Guide Association**, (520) 674-5500, at the park's visitor center. **De Chelly Tours**, (520) 674-3772 /5433, provides morning ($100) and overnight (rates vary) jeep trips. The **Thunderbird Lodge**, (520) 674-5841 or (800) 679-2473, is another option, with half-day ($36 per person) or full-day ($57) tours running April through October. Horse outings into the canyon are available through **Justin Tso Horse Rentals**, (520) 674-5678, and **Twin Trail Tours**, (520) 674-8425.

Monument Valley also features Navajo-led jeep tours and horseback rides. Prices generally run about $10 an hour for either activity. **Navajo Guided Tours**, at the visitor center, is highly recommended;

they also have an evening cookout tour. Another recommended operator is **Jackson Tours**, (801) 727-3353.

FOOD

Fine dining is not a reason to visit this area, but you will neither starve nor burn a hole in your pocket here. At Canyon de Chelly, the cafeteria at **Thunderbird Lodge** is an old standby. The Navajo taco, frybread heaped with ground beef, pinto beans, lettuce, tomatoes and cheese, will fill you up. The Thunderbird features daily specials and delicious blue-corn pancakes for breakfast.

At Monument Valley, the **Haskeneini Restaurant**, in the park visitor center, (801) 727-3312, serves up modestly priced cafeteria-style food from 6 a.m. to 10 p.m. in the summer, and 7 a.m. to 9 p.m. the rest of the year. Just across US 163 from the park entrance road, in the Goulding complex, is the **Stagecoach Dining Room**, (801) 727-3231, open for all meals.

Some 24 miles south in Kayenta are a few possibilities, including the **Amigo Café**, on US 163 just north of the intersection with US 160, (520) 697-8448, serving excellent Mexican food for breakfast, lunch, and dinner. The **Blue Coffee Pot**, intersection of US 160 and US 163, (520) 697-3396, features Navajo tacos, steaks, burgers, eggs, and sandwiches, and is open daily 6 a.m. to 9 p.m. **Pizza Edge**, in the Todineeshzhee Shopping Center, (520) 697-8427, serves pizza, calzones, and frozen yogurt from 11 a.m. to 10 p.m. daily. **Basha's Deli**, next to Pizza Edge, (520) 697-8176, specializes in sandwiches, salads, desserts, and drinks.

Unless you're the guest of a resident family, food can be hard to find at Hopi. Among the few options are the **Nova'ki**, (on Second Mesa in Shipaulovi in the Sekakuku Trading Post, 520-737-2525, open Monday through Saturday 10:30 a.m. to 8 p.m.), with sandwiches, hamburgers, and pizza; and the **Hopi Cultural Center Restaurant**, at AZ 264 mile marker 379.5, 520-734-2401, open 7 a.m. to 9 p.m., except when they run out of food or staff. It has overpriced (but who's complaining?) blue-corn pancakes for breakfast, and Hopi stew (lamb and corn), Hopi tacos, and American fare for lunch and dinner. Several villages, including **Shungopavi**, also have stores where you can have a hot dog, a slice of pizza, or an ice-cream cone.

About 15 miles east in Keams Canyon on AZ 264 is the **Keams**

Canyon Motel Restaurant, (520) 738-2297, with American and Hopi dishes as well as a fast-food counter. It's open weekdays 6:30 a.m.–8:30 p.m., and weekends 7 a.m.–6:30 p.m. in summer; closed Sunday in winter.

Window Rock has a handful of places to eat. For Navajo power-lunching, check out the **Navajo Nation Inn Dining Room**, in the middle of town at 48 W. US 264, (520) 871-4108, where members of the tribal council chow down. It's open 6:30 a.m. to 9 p.m. daily. But the homemade Mexican fare of **Los Verdes**, 3 miles west of town set back from AZ 264 across from St. Michael's Mission Road, may be the best food around.

A simple restaurant sits next to the visitor center at Petrified Forest National Park. In nearby Holbrook, at least ten restaurants exist, including a **Denny's**, 2510 E. Navajo Blvd., (520) 524-2893, and the **Plainsman**, 1001 West Dr., (520) 524-3345.

LODGING

Canyon de Chelly has a notable and attractive place to stay, the **Thunderbird Lodge**, near the visitor center, just past the campground; (520) 674-5841. It grew out of a trading post founded in 1902 and was once a stop on the Fred Harvey motor cruises. It has both lodge rooms and motel units (all with AC and private bath) for $85 and a good restaurant. The lodge also conducts guided tours of the ruins.

On the road from Chinle to the visitor center, is a **Holiday Inn**, (520) 674-5000 or (800) 465-4329, offering 100 rooms, a pool, and a fancy (for here) restaurant for $110 per night.

Monument Valley has just one accommodation, **Goulding's Lodge**, just across US 163 from the park's entrance road, 801-727-3231. It's a 62-room motel with an indoor pool and adjoining restaurant. Rates are $64–$110.

Two other options in the Monument Valley area are found in Kayenta, some 24 miles away. The **Wetherill Inn**, on US 163 1.5 miles north of US 160, (520) 697-3231, has rates varying from $50 (winter) to $80 (summer). The **Holiday Inn**, at the junction of US 163 and US 160, (520) 697-3221 or (800) 465-4329, has rates ranging by season from $70–$110. In Tsegi, 10 miles west of Kayenta along US 160, is the **Anasazi Inn**, (520) 697-3793, with 52 nice but simple motel rooms, magnificent views, and a full-service restaurant open year-round. Rates are $78.

INDIAN COUNTRY

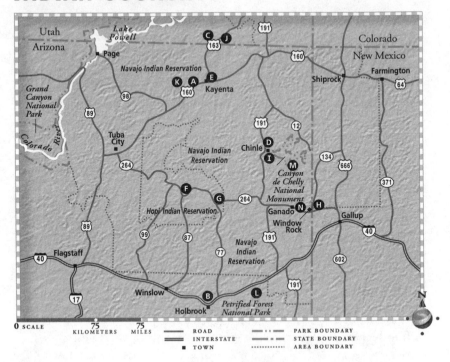

Lodging

- **A** Anasazi Inn
- **B** Best Western Adobe Inn
- **C** Goulding's Lodge
- **D** Holiday Inn–Chinle
- **E** Holiday Inn–Kayenta
- **F** Hopi Cultural Center Motel
- **G** Keams Canyon Motel
- **B** Moenkopi Motel
- **H** Navajo Nation Inn
- **I** Thunderbird Lodge
- **E** Wetherill Inn

Camping

- **I** Cottonwood Campground
- **C** Goulding's Campground
- **B** Holbrook KOA
- **J** Mitten View Campground
- **K** Navajo National Monument
- **B** OK RV Park
- **L** Petrified Forest National Park
- **F** Second Mesa Campground
- **M** Spider Rock RV Campground
- **N** Summit Campground
- **H** Tse Bonito Tribal Park

Note: Items with the same letter are located in the same town or area.

There is only one place to stay on the Hopi Mesas: the **Hopi Cultural Center Motel**, at AZ 264 mile marker 379.5, (520) 734-2401, with 30 modern, standard motel rooms and cable TV for $65. About 15 miles east, in Keams Canyon, is the **Keams Canyon Motel**, (520) 738-2297, with spartan but clean rooms for about $35.

In Window Rock, there's the **Navajo Nation Inn**, in the middle of town at 48 US 264 West, (520) 871-4108 or (800) 662-4108, a pleasant place with Navajo decor, cable TV, a pool in summer, and a restaurant. Rates are $70.

The closest accommodations to Petrified Forest National Park are in Holbrook, which has more than 1,000 motel and some hotel rooms. Choices include **Best Western Adobe Inn**, 615 West Dr., (520) 524-3948; and **Moenkopi Motel**, 464 Navajo Blvd., (520) 524-6848.

CAMPING

There are several camping options at Canyon de Chelly. **Spider Rock RV Campground**, (520) 674-8261, is owned by a Navajo businessman, and is spectacularly sited near Spider Rock at the end of the South Rim Drive (see Sightseeing Highlights). It has 44 sites with portable toilets, sites for RVs up to 44 feet long, and tent camping; $10 per night.

Another possibility is **Cottonwood Campground**, a half-mile from the visitor center, with 90 sites, restrooms, and drinking water (no hookups, no showers) on a first-come, first-served basis. This free campground is open year-round.

Monument Valley has the tribe-run **Mitten View Campground**, next to the tribal park visitor center, (801) 727-3287, open all year. It is set on an exposed ridge with tremendous views, but can be windy in winter and spring, has a slippery loop road in wet weather, and attracts flies from the nearby stables in summer. Its 99 $10 sites include 37 tent spaces, 36 RV spaces, and nine pull-through sites (no hookups). The ones on the loop's outer edge have the best views. Huge restrooms have coin-operated, warmish showers.

Another option, just across US 163 from the tribal park entrance road down a 2-mile road in Rock Door Canyon, is **Goulding's Campground**, (801) 727-3231/3235, open March 15 through October with 50 sites, laundry, hot showers, and a grocery store. Full hookups (water, sewer, electricity, and TV) run $25; tent sites, $14.

At Hopi, **Second Mesa Campground** sits next to the Cultural Center at mile marker 379.5 on AZ 264. This free area lacks water and hookups, but you can use the Center's restrooms. Another free camp-ground (no facilities) is in nearby Keams Canyon.

There are 30 nicely shaded sites at **Navajo National Monument**, open mid-April through mid-October. It provides toilets and drinking water, but no hookups, on a first-come, first-served basis. RVs longer than 25 feet aren't recommended here.

In and around Window Rock, one can camp at **Tse Bonito Tribal Park**, next to the zoo. It has no facilities but costs only $2. **Summit Campground**, in a pretty ponderosa forest, is about 10 miles west of town off AZ 264—turn north (right) onto Navajo Road 201. It has outhouses but no water. A permit from the Navajo Parks Department is required (see Window Rock).

Only dispersed, primitive camping is allowed by free permit in the wilderness sections of **Petrified Forest National Park**, (520) 524-6228. Nearby is the **Holbrook KOA**, 102 Hermosa Dr., (520) 524-6689, has full hookups, a pool, minigolf, laundry, showers, and a playground for $21. The **OK RV Park**, 1526 Navajo Blvd., Holbrook, (520) 524-3226, provides full hookups for $18.

APPENDIX

METRIC CONVERSION CHART

1 U.S. gallon = approximately 4 liters
1 liter = about 1 quart
1 Canadian gallon = approximately 4.5 liters

1 pound = approximately ½ kilogram
1 kilogram = about 2 pounds

1 foot = approximately ⅓ meter
1 meter = about 1 yard
1 yard = a little less than a meter
1 mile = approximately 1.6 kilometers
1 kilometer = about ⅔ mile

90°F = about 30°C
20°C = approximately 70°F

Planning Map: American Southwest

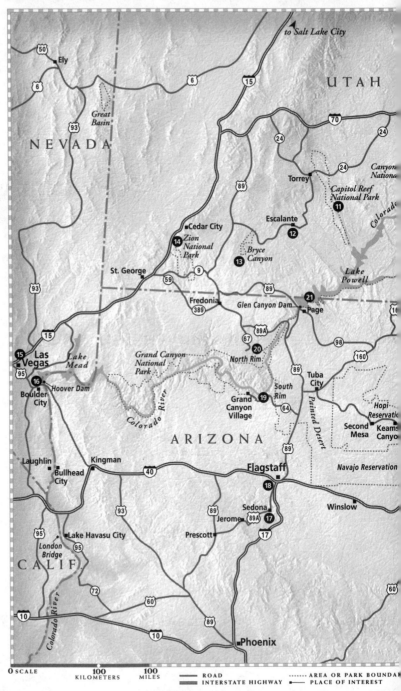

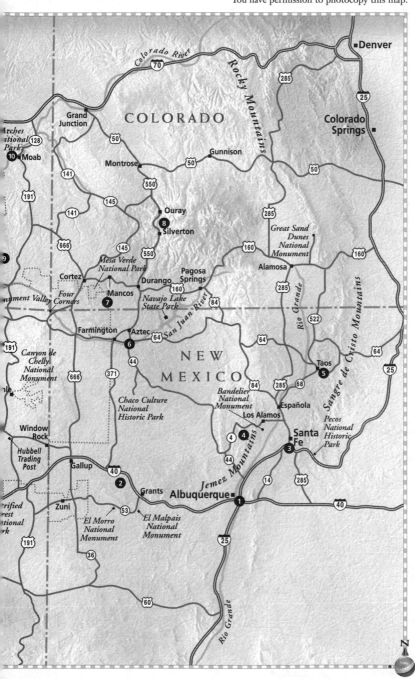

INDEX

Map Index

ABOUT THE AUTHOR

Daniel Gibson was born and raised in Albuquerque's North Valley.
After sailing across the Pacific and helping to write a book about the
experience, he went on to study journalism at the University of New
Mexico. He worked for several years as arts editor and general writer
for the now-defunct *Albuquerque News* before he took a job as a public
information officer at the Office of Indian Affairs in Santa Fe. He has
since worked as a writer and editor for numerous local, regional, and
national publications. For four years he served as an environmental and
natural history columnist for the *Santa Fe Reporter*. Gibson has also
contributed to several major guidebooks and is a founding member of
PEN New Mexico.